DISCOVERING
COMMON
GROUND

DISCOVERING
COMMON
GROUND

How FUTURE SEARCH CONFERENCES
Bring People Together to Achieve
Breakthrough Innovation,
Empowerment, Shared Vision,
and Collaborative Action

MARVIN R. WEISBORD

and 35 International Coauthors

Berrett-Koehler Publishers
San Francisco

HD 30 .28 D57 1992

Berrett-Koehler Publishers, Inc.
155 Montgomery St.
San Francisco, CA 94104-4109

Ordering Information

Orders by individuals and organizations. Berrett-Koehler publications are available through bookstores or can be ordered direct from the publisher at the Berrett-Koehler address or by calling 1 (800) 929-2929.

Quantity sales. Berrett-Koehler publications are available at special quantity discounts when purchased in bulk by corporations, associations, and others. For details, write to the "Special Sales Department" at the Berrett-Koehler address above or call (415) 288-0260.

Orders by U.S. trade bookstores and wholesalers. Please contact Prima Worldwide, P.O. Box 1260, Rocklin, CA 95677-1260; tel. (916) 786-0426; fax (916) 786-0488.

Orders for college textbook/course adoption use. Please contact Berrett-Koehler Publishers, 155 Montgomery St., San Francisco, CA 94104-4109; tel (415) 288-0260; fax (415) 362-2512.

Printed in the United States of America

 Printed on acid-free and recycled paper that meets the strictest state and U.S. guidelines for recycled paper (50 percent recycled waste, including 10 percent postconsumer waste).

Library of Congress Cataloging-in-Publication Data

Discovering common ground: how future search conferences bring people together to achieve breakthrough innovation, empowerment, shared vision, and collaborative action / Marvin R. Weisbord and 35 international co-authors.
    p.   cm.
    Includes bibliographical references and index.
    ISBN 1-881052-08-7
    1. Strategic planning.   2. Strategic planning—Employee participation.
    3. Organizational change.   I. Weisbord, Marvin Ross.
    HD30.28.D57   1993
    658.4'012—dc20
    92–28433
    CIP

First Edition
First Printing 1992

Cover Design by Jim Carpenter
Book Design by Pacific West Publishing Service, Eugene, Oregon

Dedication

**To All Who Would
Enlarge Common Ground
On a Diverse Planet**

Table of Contents

Preface

New Paradigm Planning

Nothing I have written in 30 years sparked more letters and phone calls than "Inventing the Future," a chapter in *Productive Workplaces* (Jossey-Bass 1987). There I told of my enthusiasm for "future searches" as a new planning process. As a result, I met some visionary chief executives, and got to manage strategy conferences in communications, farm banking, natural foods, office furniture, publishing, and social welfare.

More, many veteran facilitators, using Chapter 14 as a recipe, cooked up their own applications—such as revising a business school curriculum, Federal agency strategic planning, and solidifying a large medical center's mission. They confirmed not only that the method made intuitive sense, but that skilled people with similar values could repeat it.

They also supported my main theme—that the world was moving from *experts* solving problems FOR people toward *everybody*, experts included, improving whole systems. They shared my belief that getting everybody improving whole systems is the best strategy if you want long-term dignity, meaning and community.

And they validated what is by now a cliche to readers of the business press. Old management methods no longer work in the face of mind-bending technologies and economic roller coasters. A "new paradigm of work" is sweeping the post-industrial world, not easily, not painlessly, but sweeping nonetheless. The new buzz words have become learning, empowering, democratizing, partnering. Everybody, it seems, wants to bridge gaps of culture, class, race, ethnicity, gender and hierarchy. The search is on to find methods equal to these values. Future search conferences—events that bring people together across diverse and improbable boundaries to do joint planning—show unusual promise.

At the same time, only a handful of leaders have caught on to the fact that a three-day strategy conference might be the best short course in managing the future. After all, the method requires no teaching, only learning. It's too simple. The point is easy to miss when you have no lectures OR training. Instead, we rely entirely on assembling the right cast of characters for a form of "blind people and the elephant." The world we all share is the elephant. We use dialogue to describe it. People ALREADY know how to do this! They just don't know that they know it.

Now, in this book, you can get an in-depth look at strategic conferences that embody learning, empowering, democratizing and partnering. All emphasize the search for common ground in a world increasingly fragmented and conflicted. I have gathered examples from around the world to lend credibility to the hundreds of people eagerly blazing this trail. I also want to make the path less rocky for the thousands who will follow. Anyone who holds the underlying values will quickly grasp the potential of this roadmap. That's why I believe this paradigm, in the next 25 years, will replace conflict-management and problem-solving—the modes that served so many of us, and vice-versa, for the last 25.

Merging Values, Theories, and Techniques

In this volume I've sought to highlight similarities and differences of a variety of conference designs. My comments in the text reflect my wish to learn from, and to integrate into my own practice, what others have done. This is not a survey of everything out there. It's a guided visit to sources of my own practice, buttressed by side-trips down paths I stumbled on while researching my own. The common thread is my own excitement.

In these events we weave together values, theories, and techniques in a special way. This integration takes us down a path toward new management practices that really do "work." By using them, we enable more control of technology, better economic choices, and joint planning among diverse people. The conferences usually involve 30-85 people for two to three days. They have been run in every sector—public, private, voluntary, government, business, labor, health care, education, local, state, national, global.

Not Just a Meeting

This conference model represents a wholly new way of doing things, using meetings, a form most people know all too well. Managers and leaders spend a high percentage of their days attending or running meetings. That's where ideals are shaped, embodied, owned, transmitted, fine-tuned, validated or trashed—to emerge as new missions, goals, policies, procedures, or systems. Yet, as far back as I can remember, we have all been dissatisfied with meetings. Our legendary frustrations have spawned a sophisticated meeting management technology—for content and process both. It's important that this book's contents not be read as another manual on how to run better meetings.

When we speak of conferences that make possible levels of action previously unobtainable, we are way beyond "better meetings." We are sketching the parameters for a whole new way of (self) managing. We are describing a new integration of structure, function and process. This mode enables us to keep abreast of what's happening in "real time;" more, it makes possible real time course corrections.

Nor should you think of this as a cookbook. Rather, it's more like a new philosophy of eating. The authors scope out a new vision of a healthy diet for organizations seeking relevance in the global village. They offer a new way of making satisfying meals for people fed-up with piece-meal problem-solving and frustrating meetings.

Purposes

The book's purposes are three. To:

1. Show how you can use strategic conferences, based on discovering common ground and imagining ideal futures, to improve planning within and between all sectors—business, government, labor, health care, education;

2. Suggest group methods of discovery, analysis, and dialogue that broaden our global perspectives, expand our horizons, utilize self-management and lead to committed action;

3. Build a bed-rock of democratic social values and core concepts under rather simple, task-focused techniques.

Moreover, I have a personal mission. There is a growing, world-wide interest in improving the quality of life, at home and at work. I believe that represents common ground for every person now living. I would like this book to serve as a catalyst for an informal global support network of people exploring and extending the use of these conferences. We have a unique opportunity to learn from each other and to amplify one another's successes.

This book provides readers a way into this network. Here you learn who is organizing strategic future conferences, why, and with what effect. You can study the theories, methods and skills needed to organize one. You can assess various practices, different models, and varying opinions on what works. You can read cases on their unlimited uses, and ponder the dilemmas and pitfalls too. I hope to encourage concerned leaders everywhere to experiment with this format. I believe this mode constitutes a learning laboratory for 21st Century strategic management.

How Is the Book Organized?

The book's nine parts represent a cornucopia of resources assembled here for the first time. I feel fortunate to have as contributors 35 professionals working in Australia, Canada, Colombia, the Channel Islands, England, Maylasia, Norway, Pakistan, Scotland, The Windward Islands, Turkey, and the United States. You will meet them through brief biographies in each chapter. Their experience enlivens every page.

PART 1 gives my overview of methodologies and a detailed account of the first "search conference," a key source that will deepen your understanding if you want to manage similar events. I also include a summary account of the design and planning for some 88 "collaborative community" events in the 1970's that opened up new possibilities for strategic change. Here also are the basic conditions for success.

PART 2 covers generic methods, underlying theory and an example of how one consultant translated this into a document for orienting participants. It also introduces another aspect—the linkage between dialogue, search processes and new ideas of science that I consider important to a full appreciation of what makes these events different. PART 3 gives cases and examples for a wide spectrum of purposes in single business and public sector organizations.

Then in PART 4 we go to "domains" (issues shared by many diverse parties) such as electricity in Colombia or conservation in Pakistan or Canadian children—issues that require interaction among many sectors—and in PART 5 to "referent" organizations, like the Australian Diabetes Foundation. "Referents" exist as clearing houses and/or network developers for diverse institutions and persons with parallel goals.

PART 6 offers two community development models that evolved in parallel to the work in Part 1 from a similar value base. Both broaden our insight into what's possible.

PART 7 offers a pot-pourri of personal experience and advice for facilitators—the training of conference managers, and theory/practice statements by practitioners. PART 8, on pitfalls and dilemmas, illustrates what might go wrong for folks new to this way of working—and veterans too.

PART 9 has speculations on what the future holds—Fred Emery's imaginative leap into telecommunications, Steve Burgess' "creative search gatherings," and my own imagining of future applications.

I have included a collective bibliography, all sources referenced by all authors, and to make the book even more useful, there is an address list of authors. Where appropriate, I show examples of the diverse conferences authors have run. The list is impressive, growing, and provides one answer to the inevitable question, "But has it ever been done by_____?"

Learning these processes involves two kinds of exploration. One is a journey into the practical theories and methods of some folks you will meet in the opening chapters. The second takes us on a voyage of discovery into ourselves—our enthusiasms, hang-ups, and internal tugs-of-war. In writing and editing this volume, I have helped myself greatly with both trips. I hope that in reading and using it you will do likewise.

Acknowledgements

First, there are 35 coauthors who made possible this book. My friend Ivar Brokhaug especially stimulated my imagination with tales of his work with motorcycle gangs and rural villages in Norway. Fred Emery and Eric Trist were generous with their files and memories. Merrelyn Emery slowed me down, cheered me up, and challenged me to offer this material as a full banquet rather than a "dog's dinner" of half-cooked letters and papers.

I gladly acknowledge the support of Ken Ross and Don Treinan, of The Alliance for Employee Growth and Development, John Mackey of Whole Foods Markets, Randy Evans and Richard Haworth, of Haworth Inc., Jane Henry of the Farm Credit System, Robert Fishman of Resources for Human Development, Steve Piersanti, former President of Jossey-Bass, Stan Rifkin, formerly of Software Engineering Institute at Carnegie-Mellon University, Chris Dennis and Pedro Mata of Grace Cocoa, and Susan Millard and Herman Simon of Quaker Oats Pet Foods. All organized strategy conferences on the strength of a chapter in my earlier book, thus deepening our experience with "future search" and validating my belief in the method.

Steve Piersanti did more, making this book a priority at his new firm, Berrett-Koehler, shaping the framework both as a skilled editor and a successful executive building on these values and ideas. I'm grateful to Pat Anderson for her diligence in checking covers and subtitles with prospective buyers, and to Alan Trist for an imaginative book design that captures the spirit of the contents.

There are others to be thanked—Deborah Zucker for her thoughtful editing and work with authors in the early stages, Dominick Volini for years of co-facilitating conferences and reminding me of the simplicity of trusting people to do the right thing, Joseph Weisbord for opening my eyes to the implications for urban planning, and Sandra Janoff for her dedication in helping design and run practitioner workshops that enable principled applications.

Then there are hundreds of enthusiasts—experts, generalists, managers, engineers, scientists, entrepreneurs—who have phoned, written, attended workshops, and shared their designs, triumphs and dilemmas. I'm particularly thinking of Marilyn Sifford, who organized a learning project in Philadelphia that launched more than a dozen conferences among non-profit organizations, and Mary Ann Holohean of the Fund for the City of New York, who did the same in her city. Finally, thanks to Gloria Co for picking up a thousand pieces, transcribing many papers that appear here, and knowing where to find every file I ever misplaced.

Marvin R. Weisbord
Wynnewood, PA
June, 1992

The Authors

Photo by Joyce George

Marvin R. Weisbord, an entrepreneur and author, worked as a consultant to business, education, government, medical, non-profit and voluntary organizations in North America and Scandinavia from 1969 to 1991. In 1991 he started Workplace Revolution, a non-profit program to help people apply the consensus-building ideas embodied in *Discovering Common Ground*. He is a partner in Block Petrella Weisbord, a firm that helps people restructure their work, and in Blue Sky Productions, a video company documenting innovations in self-management around the world.

Biographies of the coauthors, listed here in the order in which they appear, are given in their respective chapters.

Eva Schindler-Rainman	U.S.A.	Rita Schweitz	U.S.A.
Ronald Lippitt	U.S.A.	Elaine Granata	U.S.A.
Fred E. Emery	Australia	Beth Franklin	Canada
Oguz N. Baburoglu	Turkey	Alastair Crombie	Australia
M. Andy Garr, III	U.S.A.	Alan Davies	Australia
Rolf Haugen	Norway	Dick Axelrod	U.S.A.
Ivar K. Brokhaug	Norway	Cliff McIntosh	Canada
Margaret Wheatley	U.S.A.	Margaret Wanlin	Canada
John Briggs	U.S.A.	Patricia R. Tuecke	U.S.A.
John T. Wooten	U.S.A.	Tim Hutzel	U.S.A.
Kathie M. Libby	U.S.A.	Tony Richardson	Australia
Gary Frank	U.S.A.	Merrelyn Emery	Australia
Dave Angus	U.S.A.	Mary Fambrough	U.S.A.
Bob Rehm	U.S.A.	Maurice Dubras	U.K.
Rodger Schwass	Canada	James A. Cumming	U.S.A.
William E. Smith Ph.D.	U.S.A.	Chris Kloth	U.S.A.
David Morley	Canada	M. Stephen Burgess	Scotland
Eric Trist	U.S.A.		

PART 1

ORIGINS, CORE CONCEPTS, AND VALUES

Introduction

> "I am not a creator. I am a swimmer and a dismisser of all irrelevancies. Everything we need to work with is around us, although most of it is initially confusing. To find order in what we experience, we must first inventory the total experiences, then temporarily set aside all irrelevancies. I merely separate out some local patterns from a confusing whole. The act is a dismissal of pressures. Flight was the discovery of the lift—not the push."
>
> — Buckminister Fuller
> (Seattle Science Museum exhibit, noted 11/10/87)

The opening five chapters on our journey of discovery establish the values, precedents, broad applicability, and underlying conditions for a new practice of social change.

They offer a convincing rationale for making major course corrections in the way we manage corporations, communities and governments. More, they outline a theory and practice equal to the task. These chapters are the fruits of my inventory of experiences, my own and others, making one kind of sense from a confusing whole.

In Chapter 1, I describe this book's origins. I show what makes future search conferences different from any you are likely to have attended—in their assumptions, structure, tasks, and process.

In Chapter 2, I invite you to a behind-the-scenes tour of a seminal strategic planning meeting of two merged aircraft engine companies in 1960 England. Led by Fred Emery and Eric Trist, the innovators of modern work design, it opened the doors to a new strategy for confronting technological and economic "turbulence." The Emery/Trist process made possible a radical shift in the way we think of planning—who should be there, what they should do, and how they should do it.

In Chapter 3, I have adapted material written by the late Ronald Lippitt and Eva Schindler-Rainman, on some 88 community conferences they designed and managed in the 1970's. They demonstrate a dramatic method for bringing widely-divergent communities to act on local citizens' common stakes in the future. More, we are fortunate to have Schindler-Rainman's recent reassessment of that work.

Chapter 4 outlines the historic threads that make up the tapestry of my own work in this arena and the rich potential for future vartiations.

Finally, in Chapter 5, Fred Emery and I, in a recent exchange of letters, explore the guidelines for a social change practice based on dialogue. Emery draws on 30+ years of experience as an innovative action re-searcher/theorist and I on my background in managing and consulting during the same decades. This exchange underlies my contention that the principles and conditions for successful search conferences apply not only to 3-day meetings. They can be used to conduct a wide range of human affairs in democratic societies. To the extent we master them, we stand a chance of reversing many excesses of bureaucracy, fragmentation and mistrust. – MRW

CHAPTER 1
APPLIED COMMON SENSE
Marvin R. Weisbord

V ERY FEW MANAGEMENT PRACTICES I USED AS AN EXECUTIVE IN
the 1960's or as a consultant in the 1970's work any more. I'm
thinking not only of "scientific" methods based on wrong economic assumptions, like breaking work into tiny pieces to improve
"efficiency." I include participative or any modes of management that
preserve old divisions of labor and power.

We have created a world of relentless economic and social change,
based on 21st century technologies. Now we struggle to discover management methods equal to the complexity. None of us can follow the
bouncing red ball any more. We improve our cellular phones, computers, and fax machines at warp speed, while stressing our 2,000-year-old
psyches to the breaking point.

Still we keep raising the ante. We drive relentlessly, some of us, for
total quality, *fanatical* service, *prodigious* output, *astronomical* growth. Nor
is this all. We insist on reaching, a lot of us, for the brass ring of dignity
and meaning in work.

GETTING EVERYBODY IMPROVING THE WHOLE

In *Productive Workplaces* (Jossey-Bass 1987), I outlined an emerging
strategy that offers hope for better economic results, control of technology, and dignity and meaning too. I called it "getting everybody improving whole systems." (See "Learning Curve" below.) I explored methods
that enable people to understand the impact of their work on customers

and costs, that empower people to do the right thing without asking permission, that encourage people to cooperate across lines of hierarchy, status, culture, gender, race, and class.

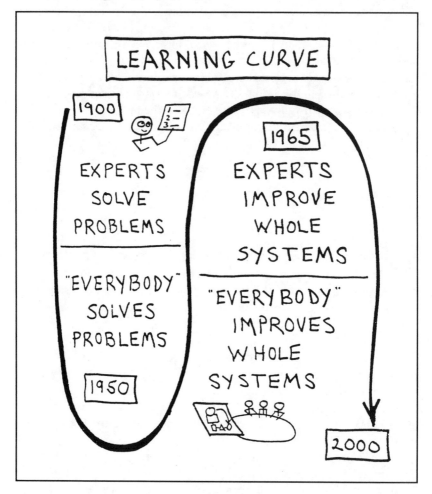

That brings us to this book. Most business meetings choose between involving "everybody" OR working on the whole system. We know how to invite large crowds for example, to hear a motivational speaker or the vision from the top.

When we do total system work, on the other hand, like strategy planning, or policy formation, we keep the group small, preferably top executives and staff experts. We farm pieces out to other small groups. Very few people ever get to help describe OR understand the whole.

As the meetings proliferate, so does the fragmentation. In a corporation of any size one senior strategy meeting can trigger 100 to 1,000 more meetings. Yet, as far back as I can remember, our dissatisfaction with meetings is legendary. The more we attend, the less we like them. Inevitably, we turn, for relief, to training workshops in the nuts and bolts of meeting management—setting agendas, using flip charts, writing down action steps, inviting comment, sticking to the subject, watching the clock. All of that is useful stuff. However none of it addresses the lessons embodied in this book. When we have large purposes and lofty goals, we need groups and agendas equal to the task.

I believe corporate and community conference strategies need significant updating. Nor is reducing the number of meetings what I'm proposing, although that would probably follow. I'm convinced that the sort of "umbrella" conference described here, if held once a quarter, would (1) obviate the need for many shorter gatherings, and (2) change the nature of, output from, and satisfaction with *all* intermediate meetings attended by the same folks. Of course, I cannot prove that. If you are persuaded by the evidence in this book, you still need to do your own experiments.

A NEW WAY OF DOING BUSINESS

To propose periodic variations on a two-and-a-half day future search conference as a substitute for dozens and maybe hundreds of meetings may seem at first glance preposterous. And it would be *unless* I can show that we can produce more whole systems learning, empowerment and teamwork with this simple mode than in dozens of separate meetings. The case would be stronger still if we could do it faster, at lower cost, and with more follow-up.

I believe that, given the right conditions, we can deliver the goods with the conferences described in this book. They represent an evolution in human thought, vision and values uniquely suited to our awesome 21st Century technical, economic, and social dilemmas. We are not talking simply meetings. We are describing another way of doing work.

These meeting designs rely on a creative interplay between two key strategic decisions. One is WHO gets to be there, the other WHAT it is they actually do. In these conferences, the WHO becomes "everybody"—a metaphor for a broad cross-section of stakeholders. The WHAT becomes scanning the whole system, not problem-solving it in bits and pieces. There is also an implicit HOW, self-managed dialogues, that we will come to shortly.

Typically, 30 to 65 or so people meet for up to two-and-a-half days. We do five tasks of about three hours each. We explore in turn the past, present, and future—of the world, ourselves, our institution. Everybody puts in information, discusses it, and decides what to do. The "technique" is a series of semi-structured dialogues. They take place in mixed, voluntary, and/or "stakeholder" groups, usually of eight people. Small groups report their conclusions to the whole. They post everything on flip charts in plain sight.

We explore and validate differences, but we don't "work" them. Should people open old wounds, fight old battles, or jump to problem-solving, we seek to have them acknowledge each other's reality and remind them that the task is finding common ground and future aspirations. As we discover them, that is where we plant our action flags. When we work on common ground and common futures, we tap deep wells of creativity and commitment.

The following box shows the "what" of one conference form, a "future search" model I have been evolving since 1983. I have put a box like this in chapters that include various conference plans.

CONFERENCE TASK: THE FUTURE OF XYZ
(Issue, company, community)

1. Review of the **PAST**: Milestones in society, self, sponsoring organization(s) over _____decades

PRESENT: 2. External—forces shaping our lives and institution right now

3. Internal—Prouds and Sorries in our relationship to "XYZ"
(Carry forward, leave behind)

4. **FUTURE**: Ideal Scenario(s)

5. ACTION PLANNING
In stakeholder, functional and/or voluntary groups

BOTH LESS PLANNING, AND MORE

In one way, these conferences require less preparation than traditional meetings. There are no rehearsals, overheads, "show and tells," keynote speeches, or training exercises. They are based on learning, not teaching. Learning, in these conferences, is not something people must "learn" how to do. They already know how. They just don't know that they know.

In another way, we need a lot more pre-planning. To find and act on common ground, we need a more diverse group than we are used to, taking a much broader view *together* of issues many have not considered in this context before.

I identify three intertwined threads that make future search conferences quite different from anything you are likely to have done before. First, we invite a much broader cross-section of "stakeholders" than is usual, widely diverse people who affect each other but rarely or never meet; Second, we have them self-manage tasks of discovery, dialogue, learning, and planning; third, we have them explore, together, the WHOLE system—its history, ideals, constraints, opportunities, global trends, within and without, rather than just the parts closest to home and soaking up the most energy.

However, the most radical aspect of these conferences is our stance toward conflict. Here we make a major break with the recent past. When we invite the right people, we will nearly always find unresolved conflicts and disagreements. Yet we discourage conferees from "working" their differences. Instead, we create a figure/ground reversal. We put the dysfunctional "shadow" dynamics in the background. People don't magically get better than they were. Rather, they tune in on different aspects of themselves—the more constructive and cooperative impulses.

Indeed, we neither avoid *nor* confront the extremes. Rather, we put our energy into staking out the widest *common ground* all can stand on without forcing or compromising. Then, from that solid base, we spontaneously invent new forms of action, using processes devised for that purpose.

In short, we seek to hear and appreciate differences, not reconcile them. We seek to validate polarities, not reduce the distance between them. We learn, innovate and act from a mutual base of discovered ideals, world views, and future goals. Above all, we stick to business. We make the conference's central task our guiding star.

It doesn't matter if people see each other once a day, once a year, or have never met. If they need each other, given a few simple tools and guidelines, they can imagine desirable futures together. More, they are likely to make action plans they may never have thought of before.

A VARIETY OF MODELS

Fred Emery and Eric Trist, pioneers of the mode, called them "search conferences." The late Ronald Lippitt and Eva Schindler-Rainman called their versions "collaborative communities." Others have dubbed them "visioning" meetings. I use both "future searches" and "strategic futures conferences."

These models are not identical. They derive from a variety of theories, experiments, and beliefs about how to improve organizational and community life. Each applier puts his or her stamp on their conferences. But most are traceable, in part, to Kurt Lewin, the social psychologist who coined that wonderful aphorism, "There's nothing so practical as a good theory." — MRW

APPLIED COMMON SENSE

The equation is something like THE RIGHT TASK + THE RIGHT PEOPLE + THE RIGHT SETTING = UNPRECEDENTED ACTIONS. That sounds a lot like applied common sense. Why, in most institutions, is it not commonly applied? I have to keep reminding myself that the (probably unconscious) function of old paradigm meetings is not breakthoughs, but control.

By hanging tight to the status quo, we maintain our control fantasies. There are two ways we use our normal meetings to maintain an illusion of control. The first is appreciating the WHOLE SYSTEM, but having only experts, staff managers, or top executives in the room to do it. They get the exercise right *cognitively*, that is, their heads are in the right place. But there are too few heads, so they never fully get the whole picture. More, they cannot easily implement what they learn from each other. They equate "understanding" with control, something that does not necessarily follow. The "big picture" is more than a static snapshot of information exchanged. It also is a moving picture dependent on how many people participate.

To implement effectively we need a shared picture of the "whole system"—future vision, values, policies and procedures in a *global* context. That calls for broad face-to-face joint planning. A lot of corporate strategy comes apart that way.

The reverse error is dynamic, getting it right *participatively*—with the wrong task. We may organize big groups into small task forces to solve narrow problems WITHOUT first joining in a shared appreciation of the whole. This kind of problem-solving takes us down numerous blind alleys. It keeps a lot of people busy, but the system gets no better. We honor democracy, but not systems thinking. Many quality circles programs came apart that way.

In short, if you have too narrow a group of people, you miss the big picture. If you seek only to solve problems and manage conflict, you miss the common ground.

The strategic conferences described here skirt both pitfalls. They uniquely meet the needs of leaders eager to upset the applecart without stirring up more resistance. This is done more easily when we shift our gaze from past problems to ideal futures, from conflict to common ground, from differences to shared assumptions, from pumping "input" into people toward *self-managed* output.

STARTLING OUTCOMES

The outcomes can be quite startling. They range from grass-roots community action to stimulate new businesses and jobs, to revitalizing a major company's total quality program, to setting future policy for a national banking system, to making policy for whole nations. Bob Rehm used the process to bring together parties feuding over the future of Colorado water (see Chapter 19). Dick Axelrod got commercial and sport fishing interests to discover their common stake in saving salt water fisheries (Chapter 23). Beth Franklin and David Morley ran a whole series of conferences that set the stage for a new industry, "nature tourism," in the Windward Islands (Chapter 20). These are a few of the many cases that follow.

The event oozes paradoxes too. Good things come of these conferences that were not planned or anticipated. They needed to happen, so they did. One example is the Haworth Corporation's discovery of the need to change its packaging practices to reduce its customers' waste disposal problems and make a cleaner environment.

Haworth's suppliers, also present, made the same discovery at the same time. So we have suppliers, company, and customers all changing their environment in "real time" while searching for *quality* in general (not environmental, or waste disposal, or ecology problems).

I suggest that *any* technique that promotes this level of systems learning, empowerment and teamwork is a good one. In my 1987 book I described two structures that I KNEW could accomplish these purposes—participative work design and future search. Both are traceable to the early coal mining studies of Eric Trist (Trist, Higgin, Murray, Pollock 1963) and later work by Fred Emery.

AN UNDERGROUND RIVER

By the late 1980's lots of cases existed on work design (e.g. "sociotechnical systems analysis"). But few business OR non-profit sector people had heard of these conferences, at least in North America. Yet, the deeper I delved the more certain I was that something important was cooking. Australians, for example, had run hundreds of "searches" that were making a big difference down under. Scandinavians and Canadians had run dozens more. There had been 100+ major community conferences in North American towns and cities congruent with these principals, and a significant scattering in South America, the Caribbean, India, Asia, Maylasia. A vast underground river flowed, unobserved by most strategy planners.

Nor was this "participative management." That concept—its heyday was the 1970's and 1980's—had been embodied largely as problem-solving task forces, quality circles and so on. The methods that had hooked me were quite distinct from breaking down issues into small, manageable chunks, the better to fix past mistakes.

Eliciting values, dreams, and innovation against a backdrop of global change, we have now discovered, is an enormous anxiety-reducer and energy source. We have learned that the more people we can get to apply their values to the whole, the more effective will be their planning. To do this we need to restructure bureaucratic hierarchies. And in this meeting—for two or three days—that is exactly what we do. A search conference provides instant relief from bureaucracy. People previously in opposition often act together across historic barriers in less than 48 hours. How does that happen? It seems to follow from our ability to combine content and process in a particular way that is more structural than interpersonal.

GETTING THE WHOLE PICTURE
REQUIRES THE WHOLE SYSTEM

The content requirement is for similar pictures in our heads of the *entire open system.* We need to bring into one room people who each have pieces of a complex puzzle. We need a shared view of what is going on in the world, our hopes for the future, what is going well for us, what not, what we want to do about it, and so forth—a moving mosaic of information captured by the phrase "whole systems learning." The starting place is NOT relationships with each other. It is our joint relationship to the wider world.

And we need to form this mosaic in a setting conducive to dialogue. We have to free ourselves up to explore, discover, learn, create, and plan together. This seems more likely to happen if we hold down exhortation and opt for self-control. And we have to skirt the bottomless pit of irreconcilable differences. That seems more likely if we make all data valid, acknowledge our differences, and agree to put our energy into working the common ground.

By 1989 I had seen remarkable discoveries made in "future searches" under these dynamic conditions. I was convinced the core process had infinite uses. I soon discovered that many experienced managers and consultants agreed.

AVERAGING APPLES AND ORANGES

So great was the hunger for more information, that I decided, somewhat naively, to put out an "international design book." When I made known my intention, Fred Emery and Eric Trist, pioneers of the methodology, were appalled. "I cannot see how any collection of instances of 'search conferences,'" wrote Emery, "can give us theoretical insight into the nature of search conferences. How do you know whether you are averaging apples, oranges or onions? More specifically, how do you know whether the different designers and managers have similar goals? Similar assumptions about how their goals are to be achieved? Similar assumptions about their role as managers?"

To this, Trist added his belief that "search conferences are a radical revolution, putting forward a new way of resolving basic human conflicts critical for securing a safe passage to a desirable human future. People will tend not to realize this or, if they do, to deny it."

Merrelyn Emery, an explorer who has influenced a generation of search managers, was blunter still. "Most of what goes under the name of 'search' in North America," she wrote, "simply isn't remotely close to the real thing. The search conference aims to do many things that include building associative communities. The foundations for this are spoken language. If people can't see that they share a world of their collective making, you've failed right at the start. The basic rules for avoiding 'in' or 'out' groups and major divisions, and for staying totally task-oriented, are violated time and again." She would not wish to perpetuate these errors, said Merrelyn.

Nor would I.

AN OPEN FORUM

So I opened the discussion to the contributors, asking for statements on their underlying theories and values. The response was quick, energetic, and gratifying.

Eva Schindler-Rainman (Chapter 4), author of several books on buiding community, cited values based on voluntary cooperation, mutual planning, and ownership by participants of their own processes. "These conferences fit into my practice of social change," she said, "because they affirm the notion that people can change the present and the future, if they become pro-active, and that I am able to help them do so in a way that transforms their desires into doable actions."

Bill Smith (Chapter 16), an international development consultant, added, "The danger is of an over-concentration on a 'thing' called a search conference, and a possible over-'technification' of what is at heart for me a very simple and powerful idea that meets a simple and urgent need. Many cultures have found their own unique ways to serve the purposes of a 'search conference.' I remember an African chief telling me how his people would gather frequently to talk about 'everything and nothing' before moving on to discuss substantive issues affecting the whole tribe. I sense that in some ways his people achieved in those far-ranging talks some of the functions of a search conference."

Mary Fambrough (Chapter 28), partner in an engineering firm, undertook some soul-searching on the relationship between teaching, learning, training and searching. "All this exploration has generated some new questions I've not come to terms with yet," she wrote. "A facilitator or conference manager has a role that is both necessary and powerful. The opportunity to manipulate outcomes is undeniable. When you have someone providing an operating structure who is called something like 'conference manager,' 'facilitator,' or 'coordinator,' the risk of creating dependency exists just as surely as if that person were a content expert."

David Angus (Chapter 15), Gary Frank and Bob Rehm (Chapter 14) cited several theoretical and value bases for their work. Their statement, I believe, captures the aspirations of many leaders today.

A NEW INTEGRATION OF VALUES AND TECHNIQUES

The techniques presented are, one by one, deceptively familiar. Anybody who practices participative or experience-based methods uses some of them. I've seen examples in strategic planning, total quality, customer service, employee development, work design, new technol-

STRATEGIC FUTURES ("SEARCH") CONFERENCES
● CORE VALUES

1. The first value is a matter of epistemology. We believe the real world is knowable to ordinary people and their knowledge can be collectively and meaningfully organized. In fact, ordinary people are an extraordinary source of information about the real world.
2. Thus, we believe people can create their own future.
3. People want opportunities to engage their heads and hearts as well as hands. They want to and are able to join the creative processes of organization rather than that being the sole domain of the organization's elite.
4. Egalitarian participation. Everyone is an equal.
5. Given the chance, people are much more likely to cooperate than fight. The consultant's task is to structure opportunities to cooperate.
6. The process should empower people to feel more knowledgeable about and in control of the future.
7. Diversity should be appreciated and valued.

David Angus, Gary Frank, Bob Rehm - 1989

ogy, cost cutting projects, stimulating product innovation. Few readers, though, will know the *integration* of these techniques into whole-cloth events that embody systems learning, self-management, and committed action. An integrated search makes a powerful antidote for bureaucracy, closed systems, narrow expertise, fragmentation and ad hoc problem-solving.

Search processes turn upside down popular beliefs about managing conflict, solving problems, learning new skills, voluntary cooperation, communications, and leadership. They do NOT make invalid other concepts and practices. Rather, these conferences provide a different lens for seeing the world, one that zeros in on perceived common ground.

That these methods work is amply documented here. That they don't *always* work is also made plain. The methods can be used as easily for amoral ends as noble ones. Techniques are easily foisted on people in the absence of commitment or perceived need. In my experience, techniques also are the major anxiety-reducers. There's an old joke about the football quarterback who always called for a punt on third down with 10 yards to go. When asked why, he replied matter-of-factly, "Because we know how to do it."

Inevitably, we must look inside ourselves if we wish to manage these conferences—to our own internal tugs of war between need and desire, creativity and control. For me, I could list a secret admiration for anarchy and a hunger for community, a need for control and a capacity to let people flounder and learn, a wish for certainty and patience with ambiguity and anxiety, an impulse to take search processes more seriously and myself less so. Even if it were possible to get others to do things we don't believe in, it is not ethical or useful. Yet, techniques don't care what we do with them. So "it" only works when WE work—with practical theories in a way that mirror values of democracy, learning, mutual respect, self-responsibility, cooperation, and wholeness.

One colleague of mine ran a group of 15 corporate personnel staffers through a one-day "future search" and concluded that "there's nothing new here, and this stuff doesn't do much anyway." We cannot expect results with discrete exercises used with too narrow a group in too short a time frame for too limited a purpose. Such applications reflect an impulse to action uninformed by any theoretical considerations.

One antidote to this impulse—that I have made infinitely more accessible here—is to explore the theories and methods of Fred Emery and Eric Trist, Kurt Lewin, Ronald Lippitt, Eva Schindler-Rainman and a host of others you will soon meet. Let me make plain that they are here entirely because those are the folks whose work excites me. Indeed, that is the main criterion for *all* the chapters.

This book reflects an ongoing dialogue among people who care deeply about improving the quality of life. We seek to expand our repertoire of methods congruently with our values and concepts. This dialogue on *what* and *why* differentiates our processes from so many others using similar techniques concerned only with *how*.

Our book contains at least six distinct strategic conference models. Many are traceable in whole or in part to the historic Barford conference (Chapter 3). The Australians—Crombie, Davies, Richardson—have been influenced most by Fred and Merrelyn Emery. Burgess in Scotland and the Canadians—Franklin, Morley, Schwass—worked with or derived their models from Eric Trist, except for Dubras who has worked with me and Brokhaug. The Norwegians—Brokhaug, Haugen—go back to Einar Thorsrud, a colleague of Emery's and Trist's from the 1960's.

Except for Smith (who studied with Trist and devised his own conceptual framework), nearly every U.S. case (e.g. Chapters 12-15) is based on my "future search" model (Weisbord, 1987, Chapter 14). That design derives from an integration of Emery/Trist and from Lippitt/Schindler-Rainman and includes other ideas I will discuss. The cases in Part 6, "Related Community Development Cases," come from other sources entirely. In both, however, we see many features in common with the other designs. (See "A Future Search Genealogy" on page 17.)

THE OUTER LIMITS

Inevitably, we come to the $64 billion question. Could these conferences make a dent in the world's most intractable conflicts—Arab/Israeli, IRA/English, black/white in South Africa, or between the republics in the newly formed Commonwealth of Independent States? Could these folks be helped this way to discover common ground? Or between cities and suburbs and among diverse ethnic groups in the United States? My answer is that I don't know. The methods reach their limits in the values of the leadership. This "works" only for people willing to engage in open dialogue based on accepting their differences. That means being open to new outcomes and unfamiliar methods influenced strongly by "real-time" creativity.

The applications that follow range from simple conferences to permutations employing search *processes* in ongoing strategic implementations. This book focuses mainly on discrete events, not entire change strategies. However, the event nearly always is a milestone, or chapter in a long story. It's not the whole drama. Nor do the sponsors imagine it to be. Yet, the processes are infinitely adaptable and could greatly improve everyday management.

I have given up trying to classify "degrees" of searching. While many of us believe we are on to the "real thing," the data here tells me there are quite a few real things going on, used in different ways by different people in different settings. The overriding reality, I conclude, is "equifinality"—lots of paths to the same place. That place, of course, is greater control of and responsibility for our own lives.

There are many ways to get there congruent with democracy, technological and economic realities, and humane values. If you want to run these conferences, put front and center the values you wish to actualize. Don't imagine you can overcome, even with elegant designs, the handicaps of weak leadership, a weak "business" rationale, a fuzzy conference task, or people who perceive no need to cooperate.

If you don't have good soil, don't waste your seeds. On the other hand, if you are working with people ripe for discovery and open to new experiences, read on. You will find here the theories, models and examples for many fruitful, home-grown harvests planted solidly in common ground.

A FUTURE SEARCH GENEALOGY

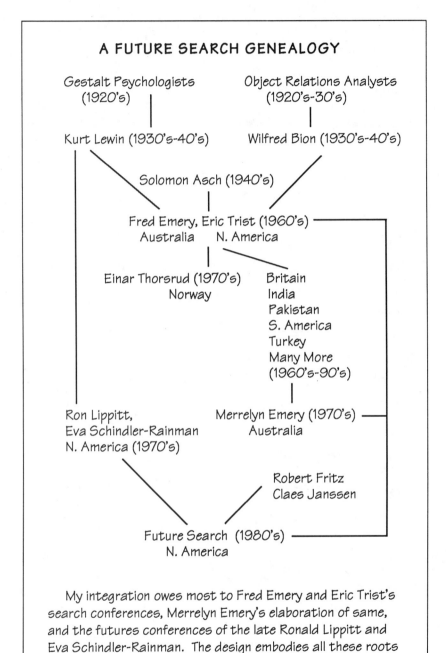

Gestalt Psychologists (1920's)

Object Relations Analysts (1920's-30's)

Kurt Lewin (1930's-40's)

Wilfred Bion (1930's-40's)

Solomon Asch (1940's)

Fred Emery, Eric Trist (1960's)
Australia   N. America

Einar Thorsrud (1970's)
Norway

Britain
India
Pakistan
S. America
Turkey
Many More
(1960's-90's)

Ron Lippitt,
Eva Schindler-Rainman
N. America (1970's)

Merrelyn Emery (1970's)
Australia

Robert Fritz
Claes Janssen

Future Search (1980's)
N. America

My integration owes most to Fred Emery and Eric Trist's search conferences, Merrelyn Emery's elaboration of same, and the futures conferences of the late Ronald Lippitt and Eva Schindler-Rainman. The design embodies all these roots and branches. — MRW

CHAPTER 2

INVENTING THE SEARCH CONFERENCE
Bristol Siddeley Aircraft Engines, 1960
Marvin R. Weisbord

I CAN IMAGINE NO BETTER WAY TO APPRECIATE THE CENTRALITY OF this book's theme to strategic planning than to climb into a time machine and revisit 1960 England. There we will observe the first search conference conducted by Eric Trist and Fred Emery for the Bristol Siddeley Aircraft Engine Company. It's a dramatic story of intellectual challenge with pointed lessons in managing strategic learning in conflicted groups.

Emery and Trist are the social scientists who in the 1950's sparked a new way of looking at workplaces, including the discovery of the power of self-managing work teams. Early on they began to think of their work as a search for more effective ways of organizing and managing congruent with democratic principles.

This objective was greatly accelerated by a request from Bristol Siddeley for an executive leadership course. Thus the first search conference became a joint action research experiment in strategic planning— an effort both to achieve strategic breakthroughs and to improve the process so others could do likewise. The intersecting needs of Bristol Siddeley and the Tavistock constitute a metaphor for discovery and learning. And their experience provides an invaluable guide to strategy formation today. Here's how it happened.

ONE WORLD, TWO CULTURES

In the 1950's the British government imposed a shotgun wedding on Armstrong-Siddeley, a piston engine company, and a world class jet pioneer, Bristol Aero Engines. The rationale was that Britain did not need three such firms, and the third, Rolls Royce, was a global leader. Now Rolls and its new rival were in a horse race to be number one in jets. Bristol Siddeley faced a classic dilemma. Its "two cultures" had merged on paper but not at the level of common plans and strategies. The potential for misunderstanding among executives was enormous.

That was a major worry for Sir Arnold Hall, the CEO, when he met Eric Trist in 1960. They were introduced by John Chandos, a mutual friend doing public relations for Hall's firm who had impressed Trist with his exploits parachuting into France in World War II and his First in History at Oxford.

"My wife and I met Hall and Chandos one evening at a local pub," Trist recalled. "Sir Arnold was bemoaning the multiplying problems in his company, given the rate of environmental change. I told him that we at Tavistock had some new ideas about coping with such problems."

Hall picked up the offer. Trist took along Fred Emery. Before lunch with Sir Arnold and his staff, Emery, Trist and Chandos met informally at Henneky's wine bar in Baker Street, for a private update (as Emery duly noted in his diary). I report this here because Chandos, an aristocrat and actor, made an indelible mark on Emery and Trist, playing a critical role in setting up a historic event.

THE FIRST SEARCH CONFERENCE

Date: July 10-16, 1960
Convener: Bristol Siddeley Aircraft Engine Co.
Conference Task: Unified Strategy/Mission/Leadership/
     Values for newly-merged company
Stakeholders: 11 – Each company's top person in design,
     production, finance, and marketing.
Length: 5 1/2 Days
Place: Barford House, Warwick, England
Conference Managers: Fred Emery and Eric Trist

As Trist recalls, "The lunch [with Sir Arnold] was set for two hours and the meeting went on another hour. The discussion, wide-ranging and sophisticated, also showed they had developed no particular ways of working together as a group, nor had they used modern methods of management. We proposed a week's residential seminar at their staff college at Barford near Warwick."

WHY BRISTOL SIDDELEY?

The new aircraft engine company offered Emery and Trist a chance to apply emerging action theories in a new arena. The two companies, Emery recalled, "were as alike as chalk and cheese. Their corporate philosophies were incompatible and they were contemptuous of each other." Sir Arnold hoped to create teamwork across the conflicting cultures. He wanted his executives to study together "the world at large to which the industry, and he as CEO, were exposed." Emery and Trist were intrigued by the dilemmas of managing large bureaucracies under "turbulent" conditions. The world was even then growing more unpredictable, less subject to rational analysis and control.

Both Tavistock and Bristol Siddeley had a lot riding on the Barford meeting. Yet their expectations were far apart. The company sought a "course" in leadership and strategy formation. Sir Arnold proposed to invite a panel of eminent experts—"the great minds"—from many walks of life to stimulate strategic thinking among his executives. Emery and Trist conceived the meeting as a process for unlocking "the internal forces of the group." They agreed the great minds had much to contribute here. They also were certain, from their experiences in Bion groups, that simply using the week for an expert lecture series would reinforce passivity and dependency.

SELZNIK, ASCH AND CONDITIONS FOR DIALOGUE

Moreover, Emery had two other conceptual frameworks he believed would increase the probability for success. One was Philip Selznick's (1957) criteria for an effective organization: (a) clear mission; (b) "distinctive competencies" to serve its market; (c) shared internal values among leaders to assure integrity despite dispersed authority.

The second framework was social psychologist Solomon Asch's (1956) "conditions for effective dialogue." Asch's research into perception and consensus had convinced Emery that these conditions would make the discovery of shared mission, competencies and values more probable in any group that could achieve them. Asch's conditions, framed by Emery, were shared assumptions that:

(a) all parties are "talking about the same world"—requiring that people back up their generalizations with concrete examples;

(b) all human beings have basic psychological similarities, as regards "laughing, loving, working, desiring, thinking, perceiving, etc."

(c) As a result of a and b, then "the facts of one person's world become part of the other's" and they develop "a shared psychological field."

Only then, Emery believed, could a genuine dialogue proceed. Its success would depend on how much people perceived an increase in freedom of choice along with increased understanding. If they did, reasoned Emery, then we could assume—final condition—that:

(d) People will experience their common dilemmas in the external demands, events, trends, developments shaping all of their lives, and plan accordingly.

ASCH AND CONDITIONS FOR DIALOGUE

Solomon Asch did a famous group pressure experiment. A subject is asked which two of four lines are of equal length. Other group members, coached in advance, unanimously pick a clearly unequal line. The dissonance is intolerable. The subjects want to belong AND to hold onto reality.

Under what conditions, Asch wondered, would people synthesize their views and agree to see the same thing?

His experiment had four features that prevented synthesis:

(1) There was no chance for dialogue: you look, listen, then decide; (2) you can only look and listen; you can't explore the source of difference; (3) you judge only on one variable, line length; (4) no complex ideas or objects are involved.

Said Asch (1952), "One fact constantly reappears in these observations. As soon as a person is in the midst of a group he is no longer indifferent to it. He may stand in a wholly unequivocal relation to an object when alone; but as soon as a group and its direction are present he ceases to be determined solely by his own coordinates."

Under the right conditions, people move toward the group and experience a shared world. They preceive themselves in common surroundings, "converging upon the same object and responding to its identical properties." Adds Asch, "Joint action and mutual understanding require this relation of intelligibility and structural simplicity."

The experimental features—no discussion, no exploration, one variable only, and over-simplified reality—can only produce false or forced consensus.

Here's what the young Fred Emery did for strategic planning using these ideas. The search, he theorized, ought to

be run so that everybody's reality is validated, considered
and explored. He took seriously Asch's admonition that,
"Consensus is valid only to the extent to which each individual
asserts his own relation to facts and retains his individuality; there can be no genuine agreement. . . unless each ad-
heres to the testimony of his experience and steadfastly
maintains his hold on reality."

Emery used the terms "extended social field" to describe
an open system's context, and "lawful relations" for the
connections among events in the extended social field. I
doubt that the Bristol Siddeley executives (or any group with
similar conflicts) could have problem-solved themselves
through to a new, successful aircraft engine in five days in
1960 with the methods and assumptions they then knew
best. Emery's innovation of having them start with the
extended social field and discover the lawful relations within
and between it, the industry, and their new company was, in
my opinion, one of the great strategic breakthroughs of this
century. — MRW

MEETING THE 'GREAT MINDS'

Emery and Trist proposed a compromise between Hall's wish for
stimulating new ideas and their emphasis on dialogue. "The 'great
minds' would be allowed in," Emery recalled, "when they would least
disrupt the continuity of the group's work. They would be selected and
briefed so that they acted to induce the group to move faster and more
widely in directions we had already established." An expert would
speak before dinner each evening and remain for an open-ended dinner
and discussion.

"All the invited speakers accepted," Trist recalled. They were the then
Chilean Ambassador who had "gained the confidence of diplomatic
London"; William Empson, an English professor, controversial poet and
critic; Seton-Watson, Oxford Professor of Politics and an expert on the
Soviet Union and Eastern Europe; Andrew Schonfield, Oxford econo-
mist and author of a book on developments in capitalism in the U.S. and
Europe "that was heralded as one of the great books of the times"; Field
Marshall Lord Slim, leader of the Burma campaign in World War II, now
ICI board member; a Catholic priest prominent in London intellectual
circles; and a controversial, conservative ex-Cabinet minister.

EXPERTS AS AN ELECTRO-MAGNETIC FIELD

Emery's metaphor for the outsiders' role was creating an electro-magnetic field. The dialogues would act as "+/-" poles keeping the whole in motion toward the twin goals of joint strategy and focused thinking, the one leading to commitment, the other to the right course of action. Here's the diagram Emery used in 1960 and recreated in 1990.

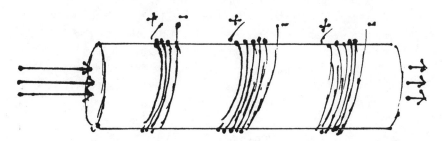

MULTIPLE REALITIES

This experiment posed several dilemmas. One, the CEO and conference managers differed on what was required. Two, Emery and Trist would play a dual role, as facilitators and action researchers. From their point of view it was not only important to pull off the merger. They also sought to learn how to improve task-centered strategic planning. This research role gave some participants fits, as we will see.

The first search was a blend of old and new consulting practices. To get ready, Emery interviewed each participant at length, wrote up his notes and got each person's agreement to the content. He then removed the names and sent all members a combined report that became their common property and the basis for the conference. And Emery based his questions on a wholly novel framework devised for the occasion.

His themes were three:

(a) What was the state of the industry in the world at large and what would the future be like over the next 15 years?

(b) What had the aero-industry become and how was it likely to develop?

(c) In relation to these, what was the state of Bristol Siddeley and how should it prepare to develop itself?

"At Emery's suggestion," writes Trist, "we proceeded from the whole outside world to the aerospace industry, to their own firm. This was the first time this order was followed. It has been retained in subsequent search conferences in the Emery/Trist tradition."

A NEW PLANNING FRAMEWORK

GLOBAL CONTEXT — The World Now and in the Future
INDUSTRY CONTEXT — Aviation Now and in the Future
COMPANY CONTEXT — Bristol Siddeley Now and in the Future
ACTION PLANNING — What Should We Do in the Future?

"Dealing with the wide world first," Trist points out, "breaks participants away from their daily concerns and centers the process on 'search' and 'appreciation' rather than decision-making. The problems of the industry are then looked at in a wide context. Their own company comes last. Its future will take place in these wider contexts, the full reality of which is not always taken into account. Any proposals for the company are future-oriented."

THE BARFORD CONFERENCE PROGRAM

Sunday Evening
Dinner with Sir Arnold Hall and informal talks afterwards.
Monday to Friday
9:00 a.m.-5:00 p.m. — Group discussions among 11 top
    executives, Emery, Trist, Chandos and staff
    (2-hour lunch break, and two 20-minute coffee breaks).
5:15 p.m.-6:30 p.m. — Address by/discussion with
    distinguished visitor.
6:30 p.m.-7:00 p.m. — "Sundowner" at pub.
7:15 p.m.-8:45 p.m. — Dinner.
8:45 p.m.-10:30 p.m. — Informal talk, group and visitor.
Saturday Morning
9:00 a.m.-12:00 noon — Group meeting with Sir Arnold Hall
    (with 20-minute coffee break).

THE BARFORD REPORT

The Barford report (Trist and Emery, 1960), is a long action research paper and a key document in management history. It is rare to find a detailed account of both content and process in a strategic conference that turned around a large firm. It is rarer still to find one written by people both central to the action and sensitive to the interplay between personal anxiety and corporate strategy.

Initially, I tried editing big excerpts from the original report. I decided it was too hard to follow. Instead, I have written a narrative, paraphrasing the content and building in Emery and Trist's recent reflections (in letters to me). This allows me to point out features that are particularly striking to me today, having run since 1983 some 20 conferences based partly on the 1960 model.

The Key Feature Was Stress

Trist and Emery open with a long commentary on "the great psychological intensity" of the course. They return often to this theme of continual stress. "The intensity," Emery wrote me in 1990, "was due to the *very high level of personal involvement in the tasks and the overriding demand for intellectual integrity.* Ideas had to be supported with everything at the individual's disposal."

A norm developed that each person was obliged to "understand and investigate the ideas of others" as a condition of belonging to the group. "Operating at this level for five-and-a-half days, was obviously very strenuous for all concerned."

Working with live issues, exchanging new information and perspectives, and balancing learning and doing in "real time" proved intensely demanding.

The emotional stress, Emery concluded, "was straight COGNITIVE overload. Five days was far too much, even for such a select group." The facilitators had forced the executives to consider every conceivable possibility. "I did not treat this as a trivial matter," Emery recalled. "Tavistock was immersed in psychoanalytic theory which held that the cognitive layer was simply a barrier of rationalizations that one had to penetrate to get to the real emotional dynamics. Our experience with Barford seemed very contrary."

Eric Trist saw the barrier as "largely true in the psychoanalytic session but not so much, or at all, in other situations." Still the pair had predicted dysfunctional group behavior—fight/flight, dependency and pairing. "We expected the conference to be disturbed by the frequent appearance of what Bion called 'basic assumptions,' unconscious material brought in to disrupt the group process," Trist recalled in 1991. "Having worked with Bion, I was there to cope with this. But it did not happen to any extent. The absence of this material caused me to remain rather silent. Subsequent experience has confirmed that these intrusions do not happen in search conferences to the extent they do in many other situations. We did not, of course, know this at the time."

Balancing Creativity and Commitment

Trist and Emery also grappled with a core issue of experience-based learning. They wanted to stimulate new ideas, creativity, and break-through thinking. They also wanted to establish common ground and stimulate new dynamics among conflicted stakeholders. "The measure of work done cannot be simply the discovery of new ideas," they wrote in their report. Any idea they turned up probably had been in *somebody's* head. The key was the discovery of common ground. This would happen if people "were able to develop new ways of looking at old problems; reach some common agreement about hoary problems that have plagued them individually; feel a new sense of personal relevance in solutions that have been officially adopted."

The pair reported several examples of "useful work."

A major piece was getting out the anxiety every person felt over an expected decline in the military aircraft engine market. While everybody was worried, no strategy had emerged. Now, after some tense discussions, they achieved a consensus on which way to go. One executive, for example, pointed out that research and development capital was a major problem for both industry and company. The group, with growing excitement, realized they could do something about this for themselves with "a scientific appraisal of the existing R&D process." Thus one executive's concern was elevated from a personal gripe to a relevant possibility sanctioned by the whole group. Trist and Emery saw that as a major advantage of the search.

The executives also considered a new organizational structure to include divisional presidents. They revisited product development and marketing, considering again a new small gas turbine engine, that led a top research person "to believe that a major technical breakthrough might be possible." In the words of the report, it showed "how looking afresh at an old problem may generate a new sense of hope, where there is a sufficient assurance that the problem is crucial to the group."

Next, they considered "distinctive competencies" and discussed making Product Manager a developmental training role for the future. "The presence of an existing Product Manager in no way inhibited discussion of this matter. In fact, the person concerned contributed greatly," reported Trist and Emery.

The group considered only aero engines, excluding industrial and marine types for lack of information. Emery and Trist could not exert enough influence to get this restriction dropped. They had counted on an expert lecture to direct attention towards marketing other kinds of engines in under-developed countries. Unfortunately, the expert took sick.

Balancing Content and Process
—The Facilitator's Dilemma

Looking back on the process, the facilitators wrote, "It was obvious that the pace [Phase 1] seemed a lot slower" to the executives than it actually was. To counteract this in future conferences, they proposed what we now call "processing the day"—reviewing what was learned in a prior phase before going forward. The group might "reassure themselves with knowledge of the results they had achieved."

Emery and Trist also held back at the start, so that the group would take initiative for their own discussion. This decision had unintended consequences. Toward the end, the executives suggested that the facilitators "should have intervened more [to speed up] the pace." In a terse comment that would tug any facilitator's heartstrings, Trist and Emery noted, "The few attempts we did make to intervene were, without exception, rejected."

The tension between the group's expectations for expert input and the facilitators' wish that the executives be more autonomous continued. The group wanted Andrew Schonfield to stay and help with the issues he had raised. Emery and Trist hoped "the group would have gone far enough in their own discussions to have been able to treat Schonfield's contribution as a parallel set of problems—a semi-neutral context within which they could argue differences that had arisen in their own field."

Here Emery and Trist encountered every consultant's dilemma. To what extent are facilitators to be "experts," and on what? "In Phase 2 the pace was rapid and the scope broad," they wrote in their report, "but quite a good deal of work failed to come to focus because of the lack of appropriate concepts. Although this was a point where we expected to make a helpful contribution, we had deliberately chosen not to [be content-focused] resource people." Rather, they opted for "keeping the group at its task."

This led to some mistrust in their roles. "We failed to come in with enough positive contributions on the problems of leadership," they wrote. They decided that in future courses their responsibility would be to describe to groups "the concepts relevant to the work (e.g., distinctive competence, organizational integrity, institutional values)."

Yet, the executives did significant work because of the facilitators' insistence that they work their own problems. "Only by doing this did they create a mutually shared goal of intellectual search and sufficient personal involvement to demand a high level of responsibility and sincerity. Outside lectures alone would not [engender] responsibility for one's views nor expose individuals to each other in ways they would feel important for their roles in Bristol Siddeley." If lectures had been central, they speculated, the conference would have been reduced to "intellectual gymnastics and entertainment."

Other Ambiguities

The role of "Great Mind" proved no less problematical.

Slim, for example, rather than the hoped for input on how leaders elicit distinctive competence, delivered "a lecture on the moral philosophy of leadership," interesting, important, and largely irrelevant. Likewise, "Seton-Watson's exercise contributed a useful and highly interesting picture of contemporary international politics, but it failed to present the matter with which the group was concerned, namely, the problems and the value attached to the deliberate creation of an institutional elite."

Trist, in a tongue-in-cheek mood, recalled some of the consequences. The Chilean Ambassador canceled at the last minute. His alternate, a psychiatry professor, got everybody's attention by remarking that one person in ten in Britain spends time in a mental hospital. "Counting Chandos and us," Trist recalled, "there were 14 people in the room. It seemed as if at least one of us was going to do time!"

Nor was this all. "Empson beguiled his audience by twisting but not spilling his sherry glass," wrote Trist, and "Seton-Watson gave a profoundly-different assessment of the Soviet Union from any they had heard. An interesting development was that quite early most participants did not go to the mess for pre-dinner cocktails but, with Emery, to the pub, for beer. This was called the 'Australian sundownder.' It was a step in establishing egalitarian relations."

Emery recalled the reaction to the visitors somewhat less-charitably. "The participants felt that the visiting lecturers, despite their eminence, were a time-wasting execresence," he wrote 30 years later, "and told us so on the last days. They did attach a lot of weight to our knowledge of what areas they should get into, what lines of enquiry should be persisted with and what lines dropped. There is still a component that touches on the 'expert' role," Emery went on. "I think conference managers should, where possible, research the field beforehand and alert themselves to emerging possibilities."

Sustaining Task Focus

The group had a hard time staying with the search rather than making decisions. Emery and Trist thought they were missing some important statistics. The resistance was low key at first. On Tuesday, "only one member was openly voicing his opposition to the search task." By Wednesday, as a range of company problems surfaced, more people became vocal. "Considerable hostility was directed at us," reported Emery and Trist, "apparently on the ground that we should not be hearing Company secrets, but really because we were seen as forcing them to go on with the task."

In mid-morning "two members blew up and demanded that the group task be abandoned because it was both sterile and illegitimate." One person felt shut off, another felt he was being pushed "further in self-exposure to the staff than he was prepared to go." A coffee break was called, "during which the members were able to reassure each other that basically they were doing a worthwhile job." After the break, tension relieved, they "recaptured their task and went at it hammer and tongs."

The group never fully got over its mistrust of the facilitators. This probably resulted from a combination of factors: tensions in the merger; the mixed focus of the conference; the various and ambiguous purposes; the complexity of the issues. Some people suspected "that the Course was being run for the Managing Director as a personnel testing and selection procedure." The greatest resistance during the meeting, for example, came from the man who had raised the selection issue in the initial interview and never let go.

Strategy Breakthroughs

Despite the mixed mode, anxiety and novelty, however, the aircraft merger partners made both social and technical breakthroughs. The two cultures discovered their common ground, AND they made critical strategic choices. "By the end of the week they were certainly thinking like one group; and not at all like Siddeley or Bristol men," recalled Emery. "They radically re-defined the business they were in: from pursuing the top-end of the big jets to mobile combustion power generation across the spectrum of internal and external combustion engines." In fact, top management had been on the verge of rolling out an expert strategy directly contradicting the plan that finally emerged.

Finally, there was a major new product breakthrough. As Emery recalled it in 1990, they came up with "the design concept for an airbus for short, dense inter-city routes. . . four small engines with the plane certified for landing on two; modular replacement of engines for overhaul; high wing for easy ground loading; small engines meant very low noise levels. That plane became the BA 146 which is Britain's winning product today."

SOME REFLECTIONS 30 YEARS LATER

The event, conclude Trist and Emery in the Barford report, "was probably successful." That, as near as I can tell, has also been the assessment of conferences I have run. The groups get more than they came for, and the facilitators are still learning new wrinkles for improving the process.

Many participants still report feeling stressed. They become deeply engaged, expend enormous energy, and always are at risk for cognitive overload. When the walls are covered with flip charts listing every issue on the minds of 40 or 50 people, it takes considerable intellectual energy to sort it all out.

In addition, regardless of the time for each task, some people may feel rushed. I do not know how to accommodate this. One way to ameliorate the stress is to quit each day by 5:00 p.m. and let people socialize and eat on their own. An "Australian sundowner" is no bad thing in this context.

A second concern is always follow-up. To what extent will we turn our dreams and schemes of the moment into reality? The answer is that rarely are strategies carried out exactly as fantasied in a conference.

At the same time, the images, metaphors, and practical ideas tend to influence a broad spectrum of future actions by participants. Because slight course corrections make a big difference the further out we go in time, these conferences probably have much more future impact than can be measured with typical evaluations.

Mixed Expectations

Identifying Barford as a "Course" set up expectations for teaching and learning. It built pressure for cognitive models by which to sort data and make sense of the experience. More, Emery and Trist felt an obligation to provide (1) models, (2) real data on the issues of merger (by way of the pre-dinner speeches), and (3) facilitation of the dialogue. Having mixed modes and expectations made this an especially stressful experience for the conference facilitators.

One consequence for me of analyzing this case is that I have come to appreciate searching as a qualitatively different activity from "training" or "management development." Encouraging full exploration of the shared environment is a positive step toward empowering people to take charge of their own experiences.

The research role—Trist as observer—raised anxiety. We see here more clearly the need for participant roles for everybody—as stakeholder, recorder, documenter, timekeeper, discussion leader. Calling the facilitators "conference managers" also reduces the social scientist/ psychologist image.

Problem-Solving vs. Searching

Years ago the late Ronald Lippitt (see next chapter) pointed out that one function of familiar problem-solving is to reduce our anxiety. Lippitt thought the anxiety, paradoxically, was caused in part by the problem-solving method itself—the relentless breaking into bite size pieces of many complex issues. So, pushing the executives to leave out "operational probabilities" in the Barford conference was a central break with the old paradigm. Today we embody this in ideal future scenarios that are highly-desirable. By putting the ideals as far into the future as the group can tolerate, we break the mindset of present constraints on time, money, and knowhow.

Projections on the Facilitators

The wish to have Emery and Trist intervene more, to make things go faster (or slower), I also have experienced. I take it to be an example of how group members project on the conference manager as authority, and expect to have all their (divergent) needs met by this person. People elicit the "parental" response, then become balky children. Every supervisor, leader, and chief executive experiences this.

Trist's observer role heightened the anxiety. Trist stayed aloof, coming across, I imagine, like a Tavistock trainer. All of us who manage large meetings experience this projection. Some people believe the leader is judging their performance, finding it wanting, and is secretly disapproving. What is projected, I think, are self-doubts among the participants that they're equal to the task. They express their doubt as dependency, e.g., "Do you want us to write or print?"

Experts as Peers

Perhaps the most significant break with the old paradigm was their positioning of experts in future conferences. They concluded that experts impeded the search unless they joined in as group members. Reducing dependency and encouraging independent thought and democratic dialogue became overriding values. These values continually challenge us as conference planners. Fred Emery wrote me recently that he thinks it's increasingly important to invite the most creative stakeholders, even at the cost of reducing numbers from some key groups.

And what can be said of the conference managers' expert role? Emery and Trist concluded they should manage the time and tasks and present only concepts that would assist the group in accepting its tasks.

Where Does Valid Data Come From?

As group size and diversity increase so does the potential for mapping the entire field, conceptually, if not technically. It's not surprising that Bristol Siddeley lacked important relevant knowledge with only 11 executives present. We now know we need at least 30 or 40 diverse stakeholders to get a solid cross section of knowledge and experience into one room.

AFTER BARFORD

In the 1960's the Human Resources Center of the Tavistock Institute conducted its own professional meetings in the search mode. Emery even used the method to develop flavor profiles for British beers, and ran three conferences in the Lyons Company on food products issues.

In 1973 a new town called Gungahlin was planned for Canberra, the capital of Australia. Merrelyn Emery (1981) and Angela Sands organized a search by young people ages 16-25. Their success sparked a rash of requests to use the method in all sorts of community development conferences. A network of practitioners inspired by the Emerys grew up in Australia. Together they began an integration of social planning and community development. They began to understand planning as something people do together rather than have done for them. This remains a problematical notion in a world overwhelmed by dazzling technologies and technologists. Yet the underlying premise is easy to test. Involve stakeholders in any institution directly in planning its future—and watch what happens!

CHAPTER 3
BUILDING COLLABORATIVE COMMUNITIES
Eva Schindler-Rainman and Ronald Lippitt

THE CHAPTER THAT FOLLOWS describes a community-building model that has had wide impact the past 20 years. I consider this an invaluable resource for anybody who cares about the future of our global society. It describes a highly-structured process that makes possible unprecedented community interaction within a few days and action projects that might continue for years. This chapter is revised with permission from *Building the Collaborative Community*, Copyright © 1980 by University of California Extension, Riverside. — MRW

W E HAVE SPENT MUCH OF OUR PROFESSIONAL LIVES HELPING groups, organizations and agencies discover values, goals and methods to improve their services and increase the satisfactions of professionals and volunteers. In the 1960's we began asking whether we could extend this work to whole communities.

Could we facilitate collaboration among many local groups and agencies toward mutual goals and action plans? Could we establish the kind of "inside-outside" consultant teams that had worked so well with organizational renewal? Could the many vested interests—public and private, professional and volunteer, profit-making and public service, disadvantaged and affluent, ethnic, racial, sex and generational divisions—be convened and find common cause?

Starting with Evansville, Indiana, in the fall of 1970, we found not only that we could do all the above, but that a great hunger for community collaboration existed everywhere, despite profound mistrust, alienation and skepticism. People *wanted* to come together. They simply did not know how. As a result, by December 1977, we had worked with 80 towns and cities and eight states or larger geographic units—88 distinct communities in all—on collaborative conferences to unite whole communities in planning their future. Some communities held one or more follow-up conferences a year or two later.

In 1978 we sent out questionnaires and documented results from 74 conferences in 60 communities. In this chapter we describe our strategies, methods, designs, and what we learned while collaborating with some 15,000 citizens over seven years. We believe our experience is relevant for national leaders seeking to establish partnerships to save, renew and strengthen our cities and neighborhoods. We also believe that our designs and tools are important resources for leaders, citizens and groups motivated to organize successful local collaboration efforts.

Extending Change Processes to Whole Communities

The communities we worked with—small, medium, large—were in the United States, Canada and islands in the mid-Pacific Ocean. They included nine towns of 5,000 to 25,000 people, 31 of medium size with 25,000 to 100,000, 20 cities from 100,000 to 500,000, and 20 metropolitan areas of 500,0000 or more.

We are describing only community activities where some form of interorganizational collaboration occurred. Usually public and private, government and business sectors were involved, as were the affluent and the disadvantaged, and urban, suburban and sometimes rural areas. Most planning activities resulted in a community conference, meeting or seminar, from half-a-day to five days in length. Most took between eight and 12 months to plan (a few took 16 months).

It is difficult to draw a participant group profile. They varied with the community, purpose, composition and values of the planners. But in every conference an effort was made to build-in "scholarships" and other enabling funds that would support participation regardless of economic resources. Participants always included both professionals and volunteers. Variations were great in age and income, life style, religious, ethnic, national and racial backgrounds. Physically-disabled persons were often important participants.

Sponsors

Activities were initiated by one or more organizations or agencies, or an ad hoc leadership group. Additional sponsors always joined during planning. Sponsorship could mean total financial support, or partial financial support with fees and others sources of funding making up the total budget. In most communities where one organization sponsored the first event, a second, if held, was always sponsored by a collaborative committee. Sponsors learned that the broader the planning team the greater the participation in the event.

The Junior Leagues initiated or co-sponsored more meetings than any other organization. A nonpolitical organization with deep community roots and wide influence, it is active, highly-respected and can involve a broad community cross-section.

Furthermore, the League generates its own funds and is therefore able to carry through projects. Ad hoc committees were initiators in 39 cases—typically including community and neighborhood organizations, some cause groups, and ad hoc community leaders.

Building Participation

To attract wide participation, we included people from all sectors in the planning group. Most planning groups included persons from upper, middle and lower income segments of the community, as well as different age, sex, race, ethnic, religious, life style and national groupings.

Publicity was important. Many planning groups arranged talk show and newspaper interviews. Some developed a speakers' bureau of planners who attended community meetings to invite people to the collaborative event. As consultants, we often were interviewed by a local paper or radio station. Another procedure was to involve a few knowledgeable resource persons or the total planning committee in nominating influential community members from various sectors to receive personalized invitations.

Defining Purposes

The purposes of each event and follow-ups varied. They ranged from information, inspiration, and education to ongoing collaborative projects and task forces; all provided opportunities to meet new people, visibility for sponsors, and exposure to new community and consultant resources. Purposes always were defined locally, and outcomes were directly tied to locally-defined hopes and needs. Most conferences developed many action projects. If the focus was future planning to improve the quality of life, for example, task forces might initiate projects ranging from developing a Voluntary Action Center to beautifying the local dump.

Ensuring Follow-Up

We learned quite a bit about voluntary action. For example, if people formed task forces during the collaborative meeting *and* conducted their first meeting on the spot, follow-up actions succeeded more often than not. Our surveys also indicated that in most communities that built follow-up into the planning process, cooperative action continued long after the event.

Conference Length

Conference lengths varied. Thirty-eight lasted from one to one-and-a-half days, 43 were two to two-and-a-half days in length, and seven lasted three or more days. Many of the one to one-and-a-half day conferences were in communities that later held a second conference, this one often a bit longer. Meeting times varied. They might be scheduled from 9 a.m. to 4 or 5 p.m. or from 1 p.m. to 8 or 9 p.m. It seems to us now that two days is about right.

Size

Conference sizes varied too. We have data on 82 meetings: ten had 30-99 participants, 44 had 100-199, and 28 had 200 or more. We estimate that 15,000 or more participants were active in all 88 meetings.

Our data came from a questionnaire sent to the organizers and sponsors of collaborative events in July 1976. We sent 88 questionnaires and got back 74 between August 1976 and the fall of 1977. Many included reports, newspaper clippings, informational materials, and often personal letters giving us details of their follow-up activities. Our survey even initiated new activities by suggesting that people get together to look at printed reports of the conferences and meetings. Most were disseminated to all conference participants. Some were placed in the local library and made available to persons and agencies not able to participate. Many participating organizations sent reports to their national headquarters. These reports constitute a rich library of community action patterns and priorities.

TOWARD THE COLLABORATIVE COMMUNITY: DESIGN CRITERIA

During our years of meetings, we evolved a generic model for helping build collaborative communities. It required managing a great many details and considerable collaboration from large numbers of people. Always we were guided by a growing awareness of the degree of fragmentation, alienation, conflict, "turfdom," competition, possessiveness, distrust between agencies, organizations, and other sectors in many communities.

The actual design, shown below, was relatively simple. However, it was not easy to implement. Rarely did we find collaborative goal setting and planning in place or hear the voices that should interact and be heard. In fact, we often found a sense of impotence, frustration, and lack of influence, discontinuity of leadership, lack of accountability, monitoring, evaluation of commitments.

COLLABORATIVE COMMUNITY DESIGN

DAY 1: 9:30 - 12:00

- Public Interviews with Community Planners Re Conferece Goals
- "Who We Are" – Introductions/Expectations
- Overview of Work Plan

THE PAST: Review Community History

THE PRESENT: Prouds and Sorries Re Community Life
- Consensus Priorities: Proudest Prouds, Sorriest Sorries

THE FUTURE: Images of Potential
- Desired Futures One Year Out

12:00 - 2:00 - Buffet Lunch

- People Read/Check Priorities on Images Lists

2:00 - 4:00

- Select Community Priorities
- Self-Select Action Groups
- Goals, Initial Action Plans
- Process Review – "Pulse Taking"

DAY 2: 9:30 - 12:00

- Testing Feasibility
- Role-Playing Skill Practice (e.g. managing resistance to ideas)

1200 - 1:30 - Buffet Lunch

- Community Leaders Comment on Plans

1:30 - 3:30

- Follow-up Planning: Who, What, When
- Task Force Reports
- Schedule Review Meeting
- Documentation Plans, Media Interviews

Converting these challenges into design strategies, we realized that to stimulate successful community action we had to:

1. Involve community leadership from "functional sectors," such as *public safety* (courts, police, probation, parole services); *recreation* (public, private, commercial); *social welfare* (private and public adult and youth service agencies); *education* (public, private and parochial); *health* (physical and mental, public and private), the *economic community* (business, industry, labor); the *political community* (elected and appointed officials as well as the more informal political influence); the *religious community* (orthodox and unorthodox belief groups — Catholic, Protestant, Jewish, Buddhist, Moslem, etc.); *mass media* (television, radio, newspapers); and the *art/cultural sector* (art, music, museums, etc.).

2. Find ways to recruit, motivate and mobilize the young, middle-aged and elderly; women and men; establishment and ad hoc informal leadership; the advantaged and disadvantaged populations; racial, national and ethnic minorities; the organized and the unorganized; handicapped community groups.

3. Develop new ways for the polarized, distrustful segments of the community to be included in the collaboration and therefore to communicate more openly and frequently and learn new designs and skills for collaborative effort.

4. Develop methods and situations that demonstrate the value of differences of traditions, ideas, beliefs, needs and expectations as a resource.

5. Help people learn the skills required to develop collaborative networks and support their effective functioning, including development and training of internal "change agents."

6. Increase the awareness, sensitivity and skills of professionals, volunteers, leaders and members to enable them to develop opportunities for, and collaborations with, underutilized citizen volunteers and groups.

7. Develop procedures for linking ad hoc initiators and groups into the ongoing structures, operating traditions and "continuities" of the community.

8. Develop commitment, designs and mechanisms for follow-up work on goals, intentions and plans discussed in the initial startup conferences.

In general, we followed the same procedure in nearly every conference. Of course, there were many local variations, depending on needs and time available. In *Building the Collaborative Community* we give detailed accounts of design options, logistical support, the required consulting skills, and suggestions for learning to manage these processes.

INFLUENCES ON FUTURE SEARCHING

The Lippitt/Schindler-Rainman model has been a major source for the "future search." Seven of the authors' eight design strategies influence my practice—involving broad leadership; including people often left out; building collaboration among opposing interests; validating differences; increasing opportunities for mutual appreciation and joint work; establishing continuity structures, follow-up and review mechanisms.

I cannot imagine improving on the political wisdom and logistical scope of the collaborative communities. I recommend the original book for its comprehensive planning advice and ingenious follow-up ideas.

Drawing on this work, I also follow the sequence of past, present, future, and action planning in future search conferences. I like the "prouds/sorries" review. It constitutes a powerful lens on the open system—how stakeholders perceive their relationship to the focal issue/task/sponsor. In dynamic terms, it enables people to own up and to move on.

The only aspects I have not embraced are this model's emphasis on training small group facilitators and including training/skill practice in the conference. The future search design relies on people self-managing their small groups. I believe in the transformational potential of diverse groups seeing themselves as living on the same planet. Rather than skill building, I see the function of future search as enabling people to do vital things that they already know how to do — and never had the chance. — MRW

THE COLLABORATIVE COMMUNITY 20 YEARS LATER

Reflections on Learning Among Diverse Community Groups

Eva Schindler-Rainman, December 1991

Collaboration was an unknown or at least an unloved concept in 1970. Some people thought it was the same as co-operation or coordination. Others thought of war time "collaborators," and that of course was totally negative. We thought of collaboration as the cooperative or joint efforts by disparate groups or systems directed to achieving an agreed upon common goal, outcome, or objective.

Collaboration was (and is) the combination of a wide variety of skills, resources, knowledge, and ideas to translate ideas, goals, and hoped for outcomes into action. It brings a wide range of people and systems together for the common good. It celebrates the beauty of difference.

We had by then written the frontier-breaking book *The Volunteer Community: Creative Use of Human Resources*, and felt we had arrived at an expanded, richer notion, namely the collaborative community. We combined Ron Lippitt's work on change and my experiences in the Volunteer or Third Sector. We both brought expertise and knowledge about individual, group, and organizational behavior, Ron from social psychology, me from social work with a special focus on community organization and development.

The *impact* of our joint ventures has been widely felt, both nationally and internationally. Reflecting on this work in 1991, I believe these are some impacts traceable to our work:

1. New concepts and language. "Volunteer Community" and "Collaborative Community" are widely used now by people who have no idea of their origins. This is also true for the concepts and strategies associated with "From Images to Action" that we also originated in the 1970's.
2. We broadened the term and concept of "community" to include functional as well as geographic conclaves.
3. It is now commonly accepted that differences or diversities are what we need to bring about common cause, common agreed-upon goals, and creative, common, concerted action.
4. When we started, people often insisted on equal effort, time, and commitment—an unrealistic aspiration. Now it is a matter of course in joint collaborative efforts that groups and individuals may contribute different efforts, time commitments, funding, etc.

5. In the 1960's, group problem-solving (looking backward) was the norm in community development. We pioneered and implemented future planning from a realistic basis of *desired* scenarios, images, and outcomes.
6. When we started, collaboration was a creative choice. Now, tighter budgets have made it a virtual necessity.
7. We changed and expanded the competencies needed by community consultants.
8. Community planning and decision making became a participatory, open system process, bringing about feelings of empowerment in all who participate.
9. We opened the door to broad participation in many communities and showed people willing to spend the necessary time and effort how to set clear goals and become community leaders.
10. Community-building has influenced macro-system change theory (Richard Beckhard, for example, invited me to the first meeting at M.I.T.'s retreat center on macro systems concepts).
11. We demonstrated the feasibility and reality of involving citizens in planning their own destinies, and implementing these plans with professional guidance and consultation.
12. We made clear that formal education, or specialized backgrounds need not be the "entrance requirements" for participation in this process.
13. We practiced our belief that local citizens know a lot about each other and the strengths and weaknesses of their community. In other words, they are the key resources for diagnosis, and realistic planning. In their diversity can be found resources of strength, commitment, knowledge, skills, time, and energy.
14. We showed how sensitive professional skill and knowledge could unlock these resources.

I am excited to feel that we contributed and impacted this world a little.

ABOUT THE AUTHORS

Dr. Eva Schindler-Rainman, an internationally-known organizational consultant, is the author of more than 250 articles and author or co-author of many books (see appendix). She is an adjunct Professor at the University of Southern California School of Social Work, and a long time member of NTL Institute. She has consulted to the U.S. and Canadian YMCAs, the American National Red Cross, the Association of Junior Leagues, the World Council of Churches, and many corporations, state volunteer offices, and corrections and human resources departments throughout North America.

The late **Ronald Lippitt** was a pioneer of group dynamics, a founder of NTL Institute and a leading innovator of social change.

The book from which this chapter is taken, *Building the Collaborative Community,* is available from ENERGIZE, Susan J. Ellis, Director, 5450 Wissahickon Ave., Suite 534, Philadelphia, PA 19144. 215 438-8342.

PARALLEL PATHS TO COMMUNITY
Equifinality in Action
Marvin R. Weisbord

I N THIS CHAPTER I WANT TO REINTERPRET STORIES FIRST TOLD TO ME, quite separately, by Eric Trist and Ronald Lippitt that form the basis for Chapters 2 and 3. They will help you appreciate my assertion that future search conferences represent a significant advance in cooperative planning. More, I write now with the advantage of 20/20 hindsight gained by putting these ideas into action the past several years.

I met Eric Trist when he was teaching at the University of Pennsylvania. We came together through a common interest in medical care systems, serving on a task force to devise an ambitious action research plan to cut costs and improve services in hospitals. It was never funded. That was the bad news. The good news was my learning about Trist's work in the 1950's with Fred Emery. Trist had a shrewd appreciation for the many dilemmas of changing large systems, and he had a talent for seeing merit in novel ideas, even improbable ones, including some of mine. Naturally I enjoyed that, and him. We remained friends.

When Fred Emery spent a year at Penn in the early 1980's Trist introduced us. Emery's legendary erudition bowled me over. He assumed I knew a host of obscure (to me) research studies in a dozen fields. I have yet to track them all down, but over the years I have honed my appreciation for Emery's ability to synthesize research findings into extremely sensible—and challenging—theories for extending democratic practices to every corner of society.

I had met the late Ronald Lippitt in Bethel, Maine some years before.

What grabbed my attention was his re-telling of the story of the discovery of the "T-Group," that included an amusing anecdote about the use of flip charts in business meetings (see below).

Kurt Lewin, the social psychologist whose fertile ideas underlie a lot of modern management practices, had a habit of using butcher's paper to make mathematical diagrams of complex human problems. He preferred paper to blackboards because he could keep his drawings in sight and show them to a lot of people at once. In 1946, driving through Connecticut to a conference in Maine, Ron Lippitt recalled, Lewin realized they had no butcher's paper. It was Sunday, the shops were closed. What to do? Newsprint, somebody suggested. Newspapers throw away the rolls at the tail end of the press run. By now they had reached Hartford, and quickly found the pressroom of the *Courant* where a friendly operator obliged with some end rolls. The group drove on to Bethel, Maine, site of the workshop. There, using rulers, they tore the newsprint into large sheets. To this day NTL Institute uses newsprint in its workshops in Bethel. Nearly everybody calls flip chart paper "newsprint" even when it isn't. In Australia, they call flip charts "butcher's paper," even when they aren't. In the United States some of us have gone back to using butcher's paper in strategic future conferences. You can paper the wall with it in a fraction of the time it takes to hang individual flip charts. We still call it "newsprint." – MRW

I soon came to appreciate Lippitt's passion for learning and pushing the boundaries of his social change practice. He had adapted as a primary change method in the 1950's what we now call "visioning," having satisfied himself with tape recordings that group problem-solving depresses people. I also learned of Lippitt's deep engagement in community building.

My attraction for these folks, and my discovery of the way their action research innovations had made my consulting practice possible, opened new doors for me. In particular, I began to experiment with getting together large, diverse groups for all sorts of reasons—re-thinking budgets, writing mission statements, reorganizing whole corporations. Over time—I'm a slow learner—I began to understand the conceptual and practical origins of the special conferences featured here.

At last I am able to describe some commonalities and contrasts of these two streams of work, both influenced by Kurt Lewin, a mutual colleague of Trist and Lippitt at different times. I consider these threads extremely important to those who want to benefit from strategic future conference methods. We can elaborate the conference designs ad infinitum. However, the underlying principles strike me as enduring, relatively simple, and not at all obvious. It has taken me a long time to catch on to what I'm going to tell you now.

My strategy in this book is to deepen and elaborate the story begun in Chapter 14 of my earlier work. As you will see, I cannot deal with the conceptual bases of "common ground" conferences independently of the problems people are trying to solve. So I want to plunge more deeply into these two refreshing streams of work, and to imagine the great river they might form as they converge.

To start, I need to reiterate a bit of management history. I consider what follows directly relevant today to our multiple economic, technical and social problems. If you hate history and want to leapfrog to "the bottom line," I suggest you start with Chapter 5—the minimum conditions for success. If you like history, you may find that you can add up what follows into a bottom line of your own.

FRED EMERY AND ERIC TRIST

Emery and Trist are the social scientists who in the 1950's sparked a new way of looking at workplaces, including the discovery of the power of self-managing teams. That 20th Century breakthrough is traceable to the Tavistock Institute of Human Relations in London, founded by Trist and other ex-British army psychologists and psychiatrists after World War II. A key goal was to help rebuild the British economy using social science knowledge gained in the war. Emery, an Australian, came to Tavistock for a year in 1952, and returned in 1958 as a senior staff member.

Trist and Emery, starting with coal miners, in the 1950's and 60's created a new method for redesigning work systems, based on self-management. One important influence on their work was Wilfred Bion, a 300-pound ex-World War I tank commander, and an Army psychiatrist in World War II. During WWII he, with Trist's help, devised a leaderless group method for selecting junior field officers for the British Army. This research, unknown in the business world, set the principles for self-managing work teams and is the basis for having groups self-manage their work in future search conferences (Weisbord, 1987, Chapters 7, 8, 15).

Bion had a dynamic model of group behavior that is useful to know when running participative conferences. He showed how groups defend against anxiety—by depending on the leader, fighting, fleeing, or pairing up. In Bion's learning groups, people studied their own reactions in an ambiguous situation that included an impassive, cryptic leader. Participants made a perceptual shift, coming to "see" in a more tangible way how uncertainty about leadership, mission, and structure affects group behavior. So self-management and group assumptions were the dynamic perspectives Emery and Trist brought to their invention of the "search conference" described in Chapter 3.

LIPPITT AND SCHINDLER-RAINMAN

Now, for the other stream. For many years before I knew the term "search" I had admired the boldness of Ronald Lippitt's and Eva Schindler-Rainman's community conferences. Lippitt, a student of Kurt Lewin at Iowa in the 1930's, helped research the differences between democratic and authoritarian leadership styles. This research established the leadership "style" appropriate both to self-managing teams and to participative events like search conferences.

Lippitt and Lewin coined the term "group dynamics" in the 1940's. Their insights laid the ground work for group problem-solving, theories of group development, leadership styles and other concepts that made possible the profession of organizational change. Lippitt, like Emery and Trist, also moved in the 1960's from small group problem-solving to future-oriented conferences with huge networks.

Eva Schindler-Rainman, a social worker with experience in community organization and development, first worked with Lippitt in 1961. She was seminar director for a project to bring Camp Fire Girls programs to the inner city, and Lippitt a planning committee member. The two went on to pioneer many NTL Institute training, consulting, and development workshops, co-authored six books, and numerous articles.

One context for their work was audio tapes Lippitt made in the 1950's of strategic planning meetings. He concluded that listing and solving problems depresses groups. He was appalled to hear people using words like "hopeless," "frustrating," and "impotent" as they applied some of his own group methods to problem-solving.

Action steps tended to be short-term, designed to deal with symptoms and reduce anxiety. The motivation, noted Lippitt, was to escape the pain induced in part by the method itself—the piece-meal listing of problems, the solution of any one of which might create still more problems. (As Lippitt told me this, sitting on the dock at his summer cottage on Lake George one August day, I recognized how much of my early consulting work had replicated the dynamics he described. I resolved to consult in a way that increased rather than drained energy.)

FROM PROBLEM-SOLVING TO FUTURING

In the 1960's Lippitt, Eva Schindler-Rainman, and Ronald Fox (1973) began speaking of "images of potential"—envisioning what could be instead of lamenting what was. In the late 1970's Lippitt teamed with the late futurist Edward Lindaman, who had directed planning for the Apollo moon shot. Lindaman believed that the future was created by our present ways of confronting "events, trends and developments" in the environment.

The "preferred future"—an image of aspiration—could be a powerful guidance mechanism for making far-reaching course corrections. Lippitt and Lindaman (1979) found that when people plan present actions by working backwards from what is really desired, they developed energy, enthusiasm, optimism, and high commitment.

"Futuring" focused awareness *away* from interpersonal relationships towards the experiences and values affecting everybody. Lippitt and his colleagues adapted that insight to national voluntary organizations like the YMCA, and to conferences for 88 cities, towns, and states (described in Chapter 3).

Diverse interest groups could jointly envision desirable futures—for example, the PTA, manufacturers association, doctors, community activists, juvenile authorities, chamber of commerce, and school board all at once. Searching together gave organizations more dependable anchor points for their own planning. It tied everybody to "reality" through their taking of joint snapshots, and became the basis for committed action based on mutual interest.

As the design evolved, one year time frames stretched to three years, five years, or even longer. More, people were asked to imagine themselves IN THE FUTURE looking back on what they had done. As time frames got longer, scenarios became more fanciful, more creative, more collaborative, and—strange to say—more actionable in the short run. That was a momentous discovery.

People learned to think of the future as a condition you create intentionally out of values, visions, and what's technically and socially feasible. Such purposeful action greatly increased the probability of making the desired future come alive. Repeating this process with relevant others could become a way of life for corporate planners if they could bring the whole system into the room.

Lippitt and Lindaman typically used one-day conferences to stimulate system-wide planning. They too devised a menu of activities geared to the past, present and future: a history, a list of events, trends and developments shaping the future, "prouds and sorries" of present operations, and detailed ideal futures.

WHAT IS THE FUTURE OF THE FUTURE?

There are still many possibilities to be discovered. I see my own "future search" as an integration of Bion/Trist's "leaderless group" studies, of Emery/Trist's global context, of Lewin/Lippitt's democratic leadership research and Lippitt/Schindler-Rainman's large communities—all tied together in a conference room to emerge as new "ahas" and action plans on Lewin's butcher's paper. How can we preserve dialogue and global understanding in a town meeting setting? That is the challenge posed by this book. It extends, sharpens, and raises our sights on what it means to get everybody improving whole systems. The exercise is made possible by including the work of so many others in diverse cultures around the world.

The Emery/Trist search grew from the inventors' realization that the world was *everybody's* domain. From systems theory they knew that each organization evolves in relation to a larger whole, that closed systems cannot change or grow. (Management "teams" who talk only among themselves often develop personal insights and warm relationships. They cannot transform their corporations.)

Lippitt and Schindler-Rainman came to roughly the same conclusion in the 1960's. They experienced the limits of working with single organizations. So they started treating a whole community as the domain, with all of its local issues and problems. The Emery/Trist search evolved into bringing people together around an issue or problem. This book is full of examples, from Australia, Canada, Norway, on issues as diverse as diabetes, child care, aging, the environment.

Searching made possible whole new structures that had not existed before. One class is what Trist calls "referent" organizations that network diverse parties with common interests (Part 5). A second is "domains," entire fields of interests composed of many referent organizations and interested parties (Part 4).

SOME COMPARISONS

In these terms, Lippitt/Schindler-Rainman brought together many community domains to consider whole arrays of local issues. The search conference usually stuck to one task—the future of "X." The collaborative communities took on as many tasks as the participants could define, with as many networks as they wished to form. Where the "search" evolved as a conference of 30-40, the "collaborative communities" sometimes brought ten times that number into one room.

Emery/Trist emphasized conditions for dialogue. Lippitt/Schindler-Rainman communities focused on linkage among diverse groups with local power brokers. The search emphasized self-managing small groups. The communities built in local volunteer facilitators trained the night before.

The search emphasized a global context—everybody sharing values and understandings about the whole. The collaborative communities emphasized local action—everybody finding new ways to act on an issue of most concern to them.

The search drew on Bion's group assumptions—fight/flight, dependency, pairing—explicated in Tavistock training groups. The collaborative community drew on experiential learning methods and group development theories derived from NTL Institute workshops.

The search emphasized an intellectual challenge—rigorous discussion, marshaling of facts, conceptual understanding of the open system. The collaborative community represented an organizational and behavioral challenge—the prospect of a substantial part of a whole community planning in one room. So in a classic search conference we have relatively small numbers thinking globally. In the classic community conference we find relatively large numbers acting locally. Neither explicitly excludes the other possibility. The value bases are wholly congruent. Yet, the emphasis and underlying purposes are ostensibly different.

The community model "empowered" a great many more people at one time. It also required enormous organizational skills, and was more dependent on the consultants' large system change strategies and training skills. The search model has tended to appeal most to "systems thinkers," people who can envision wholes, and can elicit the many linkages between world events and local issues. Neither model is something to be attempted by those inexperienced in group dynamics or untrained in managing large meetings.

THE GOAL IN COMMON IS COMMON GROUND

And yet, in terms of results, possibilities, energy released, creativity, participant satisfaction, the living out of core values, and in particular the discovery of common ground, the two models are remarkably similar. Both put the community task front and center, emphasizing the accomplishment of self-set goals. Both enabled voluntary action considered impossible when no local precedents existed. These methods seem especially relevant for building bridges, healing splits, and reducing stereotypes and prejudice between races and ethnic groups.

PREJUDICE and BIGOTRY

The concept of having people work on tasks together across lines of ethnicity, race, gender, culture, class, hierarchy and special function is strongly supported from many directions.

"Perhaps the single most successful approach to combating bias," reports Daniel Goleman (1991), "has proven to be putting people from different ethnic and racial groups into small teams where they work together regularly for some common goal. This is often accomplished with minor social engineering in the workplace and the military. In schools, it has taken the form of 'learning teams,' groups of three or four students who work together collaboratively."

He quotes Dr. Charles Green, a psychologist at Hope College, Holland, MI. "The idea that if you just get people together they'll start liking each other is naive. But if they are working together for shared goals, it breaks down the negative stereotypes they had of each other."

"This approach to attacking prejudice," writes Goleman, "is one of the oldest in psychology."

I have learned a great deal from these perspectives. Now, I would like to see us find ways to more rapidly extend the discovery of common ground into every sector. Is that possible? Can people learn about the "whole elephant" in very large groups? My growing awareness of the role of Carl Jung's "collective unconscious" in these events tells me there are discoveries still to be made. More, Margaret Wheatley's explorations of the new science—chaos theory in physics, the self-organizing properties of information as a natural life process (Chapter 10)— suggest another hypothesis. That is that these meetings engage not only our heads but our hearts, guts, and unconscious "data" in very powerful and potentially valuable ways. They can also be at times scary, leading to feelings that we are "out of control." That concern, I believe, is the single biggest reason leaders may hesitate to take this path. I hope this book will bolster the courage of those inclined toward some first steps.

Transformative change, I believe, always means a journey through denial and chaos. Fornunately our roadmaps are getting better all the time.

There is, as you will learn, a function for global data AND personal data in making our travels more satisfying, a function for dialogue, a function for visioning, a function for planning. So—like future search conferences on Day One—I leave you with many unanswered questions as you explore the many facets of this work.

CHAPTER 5

CONDITIONS FOR SUCCESS
An Exchange Between
Fred Emery and Marvin R. Weisbord

T HIS CHAPTER PROVIDES AN OVERVIEW of the central
issues in successful conference design. Our goal in
these conferences is to go beyond simply selecting from
a menu of participative exercises. Rather, it is to design into
these meetings conditions that make more probable good
dialogue, creative future scenarios, and mutual action. That
is a tall order, requiring that we separate out useful techniques from what the late Phil (later David) Herbst called the
"minimum critical specifications." These are the design
criteria that differentiate one kind of meeting from another.

I have been corresponding with Fred Emery for some time
on what makes search conferences unique. In 1989 he agreed
to "open up a debate on what searching represents" by
circulating our letters to this book's authors. Several joined
in and I again sent out the replies. This prompted Emery to
write a series reflecting on his 30 years of experience since
the Barford Conference (Chapter 3.) Now, with his permission,
I make his later letters public. I follow them with my reply,
framed as a summary of the cases in this book. I also take up
some of his key points and add my ideas on minimum conditions for success.

What are those conditions? Emery speculates on the need

> for and resistance to creativity in bureaucratic hierarchies
> and how the search amplifies the work of creative minds. And
> he reiterates his conviction that the minimum conditions can
> be found in the criteria for dialogue derived from Solomon
> Asch (Chapter 3). "I had used his concepts for seven years,"
> he says, "in agricultural diffusion, marketing and media
> studies, before drawing on them for the design of search. His
> ideas have had such lasting value that his 1952 book *Social
> Psychology* was reprinted by Oxford in 1987 despite hundreds
> of books with that title in the previous 35 years."
>
>   To Asch/Emery, I have added Robert Fritz on the dynamic
> effect of portraying our current reality against an ideal
> future. And I speculate on how "data overload" and a plunge
> into the buzzing confusion of our complex planet might
> accelerate the movement toward common ground. – MRW

EMERY, 42 SKINNER ST., COOK. 2614 AUSTRALIA

27 April 1990

Dear Marv,

Many thanks for the bundle of letters. They are a good boost to the process and suggest more convergence than I thought was out there.

It is quite possible that we will find little disagreement about an "ideal search conference." We must naturally expect considerable diversity of judgment about what is "close enough to be good enough." We cannot easily question another person's judgment that in his or her circumstances it was either their modified form or nothing. It is also very difficult to draw the line at which facilitation becomes seduction.

These sorts of differences do not bother me. I think participants make some allowance for honest mistakes by conference managers and for personal styles. I think most people who try to manage this sort of thing would have to be fairly open to learning from their experiences.

My concern is much more serious. As several have pointed out, the search conference could be reduced to a "thing," a technique; forgetting that it is the process of sustaining, for days if need be, a fully democratic dialogue. As word of their effectiveness spreads, we can expect unscrupulous consultants (independent and university based) to offer search conference packages that appear to be participative but subtly deny the participants full and democratic dialogue.

What is invariant in successful search conferences?

That is the question someone will always be asking so long as searching goes on. Hopefully our answers will always get more precise and we will see some feature we had not previously detected. However, I believe that we can (after 31 years!) detect some of the invariants. Thus it is clear the dialogue must be "democratic" if people are to believe that it is they who did the searching, and have not just been taken on a guided tour.

Asch's four criteria of a democratic dialogue are still, I think, the best we have [ed. note—see Chapter 2, page 21]. It is also clear that serious work has to be done before the dialogue can be focussed on the problem issues that have brought the participants together. Specifically, they have to convince themselves that they are living in the same world and share sufficient common ground to justify a joint effort at solving their problem. In building up a picture of the world, and their expectations and hopes, the participants are cooperating about something removed enough for them to expect some objectivity. This opening phase thus enables them to judge whether there is a shared willingness to conduct the dialogue democratically.

If this phase is successfully completed we should have what is a temporary community, not just an aggregate. The test is in the next phase—defining the problem area in a context that enables them to work on its solution. If this test is failed, one might as well close down the conference (or let it drift into an information exchange session, which is effectively the same thing in that it gives up on the joint search). If the test is passed, then work can be delegated to smaller groups acting as task forces for the temporary community. The sense of owning the product they have created needs to be reinforced by a final report that properly represents that product.

EMERY 42 SKINNER ST., COOK. 2614 AUSTRALIA

July 12, 1990

Dear Marv,

I have enclosed the unfinished letter of 27 April as I found it in my word processor. It does indicate that what is discussed in this letter was already brewing.

A great many designs are now being presented as search conferences. It is very good that people are looking in this direction, but we are uneasy about some of them. I think that this may not be as troublesome as it seems.

We have to agree, I think, that nearly all of the contenders share a quality that is not to be found in traditional conferences. They all try to maximize participation. It is obvious that we now need finer theoretical distinctions. Just making conferences more participative is not enough to define a conference as a search. As more of us can design participative conferences, we set ourselves higher goals (for some purposes) and wonder how those goals can be achieved.

At our recent conference on searching there was, for the first time, little disagreement about the sequence of phases needed for a search conference. (I guess that those who were too far out of line were not invited.) What emerged was that (a) sometimes the practical need was met by skipping some phases, i.e. using semi-search procedures, and (b) there were a lot of innovative techniques for handling each phase.

I think we need an explicit theory to enable us to distinguish between conferences that are just more participative and those that are participative *and* searches. This might help us decide what best meets particular purposes. I think that we also need some theory to choose between alternative techniques for handling the particular phases. At this conference we found ourselves using such criteria as conference outcomes and/or satisfaction of the conference managers. We did not seem very comfortable with those criteria.

My suggestion was that we look back to the Asch criteria for ABX relations that were consciously built into the original search design. Over the years I have tried to build further on Asch's propositions. I have proposed four criteria and further suggested that these constitute a serial-genetic order, i.e. that each constitutes a necessary but not sufficient condition for achieving the next.

LEVELS/ASPECT OF INTERPERSONAL SYSTEMS

Objective Level
(As seen by an outside observer)

Phenomenal Level (As seen by participants)

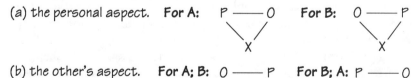

(a) the personal aspect.   **For A:**   **For B:**

(b) the other's aspect.   **For A; B:**   **For B; A:**

(Emery, F. and M. A *Choice of Futures*,
Nijhoff, Leiden. 1976. p 24.)

For an experienced person, one who has experienced all the levels of an ABX relation, I think this statement gives approximate, but adequate indices of whether a particular level has been achieved and, more importantly, indices of the transformation, or degeneration, from one level to another.

Sequences of search matched to Asch criteria:

Level 1: *Objectively ordered field* – Conference steps 1-4.
  (1. Introduction, 2. Listing of global trends, 3 & 4)
  Sorting into Consensus on Major Trends)
Level 2: *Equally human* (not same as equal humans) – 5-7
  (5. Probable Futures, 6. Desirable Futures, 7. The Planning
  Challenge—Constraints and Opportunities)
Level 3: *Shared psychological field* – 7-9
  (7. Constraints/opportunities, 8. Idealized Future Designs,
  Consensus on Key Design Features, 9. Organizing
  Task Forces)
Level 4: *Open—temporary planning community* – 9-11
  (9. Organizing Task Forces, 10. Engaging in Planning Tasks,
  11. Reporting on Next Steps and Action Plans).

We are often concerned just with helping people to get to "Asch level 3." They can then get back to their own people and do their planning with a new perspective on how the other people see things. Sometimes, e.g. with corporate searches, we can take phase 1 for granted. Sometimes, as in searches conducted for long-established voluntary associations, it might seem that we can go easy on phase 2. I grant the "sometimes" in both cases. I do feel, however, that it is precisely at these points that such organizations are likely to develop blind spots. Leaders think the world must be as they see it and followers think that power could not corrupt their leaders.

All the best,
Fred

EMERY 42 SKINNER ST., COOK. 2614 AUSTRALIA

14 July, 1990

Dear Marv,

This is a footnote to my letter of 12 July. Spelling out the phases suggests why the attempt at a "Search/Search" conference in 1976 was bound to fail. It was composed of a powerful international group but there were simply no grounds for them to accept the final step to becoming even a temporary planning community. They had parallel goals but no shared goal. Getting to the stage of having a shared psychological field was adequate to their purposes.

It would probably have been a very different matter if we had come together to design a search for, say, the Ulster Troubles; had accepted joint responsibility to see it through.

The last night of the conference we came back to the issue of technique vs. content raised in some of the letters you had received. Our two days of discussion of technique had been desirable and valuable but in evaluating alternative techniques we had, it seemed to me, forgotten the intrinsic value of the search. For us as practitioners there is the risk that it becomes a fairly mundane part of our reality. We need to remind ourselves that even the democratic dialogue that emerges at phase (level) 3 is rarely encountered in daily life.

Sure, we are constantly, in our countries, going through the various rigmaroles of pretending to be chummy, friendly and egalitarian in talking with others (even our secretaries). Labov and Fanshel have shown how hollow those deceptions are. So we should take some credit, as social scientists, that we have devised ways of creating a social space for democratic dialogue.

It is only a very limited and temporary space that we can create but at least we can plan for it and use it at socially strategic points (Our Participative Design Workshops are classic examples of a level 3 democratic dialogue. Rather more practical and of potentially greater value than so-called T-groups. But maybe that is my personal bias.)

A search conference goes way beyond a democratic dialogue in creating a uniquely-permissive atmosphere for cognitive restructuring, i.e. creativity. Since the counter-culture movement of the late 60's there has been some tolerance for creating opportunities for democratic dialogue, although it was not until 1971-72 that I was prepared to introduce Participative Design Workshops into industrial settings. (In Australia. In Europe, including Norway, I still found strong resistance in the middle 70's, and in the 80's little evidence of a permissive climate for such dialogues in either Europe or North America).

The very notion of a search conference seems to strike a much stronger cultural resistance, particularly amongst the highly-educated. Both Bion and Jung had a good clinical sense of what it means to take people to phase 4, the search conference level. Both saw it as a very human "peak experience," but both also saw it as very dangerously near-psychotic. At phase 4 the basic group assumption is that of pairing and a great deal of creativity can be released. What Bion and Jung have drawn attention to is the traditional cultural link of creativity and madness.

Or the connection that the British psychiatrist, Tom Main, used to make between the creativity of Christ and his Crucifixion. I think a very deep anxiety about creativity has been inculcated in every culture that bolsters hierarchical relations (in the same way that those cultures sustain linguistic forms and gestures that deny "democratic dialogue").

When the old hierarchical societies were threatened by creativity they could divert it into the arts or theology (up to a point). Modern hierarchies need creativity to ensure the growth of investment opportunities and maintenance of military capabilities. It is to be expected they will want constrained creativity. Such techniques as Delphi and brainstorming provide just that. Search conferences do not intrinsically meet the criteria of constraint. They could possibly be emasculated in such a way that they look like search conferences but meet the constraints. Our correspondence indicates that many people are well aware of this possibility.

I would like to think beyond just hindering corruption of the concept.

The search conference means that, in pre-planned spasms, we can release human creativity. As I have argued in my paper on "educational paradigms" this creativity is as widespread as the property of humanity itself. British studies of scientific creativity find little or no relation of this with hierarchical status. Since the days of the Egyptian priesthood, the possession of knowledge has always been used to bolster hierarchies of power. It is very disturbing to think that the means exist for genuine insights to be generated anywhere, and at any level within a hierarchical society—hardly conducive to submission and good order!

I personally think the matter goes further than that. Successful search conferences not only release the creativeness of ordinary people. They also provide a powerful amplifying system for creative minds. In the sometimes overpowering *diktat* of egalitarianism in Australian culture, I have to stop talking about this aspect. I remain convinced that this is, socially, one of the most powerful consequences of widespread use of search conferences.

> "When you have a conference in a creative mode they can tolerate and critically examine, to their satisfaction, radically new ideas. I have experienced this a number of times, even when they are the same people that I have hammered away at in committee time and again without making a mark." – FEE

This last point is not quite trivial. Our cultures, worldwide and at all levels of development, are so hostile to creativity that creative people only emerge by default; they naturally emerge in unexpected places, literally in the interstices of the web of socialization. This usually means, for obvious reasons, that they are deficient in social skills or faulted by psychological defense-mechanisms ("High grade funnies," as they were called in the British Army Selection Service). We should hope that sometime in the future we will cultivate creativity as a natural realization of human potential.

For the moment the search conference is one of the few ways I know of amplifying and benefiting from the little that gets through the net. For practical purposes this means that in selecting people for a search conference, we should be getting people to point us to the creative minds in their field. Most often these will be people who lurk in the history of the organization or community. People who have tried but been burnt out, thwarted, or rejected.

As I wrote, this is only meant as a footnote to the July 12 letter.

Very best wishes,
Fred

WEISBORD, 119 SIBLEY AVE., ARDMORE, PA 19003

January 20, 1992

Dear Fred,

Some footnote!

I have waited to respond to your letters of April-July 1990 until I had in hand all the pieces that would appear in *Discovering Common Ground*. This book would not exist but for your cautionary letter when I first started down this path. Your challenge then was to start a dialogue among practitioners that would deepen our linkage of theory and practice. As you have seen, that dialogue is well under way. Thanks for the stimulus and support. This book is testimony that the baby born in Barford has become a healthy adolescent.

I don't expect here, or ever, to finalize my understandings. But I want to sketch out what I make of the pieces in this book and the jigsaw puzzle I have been assembling. Then I want to review some concepts (in addition to Asch) that are salient for me. Finally, I want to speculate on conference structure and design from these perspectives.

Overview

What we have here, I think, is a kaleidoscope of current theory and practice. This book contains perhaps six strategic conference models with many common features. All the authors advocate careful advance planning, with the responsible leaders. All would agree, I think, that a broad cross-section of stakeholders should be involved, most that the conference should place the focal issue/institution in a global context and that the values and concrete ideas should be embodied in ideal future scenarios. Every design concludes with action planning against an ideal future.

All would agree that a major task of the conference facilitator/ manager is to minimize group dependency on experts or conference leaders. Thus, the facilitators take no positions on the conference content, and they invite people to take as much initiative as they are able for small and large group work. They seek maximum dialogue, learning, and creative ideas. They favor task group structures that equalize status and reduce hierarchy.

All the methods enable creative community action under the right conditions, else they would not be here.

Many Variations

But they are not identical. It is very common for each person to add personal wrinkles, and to modify or compromise designs based on local situations. Each practitioner develops great faith in his or her model. Nobody runs a canned design every time. And none of us, I think, are satisfied that we always get it right. I can't say for sure that every example here is the "real thing." But all, in my opinion, go well beyond participation. In putting them together this way, I hope to get us to go further still. We have a lot to learn from each other.

Each designer, no matter what their theory base, brings preferences for intellectual and/or affective tasks, based on deeply-embedded affinities. Further, designers may incorporate theories they are not aware of. (That's the story of my life, discovering theory after the fact for things I had learned intuitively.) Let me compare and contrast some design features, then go to some underlying theories.

Conference Phases (task sequence)

The dominant sequence is the one set out by Emery and Trist, growing from your Barford conference (Chapter 3). Baburoglu and Garr (Chapter 6) clearly describe a typical version. In your letter you show explicitly how you design so that your conference phases correspond to Asch's conditions for dialogue. You also suggest that unless this sequence is followed, dialogue is unlikely to take place. In particular, you make the point that for "A" and "B" to cooperate they need to agree on the nature of "X." Further, your experience, right back to Barford, is that this agreement is more probable when we start with the global situation—present and future.

Some Differences

By contrast, Brokhaug and Haugen in Norway and several of us in the United States start with a review of the past. That often means a three-pronged history—global, personal, and issue or organization—that comes right up to the present. We usually have good dialogues in our conferences. People listen to and acknowledge differences. They discover and move toward common ground. We rarely experience dysfunctional Bion group assumptions, like fighting, running away, or asking too much of the facilitator. We get imaginative future scenarios and (usually, not always) committed action plans.

That suggests to me that we have found an effective (different) way to establish the basic Asch levels. Exploring the past at the start of a future search is a powerful community builder. This step quickly moves people toward Asch's criteria—same world (that comes through in global data), psychological similarities (that come through in personal histories), and accepting each others' worlds, implicit in interpreting the various data bases in mixed groups.

As I was writing this, I received a case supporting this point. Chris Kloth's pitfall experience (Chapter 32) provides an important clue to an essential ingredient if a conference is to go beyond simple participation. Kloth thought he was choosing between two search models (either of which would have been okay). In practice, he reversed two future search phases. As a result, participants at the start got hooked into environmental demands *on the focal institution* (what you call the L21), becoming too narrowly attached to their own problems. It was not a fatal error. In phase 2, using the usual starting task, they advanced to common ground.

Letters and cases I receive regularly suggest *something* is afoot in future search that is qualitatively different from participative conferences. Starting with an open-ended global history (our legacy from Barford) strikes me as the heart of the matter. We go directly into areas never visited if we do business-as-usual. More, we find that integrating personal and focal issue histories with global data at the start helps people reorganize their experience in a way that is not all cognitive.

Personal Data

This raises a possible disagreement between us. It has to do with the function of personal data in a search conference. As near as I can tell, you believe personal history has no function except as people reveal themselves to each other in dialogue. Indeed, introducing it at the start may freeze people into past positions or roles. I believe "whole" includes each person's world in addition to a shared one. This may reflect my bias as citizen of a highly-individualistic culture. Or it may reflect a broader human need to validate ourselves and be validated. This procedure seems especially effective juxtaposed with a summary of world events.

I have found that when people reveal personal history, they become more trustful of themselves, each other, and this process; more open-minded, and more likely to shift their mental maps and behavior. The "facts of each others' worlds" form another sort of group field. Two cases in this book from high conflict domains (Colorado water in Chapter 19 and fresh-water fishing, Chapter 23) confirm separately how personal histories reveal essential values that unlock deep institutional conflicts. (An Indian colleague of mine working extensively in Asia and Africa says he sees this design feature as culture-free.)

Mixing Modes

In no cases do we find expert lectures mixed in with searching. Some managers arrange for expert input to provide useful tools or raise questions rather than supply answers. Americans also are prone to build in experiential exercises. This might take the form of get-acquainted activities that some folks have added to my future search design, although it is not my practice. Others incorporate a structured experience (e.g. training exercise) or a film followed by a process discussion. So far as I know, no conferences have fallen apart on these activities. There is no agreement in the United States on the extent to which they are necessary or desirable. I'm convinced this results from the newness (here) of searching coupled with our past successes with integrating learning and doing creatively. More, it is one way we facilitators manage our own anxiety. Even competent people are reluctant to venture into uncharted lands without proven tools in their kit.

The issue is joined, I think, in Part 7 with Merrelyn Emery's article on search manager apprentice training, followed by Mary Fambrough's do-it-yourself learning experience in her own company. Nearly every case from the USA is from people who learned on their own. Anyone who reads these chapters will be more conscious of the connections among conference structures, democratic dialogue and self-management.

Minimum Critical Specifications

Having written all that, I've put together my minimum critical specifications list below. My central hypothesis (unproven theory) goes as follows. A strategic conference is more likely to go beyond participation to the farther reaches of common ground, creativity, and committed action, to the extent we can assemble the whole system to examine all its relations and self-manage its own future planning. I hypothesize that successful strategic conferences, regardless of facilitator preferences, navigate those murky waters well enough for the planning community to get across.

MINIMUM CRITICAL SPECIFICATIONS FOR A FUTURE SEARCH CONFERENCE

1. Get the **whole system** in the room, the broadest temporary planning community feasible for the task at hand. That means maximum variety and diversity of interdependent people.

2. Have the whole conference community look at itself in a **global context**, and explore the entire open system—events, trends, relations, within and between the wider world and the focal institution/issue, in the past, present and future. That means the broadest feasible data base and common ideals before zeroing in on what to do about the issue being searched.

3. Ask people to be task-focused and to **self-manage** as much of their work as they are ready, willing and able to do. That means reducing dependency, conflict, and task avoidance.

We need all three conditions, not one or two. Simply doing things like "mapping the whole system" cannot compensate for too narrow a stakeholder group. Nor can self-managing groups, even diverse ones, compensate for tasks that restrict the field of inquiry to, say, top management's (or any one stakeholder's) views. Nor can we *facilitate* our way past too narrow a group, little interdependence, or a restricted field of inquiry. — MRW

Three Useful Concepts

I also want to mention three concepts I find useful that support or integrate with Asch. The one I consider a leading candidate for "invariant" comes from Robert Fritz, who lends considerable weight to your strong affirmation of creativity. Fritz's *The Path of Least Resistance* (1989) is a cornerstone of my practice theory.

Fritz has a proven method for releasing individual creativity. He has people imagine a concrete ideal future vision. They are asked to compare it with as clear-eyed and non-judgmental a description of their current reality as they can muster. Holding both pictures in tension, we tend toward spontaneous and persistent action to reduce the discrepancy. This is quite apart from solving problems.

The same can be said for search conferences. You, for example, have people lay out ideal against probable futures (based on what is happening now). I design a future search to help people describe and accept their (mutual) current reality—global, personal, and institutional. The more complete the descriptions, the better the ideal scenarios and the greater the impetus for action.

So I share your conviction that searching releases/enhances imagination. Many of us now have seen people who have not done any playful/creative activity since childhood produce far-out visions and action plans informed by enormous common sense. We get them as songs, stories, plays, poems, dioramas, artwork, maps, graphs, charts, that conjure up, in my opinion, aspirations deeply buried in the collective unconscious.

To cite one recent example: a drug rehab center (including recovering addicts) imagined and built a model of their 10-year vision—an integrated farm that raises its own food, provides vocational training, lives out healthy conditions and values, and incorporates the talents of the whole staff. While they have no farm yet, the values, activities, excitement and energy continue to inform their daily lives. The creative dreams in search conferences, I am convinced, live on in many ways short of literal realization. I believe, then, that successful searches build clear pictures of ideal desired futures against sharply delineated portraits of current reality."I suggest that process, in addition to Asch criteria, defines "new paradigm" conferences.

I have two other useful concepts that validate dynamic processes I might otherwise overlook, avoid, or (worst case) design out. One is Claes Janssen's (1982) idea that life is lived in a Four-Room Apartment, in rooms named Contentment, Denial, Confusion and Renewal (Chapter 9). Many practitioners (including some authors here) share my premise that the corridor to renewal goes smack through denial and confusion.

It seems to me inevitable that we make the journey into confusion—even anger, frustration, despair—to release the joy and energy that also is in us. My wish, illusion, fantasy is that every search evoke none of my negative feelings, that it be, from start to finish, pure joy. That wish is roughly like my daily dream of the transcendent cup of coffee. I have yet to taste it.

Despite this, we tend not to see much flight or fight among conferees, much less than in strategic planning sessions of yesteryear. When we do, it usually means we facilitators have done something to undercut group initiative. Moreover, unlike team-building meetings I managed in the 1970's, in search conferences people rarely personalize their negative feelings. They tend to become agitated by external data—the world, the environment, history, complexity.

"The Enemy Is Us"

I believe these feelings, in search conferences, are essential and temporary. As we accept our common fate, we turn toward each other instead of away or against. For this to happen we must each perceive that "we are the world." In many conferences we hear people quote Pogo—"We have met the enemy and he is us." I believe we come to *that* realization by encountering the "whole elephant" in a risky situation.

That's why I can accept groups mucking around in the Confusion room, even when a few people may want to blame me or my design. To make a breakthrough we have to live confused for a while. The perceptual shift comes when we realize that our diverse mental maps integrate into a larger shared whole that worries/excites us equally. The creative shift comes when we realize that together we can imagine an attractive ideal future. The action shift comes at the unconscious level as we discover that in the wider context it is *much* easier to make practical action plans and to commit ourselves willingly. Now we stand to get, at long last, what we wanted all along!

Two Cheers for Chaos

Meg Wheatley, writing on the new science (Chapter 12), is the source of my third, and most recent, hypothesis. Her paper describes the self-organizing properties of "chaotic" information. Her insights and analogies to the rest of nature strike me as intuitively right. They fit my experience. They account for data that I have puzzled over for years. She lends support to the practice of all search managers of having groups paper the walls with data and keep it in sight throughout the conference.

Wheatley offer clues for why seeking out all the "L's" (lawful relations within and between organizations and their environments) helps people shift both their feelings and cognition. The overload of an enormous data base and open-ended agenda becomes functional and perhaps essential to moving through Janssen's four rooms. Wheatley also makes a good argument, I think, against premature convergence or agreement. One way we reduce anxiety is to seize on a problem to solve. Yet anxiety fuels energy and creativity. Incidentally, she draws on physicist David Bohm and molecular biologist Rupert Sheldrake, whose works seems so supportive of this book's theme, that I introduce them in Chapter 11.

They fit with my growing interest in unconscious processes. In any case, as I have for 30 years, I cannot help but introduce threads of my present learning into whatever I work on. Of course, it is possible all these concepts, in light of Asch, are redundant to search conference design. (They might be analogous to corporate codes of ethics, all unnecessary if people only would follow the golden rule.) To orient myself in time, I've joined the branches of my practice into a "genealogy" (see page 17).

Designing Conferences

I believe strongly that our design task should not be framed as this exercise versus that one. We need to get better at creating conferences that reflect the explicit and implicit values and knowledge collectively assembled here. The right designs will follow if we seek to match our steps or phases to what we know about ourselves as a species and the sort of society we want to live in.

I believe the interplay of diverse people looking at the whole mobilizes the collective unconscious in a powerful way that I can't quite articulate. What is doable is implanted in the unconscious of every person who comes into the room. What is to be discovered is *already* there. When we focus on conflict and problems, we fence off the access to common ground.

Why is this Form Unique

What makes searching unique? I think that "whole systems" learning from assorted stakeholders talking with each other, without attacking or defending, makes *much more probable* discovery, learning, owning up, mutual support, a re-ordered world view, and changes in personal and institutional priorities. To have this level of learning, we need everybody—as broad a cross-section of the whole as feasible. The task sequence—from global to local, generic to specific—is important. Finally, we need to set up the tension between what we have and what we really want.

I believe we can get a lot more of what we really want by designing to these specifications than through conflict management or problem-solving. To one degree or another, all of our authors show how to make this happen—a hopeful sign for our beleaguered planet.

All the best,
Marv

FUNCTIONING OF FUTURE SEARCH CONFERENCES
Structure, Process, Content

Introduction

> "When you listen to somebody else, whether you like it or not, what they say becomes part of you. So if the temperature is high, a conflict is generated inside and outside. But in the dialogue, the temperature is lowered, and the common pool is created, where people begin suspending their own opinions and listening to other people's—so everybody's opinion will be held by everybody. That's what I mean by a common pool of information." – *David Bohm* (Chapter 11)

Part 2 has six chapters. The first three provide different windows on the structure and content of search processes. They answer a frequent question, "How do I explain this conference to people who never heard of it?" The authors, working in diverse cultures, employ similar, though not identical, models derived from Emery/Trist. However, each addresses a different audience.

For potential attendees, Ivar Brokhaug (Chapter 8) supplies the document he uses to inform participants of what to expect. This is "real stuff," translated from Norwegian, that has been sent to many hundreds of participants. Oguz Baburoglu and Andy Garr (Chapter 6) offer a straightforward orientation for conference managers and facilitators. Rolf Haugen (Chapter 7) addresses the scientific and academic communities. He supports broad-brush theory with many concrete examples from his native Norway. He is especially interested in the power of searching to sustain a learning organization—one that can improve continuously its own capacity for future action.

The next two chapters focus on conference dynamics. Chapter 9 describes social psychologist Claes Janssen's useful concept of dynamic change, the journey from contentment through denial and confusion to renewal, what he calls the "the four-room apartment." I have taken a big chunk of it from *Productive Workplaces* (Weisbord, 1987). I have added some thoughts on how and when we visit the rooms in future search conferences. Margaret Wheatley in Chapter 10 provides a thought-provoking explanation for how search processes help us reorganize our reality. She draws on her research into the implications of the "new science" for leadership and management.

Finally, in Chapter 11, we go more deeply into one of Wheatley's sources, in a wide-ranging conversation that integrates our global dilemmas, new concepts in science, and the centrality of dialogue. Noted physicist David Bohm validates, from a scientific standpoint, the importance of dialogue to citizens of a conflicted planet. His examples and reasoning form a harmonious counterpoint to this book's themes.

The interviewer, author John Briggs, also describes his participation over two years in an unstructured dialogue group. He experienced conflict, common ground, and in apparently aimless talk "an elegant underlying order and an often stunning logic." He also found that the group's conflicts often mirrored his own internal dilemmas, an encounter with self that I believe is of great benefit to anybody who wants to run search conferences. – MRW

CHAPTER 6

SEARCH CONFERENCE METHODOLOGY FOR PRACTITIONERS
An Introduction
Oguz N. Baburoglu and M. Andy Garr, III

THIS CHAPTER will be of most interest to those managing or hoping to manage search conferences. Baburoglu and Garr outline the rationale, key sequence of tasks, and their conditions for successful conferences. Their process is based on the original Emery formulation. They provide a clear, simple, and well-integrated view of the links between theory and practice. They also highlight key dynamics to watch for in each phase. Finally, they provide useful directions for practitioners in selecting participants, setting up ground rules, and outcomes to be expected. I have adapted this chapter from a paper they gave at the International Society for Systems Science, Edinburgh, Scotland, in 1989. – MRW

BACKGROUND

The search conference is a participatory planning method introduced by the Australian systems thinker Fred Emery (Emery and Emery 1978) that has been used in the U.S.A., Canada, Mexico, U.K., Norway, India, Sweden and Turkey for a wide range of purposes. We have applied the methodology with large and small businesses to compose mission statements and formulate competitive strategies, with state government executive and legislative branches to formulate and implement policies, with national governments to rethink strategies, with social service and grass roots organizations to refocus their efforts and improve the quality of work life, and with universities to manage long range planning.

The conference uses a systematic process in which groups design the future they want and strategies for achieving it. The "search" is for an achievable future. This may be a future that is more desirable than the one that is likely to unfold if no action is taken, or a future that is totally unexpected. Designing a future collectively unleashes a creative way of producing organizational philosophy, mission, goals and objectives enriched by shared values and beliefs of the participants. This process is especially useful in a time of social, economic and technological "turbulence."

ACTIVE ADAPTATION TO TURBULENCE

"Turbulent environment" is a phrase coined by Emery and Trist (1965) as one of four types of organizational environments. The turbulent environment brings unexpected changes, uncertainty, unintended consequences, and complexity as indicated on the chart below. It also increases the degree of interdependence among stakeholders in that environment.

Characteristics of Turbulent Environments	Active Adaptation Principles
Unexpected Changes	Flexibility
Uncertainty	Innovation/Creativity
Unintended Consequences	Social Responsibility
Complexity	Participation/Collaboration

To adapt to turbulence, say Emery and Trist, requires those principles listed on the right side of the chart—flexibility, innovation/creativity, social responsibility, and participation/collaboration. The search conference embodies all of them. So it is an excellent decision-making methodology under conditions of fast change and unpredictability (Trist 1983).

ACTIVE ADAPTATION IN SEARCH CONFERENCES

FLEXIBILITY: Searching is an extremely flexible methodology, adaptable to diverse settings and diverse planning or problem situations. The process allows for spontaneous restructuring of the conference as necessary, because the essence of the method is that participants supply all the content for discussion and regulate their own small groups. So they decide if a new task or structure is required.

INNOVATION: The search conference aims both at producing the most desirable creative ideas and making their adoption much easier. Often unconventional innovative ideas have a hard time getting the support of a larger system. Search conferences include the implementers, and brainstorming followed by evaluation of suggestions and ideas is the mode of operation at each stage. By separating imagination and judgment, we make the innovation process more likely to occur, for more ideas are likely to get a hearing.

SOCIAL RESPONSIBILITY: The key to social responsibility is that stakeholders have an equal chance to influence decisions. Each stakeholder can shape the outcome to minimize or eliminate potential harm. Moreover, small groups are likely to scrutinize carefully potentially unethical suggestions from individual stakeholders.

PARTICIPATION: This is the most critical principle for search conference design. We seek to include all stakeholders who are affected by or who affect the situation. People who may never meet can interact in "real time" and meaningful ways. Participation is not a "style" issue but a system design principle that enables us to mobilize the entire decision-making field face-to-face.

THE SEARCH CONFERENCE EVENT

In a search conference, 35-40 participants, two or three days, design the system's most desired future and formulate creative strategies to bring that future about. The process moves from the general to the specific within an agreed upon "conference task,"—the conference's central purpose. The box below represents one such guideline. Every question about the conference task must be discussed in detail and necessary changes introduced into the schedule. The significance of negotiation and mutual agreement on the conference task becomes more pertinent should the group regress into dysfunctional fight/flight or dependency.

Upon the completion of the conference task, the results are distributed to the extended stakeholders and a follow-up mechanism is designed based on the action plans. Special action implementation groups are formed at the end. If feasible, the entire group comes together later to review progress on their action plans.

A search conference is staffed by at least two facilitators who have group process skills and who have been trained in an apprenticeship position by more experienced search conference facilitators. There are several advantages to working in pairs. Facilitators must be especially sensitive to group emotional states (Bion 1961). Part of their task is helping people recognize and self-manage their way out of dependency or fight-flight, and toward creative "pairing." Two facilitators can compare their observations of the group's dynamics, help diagnose the current emotional state and intervene in ways that continue to empower the group. Another benefit of having two facilitators is to assure equal attention to process and content, which the pair can take turns in monitoring.

THE SEARCH CONFERENCE PROCESS

Phase 1   WORLD TRENDS

Desirable/Probable

Phase 2   TRENDS THAT AFFECT X

Desirable/Probable

Phase 3   THE EVOLUTION OF X

Phase 4   THE FUTURE DESIGN OF X

Desirable/Probable

Phase 5   STRATEGIES

[X can be a problem, an organization, a nation, an institution, an inter-organizational system]

X is the system that comes into organizational existence during the search conference. Stakeholders, who often plan or problem-solve in their individual departments or organizations, can now plan in the most relevant context. They help construct this context with others by creating a complete picture of the system and its environment, so they always have a fuller context than when working alone.

PHASE 1

The process starts with a scan of what's happening in the world surrounding the participants. This phase is best introduced to the participants by using a metaphor such as "waves washing over you," to indicate that the observed trends originate somewhere else and continue onwards past the point where we encounter them, or merge into other waves.

Using brainstorming, the group suspends judgment and evaluation and allows for conflicting observations to be expressed. We emphasize spontaneous sharing of mutual perceptions rather than spontaneous appraisal of others' ideas. This scanning of the environment sets the tone for the conference. This method of starting shows participants that their ideas will be registered without discrimination based on status or affiliation. We seek to build an atmosphere of trust that yields a deeper and non-superficial search of the trends in the environment.

All inputs are recorded on flip charts and hung on the walls. This simple technology assists in the symbolic representation of the shared world of the participants. They can see that their perception is legitimately a part of the whole group. The entire group embarks on this activity. We recommend it be scheduled in an evening when participants are in a more reflective mood. Furthermore, this phase is the least-demanding activity since most people are affected by the environment they live in. Hence they find it easy to participate.

Once they have a shared appreciation of the global environment, participants are now ready to appraise the trends. They usually work in four groups, choosing their own recorder and presenter, to sort out both desirable and probable trends. The desirable trends are those they want to support from a policy standpoint. The probable trends are those they consider likely to extend into the future whether they are desired or not. Thus groups place a value on the trends and inevitably bring national, regional and organizational assumptions into their judgments. The small groups present their scenarios to the large group and common themes are combined into the total group's most desirable and most probable future scenarios.

The first phase therefore accomplishes: (1) The creation of shared context, (2) the expression of values on the context, and (3) the realization of collective action and decision making as a group. Sometimes people have a tendency to move into phase two without searching into the broader environments. The facilitators' must keep the group from rushing into the second phase until they have thoroughly explored the global trends. Otherwise, they may miss significant trends relevant to the formulation or implementation of their strategies.

PHASE 2

Assuming a thorough phase one, the conference repeats the above procedure in the second phase. This time the group brainstorms trends that are washing over the focal system—X. The group then moves to sort these trends into desirable and probable categories. This phase is characterized by more detailed knowledge and would correspond to defining the operating environment of the system.

PHASE 3

In this phase attention is drawn to the evolution of system X, why and how it came into being, what sanctions it had and has, what its current character is. It is often appropriate here to identify the systems' strengths and weaknesses. The purpose is to consciously share the current system situation and to appreciate its history. Participants usually find this phase particularly engaging, especially when past constraints have inhibited the sharing of such information. A simple time line drawn on the flip chart sometimes helps to map chronologically the events that have shaped the evolution of the system.

PHASE 4

This phase explicitly calls for creativity and innovation. The future of the system can now be designed using ideal characteristics that reflect the participants' values. The resource constraint is an omnipresent deterrent for the participants to really engage in a joyful and hopeful mood and hence to release their creative imagination. So we forewarn people of this tendency and ask them to stress creativity and innovation, rather than focus on the feasibility of proposed changes.

This phase is not directed toward concrete strategies or solutions, although they might be suggested during brainstorming. On the contrary, we suggest people devise curative, unconventional and surprising conceptions of what the system ought to be. This kind of activity is best performed in small groups. When a small group generates enough design characteristics they switch their work with another group.

Thus, the selection and sorting of the most creative ideas is done by *other* groups. By introducing stakeholder scrutiny, ideas that would be supported quickly emerge and those who have selected the ideas are more likely to be committed to implementation strategies. Finally, the work of each group is merged through a discussion of differences and similarities and a consensus scenario is created.

PHASE 5

The formulation of strategies follow the same mode as the previous phase. Four small groups generate the means by which the idealized future can be attained and develop a list of strategies that the group endorses. A copy of the idealized future document is supplied to each work group so that the targeted future is the same negotiated future they can all strive for. Creative ways of bringing about the desired future are expected to be produced in the brainstorming mode. The sorting out of all the suggested strategies is done by other small groups. At this phase, more specific strategies or solutions are offered and this reflects the progression of the search conference process.

Once the strategies are articulated, the participants then self-select action plan groups to design implementation plans for their chosen strategies. Through self-selection some unpopular strategies will drop out of the agenda or to be reserved for another planning event. The products of the action groups are presented to the large group to be followed by a debate and a discussion of their desirability and feasibility. It works much better to send the same work groups back to consider the viability of their implementation plans given the contextual and operating environment trends that they have earlier identified.

Finally, each participant is asked—if they haven't already volunteered—how they will integrate the plans into their day-to-day operations when they return to work the following day. A mutually agreed upon follow-up program provides a tracking system for the whole group.

CONCLUSION: SOME DIRECTIONS FOR THE PRACTITIONER

Who To Choose As The Participants

- Stakeholders affected by or who affect the planning for the issue or situation.
- Stakeholders who have a special interest in probable outcomes.
- Decision makers, implementers, responsible or relevant people in the private sector or in government.
- Participants do not have to be experts in the planning situation.
- People who would be comfortable working in "shirt sleeves" without regard for rank or status.
- Search conference process works best with volunteers.

Conditions of Participation

- Participants must attend all the activities. Since the phases are interrelated partial attendance is not generally permitted.
- A Search Conference is not a conventional conference, and there are no speeches or testimonies.
- Participants should not be disturbed throughout the conference. They should not be receiving telephone calls, should not be leaving to go home or meet with people other than the search conference participants.
- The conference is best managed in a "social island," ideally a resort-like location away from daily disturbances of work or family.
- All opinions and perspectives must be respected by all the participants.

What Can Be Expected As The Outcomes

- Creative and achievable strategies.
- Collaborative and participative approaches.
- Consensus generation.
- Shared values.
- Commitment to strategies formulated.
- The combination of formulation and implementation.
- Learning from each other and educating members new to the situation.
- The integration of cultural, regional or value differences.
- Completing a task in two or three days that would take months if left to the specialized analysts and experts.

ABOUT THE AUTHORS

Oguz N. Baburoglu is on the management sciences faculty at Bikent University, Ankara, Turkey. His research interests are on stalemated systems, corporate entrepreneurship and participative planning.

M. Andy Garr, III is a management consultant in Atlanta, GA. He has extensive experience in the public sector, especially in the strategy formulation pertaining to legislative and executive branches of state government. Baburoglu and Garr have worked together on several projects over the last eight years.

SAMPLE CONFERENCES MANAGED

- Turkish Industrialists and Businessmen's Association: Consensus and Collaboration between Management, Unions and Government in Turkey. • IGAS (State Owned Fertilizer Manufacturer): Designing Future Corporate Strategy • Self-Privatization, January 1990. • The Ministry of Culture and Tourism, Turkish Government: Designing Turkey's Tourism Strategy, 1988. • St. Regis Mohawk Reservation: Participative Design of Economic Development Strategy, October 1988. • Georgia Governor's Commission on Children and Youth: Formulating State Strategy for Children and Youth Problems, September 1987. • Southern Legislator's Conference on Children and Youth: Planning Workshop on Southern Children, Nashville, 1986. • Chester County (PA) Nuclear Freeze Movement, Inc: Redesigning the Future of the Nuclear Freeze Movement, November 1986. • The Vermont State Legislature,:Formulating State Strategy Regarding Family and Childrens' Issues, 1986. • Pennsylvania Prison Society: Designing the Future and Quality of Work Life, 1986. • The Seneca Nation of Indians, Salamanca, NY: Resolving the Salamanca Lease Stalemate and Economic Development, 1986. • Women in Crisis, Inc., Hershey, PA: Strategic Planning and Organizational Design, 1985-86.

CHAPTER 7

ADAPTING TO RAPID CHANGE USING SEARCH CONFERENCES
Lessons from Norway
Rolf Haugen

R OLF HAUGEN provides still another design, and another look at the theory and practice of searching as it has evolved in Norway. He covers much of the same ground as Baburoglu and Garr, but from a different point of view. And he addresses an academic and largely uninformed audience. Haugen grounds his paper in eight years of experience in managing search conferences in Norway and also Uganda. He gives a concise account of his underlying theories and discusses the search as a method for creating "a learning organization," one that can improve its own capacities for future action.

He also outlines his own search methodology, and illustrates an effective way search managers can integrate the structure, process, and content of these conferences. Moreover, he puts the conference into the larger context of ongoing social change. This excerpt is from a longer paper prepared for a 1985 conference of the British Association for the Advancement of Science. I have edited it to preserve the central ideas and the thinking behind one practitioner's integration of these ideas. — MRW

1. INTRODUCTION

Formal organizations exist to meet demands for production or services. When society changes, organizations are faced with new and unfamiliar requirements. Large corporations may function for a long time "as if" market changes had not happened. They can take a long time to die. Smaller private enterprises close down more rapidly when their market position no longer can be justified in economic terms.

Public institutions endure because they are not so directly tied to markets, but may be closed by political decisions. Yet, large segments of the public question the quality and relevance of public services. In general, the need for restructuring of private and public organizations for new purposes is central for rapidly changing societies.

Here, we will look at *search conferences* as one way to plan and organize adaptation to changed environmental conditions. (Other forms serving the same function have occurred under different names throughout history.)

2. HISTORICAL BACKGROUND

Since the first modern search conference in 1960 (see Chapter 1), an increasing number have been held around the world (Williams, 1982). The first Norwegian event called a "search" was held in 1977 for the offshore oil and gas industry.

Different sectors, industries and organizations have followed. Examples: the aluminum industry, trade unions, municipal administration, garbage collection, hotel and restaurant industry, local communities (Herbst, 1980, Haugen, 1984).

The search format was of special importance for the 1982 revision of the basic agreement between the Norwegian Employer's Confederation and the Federation of Trade Unions. A supplement on organizational development, and the use of search conferences, was then included. As a result, many industries have held search conferences as part of longer-range organizational development programs.

By August 1985, programs had been initiated by the hotel and restaurant industry, printing plants, paper and pulp mills, machine workshops, security guards, furniture manufacturing, car industries (retail, service and production), wood industries, foundries (including aluminum), ship building (including construction for offshore), electronics and mining. Some of these were industry-based, others within single companies.

3. CONFERENCE DESIGN

Each conference is unique, tailored to specific requirements. However, search conferences differ from other meetings in their criteria for participants and group composition, staff roles, and how preliminary planning and follow-ups are organized. To describe this, I must distinguish between a conference's structure, process and content.

STRUCTURE means participant selection, time limits and the sequence of group and plenary sessions outlined by the program.
PROCESS refers to interpersonal and group dynamics that take place in relation to this structure.
CONTENT means views and opinions produced in the discussions.

Descriptions here are based mainly on conferences run in Norway by the Work Research Institutes (WRI). The structure described is not the only possible form. Different traditions have developed in other countries, as this book illustrates.

4. PRELIMINARY PLANNING

Search conference participants are members of a more or less ongoing social system. Such systems can be corporations, industries, voluntary associations or communities. Their point of departure could also be a composite problem area, what Trist (1983) calls a "domain," or "a problem that nobody owns"—like the environment, or mental health, or aging. No single body has clear responsibility for the whole. When we pick search conference participants, we define the domain.

Participant selection to a large extent determines the conference outcome, for participants provide the content, discussion, vision, and commitments. Selection criteria, then, is a key planning task. Our upper limit is 60 people. When the potential number exceeds 60, we select a vertical slice from an organization. If the conference includes several organizations, vertical slices may be taken from each. The slice should reflect all levels and functions. Thus, if a majority of employees are production workers, we make them a majority in the vertical slice. For local communities, key power positions are represented, as well as demographic structure—age, gender, neighborhood, different vocations or trades.

The conference staff and client committee always make planning decisions together. From companies, management and workers should be on the committee. In communities, many interests should be represented. More detailed criteria for composition of planning committees must be made in each case. Timing and location are important decisions in preliminary planning. The conference normally lasts two or two-and-a-half days, away from daily routines and telephones, on a "social island"—a place where informal evening gatherings are possible.

5. THE PROGRAM

Our program has three parts:
1) Mapping the context (trends in past and future);
2) Identification of key problem areas;
3) Making a plan for future action.

Each part involves small group discussions followed by a plenary presentation of results. Within each part, there may be one or more rounds, depending on time available.

There are no lectures or introductions in our search conferences, except welcome speeches (maximum ten minutes) and program infor-

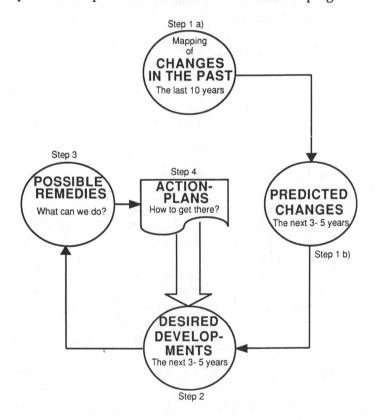

Structure of a search conference program

mation. The plenary (total group) is mostly used to hear small group reports by participants. Usually, groups have no more than ten minutes each for their presentations. Early on, there is little time for general discussions. Toward the end we make room for plenary discussions about the final action plan.

As with the conference as a whole, small group composition to a large extent determines the scope and content of these discussions. We have two criteria for group composition:

1) Homogeneous or horizontal (peer, functional) and
2) Heterogeneous groups (cross-section of whole)

We compose small groups to fit the task. For example, the first half of the program, mapping the environment and its major problem areas, is done in horizontal groups to expose divergences and overlaps in perspectives. We want participants to know others' perspectives in order to identify common ground.

In the second half, we emphasize convergence, consensus and future action planning, using heterogeneous groups. Problems are redefined and attention focused on potential areas for change where local action is likely to succeed. We achieve heterogeneity by self-selection according to interests, or "diagonal" mixing of levels and departments, or some combinations. Why heterogeneity here? To encourage coordinated action across the boundaries of levels, competence and interests.

Ground Rules

We present a set of rules for group discussions:

1) Members of horizontal groups do not need to agree among themselves. The purpose is to generate as many ideas as possible (brainstorming).
2) Heterogeneous groups are asked to find agreement, the common ground on which all can stand.
3) A general rule for all groups is that members have an equal chance to express their views.

In plenary, we use large flip-charts. Usually, one member presents, others comment. Groups are asked to find a new person to present each time. Within this framework, groups must find their own way to organize themselves. Experience indicates that the rules are respected.

Role of the Staff

Usually, our staff consists of three external consultants, at least two with previous search conference experience. We find three the most effective unit for handling the process, making decisions during the conference, giving out information about the program, presenting tasks and criteria for group composition and chairing the plenary sessions. The main structure of the program is decided in the preliminary planning. Within this framework, a number of decisions are taken during the conference, especially in the second half, when group composition and tasks may depend on the outcome of previous sessions. These decisions are based on continuous assessment of the social process and views that have evolved—who needs to discuss what with whom at this point. Staff members do not join groups. The general principle is that staff should *not* interfere with their own views on the *content* of the discussions, unless asked to do so.

Our assumption is that participants are experts on their own situation and the conference is their opportunity to act on their own. This does not mean the staff considers the content of the discussions irrelevant. On the contrary, we must consider content in formulating group tasks. Furthermore, the staff will analyze and present a condensed summary of small group reports on expected future developments after the first session. We report only the given facts, however, not our own views. Thus, staff members need to observe and understand both the social/interpersonal dynamics and the meaning of information presented throughout the program. Needless to say, this role is difficult and demanding. We need close contact and frequent consultations with representative participants during the conference. Sometimes we make decisions regarding program changes jointly with participants in plenary sessions. Sometimes we hold open staff meetings, but the staff has final responsibility for the program.

6. PREDICTED CHANGES IN THE ENVIRONMENT

The first small group task is a mapping of predicted developments viewed from different positions within the organization. The task can be formulated like this: "What important developments can be expected during the next five-ten years?"

We may frame this in different ways—for society in general, for an industry, a community, or combination of these. Predictions should be realistic judgments, not wishes. Mapping of developments in the past can also be done. This is especially useful in systems where a shared history is important.

As a staff, we analyze the predictions and present them to the plenary as an introduction to the next group task. Generally, we use the following criteria:

1) Forming categories

Predicted changes can be ordered into a limited number of categories or headings, preferably not exceeding five-six years.

2) Identifying boundary conditions beyond local control

Many external changes must be taken as given. No single company or local community, for example, can stop or reverse "macro-trends" like the increased use of computer technology, or the rising level of education in society. What is possible, however, is to meet such trends with an active, adaptive strategy.

3) Divergences and overlaps. . .

. . . in the group's views are identified. Differences in perspective are not necessarily disagreements. Views can be complementary and comprise common ground for further discussions.

4) Complexity and contradictions

The social environment may appear contradictory and so complicated that capacity for action is impaired. Contradictions can be clarified and complexity reduced.

5) Conflicts of interest. . .

. . . can be made explicit. This may form a basis not for getting rid of conflicts, but for agreement about how to handle them.

6) Rationality

Problems can be redefined in operational terms and in ways that allow open discussion.

7) Predictions as information about the present

Forecasts may turn out wrong. Search conference predictions, however, do provide valuable information about how people perceive the present. This makes a constructive basis for discussing active adaption to possible future changes, particularly in areas where there is a general agreement about future trends. So, these predictions serve as an introduction to group discussions on the key problem areas. The main purpose of these steps is identifying common ground for action.

Our experience from search conferences is that almost always there are more common interests than people expected. Probably we discover this because we live in the same external environment. External threat fosters internal solidarity. Management and workers, for example, often have a common interest in company survival and so may agree to improve product quality.

7. PLANS FOR ACTION

At the end, we produce action plans. In our process, the first step is to identify causes of problems in a definite number of areas. Groups then suggest possible remedies. The next step for each problem area is specifying *what* can be done after the conference by *whom*, *how*, and *when.*

Small groups may concentrate on different problems. We decide group composition and tasks depending on previous sessions.

Finally, groups present integrated plans with priorities on short and long term actions and discuss these in the plenary. The conference does not make formal decisions. However, groups may make commitments to seek formal sanction for their recommendations. Project groups may form and take responsibility for later implementation.

8. IMPLEMENTATION AND FOLLOW-UPS

Often, the conference is one step in a longer change project that includes:

1) Preliminary planning
2) One or more conferences
3) An implementation phase and
4) One or more follow ups. We hold the first follow-up about six months after the conference, often as a one-day-event in two parts:
    i) A summary of progress on action plans so far, and
    ii) A formulation of a new future action program.

Usually, we find that some suggestions have been implemented, others not. Implementation may have failed or may not have been tried. Either way, we want to discuss why. Some suggestions may have proved unusable, other to have been met with resistance. Still others require more time and show up on the new action program, usually in more precise form.

Sometimes people redefine earlier proposals, indicating that discussions continue and some progress has been made. Still other suggestions reappear in action plans as moral appeals without any hope of implementation. Some "problems" are not really problems and proposals for their "solution" are quietly forgotten.

We have no controlled experiments so far to show the advantages of search conferences compared to other approaches to organizational

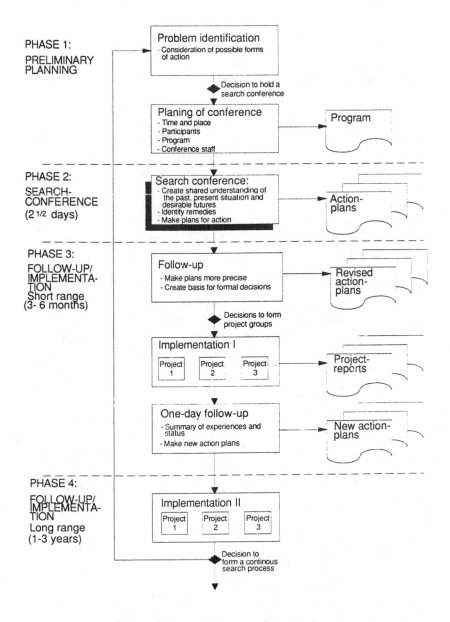

PHASE 1:
PRELIMINARY
PLANNING

Problem identification
- Consideration of possible forms
  of action

◆ Decision to hold a
  search conference

Planing of conference
- Time and place
- Participants
- Program
- Conference staff

Program

PHASE 2:
SEARCH-
CONFERENCE
(2 ½ days)

Search conference:
- Create shared understanding of
  the past, present situation and
  desirable futures
- Identify remedies
- Make plans for action

**Action-
plans**

PHASE 3:
FOLLOW-UP/
IMPLEMENTA-
TION
Short range
(3- 6 months)

Follow-up
- Make plans more precise
- Create basis for formal decisions

**Revised
action-
plans**

◆ Decisions to form
  project groups

Implementation I

| Project 1 | Project 2 | Project 3 |

**Project-
reports**

One-day follow-up
- Summary of experiences and
  status
- Make new action plans

**New action-
plans**

PHASE 4:
FOLLOW-UP/
IMPLEMENTA-
TION
Long range
(1-3 years)

Implementation II

| Project 1 | Project 2 | Project 3 |

◆ Decision to
  form a continous
  search process

Search conference in context

change. A two or two-and-a-half day conference will be minor influence and it is difficult to isolate its effects. The potential influence may, however, be consistent with other forces and strengthen developments that were already going on. Changes in organizations and in large social systems take time. Our experience in using search conferences in organizational and community development indicates that a two-five year period is realistic for substantial changes.

9. SEARCH CONFERENCES AND RESTRUCTURING ORGANIZATIONS

The search conference assumes that marketplace changes call for structural change. Relating internal structure to the nature of the environment is advocated by many researchers, among them Burns and Stalker (1961), Emery and Trist (1965), and Lawrence and Lorsch (1967). The search also assumes that organizations, communities or domains, are "open systems" in interaction with their environments (Bertalanffy, 1968, Ashby, 1956). However, various parts have different interactions. For example, top management handles a company's external relations. This does not mean, however, that lower levels (middle management or production workers) do not interact with the environment. Their interactions are of a different kind and at a different level.

The search conference makes all forms of external relations equally relevant in planning an organization's future. Top management and lower levels see different aspects of the same environment. All may be important, and related, though the parties may not know how until they discuss it. In a local community men, women, young and old perceive their social contexts differently. All these perspectives are considered equally important and valid in search conferences. The traditional hierarchy, then, is temporarily suspended and becomes a system of horizontally-coupled parts. This makes possible new understandings to every participant which would not otherwise be available. The search concept is based on two assumptions about the present state of social change:

1) That accelerating rates of change on all levels of society have created what Emery and Trist (1965) called "turbulent environments." Turbulence means that an organization's context (markets in the widest sense) has become unstable and more unpredictable.

2) An organization in a turbulent environment faces problems not clearly defined or understood by older methods. Thus, the right methods or solutions are not known. The organization (or social system) must search for new forms of functioning or, in evolutionary terms, adapt to

environmental changes by creating new behavior. This process means both redefining the environment and exploring new ways of relating to it. We call this a "search process" since a form of learning through trial and error takes place.

In turbulent environments organizations (and social systems) need to reorganize frequently. There is, in other words, a need for the capability of "learning to learn."

The search process can be defined as a form of *collective meta-learning*, where many parties learn together how to learn about themselves, each other, their common stakes, and potential new actions. This idea comes from two sources:

1)   General theories of collective behavior—within groups, organizations, movements, societies and civilizations (Buckley 1967).

2)   A theory of metalearning (Bateson 1972). We distinguish between learning on different levels, first level learning and higher order metalearning which means learning to learn.

BY COLLECTIVE LEARNING we mean learning that is shared between the members of a collective. Individual learning is required, but not sufficient. Thus, if all members of a collective were trained individually, we would not have a collective learning process.

BY COLLECTIVE METALEARNING we mean the capacity of a system to learn about and reflect on it's own learning, as advocated by Argyris and Schon (1978) and Dunn (1971). We design search conferences in hopes of creating or strengthening such capacities in social systems. We create new, temporary structures for communication, horizontal, vertical and across boundaries between departments and areas of competence. So all parties increase their awareness about how the system learns and changes.

ABOUT THE AUTHOR

Rolf Haugen is a sociologist, formerly a researcher at the Work Research Institute in Oslo, Norway (1972-86). He is currently a organizational development advisor for the Norwegian State Railways.

CONFERENCES RUN BY ROLF HAUGEN

1979   –   Local Community
1980   –   Local Municipal Administration
1981   –   Aluminum Industry on the National Level
1982   –   Local Community and Municipal Administration
1983   –   Norwegian Agency for Development Aid
1984   –   Regional Small Business Enterprises
1985   –   Teenagers, Parents, Politicians, and Local
             Administrators (on Youth Policy in a Local
             Community)
1986   –   Regional Public Health Administration,
             Planners, Politicians
1986/7–   Schools of Engineering
1987   –   Local Administration of Immigrants and
             Refugees
1987   –   Slaughterhouse Cooperative
1987   –   Top Management of Industries in Uganda
             (National Level)
1989   –   Parents and City Administrators/Planners
             of Childcare and Kindergartens
1990/1 –   Local Communities, Municipal and Regional
             Administrations

CHAPTER 8

INFORMING PARTICIPANTS OF WHAT TO EXPECT

Ivar K. Brokhaug

IVAR BROKHAUG HAS CONDUCTED 40+ search conferences in the last decade—in such diverse settings as farm and fishing villages, with motorcycle gangs, business firms, and government/industrial organizations. This paper presents a document he has developed to orient people who may be interested in search processes.

Note similarities and differences between the Brokhaug and Haugen model, especially Brokhaug's willingness to preselect participants to provide data at certain points. In addition, Haugen's model emphasizes present action, Brokhaug's the desirable future as a basis for action. Both share a key feature of all search conferences: a thorough exploration of the current environment as the shared context for dialogue and action.

Haugen provides detailed information on the theoretical underpinnings of searching in democratic societies. It is a formal conference presentation. Brokhaug gives us a model document that he uses to translate theory into practice—an orientation paper sent to all conference participants in advance. – MRW

What follows is a condensed description of the orientation I provide on search conferences for people likely to attend or prepare one. My description is based on how I manage a search conference. The orientation I describe is highly generalized. It is based on material written in Norwegian that I developed in planning and managing more than 40 search conferences over the last ten years. In practice each conference is a unique event for which I develop more event-specific materials.

The content will be revised each time, but the orientation always deals with these topics:

1. Definition
2. Process: Way of Working
3. Preparation
4. The Conference: Main Phases
5. Following up
6. Post Script

My primary intention is to prepare people mentally for the process they will attend. Secondly, it gives them an opportunity to make practical preparations, such as collecting materials and information. The conference described here will normally last for two days, with 25 to 80 participants.

What follows is the text I ask planners to send in advance.

SEARCH CONFERENCE ORIENTATION

I. Definition

A search conference is a concentrated, intense way of working, well suited for strategy and planning processes. Key actors/decision-makers (stakeholders) and representatives from all groups within "the system" (company, local community, municipality, etc.) meet for committed planning of priority activities, based on common experiences and wishes for future development. If possible all members of "the system" take part in the conference.

2. Process: Way of Working

This way of working combines system thinking with modern pedagogical principles. It differs in many ways from the traditional hierarchical and functional way of planning the future. The name "Search Conference" comes from "A Search for a Common Future," a method refined in Australia by Fred and Merrelyn Emery, that has been further developed in Norway and other countries.

The conference must be seen as a part of a process. There must be a clear reason for starting a "democratic strategy process," some preparation has to be done, and there must be willingness to follow up after the conference.

The method assumes there is (or can be built up) a consciousness about "common destiny" among the participants. And there must also be a common feeling of the need for "doing something," what I call "optimum crisis consciousness." This means a shared state of mind somewhere between "nothing is needed to be changed" and "whatever we do will not help us." The method is also based on "the whole system in one room," so that everybody can join in the necessary decisions.

Search processes also assume that development is a continuing process, where the past and the future meet in the present. You must know a system's history to understand its present situation, and you must understand the present to influence the future in desired directions. The conference focuses on the future, and on possibilities more than problems. The way of working leads to cross-disciplinary and cross-functional cooperation.

There is a clear division of labor. Conference managers provide the context and structure, participants the content. The method focuses on the participants' views and their perspectives of the future. The participants control the conference by selecting what to continue working on.

3. Preparation

Participants must always do some preparatory work. Thinking through the present situation, and how it could have been better, is one thing. Another is talking with colleagues and friends about the present and the future. Anybody who has relevant background material should bring it to the conference. The participants should not work out solutions to problems in advance. If they already have, they should bring them along "in their pockets" for introducing into the process if and when appropriate.

Every participant brings articles from papers, or other things illustrating something that will influence their future situation. Material telling about general trends in the society is as relevant as material telling about more specific things of direct relevance for "the system."

4. The Conference Itself: Main Phases

We have group-work, plenary presentations and plenary discussions, supplemented with lectures from invited persons. The groupings vary. In the first part of the conference there are homogeneous groups (people with a common background, and different from the others). They define the present situation based on historical understanding, and describe the desired future and "areas for action." Then cross-disciplinary groups are formed to search for projects/activities within the areas for action, and finally responsible groups are formed for activity planning.

A search conference can be illustrated as in the following chart:

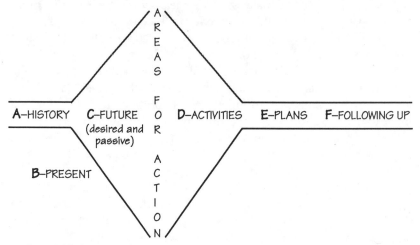

A. HISTORY

The conference starts with an orientation about the background and goals and the way of working. Then invited speaker(s) draw the lines from far history to near past.

B. THE PRESENT

The first group-work (homogeneous groups) then looks at the present situation, and how this has been created. They evaluate different sides of the present, and look for resources and limitations of "the system." The different groups present their "pictures" and evaluations of the present for the plenary, so that all participants get the results of the work from the other groups in addition to their own.

C. FUTURE

This phase starts with invited speaker(s) telling about trends that might influence "the system," but are not necessarily obvious for the participants. Then homogeneous groups look for a desired future, and for what will happen if things continue as now (passive future). They suggest "areas for action," which is where resources should be brought in to reduce the gap between the desired and the passive pictures of the future. The results from the group work are presented for the plenary and discussed.

D. ACTIVITIES

The conference staff then condenses/consolidates the presented material into a limited number of areas for action. These are presented for the participants, discussed and adjusted, and new, voluntary, cross-disciplinary groups are formed for each area. These groups search for potential activities and projects within their area, make rough outlines of these, and suggest priorities. The results are presented and discussed in the plenary session.

E. PLANS

The staff works on the suggested activities/projects based on all the presented material, and suggests single projects/activities or clusters of these for action planning. The results are presented and discussed in plenary, and final selections made from the criteria "important" and "possible." The final "responsible" groups are formed, from people who have formal responsibility and/or are willing to take personal responsibility for bringing the projects/activities from ideas to realities. For some projects/activities it is possible to implement plans immediately after the conference. For others it is necessary to make "plans for planning," where the "testing" of suggestions made at the conference is the most important thing. The plans tell what should be done, when, and who is responsible. The action plans are presented in plenary session and discussed. The plenary discussion may lead to some adjusting, coordinating between projects/activities and even changes in prioriety, when everything is presented and looked at as a whole in the light of the desired future presented earlier. The final product is a result of common work and understanding, and common responsibility for the follow-up.

5. Following Up

A few weeks after the search conference the participants meet again. The groups present in a plenary session what they have planned, what they have done and what they have learned. Then there might be a presentation of some important facts/happenings since the conference. After a break the groups revise their plans and present them for the plenary. The meeting ends with a plenary discussion, where the next steps in the continuous strategic process are the focus.

6. Post Script

The search conference process may look rather complicated. But this is what makes it possible to create a common, general understanding and strategy, based on contributions from participants with different experience and different viewpoints. The results will therefore be common property, and this is the guarantee for future success.

ABOUT THE AUTHOR

Ivar K. Brokhaug is director of the Center for Management Education at The Norwegian Institute of Technology of the University of Trondheim, and an adviser to the Norwegian Work Life Center, Oslo. He has a M.Sc. degree in Production Engineering and has consulted for 20 years in the improvement of work and community organizations in Norway and other countries.

SOME CONFERENCES RUN BY IVAR BROKHAUG

● **Budal, Mausundvaer, Salsbruket, Stongforden,** many other local communities – Improving community development, business, service, social life, and future planning. ● **SINTEF (Foundation for Scientific and Industrial Research, Norwegian Institute of Technology)** – Many conferences for whole and for departments (Transport Engineering, Production Engineering, Business Development Office and Information Section, Applied Chemistry, others) – Future planning, business and research strategies. ● **Motor Cycle Clubs of Trondheim** – Improve cooperation between clubs and with traffic police to increase traffic safety. ● **Trondheim Chamber of Commerce** – Future strategy. ● **University of Trondheim, College of Arts and Science** – Create new roles for heads of faculties and divisions. ● **Leaders in Travel and Tourism in Norway** – Develop national Travel and Tourism strategy. ● **City of Alvdal** – Revitalizing the old municipality center.

CHAPTER 9

TOURING 'THE FOUR-ROOM APARTMENT'

A Dynamic View of Future Searches

Marvin R. Weisbord

C LAES JANSSEN (1982), A SWEDISH SOCIAL PSYCHOLOGIST, has a simple tool for visualizing where energy lies, and how we focus it in the course of living our daily lives. I have found this model useful in managing conferences. So many others have now used and cited this model, I have adapted it from *Productive Workplaces* (Chapter 13) to this book's purposes. Each person, group, company, says Janssen, lives in a "four-room apartment." The tendency of people to fight, flee or become unduly dependent on conference leaders may be connected to which room they are living in at the moment.

We move from room to room, depending on internal perceptions and external events. The rooms represent cyclical phases, akin to life cycles. Indeed, change represents a "little death," a letting go of the past to actualize a desired future. We change rooms as we grow. However, it's not an ever upward spiral where things only get better. It's a circle game. Our feelings and behavior go up and down as pressures impinge on our "life space." How much energy we have for creative work is related to which room we're in. William Bridges (1980) and Robert Tannenbaum (1985) document similar dynamics.

In Contentment, we like the *status quo*. When it changes—merger, reorganization, market crisis, job threat—we move into Denial. We stay there until we own up to fear or anxiety. That moves us through the door into Confusion. Mucking about in Confusion, sorting out bits and pieces, opens the door to Renewal. The passage to Renewal leads from Denial through Confusion. You can't get there by any other route.

Anxiety, in Gestalt terminology "blocked excitement," is the emotional decor of the Confusion room. Far from a state to be avoided, it signifies readiness to learn (Perls, Hefferline, Goodman, 1956). Every new project, course correction, major change requires optimal anxiety. If there's too much, we are paralyzed, too little, unmotivated.

In every Confusion room there are people ready for constructive action—if they can be brought together to discover how their initiatives integrate with the whole. To mobilize energy, we need to be with people in Confusion or Renewal.

We can trace many failures to techniques and models foisted onto people living in Contentment or Denial. That's why there's no cause-effect connection between techniques and transforming systems. People move at their own pace from room to room.

VISITING THE ROOMS IN A FUTURE SEARCH

I experience every future search conference as a trip through the four-room apartment. These conferences, by their nature, facilitate the journey. Working with broad information, diverse participants, and open-ended opportunity maximizes our creative resources. But we all make the trip for ourselves. (Of course, it will be a "real" action planning trip only when the minimum critical specifications set out in Chapter 5 are met.)

People arrive curious, expectant, eager, mystified, open—and anxious. This is, after all, a strange group, an unfamiliar methodology, and a formidable task. Each person has an agenda, though they may not know what it is or how to work with it. That is part of the discovery.

We build lists, compare world views, listen, and seek to make order from chaos. No person has the whole. Each is tuned in to different events. But you remember what I have forgotten, and together we build a very rich portrait. Each discovery brings heightened anxiety and a release of energy. Early on people report being both confused by the multiple images, impressions, diversity, and eager to go deeper, explore more, find new action channels.

In future search conferences we usually plunge furthest into the confusion room when we make a group "mind map" of external trends affecting "X"—the focus of our search. Groups grow agitated as the map grows and grows. Gradually the realization sinks in that *this*—all of it— constitutes a mutual portrait of our world. It is complex, interconnected, hopeless, hopeful, unmanageable, inescapable. At the end of the map- making most groups fall speechless. My word for it is "awe." Awe has many meanings—shock, surprise, astonishment, dread, fear, wonder, amazement. We are awed by what we have created both in the room and in the world. We cannot imagine how we will get hold of it all, make sense of it, turn it into constructive action plans. We are deeply in the Confusion room.

That is entirely the right place to be. We get out when we take charge of the map. Every person touches it as they indicate the issues they most want to work with. Then, they start a dialogue with peers on what they are doing now and what they wish to do in the future. Within an hour, the anxiety becomes pure energy. We are moving toward renewal. We have touched down on common ground.

CHAPTER 10

FUTURE SEARCH CONFERENCES AND THE NEW SCIENCE

What Process Should We Trust?

Margaret Wheatley

THIS CHAPTER PROVIDES another perspective on the
functioning of future search conferences. Wheatley, an
experienced practitioner trained originally as a scientist,
draws on the re-thinking going on in the scientific world. From
this perspective, she provides another way of thinking about
the relationship between content and process in future
search conferences. We not only have new information available, says Wheatley, we also open up new channels for action
that did not exist before. An example of the work from which
she derives her ideas can be found in Chapter 13. This chapter
is adapted from her book, *Leadership and the New Science—
Learning About Organization from an Orderly Universe* (San
Francisco: Berrett-Koehler, 1992). – MRW

T HERE ARE MANY ASPECTS TO A FUTURE SEARCH THAT FEEL
magical. This is one of the things that draws me to them—knowing
that results will exceed expectations and that towards the end,
things will come together with a power and a sense of cohesion that I
know I did not create as the facilitator. As I've listened to other facilitators talk about their experiences, I can characterize some of the magic
that moves each of us.

Most remarkable is the similarity of visions that emerge. To have 50 or 80 people agree on something is unusual, even when what they agree on is the lowest common denominator, their dreams stripped of aspiration in an effort to reach agreement. Instead, in these conferences what emerges is a complex, finely textured vision of possibilities, more detailed and sophisticated than the individual visions that created it.

This is what I always wait for in these events—the emergence of a desired future. I and everyone else are always surprised by how similar the vision is across groups, and each of us is magnetized to that vision because of its sheer attractiveness.

Why does this occur? Is it truly a miracle, or is there an explanation for it? My own belief is that there is an explanation and that it is found in new understandings of information that have developed in the natural sciences over the past fifteen years. I have found it important to understand these conferences from the perspective of new science, because it dramatically changes the types of interventions I do as a facilitator.

CREATING NEW INFORMATION CHANNELS

Our familiar way of understanding information is as content, some *thing* that is exchanged or created in our conversations with one another. When information is viewed as a thing, our attention becomes focused on its transmission, how to move it smoothly along without distortion. We concentrate on developing clear channels that do not alter its content, and we try to hook up more and more receivers to those channels.

A future search, in bringing the whole system together, attempts to create new channels of information and to link up all parts of the organization to the same information. Also, new information is generated because of the diverse voices in the room.

But information is not only some *thing*; it is not just content. A new understanding of information has developed in the natural sciences that sees it functioning as a *structuring dynamic*, an energy that creates order and evolution. It is not just the content, but the ordering capability of information that we need to pay attention to. Information facilitates the creation of physical forms.

Let me give one example of this, an example that stretches our thinking in profound ways. Deepak Chopra, a physician, points out that the physical matter in our bodies changes regularly. Our skin is new every four weeks, our liver changes every six, and 98 percent of all the cells in our body are new every year (Chopra 1989). Given this fact, what is our body? And who are we, if our physical form is so transient?

Chopra describes us as a river of intelligent energy, where the look and shape of the river remains constant due to the information contained in our DNA. Matter keeps changing, but the information about us stays constant, directing molecules into their proper place. In this model of the body, information is a structuring dynamic. To change physical form, we need to change the information.

We can view the dual nature of information through the lens of the oft-told parable of the bricklayers. One describes his job as laying bricks, the other as building a cathedral. If we see our task as assembling more and more bricks, we are perceiving information only as a thing, as a tangible entity that builds incrementally. But if we are aware of the presence of a blueprint, of an ordering intelligence that influences the placement of the bricks, then we are perceiving information's structuring capacity as well.

Thinking about information as a process, as a structuring energy, is new to us and often difficult to grasp at an intellectual level. But we live with evidence of information's ability to create order, and see its dramatic workings in the search process. Something goes on during these conferences, invisible but felt, that organizes the flow of people, ideas and processes into the coherent structure of a shared vision. What we are experiencing is the process side of information, an energy capable of organizing matter into form. This role for information is revealed in the word itself: in-formation.

If information is the formative energy behind all life, then having more of it is the way to ensure growth and evolution. Processes that spawn new information allow life to flourish. New information is created anytime information meets other information, providing there is a context that gives meaning to the exchange. This is clearly what occurs in a search process.

TRUSTING THE "MESSINESS"

The events and processes of the first day(s) create new information, bringing together different people and perspectives, recording it all until the room is awash in flip chart papers. This stage of a search, though often well-structured in terms of group process, is somewhat chaotic. The intent is to create volumes of information without letting that information settle too early into any conclusions. It is best for things to remain messy, because that is the route to a transcendent vision.

I found that it was only after I'd been through a few searches that I

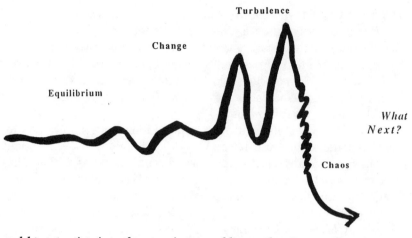

could trust going into the messiness and know that it served a purpose. It was during that period that I learned from natural scientists how messiness and chaos are part of the path to higher forms of order.

Open, natural systems use information from their environment to create new levels of organization. If the information is not suppressed, it lodges in the system and begins to grow. Different parts of the system learn of the information and amplify and change it. Finally, the disturbance becomes so great that the system can no longer remain as it is.

The presence of so much new information causes the system to fall apart. This is what we always fear, the descent into disintegration. However, natural systems possess innate properties that allow them, in most cases, to re-emerge from dissolution into new forms of organization better able to deal with the current environment. Dissolution is a necessary step on the evolutionary path. It does not signal death; it signals new forms emerging.

These natural systems are called *self-organizing* or *self-renewing,* and I believe we create them every time we run a successful search. In small groups and large, we create new and disconfirming information. In the first parts of a future search, as information is created, some of it is seized upon by participants and amplified. This information has no discernible shape yet, but it is very potent.

SELF-ORGANIZING

Finally, there is so much novelty in the room that the old order no longer makes sense. The organization or group needs to re-organize into a form that is better able to deal with the world view that has emerged. Self-organization principles are at work here, and their product is the compelling and synchronous visions that the group creates.

Working with these scientific principles has changed the way I do futures conferences (and everything else that involves information). I am much more comfortable with messiness. I have no need to fit information into categories, or models, or any kind of order too early. I know that the richness I seek will only come forth if I trust into information's self-organizing properties. My task is simply to create group processes that generate prolific amounts of information, and wait for information's structuring energy to appear.

I have even come to tolerate chaos—a condition most feared by facilitators. I have learned that if things are not under control, if I can't see the order in what is happening, this does not necessarily mean that things are out of control. There are structuring forces at work that I never knew of before, and these forces often use chaos as a necessary stage to higher levels of order. My discomfort with chaos, and my need to suppress it, only block progress.

But above all, I have come to trust in a process that a few years ago I didn't even know existed. Order is not created by rigid structures or tightly woven group processes. Order is a dynamic energy that swirls around us, creating form and shape that suit the present. Its substance is information, and I facilitate the creation of order when I facilitate the generation of information. It is surprisingly simple, perhaps fearfully so. But how good to be working in concert with natural processes, which are always simple once we understand them.

CHANGING SCIENTIFIC PARADIGMS

OLD	NEW
FATE OF LIVING SYSTEMS	
Entropy, Things Fall Apart	Self-organization
DESIRED STATE	
Equilibrium, Stasis	Non-equilibrium, Dynamic Change
STRUCTURES CREATED BY	
Man-made, Imposed	Inherent, Unfolding
ORDER FOUND IN	
Structures	Information
INFORMATION IS	
Closely Managed	Freely Generated

ABOUT THE AUTHOR

Margaret Wheatley is an Associate Professor of Management in Brigham Young University's Marriott School of Management and a practicing consultant for 20 years. She was a founding member of Goodmeasure, Inc. and a co-founder of Ibis Consulting Group in Cambridge, MA. She has consulted to many corporations, educational and non-profit organizations on work redesign, employee development and leadership teams.

In 1990 Weatley co-founded The Berkana Institute, a non-profit organization that helps facilitate communities of inquiry and support among people experimenting with new organizational forms, and with managing from a more integrated sense of self. Since 1989 she has led searches in two academic program areas, in a healthcare organization, and for a division of a large international corporation.

She has written many articles on the impact of opportunity and power in large organizations; the creation of ethical work; and the motivating power of ethics in times of corporate confusion.

DIALOGUE AS A PATH TOWARD WHOLENESS

David Bohm Interviewed by John Briggs

I
F WE SURVEY the various fields of modern science," wrote
Ludwig von Bertalanffy (1952), the biologist behind general
systems theory, "we note a dramatic and amazing evolution.
Similar conceptions and principles have arisen in quite
different realms...and the workers in the individual fields are
hardly aware of the common trend." Chapter 11 reiterates
this point. Physicist David Bohm and author John Briggs,
traveling different paths from this book's other contributors,
confirm the power of dialogue. To experience our wholeness,
Bohm prescribes conditions quite congruent with those of
Solomon Asch, iterated by Emery (Chapter 5). Bohm, however, believes real dialogue requires (1) little structure, and
(2) initially no purpose, other than to hear each other.

Bohm is one source for new theories of science used by
Wheatley in Chapter 10 to explicate search conferences and
Steven Burgess in Chapter 34 to design them. I first came
upon him in a remarkable book called *The Presence of the
Past* by Rupert Sheldrake (1990). Sheldrake's (controversial)
idea is that what makes things the way they are is memory—
of how similar things have always been in the past. This
memory sets up fields that influence both structure and
behavior, in all things inanimate and living, from tiny molecules

to whole societies. In short, we develop stable habits. Shel-drake calls the process "morphic resonance."

He imagines that we have the unique capability to tune in on our own morphic fields. Our brains may be more like radio receivers than computer disks. Hence we have the capability (unconscious and automatic) to receive relevant signals—habits from the past, that we carry on until we learn better ones. This remains a hypothesis, an unproven theory, though many experiments are underway to test it. Sheldrake sug-gests that when a critical mass of people learn something, the "gut" knowledge passes through space and time by processes so far unverifiable. It could mean that as more people experience search conferences, the event will become more natural for others to organize. As the morphic field of searching widens, the process becomes more accessible. It is a scientific description of "paradigm shift" I find easy to handle.

You don't have to believe this, of course, to learn how to run search conferences.

Meanwhile, there is David Bohm. This interview was sent to me by Bob Holder, a colleague who realized how congruent Bohm's ideas are with searching, despite his preference for low structure. Interviewer John Briggs also has joined in unstructured group dialogues—and he reports his experi-ences in an accompanying piece. My own view is that tasks that are open-ended, global in context and voluntary go a long way toward establishing Bohm's conditions, while reduc-ing anxiety to manageable levels.

"Actually," says Briggs, "Bohm doesn't specify that the dialogue be totally unstructured. He believes someone should facilitate or 'lead from behind,' as he puts it. The facilitator is not the leader however, and the dialogue has no fixed agenda or guiding theory. My own experience, however, was with a completely unstructured dialogue that we set up. It's impor-tant to note these differences."

I believe Bohm's ideas and Briggs' observations fit here because they confirm that when we get past forums and formats the shortcut to common ground starts with accept-ing each others' opinions. — MRW

CAN LESSONS LEARNED FROM SUBATOMIC PARTICLES HELP SOLVE SOCIAL PROBLEMS?

A *New Age Journal* interview with David Bohm.
September/October 1989. Reprinted by permission.

By John Briggs

Part philosopher, part mystic, part social activist, Bohm is most widely renowned as a theoretical physicist, a scientific explorer who has spent 50 years investigating the tantalizing theory that all parts of the universe are fundamentally interconnected, forming "an unbroken, flowing whole." Author of such books as *Causality and Chance in Modern Physics* (1957), *The Special Theory of Relativity* (1961), and the landmark *Wholeness and the Implicate Order* (1980), he has spun theories whose implications carry over into religion, philosophy, the arts and humanities, as well as numerous scientific fields.

JOHN BRIGGS: *What have you learned from your scientific investigations of nature that you think might be important to share with those of us who are non-scientists?*

DAVID BOHM: I've learned that we have to understand the wholeness of the world. The current way of breaking it up into fragments is not adequate. That's the reason I think we need to begin a serious dialogue, to avoid more fragmentation and repair the fragmentation now taking place.

What do you mean when you say we are breaking up the world into fragments?

Just look around. We have all kinds of division. There's the scientist, the non-scientist, the medical person, the business person. In science there are branches such as physics, biology, the social sciences. Within each branch are sub-branches, and they hardly understand each other. In medicine, specialists in one part of the body hardly understand what's going on in a closely related part. There are endless examples.

Why is that a problem? If you have something wrong with your eyes, don't you want to go to an ophthalmologist or optometrist, somebody who specializes in that part of the body?

We don't think our fragmentary approach to reality is a problem because most of us have an unconscious meta-physical assumption that nature is made of separate parts. The eye is a part, the ear is another part, and these parts interact. I'm suggesting that reality isn't that way. If you have something wrong with your eyes, our assumption is that the trouble originates in that part. But it may not. It may originate in the whole of the body, in the mind, or in society.

For example, the problem may be stress or pollution. The society we have created will cause a breakdown in all kinds of parts. You may temporarily repair the parts, but it's like pouring in pollution upstream at the same time that you're trying to remove bits of it downstream.

Everybody's doing his thing, making his bit of money, and producing his product, and therefore adding his little bit to the pollution. Because the world is finite, all these little bits affect each other, so that the soil and air are poisoned, fish die, and the climate is changed.

Is that because our technology is based on the assumption that you can extract the valuable parts out of the Earth—its uranium, gold, oil, fish—but that when you extract what you consider valuable, there are by-products you don't want?

Then, we can't get rid of these by-products. It's garbage, and nobody knows what to do with it. The idea of mining and plundering the world to get products, and as a consequence generating unwanted by-products, comes from the atomistic viewpoint. People and groups think of themselves as separate atoms.

One group wanted to make aerosols and didn't think about the results. All they were concerned with was to make aerosols and refrigerators; that was their little bit. But it turned out that the gas leaks out and attacks the ozone. Another group is burning coal just to produce energy; that's its little bit. The people in the Amazon are saying they're burning forests just to obtain their little bit of farmland. The Soviets were making nuclear power to solve their problems, but Chernobyl blew up and resulted in trouble all over northern Europe.

None of this activity takes into account the fact that everything is dynamically interconnected. Nations pretend they're sovereign, but when the climate changes there will be starvation everywhere. People sometimes talk about the whole or try to create organizations such as the United Nations, but this is only paying lip service to wholeness. The United Nations isn't allowed to do anything really serious.

Our divisions are what's really important to us. We cling to them. These divisions would make sense only if the world were in fact made of parts, and the parts were essentially independent. But they're not, so our way of going about things is a form of self-deception.

Where does this belief in parts come from?

In the seventeenth century the idea was that the universe is like a clockwork made by God. Each part is independent, interacting by the pushing and pulling of gears and rods. A machine can be disassembled and remodeled by exchanging parts. Later on, people had subtler ideas of the machine. They said it was made of atoms pushing and pulling on each other. Now they're thinking it's like a supercomputer. Whatever the latest machine is, people think that's the model of nature.

The mechanical model makes nature a means to an end. It implies that nature is there for us to get whatever we want out of it. I say this model is not adequate. I'm not against treating things as parts, but we have to understand what the word *part* means. A part has no meaning except in terms of the whole. The idea of treating everything as *only* parts may work in the short run, but it doesn't work when you follow it through.

Obviously your conviction that it doesn't work comes from your many years of studying quantum theory. Is there something about quantum physics that suggests there is a fundamental wholeness to nature?

Until the end of the nineteenth century, the idea that you could reduce everything to a machine of some kind prevailed in science. Then, in the early part of this century, it was discovered that electrons, which were supposed to be the smallest "parts" of matter, showed wavelike properties. Quantum mechanics also discovered that light waves can act like particles.

Physicists found that whether an electron acts like a wave or a wave acts like a particle depends on how you set up your experiment; in other words, it depends on the surroundings. That goes against the mechanical idea, which is that a part is independent of where it is; the environment doesn't change it, and looking at it doesn't change it. But an electron is more like a person who will behave differently if he knows he's being observed.

In quantum experiments, we find that the observer *is* the observed. What you know about the atom as a result of your attempt to see it cannot be disentangled from the context the atom exists in, which includes your observation. Again, that sounds like what happens with people who become disturbed when they're observed. The mechanical model that sees the world as parts doesn't work at the quantum level. Take superconductivity. That's good example of a phenomenon that is hard to explain with the mechanical model.

What is superconductivity?

Ordinarily, when a current is sent through a metal, the electrons that make up the current meet a lot of resistance. As they go through the metal they hit various imperfections and scatter, and they scatter each other. In this way, they fall into a random kind of movement and lose their momentum. But in superconductivity the current flows indefinitely. It has no resistance.

This property of superconductivity shows up only at fairly low temperatures at which we find the electrons suddenly start to move together with a high energy that remains orderly and does not become random. They can go around obstacles the way ballet dancers go around a piece of scenery on stage. At higher temperatures the electrons begin to break up into small, independent groups. Eventually, when the temperature is high enough, they become like people moving around independently and colliding with each other. Here we see that in one circumstance the electrons behave like parts, while in another—at a low temperature—they behave as a whole.

How do you explain such a dramatic difference in the way the electron behaves?

The electron field is affected by the whole surrounding. If you have several particles, then you have, according to my model, a single inter-woven field or pool of information for all of them. So when you touch one, it has an effect immediately on the others. They're in instant contact through the information field. This is also like what happens to human beings. If you took several humans who were closely related and someone hit one of them, the others would immediately become agitated. The agitation doesn't have to be mechanically transferred. The humans, through their minds, exist in an information field. Again we see the similarity of the sub-atomic world to our world.

And superconductivity is explained by your new electron field idea?

In superconductivity, if you have a large number of particles at low temperature, each particle will be governed by the common pool of information. Again, it's like the dancers who all have a common pool of information. But, as the temperature rises, this pool of information breaks up until there is, practically, only one pool per particle. So all the particles seem independent and seem to act mechanically, bouncing off each other. The holistic aspect comes out only when you lower the temperature.

How is your idea of dialogue connected to these scientific ideas about the underlying wholeness of nature?

I'm proposing that we need to learn how to dialogue with each other because of all the fragmentation in the world, which we talked about before. It seems to me the only way we can overcome that is by experiencing our wholeness together. We need a kind of social enlightenment to help that take place. In the past, people have developed ways to foster individual enlightenment, a higher intelligence for the individual through meditation or mystical insight or what-have-you. But we haven't worked on ways to develop a higher social intelligence.

> "We don't want to let the purpose get in the way. Once [dialogue] starts, our purposes go into the shade as it were. We discover new things shining much brighter than the purpose we started with." – David Bohm

The main difficulty is that we've organized our societies by algorithms—that is, by sets of rules by which we try to affect each other like parts of a machine. The result is that we can't talk with each other about things that are really important. This shows up internationally, where the real issues cannot be discussed at the conference table. Parties in conflict discuss mechanical details about boundary lines or arms levels. But the real issue is the professed principles and prejudices that keep us enemies.

Wouldn't it be useless? Wouldn't it just turn into a debate?

Right. But if we can't talk about the root of the problem, we'll never solve it by talking about mechanical details. The point is, as soon as people try to talk about these things, their temperature goes up. They get excited and can't listen to each other. They become like individual electrons bouncing off each other.

So in negotiations we keep the temperature down, but not much energy is involved.

The negotiators keep it down because they don't want to get too excited. They're avoiding all the fundamental issues, as people often do when they meet each other in society. They know they don't agree on important points, so they talk politely. That way of getting along doesn't have much energy. Therefore, there's not much intelligence either.

So what we can do is try to negotiate to find some common ground for our conflicting self-interests.

Which is the same metaphysics that says the world is made up of different parts. It says that each person is a separate self equipped with a set of self-interests. But you have to ask, "Why do the people in Russia have Russian self-interests while the people in the United States have American self-interests?" The same people born in different places would have had different self-interests. Such self-interest does not arise out of the self. It's picked up from the surroundings, from the culture.

OK, let's agree that we're conditioned by our environment—religious, political or whatever. But isn't that just a hard fact, a given?

But if you make that assumption, then the problem of conflict between people is insoluble. I say that at some point this atomic assumption will break down. If we could stay entirely by ourselves, we could go on thinking of ourselves as separate atoms of individuals or nations. But everybody's so crowded together that at some point the assumption that we're basically separate will be revealed as false.

You're saying that there are so many of us now on the planet that we've reached a critical mass?

That's it. It's become dangerous. People live in the city and say, "I live in my little flat and I'm separate and safe."

But when they walk out in the street, they're not safe. Because you have ignored other people and allowed them to degenerate, you're not safe. These others may attack you and kill you. The assumption that we're separate atoms just doesn't work. With our level of technology and our ability to destroy each other and the environment, to continue with that assumption could mean our extinction. The population of the planet is really too large for people to live at the standard of living they would like.

But you can't discuss this. For example, when people attempt to discuss birth control and abortion, they can't do it. Some say the fetus has an absolute right to live, and other people say the opposite. When the two try to talk, they can't. That they can't talk is much more serious than the particular issue dividing them. Those who say the fetus has a right to live don't seem to care much about it after it's born. They specialize in the fetus. At the same time, the infant mortality rate is going up and people don't seem to notice this. The fetus problem and the infant mortality problem are not separate. But each side specializes in its part of the argument and ignores the other factors.

Attempts to do so lead to confrontation and to regarding the other as evil. How are we going to talk together? That's what dialogue is aimed at, in the sense I use the word. It's not an exchange and it's not a discussion. Discussion means batting it back and forth like a ping-pong game. That has some value, but in dialogue we try to go deeper.

Specifically what is your proposal?

To create a situation where we can suspend our opinions and judgments in order to be able to listen to each other. The idea is that we might generate a kind of social superconductivity by having lots of energy in the interchange, while keeping the temperature low. To do that you need a situation in which people can talk together freely without a specific agenda or purpose to guide the proceedings, and you need a group large enough to develop a number of subcultures. If two people get together with different views, they will generally avoid real issues. They will protect their separate information pools by avoiding connections that will agitate them. But when you have twenty or thirty people, there are bound to be subgroups wherein those deeper issues will come up. It's not controllable anymore. Eventually, the dialogue is going to touch an individual's non-negotiable assumptions, which will liberate high energy.

Do you have an example?

In Israel we held a dialogue group and the subject of Zionism came up. Somebody in the group said that Zionism makes the Arab-Jewish problem insoluble. At this point, a man popped up and said that without Zionism Israel and the Jews would go to pieces. He was very disturbed. The discussion had struck one of his non-negotiable assumptions. Other people began to get excited. There was danger. The whole meeting might have blown up, except that there were still other people who were not quite that involved, and they came in tangentially and kept the temperature down so that we could begin to face these issues.

Even the fellow who had gotten so excited about Zionism didn't get angry enough to walk out. Had he walked out, it would have stopped the dialogue. Eventually things cooled down and he was looking at his own view and the other views together. That created a common pool of information. Everybody began operating from the same pool of information.

When you listen to somebody else, whether you like it or not, what they say becomes part of you. So if the temperature is high, a conflict is generated inside and outside. But in the dialogue, the temperature is lowered, and the common pool is created, where people begin suspending their own opinions and listening to other people's—so everybody's opinion will be held by everybody. That's what I mean by a common pool of information.

At some point, people recognize that this common pool is more important than the separate pools. A state of high intelligence, social intelligence, unfolds from this; call it a kind of superconductive state. Just as superconductivity makes possible marvelous things such as trains that can move without friction, or circuits where electricity flows at incredible speed, so the intelligence that comes from dialogue may make it possible for something new to come into human relations.

The purpose of dialogue is to discover the holistic ground that has been ignored by the way we operate as individual and group atoms.

Let's say we start with that purpose, but that the more we participate, the more that purpose will slip into the background as we are achieving it. We don't want to let the purpose get in the way. Once this starts, our purposes go into the shade, as it were. We discover new things shining much brighter than the purpose we started with.

Dialogue as you describe it means learning to suspend one's position. But isn't it basic to humans to operate from a position and have instantaneous judgments and opinions about other people's positions?

Anthropologists who have studied hunter-gatherer groups say many of these people sit around in a circle without making decisions, and then they seem to know what to do. They don't have complete individualism, nor do they have collective pressure. It's a kind of life that doesn't lead to the stress we have now. It was only with the growth of technology that we developed authority and punishment and rewards to get other people to adopt our positions. We had to have armies to protect these positions, and all sorts of cruelty and torture and deception. In other words, the growth of technology has led to a worsening of our psychological situation.

But don't anthropologists also argue that it is the growth of technology, our ability to make tools, that makes us different from other species?

I don't think that's a good measure of intelligence. Look at the dolphins or the Orca whale. They don't have toolmaking capacity. They have large brains, but apparently their intelligence is directed a different way. Somebody told me about a case of eight dolphins getting together when one of them was being attacked by a shark. They formed a ring around the shark and came into the center and crushed it. It was collective action, like superconductivity, and it evidently came through their communicating faculty.

I'm not sure that the toolmaking ability is really the crucial feature of intelligence. Perhaps speech is the most crucial. I think that dialogue will liberate a more subtle kind of intelligence than that used in making tools. The intelligence that creates and uses tools is not able to organize society properly so as to take into account the consequences of those tools.

The intelligence that uses tools is the intelligence that emphasizes parts.

It also emphasizes using things as a means to an end. In dialogue we don't emphasize the parts. We don't have a means to an end. The dialogue does not work by saying that we are trying to manipulate each other to an end, or the group to an end. Rather, we're participating, talking together, exploring, creating. The end is not known.

Usually, when people talk about a higher intelligence, they are talking about an individual tapping into his or her higher intelligence, attaining individual realization. You think a group intelligence is available?

Perhaps an individual can tap into a higher mind, but in addition we need this higher intelligence to operate socially, or else we're not going to survive. Most of our life is social. If we don't manage things socially, individual higher, intelligence is not going to make much difference.

As you know, you have critics. Scientists claim that you're too philosophical to be a scientist, philosophers claim you're too scientific to be a philosopher. You sometimes talk about doing science the way an artist does art, and there's obviously a great deal of the psychologist and sociologist in your discussions of dialogue. Just how would you define yourself?

Frankly, I think it's sign of degeneration and fragmentation to want to arbitrarily put people into pigeonholes.

Then how would you describe a person who is interested in the whole?

I don't think we need to label people beyond saying that they're human beings. You can say you're interested in questioning the basis of things. You can say that.

Can you remember as a child being concerned about the issues we've been discussing here?

When I was in fourth grade, I was very much influenced in the direction of science by a book on astronomy that the teacher passed out. It told about the sun, Earth, and planets, which fascinated me very much. I felt it was something beyond all the chaos and smallness of what we were doing in our small town. The book began with a little poem in the frontispiece by Francis Bourdillon: "The nigh has a thousand eyes,/ And the day but one;/ Yet the light of the bright world dies/ With the dying sun./ The mind has a thousand eyes,/ And the heart but one;/ Yet the light of a whole life dies,/ When love is done." It was a kind of warning not to give too much value to this fascinating intellectual stuff. It all could be just starlight. It was a sort of chilling notion. It later became clear to me that no matter what we do in science or any other area, it will not help if we don't find a way to be related to each other at a deep level.

EXPLORING THE GROUP MIND
AN EXPERIMENT IN DIALOGUE

The form of group dialogue David Bohm invites us to undertake in order to save the planet is difficult to describe, because most of our language emphasizes our experiences as individuals or as members of organized groups. Bohm asks us to explore another kind of experience entirely, one he believes could radically transform the whole of human consciousness. A few years ago, I participated in an experiment along the lines Bohm suggests.

I had met Bohm and learned about his scientific ideas though an old friend, a psychiatrist-turned-painter, David Shainberg. One summer afternoon on Cape Cod, Shainberg and I discussed some of Bohm's ideas and speculated on the possibility that there might indeed be such a phenomenon as a group mind, or a collective consciousness, and that it might hold potential for addressing the universal problems of selfishness, war, and hatred. We wondered if there might be a way for us to contact our group mind, to learn if it might contain some new form of intelligence.

It was an ironic idea. As both Bohm and Indian philosopher Jiddu Krishnamurti have insisted, groups are, generally speaking, the cause of our conflicts rather than the cure. Any group organized around a leader, ideology, theory, or agenda creates a group identity that inevitably brings it to blows with other groups and individuals. The sad but obvious fact is that even organized groups with the highest ideals end up adding to the general cacophony of organized groups vying to solve the world's problems.

But what if a group of people were to gather with no leader, no ideology, and no specified purpose? What would happen if 20 or 30 individuals—who had in common only an uneasiness over the current state of humankind—simply met to attempt a dialogue? Would such a group quickly form an agenda and raise up a leader? Would it break up into warring subgroups? Would it develop a new way to communicate, or would communication degenerate into discussions about baseball? To find out, we launched an experiment with about twenty-five people who agreed to meet once a month at Shainberg's apartment in New York.

At the time, we were vaguely aware that Bohm was engaged in a group dialogue experiment of his own, in London. We later learned that the dialogue experiments on both sides of the Atlantic contained some striking similarities—most notably the discovery of what appeared to be a collective consciousness.

We found our Sunday afternoon discussions in New York a frustrating mix of aimless chat and deep communion. We talked a lot about whether, though there were no formal agendas or leaders for our meetings, there might be hidden ones. We found that the large size of the group and the stubborn individuality of its members made it impossible to stick to any subject very long, and we yearned to set some specified purposes or rules. But we never set them.

We taped the meetings, and volunteers reviewed the tapes and wrote up summaries, which frequently revealed that the apparent meandering of our conversations disguised an elegant underlying order and an often stunning logic. Sometimes what took place was quite eerie. We would actually seem to feel the presence of the group mind, separate from our individual minds, having its own will or intention and speaking in our various voices.

I would often times feel myself pitted against the group, unable to persuade the other members to see my point of view. However, when I would listen to the tapes I would realize that my point of view had been subtly adopted by everyone. Other people also reported having this experience. I compare it to the way an author feels about a story he is writing when it takes on a life of its own, frustrating his plans and intentions while at the same time being shaped by those intentions.

Another phenomenon I noticed in the strange communal currents that ran through our Sunday afternoons was that conflicts that arose among group members mirrored conflicts taking place within my own mind—as if the group's dialogue were a psychodrama of my interior monologue. One example of this was that many of us became quite angry at one fellow who badgered us with his skepticism about the dialogue project and was always threatening to leave the group. In fact, though we vigorously opposed him, his position reflected shadows of skepticism that existed within each of us. At least, that was my impression.

Other people had other impressions, and one of the irritating aspects of "dialoguing" was our inability to agree on any theory about what was going on. Yet, that seemed fitting, because we began to appreciate our different points of view not as sources of conflict but as sources of dialogue itself—a basis for social creativity. Of course, not everybody in the group agreed with that point of view, either.

After two years I dropped out of our group, abandoning the long car trip from Massachusetts to New York under the pressure of other commitments. Also, I wanted to try out the dialogue in "the real world." On those Sundays we had more than once discussed the fact that we were doing what we were doing with a hot house collection of people who not only had a global outlook but also had the luxury of enough time to indulge an interest in abstract, philosophical talk. It was quite another thing to enter into a creative dialogue with the IRS, the boss, or a cranky cab driver.

I have spent my adult life as a professional observer, journalist, and writer—and I consider myself a detached and basically antisocial individual. Part of that self-perception derives from having always felt inadequate and self-conscious in social situations. After two years of participating in the Sunday dialogue group, I was astonished to find myself eagerly and relatively comfortably taking on a job as an elected official in my small Berkshire hill town.

I attribute that change in myself to my experience in dialoguing.

Something essential in my relationship to society had changed. I continue to feel it operating like a smooth current amid the usual cauldron of conflicts that constitutes small-town New England politics. I haven't the slightest idea what that current is—except that it seems a continuation of what was begun in our group.

ABOUT THE AUTHOR

John Briggs received his doctorate from The Union Institute in aesthetics and psychology. He is author of *Fire in the Crucible: The Self-Creation of Creativity and Genius;* and *Fractals: The Patterns of Chaos;* and he is co-author of *Metaphor: The Logic of Poetry; Looking Glass Universe;* and *Turbulent Mirror.* Briggs is a professor of aesthetics and journalism at Western Connecticut State University and has been a Selectman in his hometown of Granville, MA since 1987.

PART 3

SINGLE-ORGANIZATION CASES

Introduction

"We can take the view that our organization has an appropriate place in the larger system, and that our task as management and leaders is to attune our organization to its environment... to discover what our part is and play it.... From a system point of view, then, strategic thinking is a search for meaning, rather than a search for advantage."

— Roger Harrison (1983)

The cases in Part 3 derive from a design I worked out in many conferences between 1983 and 1987. I outlined the rationale and methodology in Chapter 14 of *Productive Workplaces*. Indeed, it was the response to that chapter that started me thinking about this book. My generic plan reflects the concepts/methods discussed at length in Part One. I cannot emphasize too strongly that what attracted me was not any particular technique but the powerful shift toward constructive action made possible by a shift in conference structure. Even self-defined "powerless" single organizations, I discovered, could find the means to do extraordinary things if they invited a broader group to help them and shifted their focus toward the wider world.

The authors here are experienced consultants who read the earlier book, set out to apply the concepts, and modified my design. Two describe public sector cases—the Health and Human Services Agency of the United States Government, and the School of Management at Brigham Young University. Two others report on business conferences—from StorageTek, manufacturer of computer components, and St. Lukes/ Presbyterian Medical Center in Denver, a private hospital.

Each facilitator added personal wrinkles to the process. I am especially struck by their efforts to engage group creativity and to tap into unconscious processes. (This mode has been carried further still by Stephen Burgess in Scotland. See Chapter 34). Margaret Wheatley, of Brigham Young University, describes one experience that led her to the connections between search processes and new developments in science (Chapter 10).

Angus, Frank and Rehm work from a set of concepts they describe in "Concept: Theory and Practice" (page 141). All used guided fantasy to elicit creative visions for the future—a predisposition of conference facilitators in the United States. They also had people do individual futures scenarios as "letters from the future" before sharing them in small groups and merging them into a whole conference product. Wooten and Libby, who incorporated animated films to stimulate creativity, also make the point that the search mode is especially useful in large government bureaucracies to help people cut through a tangled web of competing special interests. – MRW

CHAPTER 12

STRATEGIC PLANNING IN THE U.S. DEPARTMENT OF HEALTH AND HUMAN SERVICES

John T. Wooten and Kathie M. Libby

JOHN WOOTEN AND KATHIE LIBBY have used variations on the "future search" in more than 20 conferences since 1983. Their main context is especially notable—the federal bureaucracy within the U.S. government's most pervasive agency. Here they sketch the context and potential importance of this work for public services, and give a typical design. At the end are a list of conferences they have managed using variations on this design. — MRW

W E WANT TO ADDRESS SEVERAL POINTS WE FEEL ARE CRITICAL to the dialogue about search conferences. In particular we want to express the values and assumptions underpinning our work experience, and suggest important design considerations that flow from them. We have a clear bias for action and empowerment, and have found that the search design values can be maintained in many environments where it is traditionally difficult to practice organization development.

Much of our work has been in adapting this conference approach to planning and priority setting in U.S. government institutions, notably The Department of Health and Human Services (HHS), formally Health, Education and Welfare.

The assumptions inherent to search processes—participation, shared power, influence and support—are historic hallmarks of democracy and public service in the U.S., hence are easily embraced intellectually by public servants. At the same time, the extreme complexity of the federal structure, with its constitutionally shared powers, is magnified at HHS because State and local rather than Federal governments administer many of its large social programs and are responsible for the delivery of day-to-day services to millions of people.

The HHS organization challenges its managers not only by its magnitude—approximately 140,000 people and the third largest budget in the U.S.—but by the sheer complexity and volatility of its responsibilities. It is said that HHS programs touch all American citizens from birth to death. It manages the social security trust fund; provides health coverage for the aged, the poor and Native Americans; conducts and funds basic bio-medical research; regulates drugs and food purity; and funds a variety of educational support programs such as Head Start.

The Department tests food and water for safety and assessed the health impact of the radiation after the Three Mile Island accident. It did the background work to find the cause of Legionnaire's disease. Now it makes decisions on compounds to be tested for their usefulness in abating the dreaded AIDS epidemic.

HHS is charged by law to solve human problems that other institutions—the family, the schools, the economy, and local governments—had ignored or failed to solve. The Department is the focal point for special interests of the poor, racial and ethnic minorities, and the elderly. In carrying out programs that touch all aspects of citizens lives, it must fight discrimination based on race, religion, ethnic origin, sex handicap and age.

The public program management environment in the 80's and the associated processes for distributing federal funds provided us a unique opportunity to introduce search ideas and technologies to the career and political stewards of the Department.

The Social Security Administration (SSA), an agency of HHS in which we utilized variations on the accompanying design, employs over 80,000 people. In the mid 70's it had been opened up to the world of special interest politics, primarily through the designation of its *first* political chief.

The dimensions of the future search that treat stakeholder interests were particularly powerful in our work with SSA in the early to mid-1980's, because the agency was no longer insulated from external interests and the national policy debate was, for the first time, brought directly into the agency's program operating level.

Few Americans appreciate how much these special interests have been institutionalized in law and regulations. Numerous Congressional committees and subcommittees claim jurisdiction over parts of SSA. Each month top departmental appointees give hundreds of hours of testimony to Congress and produce thousands of documents. We found the future search compatible with SSA's need for new planning and survival approaches that took into account these external forces and competing trends.

SSA organizations where we used this conference model were especially ready for this approach for two reasons. First, they were under pressure to become more strategic in managing their far-reaching programs; second, they needed to discover a sense of the possible as they entered the quagmire of the public arena in the 80's.

In each conference reviewing the global events of the preceding decades proved to be an exciting journey through SSA's past and present. As a result of this exploration, the need for programmatic and policy changes impacting services came sharply into focus, resulting in a mutual recognition of an expanded mission for the agency.

The subsequent discussions provided all participants with opportunities to identify and make clear their own values as public servants, in relation to the values inherent in current programs. More importantly the process awakened participants in a different way to the ever-present responsibilities of public stewardship during the difficult times brought on by an environment of dwindling resources, large scale structural changes and plans for major technological improvements.

We believe that the principles and values of the search process should be made widely available. We know of no other conference framework that so effectively empowers individuals toward collective action in the light of a greater public good.

LEARNING AND THE FUTURE OF THE WORK

The most important learning from our experiences with the future search is its capacity to free people to recognize their own capacity to influence the forward direction of a whole enterprise. We have also learned how to adapt the design to the arena of institutional policy-making and administration. Even when key stakeholders cannot be physically present, their interests and claims can be artfully attended to.

For example, in the case that follows, the Associate Commissioner and top managers organized a conference call prior to the start of the conference. It included key people from state offices, industry and client groups. These representatives were able to brainstorm significant environmental impacts and major service issues of importance to them.

Additionally, since much recently had been written about the conference issues, special reports, speeches, bulletins and news clippings from the stakeholders' perspectives were made available and used at strategic points during the conference.

As we begin the decade of the 90's, it is apparent that the themes of retrenchment, recession and budgetary constraints will be milestones in our ascension to the 21st century. The world around us has undergone tremendous change. The repercussions are yet to be fully realized. Retrenchment, recession and budgetary constraints are just that—constraints on peoples' motivation, drive, and creativity.

Search processes enable people to free themselves enough so they can recognize and act in ways that are not obvious day-to-day. We strongly believe search processes also can become an important tool for the emerging democracies in Eastern Europe, Central and South America, and for capacity building in parts of Africa.

It is still an open question, too early to answer, whether the use of this form of strategic planning by institutional stewards will result in improved decision-making and program implementation and management.

[Note: The following is our actual planning document. – JTW/KML]

FUTURE SEARCH CONFERENCE

OFFICE OF DISABILITY
SOCIAL SECURITY ADMINISTRATION

NOVEMBER 17-18, 1983

BACKGROUND

Conference managers met with Associate Commissioner of Disability in late October following an unsuccessful attempt at designing their own retreat. This organization of 300+ people sets policy and pays SSA disability claims. It had experienced several months of bad press and Congressional criticism resulting from decisions made at the political level. Conference managers met with retreat planning committee which agreed to use the Search approach.

PURPOSES
   Develop a spirit of belonging and cooperation
among the management team
   Establish clear direction in the face of
conflicting demands
   Make disability programs dynamic and proactive,
therefore more in control of their own destiny
   Time: 8:30 Wednesday 11/17-4:30 Thursday 11/18
   Place: Marriottesville Conference Center
       Marriottesville, Maryland
   Participants: 45
       Mngt: 40   Conf. Mngers: 2
       Admin staff: 5

PRE-WORK:
   Read Ron Lippitt's *Future Before You Plan*
   Materials required: flip charts (6), easel, paper
and markers (many, 35 mm projector, music system
and tapes)

DETAILED SEARCH AGENDA - DISABILITY

   8:30 Coffee/arrival

   9:00 Opening:
Commissioner states her hopes for program and the
Associate Commissioner states how much she values
staff and needs their participation
   Introductions: all
   Expectations: select a number from 1 (low) to 7
(high) that reflects your expectations for a
successful meeting; record numbers on flip chart -
discuss: "What will hinder a successful experience"
   Share overall agenda for the 2 days, elaborating
on "Why a Search design?"

   9:45 Environmental Scanning
   Review Past: describe significant events, trends
and developments that helped shape today's program/
organization
   Record ideas on flip charts on the walls
   Charts: 50's, 60's, 70's charts for each of

Economic/Political/Social/Technological/Organiza-
tional background music for each decade

10:15 Review lists and clarity, share and
appreciate different perspectives. Identify themes
and patterns for each decade.
Have volunteers lead discussions, making sure to
manage time carefully

11:00 Describe Present
List events happening right now in the organization and society that will shape disability's
future
Review lists and discuss as previously

12:00 LUNCH

1:30 Identify Prouds and Sorries from the lists
of events happening in the organization right now.
Make individual lists then join in mixed groups of
6/7 to share Groups consolidate list of things to
keep for the future (desirable) and things not to
keep (undesirable)

2:30 Groups report Out and Consolidate Lists

3:00 Break

3:15 Joshua in the Box
Introduce and present this 5 min. un-narrated,
animated film that provokes creative thinking about
our constraints and possibilities
Discuss meaning to participants

3:45 Preview Day 2

4:00 Social

DAY 2

8:30 Coffee/opening remarks about future
scenarios: ask participants to share ideas from
Future article

9:00 Future Scenarios—Blue Sky
In mixed groups of 6/7 identify desired/preferred
scenarios for OD. Consider the newspaper article
you want to read about OD in 5 years - what does it

say/what is OD doing worthy of note - re: services, employees, practices, policy
   Don't do problem-solving at this point

   10:00   Report Out
   Discuss and identify commonalities
   Prioritize: each has $10.00 to spend on priority
items

   11:00   Action Planning
   Note: set up action planning before lunch - have groups and task clear — allow groups to meet anywhere they feel comfortable
   In organizational groupings, identify possible actions to achieve high priority future scenarios
      brainstorm actions
      identify others who would need to be involved

12:00   LUNCH
   go to lunch in organizational groupings

   2:45   Report out Action Plans
   Associate Commissioner responds to and leads discussion on actions proposed, noting particularly those actions she is willing to support, those which may need further discussion

   3:30   Top Management Staff Meeting
   In fishbowl, staff meeting regulars discuss next steps, how to monitor progress, etc.
   Open chair available to anyone for up to 2 minutes

   4:00   Closing
   Review goals and expectations scale, test how well expectations were met, allow for general comment
   Associate Commissioner leads discussion on what each is willing to do to make this work and to make a difference.

   4:30   THE BEGINNING

EXAMPLES OF STRATEGIC DECISIONS FROM WOOTEN/LIBBY CONFERENCES IN THE DEPARTMENT OF HEALTH AND HUMAN SERVICES

1. Social Security Administration: Office of Disability

TASK: Strategic Planning for FY 1984 and setting overall Office direction.

OUTCOME: Managers reached agreement to monitor the disability incidence rate versus the quality of decisions made, with respect to their supportability, and to monitor these decisions to assure their quality is consistent throughout the country.

2. Social Security Administration: Office of Central Records

TASK: Planning for the impact of technology and improving service quality and timeliness.

OUTCOME: Agreement was reached on an implementation plan to utilize the project management approach to reach overall agency objectives and alignment with SSA values, i.e. providing timely and accurate payment services; administering efficiently and effectively; providing courteous sensitive and dignified service to the public; maintaining a positive work climate for all employees.

3. Office of the Secretary, Grants Appeals Board

TASK: Reexamination and commitment to the consensus process for dispute resolution.

OUTCOME: The importance of the Board's role in providing grantees a fair opportunity to present their position requires a consensus decision process. The stress, frustration, and time costs produced by this process are outweighed by the value of a fair hearing.

4. Regional Personnel Office

TASK: Planning for fundamental changes in processes and services as a result of new technology.

OUTCOME: Retrenchment activities require consolidating geographic services for all major administrative systems to achieve greater cost efficiencies and economies of scale. Enhanced automated support is needed.

5. Health Care Financing Administration: Regional Office

TASK: Adaptation to current agency trends suggesting the need for strategic planning and cutback management.

OUTCOME: Discovery that the political emphasis away from a strict service orientation and toward fiscal accountability in Medicaid and Medicare requires a restructuring and clarification of the role of the Financial Operations Division.

6. U.S. Public Health Service: Office of the Surgeon-General

TASK: Assessment of PHS Commissioned Corps' direction and operations in light of changed public health priorities.

OUTCOME: Clarified that the curative and reparative orientation of the Commissioned Corps is ill-suited to the prevention focus required for meeting society's behaviorally-induced public health problems. Plans were developed to refocus training, recruitment, and placement of Corps members to better position them to address major health issues of the 21st Century.

THE AUTHORS...

John T. Wooten and Kathie M. Libby are partners in Management Consulting Services, a consulting firm that emphasizes planning and priority-setting, team building, transition management and leadership development. Each has more than 15 years experience consulting and managing. They have conducted training and strategic planning sessions in agencies responsible for health, income security, insurance, family counseling, legal and personnel programs.

They have worked at all levels—from local community organizations to international programs in health care, social services, food, agriculture, and the environment. Both have academic and professional backgrounds in Public Management and Organizational Development.

CHAPTER 13
REVISING BRIGHAM YOUNG UNIVERSITY'S BUSINESS SCHOOL CURRICULUM
Margaret Wheatley

NOTE: This case should be read in conjunction with Chapter 10 where Wheatley speculates on how the new science puts these processes into another theoretical context. – MRW

I N ACADEMIC INSTITUTIONS, THE TRADITIONAL FORM OF DECISION-making is that of faculty consensus. Faculty usually experience this process as time-consuming and cumbersome; change is slow, painful and boring. Any new initiative is subjected to study, deliberation, comparison, discussion—in short, the skills of research and analysis are transferred to the sphere of action. There is little or no experience with participative forms that include more than faculty and administration.

It was into this type of setting that we introduced the idea of a future search conference. The issue at hand was the design and approval of a new Master of Business Administration program for Brigham Young University's Marriott School of Management, a program that would better suit the needs of the rapidly changing field of management.

A traditional academic decision-making model had been created for this project. A committee of eight influential senior faculty and administrators had been meeting for a few months, collecting information from other MBA programs, exchanging opinions, putting forward personal recommendations for a new program design. It is fair to say that their idea of a participative process extended only so far as the possibility that they might interview a few students.

The idea of a different kind of process, one that would involve all significant stakeholders, was introduced to the committee over the course of several meetings. They became more intrigued with the possibility as it was discussed, and finally agreed to take the risk of spending two days, and involving several stakeholders, for the chance that they might discover some additional insights for a new MBA program.

The list of attendees (totaling 48) included a good representation of major stakeholders. Students were invited from each department, from each year of the program, and included international students. Faculty from all departments participated, as well as department chairs, even those that did not directly deal with the MBA program. Within each stakeholder group, we sought as much diversity as possible.

DIVERSE STAKEHOLDERS

Faculty and students were in equal numbers, each group representing one-third of the total. The last third was composed of employers, senior corporate managers and program alumni, as well as one administrator from the university. A visiting professor from Moscow State University also was a lively contributor in the conference.

The design for the two days was taken directly from Weisbord's design for Whole Foods Market, as outlined in *Productive Workplaces*. Our one innovation was to begin with a group warm-up activity (Group Juggling) that gives people experience with dramatic quantum leaps in performance once they break out of preconceived patterns of organizing. We spent the first morning focused on the past, using the Three Decades Exercise.

We were impressed by the willingness of people to record publicly some very personal changes and feelings they had experienced over time. We came to understand that this first activity not only provides useful historical data, but also opens people up very quickly both to one another and to the process.

The other activities in order were: Present External Trends (using clippings); Present Internal State (Prouds and Sorries); Creation of New Futures, and presentation of these in skit form.

This search did not include any plans to involve stakeholders in follow-up planning or actions. We had agreed that the recommendations, visions, and ideas presented would be entrusted to the Faculty Strategy Committee charged with responsibility for the new program design. Their design and recommendations would be channeled back into the normal faculty decision-making process. Search conference attendees were promised a copy of the report, but were not expected to participate further.

Six weeks after the Search Conference, over 120 faculty were presented with a radically new program, one that would affect the teaching load and course content of every teacher involved with the MBA program. The new design also would have profound effects on the functioning of other, non-MBA programs. The design incorporated all of the major ideas that had emerged during the search. The projected futures were so similar in their ideas and goals that it was relatively easy to fully represent them in the final plans.

Two weeks after presentation of the new program, the faculty met to vote. The strategy committee anticipated a difficult session and had prepared itself to deal with opposition; a long meeting was expected, no different from any other faculty meeting.

What occurred caught everyone by surprise. A few questions were asked, the vote was called, and the program passed with only five abstentions and no opponents. Those who had been involved in the design process were pleased, but stunned. No one could recall such an easy vote, especially for a proposal that would affect the teaching lives of everyone.

BROAD FACULTY SUPPORT

Although it is difficult to ascribe causality to any sequence of organizational events, it seems clear that the open and participative nature of the search conference influenced not only the quality of design, but the faculty decision-making process in a dramatic way.

For those 18 faculty and administrators who had attended, the search conference seemed to give them a clarity of direction and excitement for the future. All members of the strategy committee participated in the conference, and many reported that their ideas for a new program had been validated. They felt encouraged, also, because support came from such a broad constituency of stakeholders.

In fact, some of the most dramatic moments of the conference came from the comments of employers—those who saw the fruits of our labors. Employers and alumni spoke of the dramatic changes occurring in their industries, and how alarmed they were at the university's serene focus on the status quo. One said that he was "singularly unimpressed" by the student resumes that passed over his desk; he got everyone's attention. That phrase became a *leitmotif* of the conference, reappearing in jokes and skits. At the conference end, the same employer who had been so critical stood and said that he was now "singularly impressed" by both the process and the output. Everyone cheered.

The search process seemed to have affected the faculty who weren't there as well. The excitement felt by those who attended spilt over into the halls of faculty offices; those who hadn't been there sensed that something important, different, and exciting had occurred. This seems to have given momentum to the process, and in some way none of us have figured out, contributed to the easy acceptance of the new program.

The credibility of what was recommended seems to have increased as a result of the search process. In particular, the inclusion of so many stakeholders in the design process may have increased the stature or inviolability of the final product in the eyes of those who had not been part of the process.

Two other points are worth mentioning. The search process, which is always high energy, creative and involving, is a wonderful means for introducing faculty and administrators to the benefits of a participative process. Unlike the experience of committees, boards and task forces, searches exemplify the best of participation. It becomes much easier, after a search has been experienced, to invoke support for more open and participative processes in general.

Secondly, the structure of a search presents faculty with the opportunity to experiment with new ways of data-gathering and assimilation. The majority of activities are well-structured, move at a brisk pace, and generate lots of fairly messy data. We stressed the "right brain" nature of the activities and kept urging people to stay playful.

We had to keep encouraging faculty, in particular, to generate the data and not get hooked into interpreting it, analyzing it, or any of the other traditional activities of academics. Faculty responded well to this, in part, we believe, because things move so quickly during a search. Their final presentations, skits of future ideal scenarios, were not only creative, but richly textured, containing many levels of analysis and description.

For us, the most difficult aspect of creating a futures search in an academic institution was convincing faculty and administrators to take the plunge. They were moving into strange territory and feared that the process could not be controlled, or that it would be filled with conflict, or worse yet, that it would be like a faculty meeting that went on for days.

Their past experience provided no frame of reference for understanding the nature of the search process. They needed first to be educated to the benefits of a participative process, and then to be reassured with examples of other searches. But once they decided to be experimental and to try it, they were strong supporters. And for many faculty, the actual conference was not only new and different, but memorable.

Margaret Wheatley's biography appears at the end of Chapter 10.

THEORY INTO PRACTICE
A Prelude to Chapters 14 and 15

By Gary Frank, Dave Angus, Bob Rehm

We are practitioners, not researchers or theoreticians. However, we rely on three explicit theories for future search conferences. They are (1) "appreciative inquiry," a recent derivative of action research (Cooperrider and Srivastva, 1987), (2) open systems theory, and (3) Kurt Lewin's field theory concept of change.

First, we see appreciative inquiry as very consistent with our understanding of the basic assumption of the future search conference. It is the "generative" side of action research as opposed to the traditional problem-solving, "deficiency" approach to action research. The latter serves primarily to constrain thinking, imagination, and the creation of a preferred future. However, through a process of appreciative inquiry, action research can be used for social innovation.

The process encompasses appreciating the best of what is (analogous to "prouds and sorries"), exploring ideals of what might be (visioning), agreeing on what should be, and finally experiencing what can be. While the dimensions of the appreciative inquiry are not completely analogous to the search conference activities, we believe there is a close relationship in the underlying assumptions and approach of the two.

Second, open systems theory is the basis of our approach at two levels. It is important to get as much if not the whole system in the room at once. This represents the internal ecology of the organization and must be understood within the context of the search. The search ALSO is about the organization as a part of a larger system. The relationship of the organization to its external environment, how that environment is changing, what the change either means to us (reactive) or how we can influence the change (proactive) are the key ingredients of the search.

Third, the Lewinian model of change is fundamental to our conference approach. The essence of the future search is to unfreeze and move a system in the direction of meaningful, deliberate, agreed-upon, preferred change. The change model structures this journey. It also occurs to us that pieces of field theory like cognitive dissonance and the creation of our "own" (internal) forces in the direction of change instead of imposed (external) forces are implicit to the search process.

The future search brings diverse people together in a cooperative setting and asks them to use their knowledge to explore and create a preferred future state. Strong values of human diversity, cooperation, knowledge, and creativity underlie this statement. We believe that the values and practices exemplified in these conferences are also values and practices that best facilitate social change and comprise the ideal future of society.

The diffusion of these conferences moves society in a direction consistent with widely-shared values. It is truly a recursive exercise in that it enables us to practice what we preach. A bumper sticker popular in our area reads:

"THINK GLOBALLY, ACT LOCALLY."

We know that when we conduct a future search conference in our "local" organization, we are joining a "global" social change movement consistent with our beliefs.

CHAPTER 14

HUMAN RESOURCE FUTURE STRATEGY AT STORAGETEK

By Gary Frank and Bob Rehm

W E HAVE CONDUCTED THREE CONFERENCES HERE AT StorageTek based on *Productive Workplaces* and are reporting on the one we did for our human resources strategic planning process. The three principles important to us in our work are:

> "Get the whole system in the room."
> "Structure tasks people can do themselves."
> "Focus on the future."

We believe the search is a helpful mechanism for realizing these principles. The conference works best when people from all levels of an organization and external stakeholders come together in an egalitarian environment. This delivers a strong message that everyone is knowledgeable and has something valuable to contribute.

In our conferences we provide tasks for the group to work on and then use our process consultation skills to facilitate the conference. This is an effective use of our skills that allows participants to unleash their energy and knowledge.

The future focus of the search conference encourages people to appreciate the possibilities of whatever situations they face together. In fact, we believe appreciating the future actually helps create it. The "focus on the past" and the "prouds and sorries" exercises provide a useful context for jumping into the future. In our Human Resources (HR) strategic planning conference we encouraged the inclusion of these activities, but the client decided to focus exclusively on the external environment and preferred future state for HR. Our own "Volume to Value" exercise helped somewhat, but we could sense the lack of historical context the group experienced.

SPONSOR: HUMAN RESOURCES, STORAGE TECHNOLOGY CORPORATION

Conference Task: Future Scenarios Five Years Out

Stakeholders: HR Staff (30), HR Managers (6), Corporate Education (6), Product Marketing (1), Manufacturing (2), Development Engineering, Corporate Services, Field Sales and Service, Customer Services (2).

Length: Two Days

Place: Louisville, Colorado

Conference Managers: Gary Frank, Bob Rehm

INTRODUCTION

The Storage Technology Corporation (StorageTek) is a manufacturer of computer information storage and retrieval systems. StorageTek employs more than 8,000 people and markets its products throughout the world. After experiencing Chapter 11 bankruptcy in 1984, the organization bounced back and is reasserting its competitive place in the marketplace.

As StorageTek moved from a survival orientation to long term achievement, the company began to focus on a comprehensive strategic planning process. In January, 1989, the newly appointed vice president of human resources enlisted the support of his organization development staff to develop a process to create HR's first ever strategic plan. He wanted a plan that would explore human resource issues to 1994 and fit into StorageTek's overall strategic plan.

In March, the vice president and his HR managers endorsed a process that integrated strategic planning and organization development approaches. The major kickoff event would be a two-day futures conference based on the model described in Weisbord's book, *Productive Workplaces*. The rest of this paper describes the design of the conference.

THE EVENT

About 50 StorageTek people came together in a two day conference to help create the future of human resources for the corporation. A cross section of HR staff and managers attended as well as representatives from several internal client groups such as manufacturing, marketing and customer services. The HR vice president welcomed participants and stated the purpose of the conference:

- To generate and analyze the forces that will affect the human resources function at StorageTek over the next five years;
- To create ideal future scenarios for HR;
- To make recommendations to HR as they prepare their strategic plan.

The organization development staff facilitated the event. Ground rules describing the collaborative, idea generation nature of the event were discussed and clarified to make sure everyone understood the participatory purpose of the futures conference. Then participants introduced themselves stating their hopes for the conference.

The first activity was a private one in which each participant identified the trends, forces, changes expected in the next five years that will affect human resources at StorageTek. Participants came to the conference prepared for this activity. Many had articles and clippings to support their viewpoints. People shared their trends and forces in small groups.

Each group then prepared a list of what they considered their group's hot trends and they posted these on the wall under the categories: social, technological, political or economic. Time was then taken for everyone to read and clarify all the hot issues listed on the wall. A voting process followed in which each person marked the issues he or she felt were the hottest of the hot.

Through large group facilitation, the 15 hottest trends, forces, and changes were identified. Each person selected the trend that he or she most wanted to analyze and signed up with others to form small groups for this purpose. Seven groups worked for some time analyzing their selected trend by answering the following questions:

1. What are the implications of this trend for human resources?
2. What happens if we fail to address this?
3. What is HR's current response?
4. How well does current response meet StorageTek's needs?
5. What is HR's desired response?

STORAGETEK HUMAN RESOURCES FUTURES
CONFERENCE: APRIL 19-20, 1989
AGENDA

WEDNESDAY, A.M.

INTRODUCTION – HR STRATEGIC PLANNING
● Strategic planning process in HR
● Orientation to conference/ground rules
ACTIVITY ONE – IDENTIFY TRENDS/FORCES THAT
   IMPACT HR
● Identify social, technological, political, and economic
      trends/forces
● Develop environmental map of these trends/forces
ACTIVITY TWO – ANALYZE TRENDS/FORCES
● Analyze one trend/force in small group
● Present analysis to entire group

WEDNESDAY, P.M.

ACTIVITY TWO, CONTINUED
● Analyze another trend/force in small group
● Present analysis to entire group

THURSDAY, A.M.

ACTIVITY THREE – BELIEFS ABOUT PEOPLE AT
   STORAGETEK
● Generate lists of how we value people at StorkageTek
● Find common themes
ACTIVITY FOUR – THE HR FUTURE AT STORAGETEK
● Create scenarios of the ideal StorageTek HR
      organization five years out
● Find common themes

THURSDAY, P.M.

ACTIVITY FIVE - WHERE DO WE GO FROM HERE?
● Make recommendations to HR managers
● Conclude conference

The results of this analysis were reported and discussed. Then the process was repeated with the remaining hottest trends to finish day one.

The first exercise on the second day of the conference was designed to explore "our beliefs about people" at StorageTek. This began with a brief statement of the theory that successful organizations need to move from a paradigm of "volume" to a paradigm of "value." In other words, quality needs to overtake quantity as a valuable way of doing business and people make the difference in that change.

A large group brainstorm activity identified "what we believe about people" from both the volume and value perspectives. The exercise provided some useful comparisons and resulted in common beliefs about the value of people in the StorageTek workplace. This was also a helpful preparation for the next session on visioning.

After considering the impact of environmental trends, forces, and changes on Human Resources at StorageTek and creating common ground about "our beliefs about people," the group was ready to look into the future. The participants were asked to relax, close their eyes and engage in a guided group fantasy trip to HR in 1994. Once in the future, people were asked what they could see, hear, and feel at the workplace.

Then each person wrote a detailed story, article, or letter to a friend describing Human Resources in 1994 at StorageTek. People spent up to thirty minutes writing down their experience and then gathered in natural work groups to share their stories. Once the stories were shared, each group was asked to develop a creative display capturing the essence of their group's common vision. Groups used everything from flip-chart paper drawings to cardboard cut-outs.

When the displays were finished they were brought into the main conference room for a "Futures Fair" in which each participant wandered from display to display asking questions and writing down recurring themes of the future. All the recurring themes were summarized through a facilitated process and became a strong statement of the conference's view of the ideal future of human resources at StorageTek.

The last activity was a fishbowl exercise in which the conference participants answered the question, "What advice do you have for the Human Resources as it takes the ideas from the conference and develops the HR strategic plan?" The conference ended with participants reflecting on the Futures Conference experience.

EPILOGUE (November 17, 1989)

The HR management team spent three months drafting the strategic plan from the results of the conference. The trends exercise became the situation analysis that provided the foundation for the plan. The "volume to value" exercise and the visioning session provided useful frameworks for the HR mission statement and strategic goals.

Individual HR managers, who were involved in creating the final plan, continued to gather employee and stakeholder feedback as the planning progressed. By the time the plan was finished, HR staff and many clients had made their personal mark on the plan. The final feedback meeting in which the plan was reported to all employees seem almost anti-climatic. There were no surprises.

The human resources strategic plan was the first one presented to the StorageTek management committee and it was the only one accepted without revisions. Two other corporate departments used variations of the Futures Conference to complete their own strategic plans, and this approach to planning is gaining wider acceptance in the corporation.

THE AUTHORS

Gary Frank, now an independent consultant, is the former manager of Organization Development at StorageTek. While at StorageTek he and his colleague Bob Rehm focused on work system design, but were often called upon for other services, including strategic planning. He also worked on the search conference that created a new mission statement for two AMI hospitals. (See Chapter 15.)

Bob Rehm, has facilitated search conferences in both the private and public sectors. His experiences with Colorado water quality issues are recorded in Chapter 19, at the end of which you will find his biography.

CHAPTER 15

Presbyterian/St. Luke's
MEDICAL CENTER
DEVELOPS A NEW VISION

David W. Angus

THE FOLLOWING NEWS STORY, provided by David Angus, is reprinted by permission from the Presbyterian/St. Luke's Medical Center publication, Scanner II, Volume 1, No. 1, June, 1989. This gives a good overview of the conference. Angus then follows up with his notes on the methods and design.

MEDICAL CENTER VISION STATEMENT DEVELOPED
By Bert Newman

At a two-day conference in late April, members of the P/SL board of directors, nurses, administrators, medical staff members, and employees from every area of the downtown hospitals developed a vision statement, an explanation of purpose for our institutions and a map for us to use in planning our future.

Vision Statement
"We are dedicated to blending and continuing traditions of excellence in the practice and delivery of health care. We are enriched by pride of purpose, sense of community, personal loyalty and medical leadership.

"With a spirit of cooperation, compassion and commitment to all we serve, we assume the absolute success of Presbyterian Saint Luke's Regional Medical Center." (*April 28, 1989*)

The process was led by David Angus, Gary Frank and Chris Trani-Shirley, who took participants on a journey of clarification and discovery from decade to decade within and without the hospitals, finally focusing on the elements of the new medical center which everyone felt were absolutely crucial to its success. This process was "not a problem-solving conference, but rather an exercise in learning, awareness, understanding and mutual support."

To clarify who we are personally and as an institution, program participants examined events and issues which affected society, themselves and Presbyterian/Saint Luke's Medical Center during the last three decades—the 60's, 70's and 80's. Results of this time traveling were mixed, and brought up everything from the assassinations of the 60's, the Peace Corps and Vietnam, to loss of innocence and the emergence of television and media as prominent features in our society.

For P/SL, the 60's were felt to represent a period of stability, with good patient censuses, abundant staffing resources and financial strength. By the 70's, participants felt, things began to change, bringing heavy regulation, the hi-tech revolution, and centers of medical excellence. Then the 80's brought a period of medical revolution—shortages of personnel, increased age and acuity of patients, the decline of reimbursement, medical competition and resulting need for marketing and, of course, the sale of Presbyterian Denver and Saint Luke's hospitals to American Medical International (AMI).

What will the 1990s bring? For P/SL the group guessed that a return to the stability of the 1960s was a distinct possibility, for something must change in healthcare in the very near future. Also, technology will increasingly affect healthcare and an aging population will have an impact as well.

From this reminiscing, participants divided into subgroups to report on major events, trends and developments that are now affecting our medical center. The object of this exercise was to illustrate how all these events are interconnected, for as John Kennedy reminded us, "Those who forget the past are condemned to relive it."

What are some of these forces which are currently shaping the healthcare world that we work in?

Participants developed the following short list, in this order of importance, from among approximately 60 concerns and challenges facing Presbyterian St. Lukes Medical Center.

CONCERNS AND CHALLENGES

Restrictive healthcare financing
Consolidation
Shortage of skilled personnel
High-tech/increased specialization
Competition
Increased violence and drug use
Payer mix
AIDS
Aging population

After these nine issues were isolated as the most important, participants chose which challenge to address according to two criteria: What we are doing now; What we should do in the future. The group considering the present shortage of skilled personnel (number three above), for example, suggested that as a medical center we could increase our contacts with high school students, increase tuition reimbursement, lobby to offer the state board nursing exam more than once, enhance positive images of healthcare workers, establish an on-site RN–BSN program and develop an increased sensitivity to staff needs.

On the second day of the conference, participants began by developing two lists—one of things which we would like to carry into the future, the other of things which we would like to leave behind.

To be left behind were, in order to importance: Lack of public image, resistance to change, negative attitudes, a sense of division, physician attrition, crisis management, and worry about safety in the hospital. Other issues/conditions not to be carried into the future, included nostalgia-depression, lack of dollars and being understaffed and overworked.

On the brighter side, there were a great many things which people wanted to incorporate into the future and make part of Presbyterian Saint Luke's Medical Center. Among them, again in order of importance, were: Participative problem solving, a tradition of excellence, our high-quality medical staff, the Gold Star Program, the traditional theme parties, laughter, and a strong marketing effort. Other things to be brought into the future included ease of access to the top, employees who care, good ethics and a caring spirit for patients and families.

By clarifying these values—both those that they respected and those that they wished to leave behind—the group was moving closer to a vision of what they wanted our medical center to be.

The next step was to envision what they would see during a visit to

Presbyterian Saint Luke's Medical Center in 1993. The fictional visit began with a helicopter flight to the new medical center, and concluded with a look inside at the new facility as it will be operating in four years.

These descriptions of 1993 visits to P/SL Regional Medical center were remarkably similar. They portrayed a regional center for new technologies with warm, human values and ambiance. It will be the newest and best planned facility in the region with strong, well-defined public image and will display compassion, caring and concern. There will be a sense of pride in both the facility and what it has done for the neighborhood surrounding it. Some quotes from descriptions of this future visit include: "A mecca of healthcare and education," "An aura of dedication," "A 'will do it today' attitude," "The hospital is the employer and provider of choice."

Following this exercise, all the pieces were in place. The group knew what it did not want to include in the new medical center, it knew what it did want to include, and it had a vision of how that center will operate. It was time to construct the Vision Statement—an expression of aspirations, commitment and requirements for our medical center.

A shared sentiment of the group was that the Vision Statement was important, but that the process used to develop the statement was equally important. This Vision Statement takes into account both the past and the future, and should provide a focus of inspiration for all of us at Presbytarian/St. Lukes.

This is our opportunity to define our future, determine for ourselves, for our community and for our patients the success of the great venture we are undertaking.

SPONSOR: PRESBYTERIAN/ST.LUKE'S MEDICAL CENTER

Conference Task: Merged Vision and Action Plans for Future

Stakeholders: Board of Directors (6), Senior Management (2), Vice Presidents (3), Physicians (2), Middle Managers (6), Hospital Staff (8),

Length: Two Days

Place: Englewood, Colorado, Conference

Managers: David Angus, Gary Frank and Chris Trani-Shirley

NOTES ON THE METHOD & DESIGN By David W. Angus

Our conference grew from a plan to consolidate our two 400-bed hospitals on to a single campus. It was one of several organizational development activities in support of the merger. As construction began for the new buildings, we thought it was important to create a "vision of our future" to serve as an anchor point through this major change and transition.

Actually, we explored several methods for doing this. Initially, our CEO wanted a low-key process, in which he and a few board members would develop the vision. He was urged to consider a process that would engage and excite participants, produce new awareness of our organization, and build a common framework of purpose and values.

Reading Weisbord's (1987) account of "future search," I was taken by the statement that this method was "especially attractive to organizations faced with significant change: markets, mergers, reorganizations, new technologies, new leadership, the wish for a coherent culture and corporate philosophy." That described our needs exactly.

After considerable discussion we decided we liked the idea of involving key stakeholders from all levels. It was a concrete way to reinforced our stated philosophy of participation at all levels. However, applying the search method for the first time caused us some concern and anxiety. None of us had attended or participated in a search conference. We weren't sure exactly how to go about preparing for such an event. Our only exposure was Chapter 14 of Weisbord's book. However, we did speak with Weisbord and one of his associates, who were helpful in answering our questions, providing reading, ideas, and materials from their own conferences. We pretty much followed Weisbord's procedure in the first stages, starting by presenting the following guidelines.

GROUND RULES

1. No problem-solving. Learning, awareness, understanding, and mutual support will be the focus.
2. Every idea and comment is valid. People need not agree.
3. All items written on flip-charts as community record.
4. Task-oriented activity. We will stick to time frames.
5. No lectures.
6. No pleading self-interests or personal agendas.
7. Facilitators structure tasks and manage time.
8. Participants generate and analyze information, derive meanings, propose action, and take responsibility for output.

We had participants reflect on their collective history from three perspectives: self, organization, and society. We then took up present trends significantly shaping the future of our medical center. At the start we worried that participants might not engage themselves. What would we do then? Our concerns proved unfounded. As participants completed and reported on these opening tasks, not only did their understanding grow, the focus of the group came together as well. They identified and discussed major themes with enthusiasm. This task led nicely into exploring trends and developments currently shaping the hospital/medical care industry.

To transition to the future focus, we use a video clip of President John F. Kennedy's inaugural as an example of visionary leadership. We did this out of concern that the futures task might otherwise seem too "airy-fairy" for our participants.

We also presented to the group an architect's model of the new center and invited people to look it over. Then we took them on a guided journey into the future, asking them to imagine they had left the center for some years and were returning for the first time. We had people imagine a visit to the medical center, observing how people were interacting with each other, engaging all the senses—how it felt, looked, sounded, smelled, etc.

LETTERS FROM THE FUTURE

Drawing on our "experiential learning" repertoire, we asked each person to write a letter to a close friend or relative describing their return visit. This turned out to be a powerful exercise. People were asked to share their letters in small groups and to identify common themes and values. This proved to be an extremely engaging experience. It made no differences what a person's role was, whether executive, medical, or staff support. All showed a genuine interest and sincere commitment to the whole future organization they had envisioned. Each small group was asked to select a letter that best represented their collective future vision, and those letters were presented in the large group. Participants were amazed and extremely enthused.

It was as if none had really thought it possible that so many people across the organization share the same goals and values. The six authors of the letters actually chosen by the small groups were then charged as a task group to develop a vision statement reflecting the feelings and visions of the whole. This was not an easy process but it did generate tremendous pride and energy. The task group presented their proposed vision statement to the rest of the participants and welcomed their thoughts, feelings and criticisms. Several questions were asked, and alternative syntax and semantic changes considered. The group then overwhelmingly agreed to support and embrace the vision statement as it had been presented to the total group (see page 149). This process proved extremely powerful and inspiring.

Action plans

We asked each stakeholder group to prepare action plans based on their joint work. Members of the Board of Directors, for examples, developed plans and strategies for taking the newly-created vision to their fellow board members and associates. Top management, physicians, middle managers and line staff did likewise.

To conclude the conference people presented their action plans and discussed what kind of commitment was needed to carry out our vision. As a closing touch, we showed a video of Martin Luther King's "I Have a Dream" speech at the Lincoln Memorial as an example of commitment and devotion to a vision.

At the end our CEO described this two-day conference as one of the most important meetings he had been a part of in his ten years with the organization. He declared his commitment to the vision and invited others to do the same. One group member joined him; then she asked that the entire group read the vision aloud and sign the newsprint on which it was written as a symbol of their mutual commitment. This suggestion was embraced unanimously.

Epilogue

As the action plans from the conference were implemented, the underlying vision also was made public. It has been very favorably received and embraced in our medical center. This vision also has served as a stabilizing factor during our major consolidation process. At one point, our parent organization stopped construction of the new center due to cost miscalculations. This situation (not well-founded) nonetheless caused great turmoil and doubt. When the hospitals were then put up for sale, our local Board moved to purchase them. With the consummation of the sale, the medical center was once again on track to pursue its vision.

In my opinion, our Search Conference, vision statement, and action plans strengthened the resolve of our local leadership to change a negative situation into a new opportunity. As I write this, we still are very much creating our future!

THE AUTHOR

David Angus is Vice President of Organization and Management Development for P/SL Healthcare System in Denver, Colorado. He has worked in health care organizations since 1985.

ISSUE-FOCUSED CASES

Introduction

"The idea that if you just get people together they'll start liking each other is naive. But if they are working together for shared goals, it breaks down the negative stereotypes they had of each other."
— Dr. Charles Green, psychologist (Goleman, 1991)

Part 4 takes on a journey of discovery into "domains." A "domain" in search conference language is an amorphous region inhabited by people united by common interest in an issue without boundaries. The issues are often sticky, complicated, tangled, and conflicted affairs. They reflect the coalescing of many ongoing social, technical, and political dilemmas that cut across organizations, nations and communities.

The five chapters here constitute an advanced course in domain formation and management. They cover the globe—from Colorado to Pakistan, from Ontario to the Windward Islands, from Saskatchewan to Columbia. The pieces center on strategy development in many sectors—conservation and electric power, local water quality, community day care, tourism strategies, waste management, developmentally handicapped people. In each case we learn the political context, detailed conference designs, and the authors' reflections on their experience. Search conferences constitute one proven method for helping people overcome negative stereotypes and shape new domains.

There are further conceptual benefits here. William Smith, in Chapter 16, and Beth Franklin and David Morley in Chapter 19, provide us with additional theoretical links to their search models, deepening our understanding of how experienced practitioners use theory to practice in highly-charged situations. – MRW

CHAPTER 16

A CONSERVATION STRATEGY FOR PAKISTAN

Rodger Schwass

NEARLY 30 COUNTRIES in the world, notes Rodger Schwass, have comprehensive conservation strategies. Pakistan's is one of the more successful. In this chapter Schwass documents the use of search processes in what many would consider a superhuman task. His case represents the most far-reaching strategic futures conference application I have discovered in the three years of developing this book.

"Pakistan provides a good example of the way the search process enables groups of people to design, plan and implement their national conservation and sustainable development strategies," writes Schwass. His report strongly supports the case for search processes as among the very few innovations that "work" in highly complex, conflicted situations that cut across communities, government agencies, business and other boundaries.

Schwass does more than describe a single conference. The conference is just one step in a multi-phase, long-term strategy that has had significant impact on national policy in Pakistan. He shows the detailed preparation, including 80+ interviews and 30 expert position papers. While many search managers discourage "keynotes" and expert speeches, here

Schwass brings experts into intensive dialogue with other stakeholders, including senior politicians, in a one-day workshop preceding the actual search. I see this as a practical way to use technical expertise and factual analyses to scope out a very complex issue, achieve breakthrough understandings in a large group, and set the stage for far-reaching decisions in a democratic spirit.

Schwass illustrates the interplay between content and process in the search conference itself. After the initial search Pakistani action teams skillfully thread content and process into a rich, ongoing tapestry—five years in the weaving—of national awareness and action by hundreds of concerned people in conferences and workshops all over Pakistan. As this book goes to press, the efforts initiated in 1984 continue, with major positive impact on the nation's environment.

This case suggests that the only limits on using these methods are to be found in our own imaginations. – MRW

Pakistan is a country which has grown from 34 millions to 110 millions since independence in 1947. It is one of about 30 countries in the world today that have national conservation strategies. Here I want to describe how search processes helped to bring this about.

The World Bank forecasts a population of 280 millions for Pakistan by the year 2025. Economic growth has been fairly rapid, due to strong financial support from the US government, large annual remittances from expatriate Pakistanis working in the Middle East, and government borrowing from international lending agencies such as the World Bank. Yet the environment has been devastated by increasing numbers of people, the long-term impact of over-irrigation with inadequate drainage, deforestation and overgrazing. The ingestion of resources by the Pakistan economy, together with the excretion of large volumes of waste that have not been properly treated or disposed of, are causing a visible decline in the state of the environment, even while economic indicators remain temporarily favorable. The present development process in Pakistan is clearly unsustainable.

Against this backdrop, the International Union for the Conservation of Nature and Natural Resources (IUCN) decided in 1984 to assist the World Wildlife Fund and other organizations in Pakistan to undertake the development of a National Conservation Strategy. The Strategy would attempt to bring together all the stakeholders in the Pakistan economy (leaders in government-both State and Federal), business, media and non-governmental organizations to try to formulate a design for the future which would be sustainable in both environmental and economic terms (Schwass, 1984).

Mrs. Aban Kabraji, Karachi Director of the World Wildlife Fund (Pakistan) and Manager of the IUCN office in Pakistan, and the author organized the process. The Urban Affairs Division, which had a small environmental division located within it, was designated as the lead agency. The Urban Affairs Division had been largely dormant on environmental matters, but for this purpose, it seemed to be the most appropriate location for the development of the Strategy.

I was asked to help facilitate the first stage of the process. The first step was to interview some 80 key people in the various stakeholder organizations, but with special focus on the public service where much of the research and implementation capacity are located. The interviews, up to two hours each, helped identify the key issues to be addressed.

Most individuals felt they had little influence and lacked a mechanism to relate their concerns to one another. Boundaries between Ministries were perceived to be a major blockage to communication. An economic and financial mindset that focused on economic growth indicators but ignored resource depletion and environmental degradation was also a problem. A further complication was that military control of the government inhibited open discussion of performance or allocation of resources.

UTILIZING EXPERTISE

After the interviews, I prepared a report entitled "A Conservation Strategy for Pakistan: Basic Issues." A Technical Steering Committee of the most senior government and private sector activists was created to press forward with the Strategy development. They identified 30 issues requiring detailed attention and commissioned papers by 30 experts who had the specialized background to address them.

The papers followed a consistent format. The first section set out the present situation in detail and indicated where it would lead if action was not taken. The second section identified desirable goals attainable in the future if proper action was taken. The third section identified the principal constraints and obstacles and possible means of dealing with them, and the final section indicated what the writer believed would be the most desirable lines of action.

Thirty papers were eventually produced, ranging from population to resource depletion to waste management. These embraced all the key issues of sustainable development. The papers were completed in about three months, with the assistance of Mrs. Kabraji and her staff, and a workshop was scheduled for September, 1986, in Islamabad. Senior ministers in all key areas were briefed on the purpose and approach. They were asked to attend the opening session to indicate their strong support for the Conservation Strategy and their intention to use the output. They also were invited to the closing session to hear and to respond to the Action Plan recommended by the Workshop participants.

All background papers were to be mailed to workshop participants three weeks in advance, to provide time for reading and reflection. This was not accomplished, unfortunately, so the bulky kits of background material were handed out at the conference registration desk. This proved to be a serious limitation on the depth of workshop discussions.

On the first day, the 30 papers were summarized in short presentations by their authors. Key issues were identified and possible courses of action were recommended. Five minutes was allowed after each paper for clarifying questions and responses but no detailed discussion of the issues was permitted at this stage. It was possible to get through the 30 papers in ten hours of presentations. Over 100 people, including a number of senior ministers, remained to the end of the sessions.

The result of these presentations was a powerful sense of a truly stupendous set of problems that interlocked in hundreds of ways. Courses of action that might solve one set of problems would exacerbate others. Most participants were familiar with a small part of the total situation revealed in the papers, but quite unfamiliar with the rest of it. The environmental plight of the country came into focus for perhaps the first time.

SPONSOR: WORLD WILDLIFE FUND (KARACHI) AND MINISTRY OF URBAN AFFAIRS

Conference Task: A National Conservation Strategy

Stakeholders: Representatives from Agriculture, Forestry, Range Management, Fisheries, Water Resources, Energy, Industry, Governments

Length of Conference: Three Days, preceded by one day of expert position papers

Place and Time: Islamabad, Pakistan, September 1986

Conference Managers: Rodger Schwass and Mary Schwass

STRATEGY/CONFERENCE DESIGN

1. **1985** – 80 interviews of key people.
2. **1986** – Government/private sector committee selects 30 themes
3. **SEPTEMBER 1986** – 3-Day Search Conference convened
   Pre-conference briefing: 30 position papers summarized for 100 people.
   Search conference begins – 85 people
   DAY 1: The Present & Where We Are Headed
   DAY 2: Desirable Futures
   Constraints and Obstacles
   DAY 3: Opportunities
   Action Plans Presentations/Reporting to Government Ministers
4. **1987** – Team edits papers, starts media campaign, fund raising
5. **1987-88** – Teams work with planners and economists on national five-year plan
6. **1988-91** – Modified Searches in Peshawar, Karachi, Lahore; Quetta propose more than 100 demonstration projects for sustainable development
7. **1991-92** – Implementation

STARTING THE SEARCH

On the second day of the workshop, about 85 remaining participants came together and began a Search Conference of three days duration. In the first day, five groups, each a microcosm of the larger conference and the country, examined the present situation and where it would lead. These groups reinforced the dramatic evidence presented on the first day and showed how optimistic economic statistics had hidden the true decline in living conditions, including health, literacy, education and social participation. Even though statistics indicated improved survival rates for mothers and infants in the 1960's and 1970's, most of these trends now had reversed. Birthrates remained high and literacy levels for women were about four percent compared to 50 percent for men. However, the term "literacy" had ceased to have much meaning. In many cases, it merely meant that people could write their name and a few simple facts about themselves.

The extreme pressure on the natural environment was revealed by all of the speakers from agriculture, forestry, wildlife, range management, fisheries and the like. Those from water resources, energy, and other industrial fields related the imminence of economic as well as environmental decline.

On the second day, an effort was made to create scenarios for a more desirable future. Some aspects of a desirable future—the re-emergence of democracy, for example—were beyond the powers of those attending. But other goals could be achieved by people operating in collaboration with a clearer sense of their mutual objectives.

Thus, the Workshop concluded that a dramatically improved environment could be combined with rapid economic growth under certain conditions. Late on the second day, the groups listed the constraints to achieving the desirable future and identified some of the more formidable obstacles that had to be overcome. By the third morning, the groups were ready to examine these constraints and obstacles and to find means of circumventing or overcoming them and identifying opportunities that could be pursued immediately. This led in turn, to a session on building an action plan in preparation for the return of the Ministers. The Conference worked in plenary session for several hours to refine the action plan to make it suitable for ministerial presentation. In the final session, they presented their Action Plan to the Ministers with a strong recommendation for a new senior steering group at the political level, chaired by the Prime Minister and dedicated to carrying forward the work plan.

FORMING A HIGH LEVEL ACTION GROUP

The ministers responded warmly. They assured the group that action would be taken as soon as possible. Indeed, a high level committee was struck and the Chief of the Central Planning Unit responsible for five-year planning in Pakistan became a leading figure for follow-up. The Prime Minister at that time, Muhammed Khan Junejo, while not at the Workshop, agreed to be chairman of the Political Steering Committee. At a lower level, the Technical Committee described earlier would continue to pursue the day-to-day work involved in creating a new National Conservation Strategy for Pakistan.

The next stage was to carry the recommendations from the Conference forward in written form. Accordingly, I submitted a report to the Technical Committee, and a team was assigned to edit and publish the 30 key papers in a book, *Toward a National Conservation Strategy For Pakistan* (Schwass, 1986). While this work went forward, efforts were made to raise funds for Phase II of the Project (the Action Plan). It would take many new activities to embed the Conference suggestions in new legislation, research and to undertake a very large media campaign to raise the consciousness of Pakistanis to the threats they faced and opportunities inherent in sustainable development.

FUNDING THE SECOND STAGE

About a year later, CIDA (Canadian International Development Agency), agreed to support the second stage with more than a million dollars. IUCN recruited a team consisting of Mr. Alistair Crerar, former Director of the Alberta Conservation Society in Edmonton, Alberta, and Dr. Ayub Qutub, a senior public servant with an outstanding research record in Islamabad. A Secretariat was created and a Director of Communications and Public Relations hired to work with the media. In Karachi, IUCN expanded significantly and developed a Resource Centre for environmental journalists.

The National Conservation Strategy team established a close working relationship with economists and planners responsible for the next Five-Year Plan, to ensure that the concept of sustainable development would be incorporated into the plan at all levels. Wasim Jafarey, head of the Central Planning Unit, who had taken part in the interviews and followed the Workshop and Search Process with great interest, became the pivotal figure in this work. On his retirement, his successor, A.G.N. Kazi, assumed the chair.

The team also sought to generate widespread public understanding of the environmental situation facing Pakistan. Aban Kabraji and a new staff member, Saneeya Hussain, began to publish a quarterly newsletter to acquaint the media and the public with the situation facing the country and the objectives of the National Conservation Strategy. A Journalists' Resource Centre was set up to work with journalists and broadcasters in both Urdu and English.

FOLLOW-UP SEARCH CONFERENCES

Another effort centered on decentralizing the activity, first to the state level and then to assist leaders at the community level to generate activity leading to sustainable development. Workshops were held in December 1988 and January 1989 in Peshawar, Karachi, Lahore and Quetta, and organized as modified Search Conferences. They were attended by about 300 state and local representatives, businessmen, media representatives and leading public figures. Over 100 demonstration projects were proposed, ranging from new approaches to rangeland management to urban gardens on rooftops in Karachi, to sewing and food processing classes for girls and women. About 40 pilot projects were funded. Financing came from aid agencies in a number of countries.

Although it is too early to assess the final outcome, it appears that the Search Conference process used in Pakistan has worked well in developing an understanding of the environmental issues facing the country and in breaking down institutional barriers to dealing with the issues. The process allowed people who normally were not expected to work together, to develop common objectives and to collaborate as a team to achieve them. Because high-level support was provided, both within Pakistan and by aid agencies outside (the Benazir Bhutto government, which took power in mid-project, has continued and increased support), there is a good prospect that the decisions made at the Search Conferences will be carried to fruition.

> "The search process itself is not sufficient to ensure action
> . . . There must be common ground on which various groups
> can stand together and there must be some common elements in their visions of the future." — *Rodger Schwass*

A SEARCH CONFERENCE IS JUST THE BEGINNING

The search process itself is not sufficient to ensure action. It must be embedded in a setting that permits an action team to form. There must be common ground on which various groups can stand together and there must be some common elements in their visions of the future. Committed people, with enough resources at their disposal, are the essential factor, if the plans that are made are to be translated into action.

Ideally, all relevant stakeholders should be present and capable of taking action, the environment should be open, and senior authorities should be receptive. At least some resources need to be available if there is to be hope of reform and new investment.

SEQUEL: JUNE, 1992

Since this document was written, the Pakistan National Conservation Strategy (NCS) has proceeded rapidly to completion and implementation. The Final Report was approved by the Steering Committee in July of 1991. A Committee of Donors was formed, including aid agencies ranging from the World Bank and Asian Development Bank to national aid agencies in the US, Canada, the UK, Holland, Norway, Denmark and Germany. They are working on "projectizing" the NCS, to make it compatible with their funding procedures.

The Canadian International Development Agency has provided the International Union for the Conservation of Nature (World Conservation Union) and the relevant units of the Government of Pakistan with funds to proceed with implementation.

At the same time, a detailed Implementation Process has been developed to ensure that the 68 programs in the NCS are implemented. The Pakistan Cabinet approved the NCS in March 1991. A Media Launch was held in May, 1992. In October, 1992, an Implementation Conference will bring together the major donors and senior government officials to finance the next five years of implementation.

Pakistan is currently developing the Eighth Five-Year Plan, to guide development to the end of the century. A special section is being developed in the Division of Planning and Development in the Government of Pakistan, to ensure that the NCS recommendations are incorporated in the Plan.

The Ministry of Environment and Urban Affairs is being expanded to implement the NCS. An NCS Division is being established to implement the NCS and to develop national awareness of the problems the country faces. Population and environmental issues are to be linked with education and programs to enhance the status of women.

The President has recently announced the formation of the Pakistan Environmental Protection Council, which will bring into force the Pakistan Environmental Protection Ordinance. The Ordinance provides the basis for environmental protection and control legislation and will bring into force a wide range of new environmental regulations.

At the same time, a Business-Industry Round Table has been set up to discuss the implementation of the new regulations. To accomplish this, the Pakistan Environmental Protection Agency has been developed, within the Division of Environment and Urban Affairs. A consultant has been assigned to this group by the Asian Development Bank. Provincial Environmental Protection Agencies have been established in all provinces, to enforce the new laws and regulations.

Senior officials in the North West Frontier Province have requested that a process for implementing the NCS in the province be undertaken immediately. The challenge is to develop effective local governments and non-governmental organizations to assume environmental management at the community level. Design work is going on now and a major workshop (search conference) was held in early January (1992) involving Ministers and Secretaries in the Government of NWFP. NWFP has launched a crash program to achieve sustainable development through local government and selp-help organizations, based on the recommendations of this workshop. International donors have pledged their support.

OTHER APPLICATIONS TO THE ENVIRONMENT

The Pakistan process was earlier used in Tanzania. Despite excellent support at the top and at the technical level, and an excellent Search Conference, the Action Plan was never completed. It was turned over to a technical agency that did not follow up. Nevertheless, some 80 senior administrators and politicians emerged from the workshop with a clearer perception of the environmental decline in Tanzania. This knowledge has apparently been of importance in the recent liberalization and privatization of the Tanzanian economy.

The Search Conference process was also used in Canada for a wide variety of environmental/economic planning activities from 1977 to the present. Examples include Search Conferences which led to the formation of the Task Force on Northern Conservation (1984), the forerunner of extensive land claim negotiation and social mediation in the Yukon and Northwest Territories, and the Search Conference on a Circumpolar Conservation Strategy, held in Vancouver in February 1988 (Schwass, 1988). The latter led to a major international conference held the summer of 1989 in Greenland.

Other searches were used by Environment Canada to examine prospects for Canada's parks and protected areas and to draw together business, government, non-governmental organizations, labor unions and the media to discuss the modernization of Canadian industry and the cleanup of toxic wastes. These search conferences have led to concerted action by many diverse agencies, a very effective and productive means of launching multi-organization action.

The focus on "sustainable development" in the past two years has created a world-wide demand for a simple, reliable process wherein individuals and organizations with disparate goals can develop shared goals and plans to achieve them. The search process is a valuable tool for this purpose.

ABOUT THE AUTHOR

Rodger Schwass is Professor, Faculty of Environmental Studies at York University, Toronto. Since 1976 he has worked with Eric Trist and others to to adapt search conferences to environmental planning. He has facilitated more than 50 strategic planning/search conferences in Canada, Jamaica, Barbadoes, Kenya, Tanzania, Pakistan, and Indonesia. Most have led to long-term, sustainable development programs. At York University Dr. Schwass has served as Dean of Faculty (1976-82), and Director of the Office of International Services (1982-85). From 1968-76 he was a Vice President of Acres, a major Canadian consulting firm specializing in resources management and developmental studies.

CHAPTER 17

PLANNING FOR THE ELECTRICITY SECTOR IN COLOMBIA

William E. Smith Ph.D.

W ILLIAM SMITH has worked in many countries on economic, technical, and social development. In this chapter he puts search conference processes into a broad framework, based on his theory about how to increase everybody's power in relation to a given issue. His conceptual base was developed in collaboration with Eric Trist and Russell Ackoff in the Doctoral program in Social Systems Sciences at the Wharton Graduate School of Business. It combines search processes with a cognitive framework based on what we can and cannot control in making future plans.

Not only does Smith address issues of domain formation (what he calls a "sector"). He also shows how different levels of hierarchy deal with different issues, and why increasing power at all levels means sharing information and increasing learning processes between them. This requires getting all the parties into the same room.

Smith uses his theory in improving Colombia's management of energy resources. He also gives a brief description of the electricity sector's future search conference and its results. At the end he describes his views on the role of searching and includes a detailed conference design. Note the similarities between his creative feedback exercises (drawing on unconscious processes in each person), and Burgess' "creative search gathering" in Chapter 34. Parts of this chapter are adapted from a paper written for the World Bank. — MRW

A POWER FRAMEWORK FOR POLICY FORMULATION

Searching for a New Approach

During the early 1970's, the World Bank shifted its emphasis away from physical infrastructure towards agriculture and the social sectors. This required major changes in the Bank's organization and in its investment and technical assistance tools. It became difficult for its development clients to adapt to new policies, shift priorities, and organize projects under the new policies.

A study of agricultural and rural development projects (Smith, Lethem, Thoolen 1980) under the new policies revealed that borrowers lacked commitment to policy objectives, project designs left out environmental variables affecting implementation, and programs relied too much on earlier rational, technical approaches, paying too little attention to social and political realities.

The Bank also began to shift its loans from projects to whole economic sectors, such as agriculture, transportation, and trade. This changed relations between levels within the Bank and with its clients. Donors tried to redesign existing organizations for the program's enlarged scope, but found it difficult. The Bank and government agencies reached the limits, not only of their own organizing experience, but of what was known in the field.

Power and Policy

In the 1980's we began an Action Research Program to improve the Bank's development projects. Our model was based on a particular understanding of power. Chart 1 shows how potential power increases as our purposes expand from individual, short-term problem-solving to serve medium-term community values, and still more when we serve the long-term ideals of a whole system.

For example, while several hundred people might share the goal of increasing one private company's profits, the goal of eliminating hunger might be shared by a whole nation, creating much more potential power. A policy power field consists of all related actors, organizations, and events. The field extends horizontally to include all inputs to policy makers and to those affected.

It extends upward to include levels of regulation/supervision, such as planning, budgeting, evaluation and oversight committees. It extends downwards to units that formulate and implement strategy. Our research identified three distinct power relationships in each power field (Chart 2).

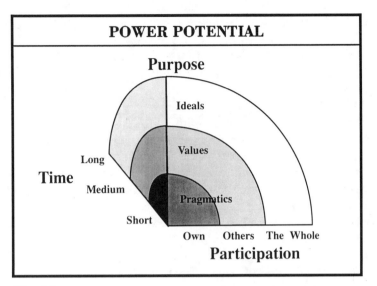

Chart 1

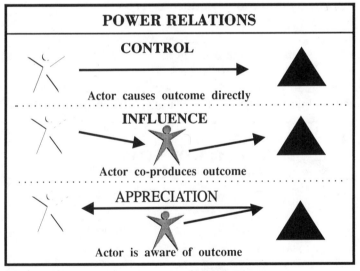

Chart 2

I) *CONTROL*, at the center, means causing something to happen directly without having to persuade others or to do something else first. For example, cabinet ministers can control their management priorities, time, and how much of their energies and emotions they invest in each priority.

II) INFLUENCE means indirect causation, a lesser degree of power. Influence means being from one to 99 percent sure of obtaining a desired outcome, but not 100%. A marketing board cannot control suppliers or customers. It can influence them through the terms negotiated for the delivery of goods or services.

III) APPRECIATION means understanding and valuing external events over which we have no control or influence. It's another way of saying "knowledge is power." For managers, appreciation consists of evaluating the impact of external factors they cannot control or influence. Such factors include the likely impact of regulatory agencies, research institutes, climatic conditions, and economic, social, and political events.

So, we increase the power potential of a policy initiative as we (1) serve higher purposes, (2) have it owned by larger numbers of people, and (3) keep it alive over time.

As Chart 3 shows, this developmental perspective is quite different from traditional views of power. The usual model puts us in the midst of a control-centered world battling an often hostile, uncontrolled environment hoping to tame it. The developmental model (Chart 4) has us living primarily in a world of influence, forever appreciating the larger world and bringing what is controllable under control. It gives us many more options, and ultimately, more power.

So an organization will become more successful as it increases its ability to manage power processes. That means creating a flow of appreciation, influence, and control across levels and reducing power differences between them. This is best done by raising the level of

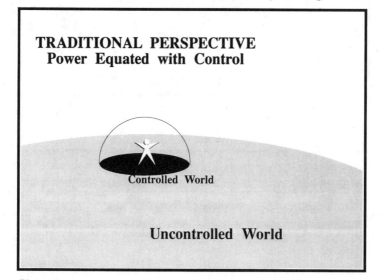

TRADITIONAL PERSPECTIVE
Power Equated with Control

Controlled World

Uncontrolled World

Chart 3a

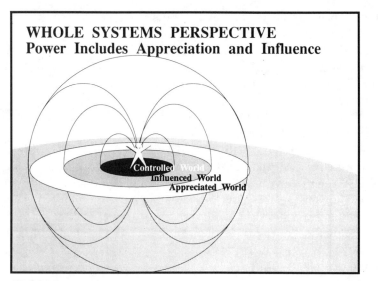

WHOLE SYSTEMS PERSPECTIVE
Power Includes Appreciation and Influence

Controlled World
Influenced World
Appreciated World

Chart 3b

purpose served, increasing the time horizon, and serving the needs of growing numbers of people.

Raising Level of Purpose

We can raise the level of purpose by working toward broad ideals and widely-shared needs over time. Working on mission statements or envisioning desirable futures are ways we do that. Ackoff (1981), for example, describes idealized planning and an interactive process linking an organization's objectives to broad needs and values. This brings separate divisions that might be in conflict closer together.

Development organizations have the opposite problem: they often have high-level, widely-supported purposes but they need organizational relationships and resources to carry them out.

Unfortunately, governments and organizations trying to operate at the development level often use criteria more suited to the technical or control level. They have no way of valuing appreciation, based on direction, survivability, and legitimacy of purpose.

Using All Levels of Power

Understanding an organization's power relative to its environment helps us understand its internal flow of power too.

a) An organization's boundaries define the limits of its control. It attempts to control all elements necessary to achieve its policy objectives.

b) What the organization cannot control, it tries to influence. Its area of influence extends to sources of inputs and outputs—suppliers, customers or clients.

c) What the organization cannot control or influence, it ought to understand. How does contextual environment affect us in the long term? Is our general direction sustainable?

Parsons (1960) noted three hierarchical levels within any large organization, shown on Chart 4. Each concentrates on only one environment, and thus deals with one type of power.

a) At the top, the "institutional" level deals with the appreciated environment, ensuring survivability by linking to needs valued by society. Their main output is policy.

b) The "managerial" level chooses the most influential means for implementing policy. Its output is strategy and structure.

c) Only the "technical" level ought be most concerned with control. The key issue is reducing uncertainty, through concrete planning, rules, and regulation.

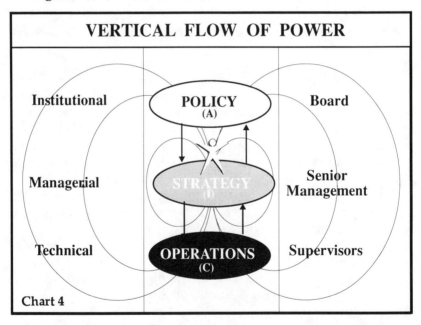

Chart 4

To apply this model, we need to overcome power differences, *and* provide each level a chance to influence decision-makers. We can best do this by introducing a power flow across the organization to counterbalance the vertical flow (see Chart 5). We ensure that each level carries out its own appreciative process and has an opportunity to influence decisions that affect it before being controlled by the results.

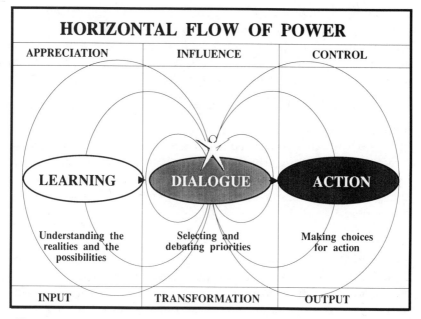

HORIZONTAL FLOW OF POWER

APPRECIATION · **INFLUENCE** · **CONTROL**

LEARNING ▶ **DIALOGUE** ▶ **ACTION**

Understanding the realities and the possibilities · Selecting and debating priorities · Making choices for action

INPUT · **TRANSFORMATION** · **OUTPUT**

Chart 5

Search conferences are particularly useful for this purpose. In the case that follows, I will use the example of the creation of energy policy in Colombia to show how a conference was used to balance power and improve policy making.

BALANCING POWER – THE COLOMBIA CASE

During the 1980's, the Colombian electricity sector was buffeted by adversity—world-wide recession, devaluation of the peso, and a lower rate of demand than forecast. The sector already had underway many capital-intensive hydro-projects not easily postponed. Its tariff policies generated too little cash to pay for the investments. Institutional jealousies within the sector made developing common strategies difficult, many government agencies did not pay their electric bills, and losses due to illegal tapping were estimated at 25 percent.

The sector faced an external debt of some $3 billion—about 40 percent of the country's foreign debt—and it had an over-capacity in generation of 45 percent. Until the early 1970's, each major city—Bogota, Medellin, and Cali—had its own self-contained utility and investment plan. Little environmental contact was involved. Then, the World Bank encouraged the utilities toward greater physical interconnection and coordination. They set up a new organization, ISA, to coordinate their activities of all the utilities in the country.

Discovering substantial over-capacity in the sector and devaluing the peso in 1984 (doubling the sector's external debt) sounded the death knell for the current policies. It dramatized the effect of the external environment on sector plans and revealed faulty assumptions about demand levels, opportunity costs of capital, and the inflexibility built into heavy dependence on large hydroelectric projects.

In January 1985, the Minister of Finance appealed to the World Bank for help in what he perceived to be a serious financial and institutional problem. The Bank responded with new concepts of shared power rather than the traditional hierarchical method of providing the electricity sector policy makers with expert solutions. Instead, it facilitated a conference in Santa Marta to develop an appreciation of the sector's total power field.

Raising the Level of Purpose

We deliberately elevated the level of purpose in the conference by visualizing the electricity sector's problems as those of the whole Colombian economy. In an idealization exercise participants were asked to play the role of concerned Colombian citizens rather than their normal sector roles. The electricity sector was figuratively destroyed and the participants were asked to produce the best design possible for the future of their country in the next 24 hours.

Using all Levels of Power

Some 60 participants attended the workshop, drawn from a bipartisan list to represent all three system levels (see Chart 6). From the national policy level came the sponsoring agencies—Mines & Energy, Planning, and Finance, and academics from local universities specializ-

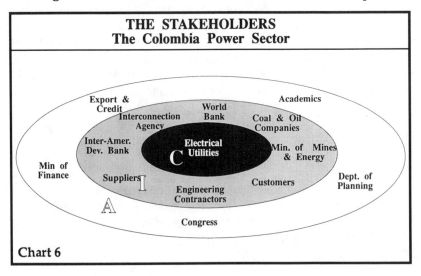

THE STAKEHOLDERS
The Colombia Power Sector

Export & Credit · Interconnection Agency · World Bank · Academics · Coal & Oil Companies · Inter-Amer. Dev. Bank · Electrical Utilities · Min. of Mines & Energy · Min of Finance · Suppliers · Engineering Contraactors · Customers · Dept. of Planning · Congress

Chart 6

ing in energy policy (appreciated environment). From the influence level we drew heads and key staff of energy sub-sectors like coal and oil (influenced environment).

The subordinate level was represented by key power sector institutions like major city and regional utilities (controlled environment). Several congressmen and senators represented consumers. In addition, academics and consultants with knowledge of the sector were invited. Three World Bank and Inter-American Development Bank staff attended as observers.

Creating a Horizontal Flow of Power

The workshop was designed as the first of the three horizontal power processes: learning, politics, and planning.

1) The workshop's *learning* function provided all three levels of the hierarchy with a common appreciation of the electricity sector's realities and possibilities. It was organized into three parts: creating an ideal future; examining the present realities and possibilities, and a search for options to move toward the ideal.

The broader environmental perspective adopted at the workshop revealed that most of the problems could not be *solved* by measures within the power sector's internal or controlled environment. These problems could only be *resolved* through participation with external stakeholders, broadening the horizontal dimension of the power field as far as possible. A new "sector" was required to mediate between the interests of energy sub-sectors like coal, electricity, and oil, and those of the nation. The workshop thus provided a common appreciation across three levels: the electricity sector; its superior, the national energy planning level; and its subordinate, productive enterprises.

2) The influence or *political* phase involved taking the workshop proposals, identifying the most influential stakeholders from each level, and forming a steering committee—the Technical Energy Board—to mediate major stakeholder interests. Its tasks were to:

- test the basic directions indicated by the Santa Marta workshop and to formalize the sector decisions that would be made by the national government;
- examine the sector's strategic alternatives in the national economy, and the roles of four subsectors;
- test the new organizing approach through a new working relationship.

The World Bank facilitated the process. The Colombians made their own diagnosis and recommendations. The Board influenced by appraising the recommendations, provided inputs to the government's political negotiation process at CONPES, the parliament.

3) In the "planning" phase the Technical Energy Board negotiated objectives with each energy enterprise, and provided political and strategic support necessary to achieve the objectives. The enterprise implemented the objectives. The Board thus became the enterprises' ally in managing their influenced and appreciated environments.

By sharing power, the parties moved from joint appreciation of the problem to joint influence and shared control. This horizontal flow overcame the shortcomings of the more traditional and limited vertical flow of power between government and the enterprises.

Outcomes

So successful was this approach that one Technical Board energy consultant, Guillermo Perry, became the next Minister of Mines. He was regarded as the only minister with a plan, and was able to introduce fairly unpopular and drastic changes such as cutting the size of the sector by 25 percent and raising rates. The extensive appreciative work gave the country an understanding of the realities of the current situation and hope that the new lines of action that had been developed would solve the basic problem. The influence work ensured that the right people were in the right place to influence movement in the policy directions.

Conference Design

The detailed conference plan follows. It includes six major tasks or exercises, to be self-managed by small groups using facilitators and reporters.

SEARCH CONFERENCE DESIGN

"The search conference provides a way to enable stake-holders (those involved in and affected by an organization's decisions) to develop a picture of the whole situation that affects their purposes. That means to see the social, political and cultural as well as the economic and technical factors that affect them, to see the past and the future influencing equally interaction in the present. I treat such conferences as part of a wider organizing process. So I'm particularly interested in the specific role such conferences play in that broader process.

"For example, my own idea goes something like this. Organizing requires managing three sets of relations—to

---

ourselves (control), to others (influence), and to the whole (appreciation). Search conferences are concerned with the third relationship. They help participants better understand the whole of which they are a part. To effectively focus on relationships to the whole, we have to limit peoples' concern with relationships to others or with the self. Search conferences may possibly be judged by how well they meet such simple criteria.

"From these simple criteria, we can identify relevant principles, for example, the needs to:

(a) eliminate power differences between the participants (that would divert energy to relationships to others),

(b) ensure that information flows with equal probability between any of the participants, thus ensuring equal access to all aspects of the whole that each appreciates,

(c) allow participants their own interpretation of results, accepting that the whole is too huge and complex to be analyzed, categorized, by any one person.

"Once such principles are identified, designers can find many ways to use the principles not only to plan conferences but to provide other means for meeting the same needs.

"My approach has basically evolved over time working with teams of managers. I discovered that most problems could not be addressed (i.e. controlled) from within the team and needed other people from the external environment. Getting managers to include outsiders was difficult because of their sense of lack of control.

"Eventually I began treating contracting as a 'framing' problem, and discussed with potential clients the balance necessary between the presenting issues and the 'power' to address them. We would then adjust either the size of the problem or the extent of participation to ensure that we had all three levels of power present in order to effectively address the issues in the center.

"If we are unable to obtain a match between the issue and the relevant 'power field,' we do not proceed. The appreciative part of the design owes much to the search conference and to Russell Ackoff's idealized planning. The influence part owes much to negotiating theory, and some technology from organization development, e.g. 'fish-bowls' for debate."

— William E. Smith

AN EXPLORATORY PLANNING WORKSHOP
The Electricity Sector, Colombia, Latin America

Objectives

1. Develop improved policies to overcome and prevent future financial and institutional crises in the sector.
2. Develop new linkages between groups, organizations and institutions affecting and affected by those policies.
3. Provide a support network to individuals as they implement the policies.
4. Prepare an action plan that includes all participants.

SPONSOR: WORLD BANK AND MINISTRIES OF FINANCE, PLANNING AND MINES AND ENERGY, COLOMBIA CONFERENCE

Task: Diagnose of financial collapse of the electricity sector and develop lines of action and policy recommendations to remedy the situation.

Stakeholders: 60 people—Mines & Energy, Planning, Budgeting Departments; coal and oil companies, senators, congressmen, academics, consultants, World Bank staff, IDB staff

Length: Three Days

Place: Santa Marta, Colombia

Conference Managers: William E. Smith, Turid Sato, Arnoldo Martinez

---

Role of Facilitators

Each small group will have a facilitator and elect a reporter. The facilitator will: read the instructions for each exercise and ensure that they are understood; inform the principal facilitator if more time is needed; ensure that each participant has equal opportunity to contribute; ensure that materials are available for the group (paper, pens, flipcharts, transparencies); organize papers from presentations.

Role of Reporters

Reporters will keep track of major points made; prepare a summary for presentation and ensure that it represents the team's views; present summary reports to plenary sessions.

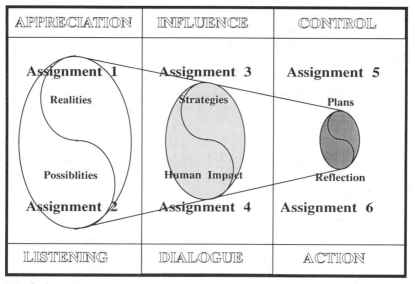

Workshop Process

Excercise 1: Image of Current Realities

PURPOSES: ● Create increased awareness of the current state of economic development and its effect on participants. ● Explore the realities facing any program of economic development. ● Bring out the richness of the experience represented by all participants.

INDIVIDUAL TASK: Think about the current state of the electricity sector. Imagine what would happen to Colombia in the next ten years if nobody took any new initiatives. To help communicate your insights in a meaningful way draw a picture that captures, as best you can, what you see and what you feel about that future. When you finish join your small group to share your picture, and the thoughts and feelings you had in creating it.

TEAM TASK: Each in turn share your image, thoughts and provide a brief explanation. Listen carefully. You may ask questions but this is not the time for critical questions or analysis. Your group then draws an image putting together as many of the group's ideas as possible. The reporter will: Make notes of key points and copy the image and a brief written explanation of the image onto a flip chart for presentation to the plenary; organize the group picture and the individual pictures into a group to place on the wall to form an "art gallery" of current realities.

PLENARY TASK: The reporter of each team presents the group image. Each individual adds comments about their picture and its relation to the group.

Excercise 2: The Ideal Design of the Electricity Sector

PURPOSES: ● Imagine the future of the electricity sector if you were able to implement any policies you wished. How would the area be different from now? Assume that you have all the power necessary to implement your proposals.

INDIVIDUAL TASK: You no longer have your current position. You are acting as a group of concerned Colombian citizens. What would the sector look like? Try to imagine it.

TEAM TASK: The facilitator reviews the instructions, timing and obtains a volunteer to act as reporter. Share, in turn, one of your major ideas. Continue the round until all major ideas have been shared. Discuss commonalties and differences. The reporter will record the major ideas on flip-chart. Together with the group select the most creative way possible to present a synthesis of the ideas—image, metaphor, story, proverb, dance, theater, etc. Put visuals on a flip chart e.g. images, brief explanation of any dance or theater, for inclusion in the final report.

PLENARY TASK: The reporter organizes the group to make a presentation.

Excercise 3: Strategies for Approaching the Ideal

PURPOSES: ● Develop creative approaches, models, processes and techniques for improving economic development. ● Ensure that the most influential factors are taken into account when developing a strategy. ● Ensure that key elements of the strategy are fully debated.

INDIVIDUAL TASK: Imagine that you are in the future and the policies you created have been implemented. Look back to the past and identify two or three key events that made your ideal feasible. Think why these events were so important. Make notes to share with your group.

TEAM TASK: The reporter helps the group discuss and review their list of events and record them in the form of a causal map. The group then discusses the implications of these events for a strategy of economic development. Produce a map showing the relationships between the major events and a brief explanation of any strategic implications.

PLENARY TASK: Each reporter presents their joint causal map and implications.

Excercise 4: Stakeholder Reactions

PURPOSES: ● To trace the effects of the events you mapped in the previous exercise on the people involved and affected. Who were the key individuals, groups, organizations and institutions? How did they feel and how did they react?

INDIVIDUAL TASK: Review the events you created in the previous exercise and imagine specifically who—what persons, groups or institutions were involved. Try to put yourself in their shoes and ask yourself how they felt when the event occurred. Look at all facets of their life to assess the effects—social, cultural, political as well as economic.

TEAM TASK: Discuss your findings in your group and produce a group picture of the effects of the events on the people of the Colombia.

PLENARY TASK: Role play of debate between major actors involved in and affected by economic development.

Excercise 5: Creating a Plan of Action

PURPOSES: ● Design the specifics of an approach to improvement in the electricity sector, taking into account your learning from the previous exercises. ● Develop support for actions you wish to take. ● Build on the commitment of the participants.

INDIVIDUAL TASK: Take a look at all the events that you considered crucial for creating your ideal design of the electricity sector and the reactions of people to those events. Devise a line of action that you could contribute to that would overcome some of the difficulties outlined and contribute to some of the positive outcomes you envisaged. What would you like to accomplish? How can you leverage your influence to encourage others to participate?

TEAM TASK: Discuss your list of key actions with your team.

Synthesize discussion in the form of a plan of action.

Who should have responsibility and who will provide support?

What resources are required? What is the time frame for action? Where should future sharing take place?

PLENARY TASK: Presentation from teams. Discussion of Next Steps.

Excercise 6: Reflections

PURPOSES: ● Reflect on the work achieved. ● Prepare for return to normal work. ● Gain perspective on achievements.

PLENARY TASK: Open reflection on results vs. expectations. Statements of actions and difficulties anticipated. Feelings about accomplishments.

ABOUT THE AUTHOR

William E. Smith, PhD, is a Director and Founder of Organizing for Development, An International Institute. It was founded in 1988 to foster the more holistic approaches to organizing he describes here. He previously worked as an overseas manager for British Airways, and as a consultant in Organization.

His recent work draws on the cultural implications of the three power relations discussed in this chapter. With his partner Turid Sato he is using search processes to build more holistic developmental partnerships across cultures—African, Asian, European, and Latin American—based on their different ways of learning.

CONFERENCES RUN USING ODII MODEL

● The Design of a National Information System for Columbia, 1986 ● Strategic Planning for Ecopetrol (State Oil Company Columbia), 1988 ● The Re-Design of the "Office Du Niger," a State Agricultural Company, Mali, 1989 ● An International Search for New Approaches to Decentralization — Sundvolen, Norway, 1990 ● Women's Organizing Abilities in Development — An international search for a strategy for making better use of feminine organizing skills, Virginia, 1990 ● Organizing for Economic Development — A grass roots search for alternative means for creating economic development, Maine, 1991 ● Design for Village Development Linkage to NGO's and Government Policy Makers, Thailand, 1991 ● Cambodia Workshop for Reconstruction and Development — A search for a framework for development by experts from within and from outside Cambodia prior to the peace resolution, 1991 ● New Strategies for Development Assistance, NORAD and Ministry of Foreign Affairs, Norway. 1991 ● Indonesia, Workshop on Administrative Reform — A search for ways to make better linkages between districts, provinces and national government, 1991 ● Hungary, Product Market Development — A search for ways to create the middle level systems between producers, planners, and policy makers, 1992.

CHAPTER 18

PLANNING, DESIGNING AND MANAGING LARGE-SCALE SEARCHES
Day Care in Saskatchewan
By David Morley and Eric Trist

THIS CHAPTER HAS TWO PARTS. In the first, Morley and Trist give a moving, personal account of the hidden dynamics that occur, in various forms, in many conferences. Participants often hit what runners call "the wall," when it seems impossible to keep going. The test of a search process is not whether people go the first mile, but rather how they get their second wind.

Here the group gets off schedule, fails to compare notes on proposed future scenarios, and falls into a futile competition in front of outside invited guests. The authors show why and how the later "process" discussion leads to a reaffirmation of cooperation much stronger for having been tested.

The second part presents selections from the final report to sponsors and participants. It provides unique insights into the planning, group selection, and design process.

This conference is especially instructive for its testing of the potential for a new "referent" group on day care in a Canadian province. The authors give explicit detail on the way diverse stakeholders are mobilized to select issues and groups to work on various scenarios during the conference. This step is especially important where no one agency, group, or organization is the sanctioned center of the informal network.

I have let stand much of the verbatim final discussion.
There the reader can trace the turn around from anger and
disappointment to a restoration of and commitment to
common ground on day care. — MRW

This is a personal reflection on the Saskatchewan Day Care Search Conference from the only real "outsiders"—the staff. Many important search conference events are never recorded, not on flip-charts or in a final report. Rarely is the social experience with its own particular character and atmosphere documented.

This short "story" is our attempt to record these dimensions of the Day Care Search Conference and to reflect on the contribution of its social/political atmosphere to its possible outcomes. There were three sequences of events that particularly impressed the staff. On reflection, they seem important as measures of the conference's worth and its capacity to "survive" through future activities by the participants.

THE ARRIVAL. . . AND ADAPTATION
OF THE WORK/FAMILY ENVIRONMENT

The hour or so before a search conference begins is always a tense one for the staff. Nobody can predict the effect of bringing together this mix of special interests around a particular social issue—whether the chemistry of the "mix" will be explosive, or flat. . . or merely fizzy! To compensate for this uncertainty, the staff wander around getting the feel of the conference's spaces, shifting the chairs and tables into the patterns demanded by the conference's social settings, and imagining what this one will be like.

Camp Rayner upset our tranquility, because it is not well designed for a search conference. The impression was of a dark underground space that brought back lurking memories of air-raid shelters! Perhaps it was the smell, of emptiness, of the winter damp not yet dispersed. Bleak and, in some cases, windowless rooms for the small groups; a huge, bare "dungeon" in which 50 people were to spend a good many hours. The impression was dispiriting. Could the subtle communications involved in this kind of experiential learning "happen" in such a place?

The fact is that they *could* and *did* occur. Our gloomy, environmental-determinist thinking dispersed with the arrival of participants. And this "arrival" was different. As cars appeared across the flat Saskatchewan farmland and passengers disgorged, the rightness of the unusual social scene that was to become our conference was quickly apparent.

We had forgotten the children, the 18 or so youngsters who accompanied their parents and were to form a permanent, tumultuous backdrop. And, as the parents struggled through the prairie dust of the car park—children and luggage under their arms—with cots, toys, and other familiar paraphernalia—it became clear that they were spontaneously mobilizing in response to a new environment, precisely as the conference would encourage participants to create new coping mechanisms for day care. The conference (work) and the children (family) had to co-exist in a relatively inadequate environment. Such co-existence is what day care is all about.

So the children were critical, both as symbols and a reality in the conference. They were also a stimulus for innovation. The parents were soon looking for space for their own day care center, so that they could turn their attention fully to the conference. Since "getting children out of church basements" became a conference slogan, it is not surprising that these parents wished to get their children out of the Camp Rayner "basements."

Providing for the Children

Their demands, indeed, led to a lesson for staff, conference organizers, and parents alike. Light, airy rooms had been found in another building for small working groups originally scheduled to occupy windowless rooms. The same space also was discovered by the parents.

For a moment the trust and sympathy between staff and participants that is essential for a search conference was in the balance. Of course, the groups occupying the sunny, airy, domestic-scale space now requested for the children, were quite willing to move. As a result of this first successful negotiation, there was an increase in trust between staff and "inmates."

So the conferees' children and their day care needs became intertwined with our conference focus—the children of Saskatchewan and *their* day care needs. This made the conference a *real* social process, not an artificial gaming exercise. The conference was modeling at every level a new approach to family/work relationships, providing a projection screen for the real process.

Other changes were made to meet the needs of conference families, like taking earlier lunch and dinner times. A four-hour break was negotiated between afternoon and evening sessions so that parents and children could be together for bedtime. Responding to the demands of both conference *and* children made it very much easier for the parents.

The conference "lived" in the whole social texture of the lives between the parents and children.

All had settled down by the end of the morning of the second day. The displaced working groups, after intense negotiation by the conference coordinator, had found pleasant rooms in another building. Even the dungeon-like plenary room was transformed when a staff member discovered that two sets of wide, resolutely-shut doors, could be opened.

The damp was let out and the sunlight in. Prairie bird song replaced the dank smell. The chairs were rearranged in semi-circles looking out into woodland. A routine had been established and the environment had come to life out of the intensity of participation in the experience by *all* the participants—children as well as adults.

Participants had demonstrated that sustained and creative labor is not necessarily inhibited by the presence of children and the sense of family. Indeed the sad irony is that no employers' representatives attended; so this practical workplace issue was not addressed again. The conference itself was an experiment in balancing work and family, but the group with so much to gain from the implications could not observe the results.

THE SYMBIOSIS OF WORK, PLAY, AND CREATIVITY

Several participants described to us their feelings on attending yet another day care conference. "Here I go again, why do I keep going?" They recognized their response as a classic symptom of "burn out" for volunteers in a social change process—the sense of inevitably being blocked and the almost reflex-response to attend, the syndrome of hopelessness. And yet here they all were again, reflecting in their determination a strong sense that the cause is right.

Very exciting for us as outsiders was the response to this new mode of social learning. Generally, in small group search sessions, as people explore areas they jointly recognize as critical, both individual and group learning appears in three forms. It is *experiential*—problems are worked through in the present setting. It is *co-operative*—learning is jointly attained. It is *participative*—each individual has a stake in the outcome, a sense of ownership.

For some in this conference, too, "the wall" could be maneuvered around, the constraints pushed back, with a liberating effect. Not only were new notions of child care jointly defined out of collective experience, a new idiom emerged that felt realistic because it was adjusted to existing conditions. The experience was truly existential, based on a real experience created by the participants and sustained for the week.

Most remarkable in this process was the symbiosis among conference elements over the last 36 hours. Wednesday evening we had a conference party. The groups had worked long hours on unfamiliar tasks. On Thursday morning they were to negotiate task group themes to be worked into presentations for the "outsiders" who would arrive Friday morning. It was important that the recreation be of high quality.

To generate the right atmosphere, a good folk-rock group was invited out from Saskatoon. The musicians soon had most of the participants dancing and singing. The volume of informal social interaction trebled. . . quadrupled. As much energy was spent in having fun as in working. The party continued into the early hours, but people seemed refreshed rather than exhausted when the critical negotiating session began next morning.

The action tasks necessary to re-enter the "outside" world were now undertaken. Small group facilitators withdrew, and the task groups developed their presentations. There followed a period of intense activity, full of energy and commitment. The mood was the very opposite of burn out.

A glance at the presentation graphics reproduced in the report is enough to recognize that this is not merely our hyperbole. The flow diagrams, slogan writing, visual expressions were created during a hectic Thursday evening which saw clusters of people around the tables in the Camp Rayner dining room—sharing, explaining, helping—late into the night.

One group worked until 4:00 Friday morning, another until 5:30. This was not dull work, nor were the workers driven to impress or influence the visitors next morning. This was a release from constraint long enough to re-frame often-repeated issues and emerge with new proposals for change.

The conference slogans may have seemed commonplace to the visitors, but they were deeply felt expressions of rediscovery. "UNIVERSAL DAY CARE IS AN IDEA WHOSE TIME HAS COME," and most of all, "CHILDREN ARE OUR NUMBER ONE RESOURCE."

THE CONFERENCE AND THE REAL WORLD

Yet, the conference missed one vital "heart beat," an important lesson for those who would avoid similar pitfalls. There was no time for participants to hear each other's group presentations before they were delivered "live" to the outsiders. The original agenda called for this to happen Friday morning. But we fell behind schedule and the task groups needed more time to complete their work.

As a result, the atmosphere of enthusiasm and fun ended abruptly and harshly. Real world memberships and loyalties, reinforced by lack of time to *share* and integrate the groups' conclusions "in-house," exerted a greater pull at this stage. Each group found itself presenting "cold" to the outsiders, making separate cases for their own ideas.

This was a major design error on our part. We were deceived by the unusual cohesion that arose in the temporary conference community, and did not expect the re-appearance during the final conference sessions of the many differences that existed among the participants' organizations. However, the inherent disagreements between participants, suppressed in favor of a common purpose for four days, now emerged in their full complexity.

A Series of Disasters

To the initial design error, must be added a set of "disasters" that further unsettled this critical final presentation. First the Minister (viewed by many as the key visitor) and his party were late. His plane had broken down, and a climate of great uncertainty developed that stirred up considerable anxiety.

When at last the Minister arrived, participants decided to make all reports in one session so he could hear them before returning to Regina for a budget meeting two hours later. This meant postponing lunch, which produced vigorous protest from mothers with young children who felt that their needs were being sacrificed, since they would not leave the day care staff to cope with lunch alone. So they had to miss the last two presentations.

Next, the session chairman, who had been called away from the conference, was insufficiently briefed and missed giving a critical introduction to the search conference process. So the visitors were not clear as to what they were hearing or how to respond. Added to all this, the electric power went off, making the plenary space look like a "dungeon" again!

Nevertheless, task group presentations were made in style. The guests listened intently, and the Minister, on departure, declared himself interested and impressed. A number of people succeeded in making their particular points to him as he was leaving. Most guests stayed a while, and a few remained until the end of the final plenary, when the conflicts stirred up by the unprepared encounter with powerful outsiders surfaced and ultimately were resolved.

It's too bad more guests were not present, because the group process through which this took place was a remarkable phenomenon that points both to the robustness of the search conference process *and* to the maturity of these participants.

Still, the group cohesion and sense of common purpose generated in the temporary conference community seemed to be shattered by this first encounter with the "power field" of the real world. Was their accomplishment so fragile? Was all their work in vain? Many had taken risks, opening up and venturing into relationships with people who were strangers or even opponents. Now they were flung into competition. They began to regret having ventured forth, and became angry and depressed.

No one expected task groups to make their proposals ends in themselves, or that anyone would start lobbying for them there and then. But this is what seemed to happen. The old familiar in-fighting, competitive advantage-seeking, and individual pressuring seemed to return. It is good that this was faced. The issue was made public and analyzed in a collective group process, where it was shown not to have a monopoly of the truth. The final plenary transcript traces the constructive path taken that led to a unanimous day care resolution, and the formation of an interim committee to work towards a province-wide "alliance." The suggestion that this might be the way to go first appears in the remarks of the fifth participant to speak.

The first half of the session, however, is taken up with a full confrontation of differences and of the individualistic behavior felt to have disrupted collective process. There is considerable confusion and ascription of motive. Nevertheless everyone is heard in a very civilized way.

In the second half of the session, contributions that seek to re-unify the group become more numerous and are applauded. The suggestion of a joint resolution is put first by one participant, then by another, and is finally proposed. (You can follow this in the edited account starting on page 206.)

The proposals of the five task groups were not inherently incompatible. The first two were concerned with problems internal to the day care system. The last three with its relations with wider systems in government, the community, and in the networking together of many diverse interests. All five could be expected to have a role in an evolving system, although much further dialogue would be needed before an acceptable balance could be struck between the various emphases.

Moreover, the continuation of this dialogue would generate still more ideas. This is what is meant by "social learning." Through time and continued effort it can lead to legitimate and viable institution building.

These are our impressions. Whatever their long-term outcomes, search conferences tend to create intense environments for learning and socializing. People with common interests, but often widely differing perspectives, explore the concerns that they share, and appreciate more clearly those they do not. They also come to discover jointly the areas that are not normally considered—particularly as they relate to the future. All of this promotes skepticism and uncertainty, questioning and discovery, excitement and disagreement, and hope and disillusionment too.

Whether this experience can have any lasting effect in Saskatchewan is in the hands of the participants. It will depend on their capacity to extend this social learning mode among their co-workers and others in Saskatchewan who will have a hand forming the future of childcare.

CHILDREN: OUR NUMBER ONE RESOURCE
A Report on the Saskatchewan Search Conference on Day Care

By David Morley and Eric Trist
Faculty of Environmental Studies
York University, Toronto

This conference was held in Canada from June 1 to June 5, 1981. Morley and Trist co-managed it with the help of several local facilitators. They kept careful notes, saved the flip charts, and put together the report that follows. I have edited this document at their direction to highlight information that will be of most use to others. The full report, nearly 100 pages in length, was published originally by The Co-operative College of Canada in June 1981. – MRW

Origins of a Day Care Search Conference

The Saskatchewan Search Conference on Day Care emerged in the context of an increasing need for day care services and public debate set off by a Needs Survey for Child Care carried out by an inter-ministerial review committee. The conference form and timing resulted from contacts among the Co-operative College of Canada, the Saskatchewan Department of Co-operation and Co-operative Development, and the Faculty of Environmental Studies at York University.

As a result of the experience of a Search facilitated by York Environmental Studies members on the future of co-operatives in Winnipeg in 1980, the Executive Director of the Co-operative College, proposed a similar conference on the future of day care in Saskatchewan. The Department of Co-operation agreed to fund it.

The authors, who had managed several similar events, were invited to design and run the conference. The Day Care Search Conference was seen as a model for policy-making under conditions of rapid change, capable of further applications in Saskatchewan.

Purpose of the Conference

Day care is reaching crisis proportions in Canada as in many industrial countries. The problem results from profound social changes—families in which both parents work and single parent families—that reflect industrialization, urbanization and the rise of the women's movement. These trends are expected to increase in the future.

The *Regina Leader Post* (August 22, 1980) summarized the situation:

"The most vulnerable families—single parent and those with two breadwinners but low incomes—have been showing signs of intolerable stress that is beginning to manifest itself in a mounting casualty... For infants and children of school age there is virtually no provision... Among day care workers, there has been increasing signs of 'burn out.'"

The day care scene is fragmented. Organizations pull in different directions. Womens' groups press their demands urgently, frustrated that their views receive scant attention. No single entity, governmental or independent, existed to receive inputs from these organizations, to facilitate their inter-relations or to provide conditions that could encourage them to find common ground among divergent but not necessarily incompatible positions.

For these reasons the Department of Co-operation decided to call together individuals from a wide range of concerned organizations for an uninterrupted dialogue on all aspects of day-care. It was hoped that enough common ground would be established to allow for developing long-range policy based on consensus, and that new and creative options would enable actions that would gain wide public support.

Planning Process

A six person planning committee met in March 1981 to develop the conference design, identify day care constituency groups, invite participants, and set up a managing process. Planners came from the Departments of Social Services, Co-operation and Co-operative Development, the Society for Involvement of Good Neighbors (SIGN), the Co-operative College of Canada, the Regina Day Care Co-operative, Saskatchewan Public School Board, and included the Secretary of State for Saskatchewan.

Three meetings were held between March and May. The authors attended two of them. A secretariat based at the Co-operative College of Canada carried out day-to-day co-ordinating tasks.

At the first meeting, key tasks were defining the purpose of the conference and its expression in the search process, establishing key constituencies, and inviting participants.

The following day care *interests* were identified to ensure coverage of the full range of concerns and perspectives:

Users and Providers of Day Care Services
Parents/Children (day care boards, parents)
User Organizations (child/day care associations)
Providers (coops, non-profit, private, family)
Associated Interest Groups (women's groups, native people's organizations, unions, social planners, rural organizations, political parties, schools, churches, human services)
Government (Social Services Co-operation and Co-operative Development, Education, Culture and Youth, Health, Tourism and Recreation, Labor, Association of Rural Municipalities, Association of Urban School Boards)
Employers: co-operative organizations, crown and private corporations, the public service commission, banks, retail firms.

The conference would be limited to 60—a manageable number. Local leaders and people with authority to follow through at policy and decision-making levels would be invited, plus a number of guests influential to the future of child care to hear the final task group reports.

The second planning meeting focussed on conference development, participants, guests, and small-group facilitators, the final meeting on design and invitation lists. Efforts to attract employer and further government involvement prior to the conference were unsuccessful. The final participant list includes each constituency group (see Table 1).

Invitations included information on the search process and the preliminary program—to introduce the idea that the search would make demands on participants different from a traditional conference. It was emphasized that final presentations "will be given to an invited audience of key decision makers."

Table 1: Saskatchewan Search Conference on Day Care
INTEREST BASES OF PARTICIPANTS*

	March 27 Original Estimate	May 6 Accepts	June 1-5 Conf.	Diff. from Original Estimate
Users and Providers	20	17	16	- 4
Native People	8	1	4	- 4
Associated Interest Groups	9	4	14	+ 5
Government	17	6	8	- 9
Employers	3	–	–	- 3
Educational Institutions	3	2	2	- 1
Totals	60	30	44	-16

*Many participants have interests involving several categories. These data are based on assumed primary association.

Six small-group facilitators were recruited from Saskatchewan organizations. Most attended the May 6 planning meeting on conference design, and their role was fully discussed. Camp Rayner was selected as conference site to fit the "social island" requirements of the search process—a residential setting remote from day-to-day occupational demands.

FINAL PROGRAM: SASKATCHEWAN SEARCH CONFERENCE
ON DAY CARE (June 1 to 5, 1981)

MONDAY, JUNE 1

mid p.m.   CONFERENCE REGISTRATION
6:00   Dinner
7:15   INTRODUCTORY PLENARY SESSION
             • introduction to conference process
               general conference information
9:00   SMALL GROUP SESSION 1
             Scanning the Wider Environment
             • issues and trends/past into future
             • 6 groups with 7/8 persons
             • representation from each main interest/group
               pre-selected by staff

TUESDAY, JUNE 2

8:00 am	Breakfast
9:00	SMALL GROUP SESSION 2
	Scanning (continued)
	• review of small group work
	• prepare summary for presentation
10:15	Coffee
	• "Village Fair" atmosphere/informal discussion of group reports headlined on charts hung around the walls.
10:45	PLENARY REPORTING AND DISCUSSION SESSION
	• 5-minute presentations of key issues
	• general discussion – comparison of group viewpoints
	• introduction to session 3
12:00	Lunch
1:30 pm	SMALL GROUP SESSION 3
	Assessment of Current Day Care System
	• day care from the standpoints of the various interests represented in the groups
	• organizational capacities to respond to trends
3:30-4:30	PLENARY REPORTING SESSION
	• group presentations and general discussion from session 3
	• posting of session 3 flip-charts
5:30	Dinner
9:00-10:00	INTEREST GROUP CLUSTER MEETINGS
	• participants' caucus in special interest clusters: users, providers, government, etc.
	• review of discussion/conference process

WEDNESDAY, JUNE 3

8:00 am	Breakfast
9:00	PLENARY SESSION
	introduction to session 4
9:15	SMALL GROUP SESSION 4
	Desirable Futures for Day Care
	• long-range visions of day care
	• a constraint-free approach
	Coffee

11:30	PLENARY REPORTING SESSION
	• group reports/general discussion on desirable futures
12:00	Lunch
1:30	PLENARY SESSION (continued)
2:00-4:30	SMALL GROUP SESSION 5
	Constraints and Opportunities for Day Care
	• focus on existing limits to change and opportunities available to unblock the future and establish areas for action
5:30	Dinner
8:00	FREE EVENING – Conference Party

THURSDAY, JUNE 4

8:00 am	Breakfast
9:30	PLENARY REPORTING SESSION
	• small group reports/constraints and opportunities session
	Coffee
10:30	PLENARY NEGOTIATING SESSION
	Selection of Task Group Themes
	• agreement on key themes for action
	• establish task groups/membership self-selected by participants/facilitators withdrawn
12:00	Lunch
1:30	PLENARY NEGOTIATING SESSION (continued)
2:00-4:00	TASK GROUP SESSION 1
	• establish agenda/working timetable
5:30	Dinner
7:30	TASK GROUP SESSION 2
	• each group continues to work on aspects of its related theme
	• interaction between groups/exchange of information and ideas

FRIDAY, JUNE 5

8:00 am	Breakfast
8:30	TASK GROUP SESSION 3
	• finalize presentations
10:00	Coffee/Arrival of Visitors
10:30	PLENARY: TASK GROUP PRESENTATIONS

1. A model for Delivery of Child Care Services
2. Universal free Child Care
3. A Department of Children and Youth
4. Community-Based Child Care
5. Networking

1:15	Lunch
2:15	FINAL PLENARY: REVIEW OF PRESENTATIONS
	• discussion of presentations/comments from visitors
	• decisions on the form and direction of future actions
4:00	CONFERENCE CLOSES

THE SEARCH PHASE

The search phase had four elements, titled:

1. Scanning the Wider Environment
2. Assessment of the Current Day Care System
3. Desirable Futures for Day Care
4. Constraints and Opportunities for Day Care

SELECTION OF TASK GROUP THEMES

The search phase ends with conference participants selecting tasks to focus upon during the final stages. The critical turning point is the plenary negotiating session in which people select task themes and groups to work on them. Participants are then required to make a basic philosophic choice. In this case, the choices were:

1. Revert to *"old paradigm"* frameworks (e.g. a welfare approach to child care, "dampening the scream" of the disadvantaged, based on fragmenting and competing interests)

OR

2. Adopt *"new paradigm" assumptions* (e.g. universal day care as a human right, accessible and available for all, child care integral to human development).

The basic conference assumption soon emerged. The "child care" issue was not going to disappear. Indeed it will tend to intensify from major social shifts like continued inflation, unemployment, major changes in workplace, technological innovation, family structures (single parents, two-career families), roles of women, and demographic discontinuities like baby boomers, aging population, declining birth rates, ideological and value conflicts in society, and changing attitudes towards children.

These interconnected trends conflict with the existing paradigm and set up demands for a new paradigm of child care. However, it is often found in search conferences, which mirror the real world, that agreement on new paradigm long-range values and objectives is not hard to achieve. Agreement on *means* is much more difficult. Our task groups face the challenge of discovering the "means"—inventing processes that did not exist before. Their proposals go beyond special pleading and often take the form of continuing joint action steps towards desired alternative futures.

Selection of Themes

Task group themes typically emerge from an ends/means dialogue on "desirable futures" compared with "constraints and opportunities." Table 2 lists the topics generated by the day care search conference, through three iterations—one proposed by staff after hearing group presentations, the second amended and voted on for viability by participants, and the third defined and selected during the negotiating session.

TABLE 2: TASK GROUP THEMES

Proposed by Conference Staff from Analysis of Reports	Amended by Participants (multiple votes per person)		Final Task Group Selection by Group Participants (one vote each)	
Dept of the Child and Youth	Dept of the Child	14*	Dept of Children	7
Community-Based Child Care	Community-Based Child Care	15	Community-Based Child Care	8
Child Care Networks and Coalitions	Child Care Networks 1and Coalitions	17	Child Care Networks	9
Changing Public Attitudes to Child Care				
Lobbying Government and Other Interest Groups				
Child Care Personnel and Training	Child Care Personnel and Training	16	Universal/Free Child Care	8
Employers/Work Environments	Employers/Work Environment	11		
Redesign Day Care Organizations	Redesign Day Care Organizations	9	Child Care Delivery Model	8
Quality Child Care: Availability and Accessibility	Quality Child Care: Availability and Accessibility	13		
Funding	Funding	6		

*Numbers = votes for that issue

Task Group Make-Up

Each task group was made up of volunteers representing diverse interests. However, their work suggested they were by no means homogeneous, and several sharp edges of opinion emerged regarding child care.

Editor's Note: You see here the creative charts the authors mention in Part One. Each reflects the work of a task group, showing many (not necessarily incompatible) approaches to day care. These reports were not shared among participants prior to their presentations to invited influential guests. The authors flag this omission as a crucial strategic mistake that, however, the group recovered from as will be seen below. Reports are identified by group number or task group name in the transcript that follows. — MRW

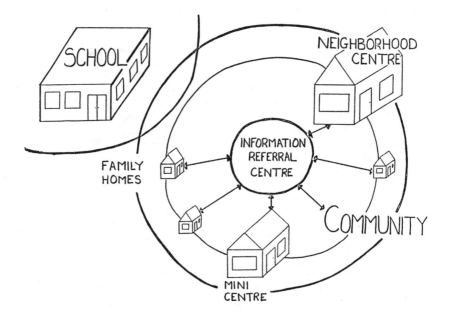

CHILDCARE BALLOON

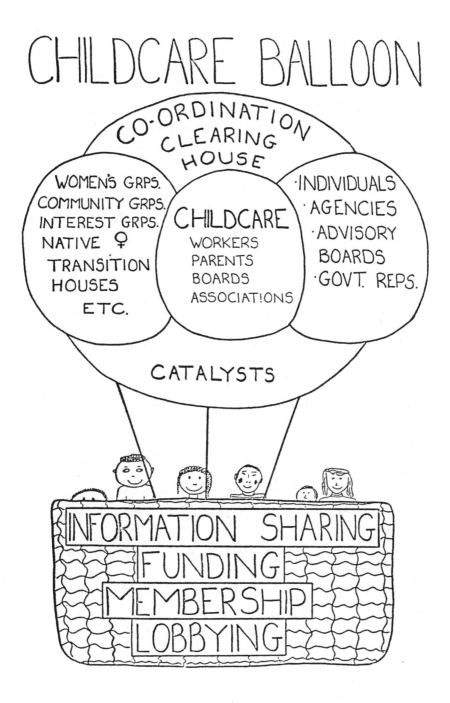

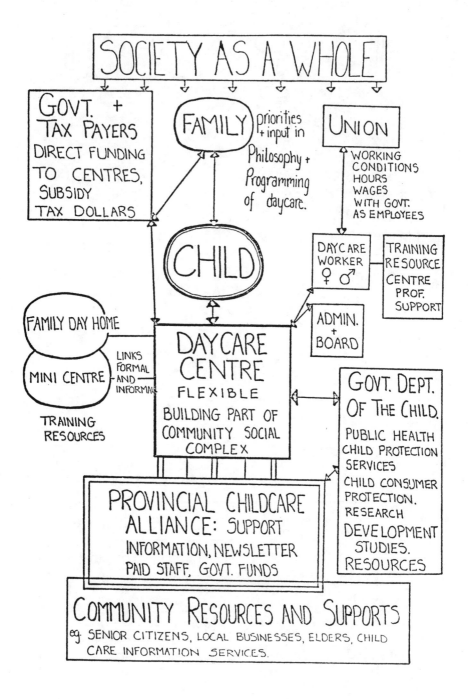

OUR VISION

THE ATTRIBUTES OF THE NEW PARADIGM OF CHILD CARE

1. Our *vision* is a society that places CHILDCARE as its *highest priority*.

2. Our *vision* recognizes the *development* and *growth* of CHILDREN as *essential* in the CREATION of a *humane productive* future.

3. Our *vision* will ENSURE the *basic human rights* of *all* CHILDREN through the *provision* of a *variety* of community based CHILDCARE RESOURCES which *support* and *enhance* FAMILY Life.

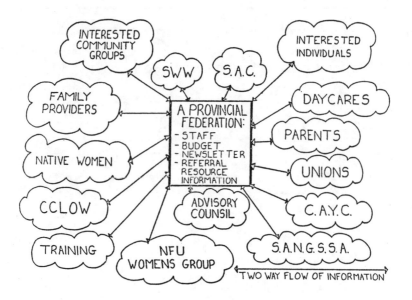

FINAL PLENARY SESSION
– REVIEW OF TASK GROUP PRESENTATIONS
Friday, June 5, 1981, 2:30 TO 4:00 P.M.

Introduction

What follows is an abridged transcript of the critical discussion leading to the meeting's major action agreements. It shows participants reflecting on their work in a way that deepens our understanding both of search processes and new day care initiatives. It documents the origins of a proposed provincial day care alliance, and can clarify misperceptions that may emerge based on incomplete information. It is the final "minute" of the session that crystallized the conference participants' collective intent.

Discussion Transcript

STAFF 1: We are here to pick up the energy generated by the search process and to decide how to continue.

STAFF 2: Any way you can take advantage of this last hour together to find ways of maintaining the conference network and moving towards an alliance or community will be useful, since it will be hard to get as many of you together again.

PARTICIPANT A: Could we get some feedback on how people feel the presentations went over?

PARTICIPANT B: A strong sense of lobbying for core funding is the main thrust for Group 1 (A Model for the Delivery of Child Care Services). I don't think we can work on other things until we have assurance of funding.

PARTICIPANT C: In Group 2 (Universal-Free Child Care) much emphasis was put on organized labor (whether parents or workers); that still seems to me the logical constituency that I would look to. There are many ways I can see that happening—resolutions at union conventions, pressures on our own union contracts, benefits for parents [that we can] win in these contracts.

PARTICIPANT D: We also can make representations to the Minister of Labour for changes to the Labour Standards Act when it comes to things like flex-time or earned days off as a right, dependents' need over and above normal sick leave. Not all people choose to be unionized. We need minimum protection through the Standards Act. Also, capital grants for space. . . We have to take our children out of church basements into healthy, happy environments.

PARTICIPANT E: I want to get back to the idea of an interim board with provincial aims, [not] go to government for this. I feel we will have a lot better chance of getting what we want if we unite provincially. I would like to see people put themselves on that interim board (representing all day care interests). If we leave with that in place, then we do have something to go ahead with. Who is going to lobby for core funding? There will be Action Child Care over here, and Saskatoon Day Care Association over here, and Status of Women over there. Why don't we get together? We are all asking for the same thing.

PARTICIPANT F: Can I comment as an outsider? I heard core funding come up in every presentation. It would be useful if this body today could come up with one pointed thing they would like to see implemented in the next budget. This is possible right now. Budget estimates for next year are being formulated. Now is the time to say that we want core funding and recommendations for Day Care Review. Something like this could be the consensus of the whole group. Perhaps you can send a telegram from this group to the Minister.

PARTICIPANT G: Group 3 (Department of Children and Youth) have suggested that it go to the Minister of Social Services, to the Day Care Advisory Board. I like the idea of forming a core here so that we could get started. We would also like to see it go to the many support groups that we didn't know existed... hopefully everyone will take it up in their own groups and carry the torch.

PARTICIPANT H: Group 4 (Community-Based Child Care) had a fair amount of positive feedback from the provincial guests. So on Monday we are going to pursue the contacts we made with the senior officials today. We don't want to disband because we are afraid if we drop it, or leave it for a provincial association, nothing will be done this year. Our proposal is that we flesh out what we said this morning, and meet with the Department of Social Services the following week to see what can be accomplished in next year's budget. We need both formal and informal networks to sell this proposal to the broader public.

We would like some feedback on this.

PARTICIPANT I: I would like to give some feedback. There was an unfortunate situation here today that made me feel extremely angry—that we changed our process to accommodate certain people in the room. I would really have liked to listen to your presentation. I would like to be able to sit down and go through the implications and look at the pros and cons before you go any further.

PARTICIPANT H: We are not proposing to speak for everybody in this room. We think the community-based proposal is a structure that is acceptable, that is all we are talking about; we are not talking about writing in the fine points about community representation or structure. . . We are concerned with the concept of community basis versus adding more money to the Day Care Division. We want the control.

PARTICIPANT K: I observed quite a change today. For four days we developed a sense of unity with mutual goals, drawing on each other's resources. Something shifted dramatically today. Some outsiders came in perceived as the higher powers. Instead of looking to our group to pull together, we suddenly found people saying, "Well, we can forget about the grass-roots, now we are going to head for the bigwigs with all the money." It is destroying the community that was here.

APPLAUSE

During three or four days we lit some torches. If we pass them to elected representatives we are lost. We have to all take them with us and work on them communally.

PARTICIPANT C: I haven't been feeling very good this morning. I saw people I've put a great deal of trust and faith in reacting all over the place. Instead of acting together, people are splintering up and struggling for power. I don't think the power is with the government bureaucrats who were here. The power is us. I think we want to go on as far as we can together.

APPLAUSE

PARTICIPANT L: I don't think that people *are* separated. I think that all the things that were presented today are compatible in a lot of ways. Nobody has said they are going to do something that will interfere with anyone else's ideas.

PARTICIPANT M: We are native people and we need this victory to go on fighting and lobbying for our children.

PARTICIPANT N: I don't think it is realistic for us to expect to move on a very significant set of actions unless we maintain the communication network that we have here. I think we should concentrate on proposals that came out of the group presentation on networking—to maintain what is begun here.

PARTICIPANT F: The group I come from would be very upset if our people were supporting something going to higher levels before they checked back with the many community groups involved in day care. They should reflect on it, discuss it and send comments back.

APPLAUSE

PARTICIPANT J: There are things we can do as individuals, but our key point was establishing an "alliance." We have to be united. Maybe we can't agree on every point, but we all agreed that we want better child care. We need volunteers until we get funded, willing to take it back to your own organizations and convince them they should be behind this. It is not setting up another organization. It is a "wall" for everybody to get behind; maybe you're standing at different points of the wall, but we are all going to push together.

PARTICIPANT K: I was shocked at the request that each task group reports separately. I don't think that is possible. Our suggestion was that if we believe this should be an alliance of interests, put your name on the chart. We need some co-ordination. Maybe only three names go on the list today, but perhaps within a month these three will hear from ten more who say "Yes, I want to be in it." Because all the committed people are not here today. It could either grow or die.

PARTICIPANT I: What I would like to see is a resolution that we are all united and that we stand behind a vision, a new paradigm of child care that we would take back and publicize and promote. Then maybe people from each task group could sit on an interim board.

PARTICIPANT P: I would like to support the last speaker in the idea of a resolution. There has to be some kind of unification or this thing is going to die.

STAFF 2: We are talking about taking some institution-building steps. I have a feeling that without this, the process, even if it doesn't die, would be severely slowed down. I sense a feeling of the death of this group. It's a hard moment, especially after a relatively successful interchange with the Minister... The objective is to share all these ideas and find out if there is a common direction. The cost of doing nothing is the loss of the continuing process.

STAFF 1: Perhaps the question in the balance is: Is there a possibility of a loose, informal network made up of members of organizations or not— crossing boundaries, temporary or permanent, intended to transmit the energy and ideas through the more formal organizations to which you may belong?

PARTICIPANT R: As a member of the group that put the community proposal together, I thought we were to take those ideas back to our organizations.

PARTICIPANT O: There is a lot of vested interest in every proposition that came up here. Any interest that looks as if it is going to be threatened is the first one to go_it's natural.

PARTICIPANT C: We are not saying as a group that we are disagreeing or agreeing with what your group is planning on presenting on Monday. But what we are saying is that we would like to go back to the groups that we represent to discuss all the proposals and perhaps meet together again at the October Day Care Conference. I don't want to put up our hands right now to say we do or don't support the community-based group proposal.

PARTICIPANT L: I would like to suggest a resolution that we all support a new vision, that we all agree that a provincial alliance is necessary to fight for this new vision. Therefore, this conference as an ad hoc group will support such a body. Take the idea first back to our own groups— and support an interim board in the attempt to form the alliance. I suggest a statement of our commitment to that idea.

PARTICIPANT R: Let's keep ourselves together and let's do the best we can; get the group together and do it with the feeling of holding each other's hands.

APPLAUSE

PARTICIPANT S: I have a sense that we can probably get consensus on the vision that is sitting there. I think what we *can't* get consensus on is the means of achieving that vision in structural terms and organizational terms, be it government providing everything or being more commu-nity-based. I support an alliance, because there has to be a forum that brings together the various groups, including those that have not appeared here yet. The alliance could explore in greater detail options presented here.

STAFF 2: We have in embryo the alliance here. And the problems of the alliance! This conference has created the possibility and enabled us to make the initial confrontation with the problems. Search conferences do frequently generate a new vision. The task for people here is to carry this understanding outside. If the vision is not shared very widely we would never face the structural problems. There is broad agreement on the ends, what we are calling the "vision," but, to work out the various options is a very difficult and serious task.

There is a good rule that when facing a process of this kind you try to take the minimum decision that you've got to take to advance the process and leave the options open. The aim is to keep the trail open so that the problems can be more exhaustively discussed further down the road.

[At this point STAFF 1 presented a flip-chart headed "Summary of Possible Steps To Be Taken." It showed a consensus on (1) a shared vision and (2) a need to maintain conference initiatives through reports to home groups and a temporary networking group to organize responses from the many organizations. Finally, (3) these would be discussed at the October day care conference.]

STAFF 2: I didn't sense any fracture in this conference until after this morning. We were growing in unity around the vision, but we have had the intervention of power systems from the outside and the making of separate contacts with them. It certainly wasn't the intention of the conference design that separate task groups should become a number of run-away chariots on their own. We are suffering the necessary and beneficial intrusion of the outside.

We have established the need for the collective response. Now we have to decide what the whole of this group is going to do. There is always danger in rushing an operational decision. This process is geared to much longer time frames. We're trying to open up a base for "thinking and therefore doing." If we don't have some temporary reference point, then we scatter and that is that. People will in their own way carry the vision. We will never know.

PARTICIPANT T: I want to comment on the search conference process. With the formation of task groups at the same time, there grew the formation of a competitive era. This was because we didn't hear task groups' presentations before they were presented to the outsiders.

STAFF 1: There is obviously a need to build into the search conference a preliminary session to share the participants' ideas before they go public. If we had done that here we may have gone through a lot of the discussion then and felt that what was coming out of the task group presentations was something we have already shared, rather than something that belongs separately to each group. People felt they had lost ownership of something important that was happening. I think you've put your finger exactly on a significant design problem—the time for the pre-presentation discussion was sacrificed for other time demands and was sadly missed.

PARTICIPANT U: Can we vote on the resolution?

GENERAL ASSENT

[Two flip charts were presented with the consensus vision and resolution]

A NEW VISION FOR CHILD CARE

1. Our vision is a society that places CHILD CARE as its highest priority.

2. Our vision recognizes the development and growth of CHILDREN as essential in the creation of a humane productive future.

3. Our vision will ensure the human rights of all CHILDREN through the provision of a variety of community-based CHILD CARE RESOURCES which will support and enhance FAMILY LIFE.

RESOLUTION

Whereas we all support the new vision or paradigm of child care; and that we all agree that a Provincial Alliance is needed to support and work together toward achieving a new vision,

Therefore, we as the participants of the Search Conference on Day Care, support:

1. The formation of such an Alliance,

2. The formation of an interim founding group,

And we will report this commitment back to our organizations to discover if there is a wide community support for such an Alliance.

PASSED UNANIMOUSLY — Friday, June 5, 1981.

A significant majority then agreed that the interim group be empowered to obtain the funds needed to assist in developing a provincial alliance of day care interests.

It was also agreed that the interim group should be made up of those people who signed their names as willing to assist and able to get together in the immediate future. Others could be added to the interim group who were not present at the conference. Further general meetings of those committed to a provincial alliance would be arranged at the Day Care Conference planned for October, 1981 in Saskatoon.

ABOUT THE AUTHORS

Notes on **David Morley's** background appear at the end of Chapter 20. **Eric Trist**, whose pioneer effort is the focus of Chapter 3, now lives in Carmel-by-the-Sea, California, where he is completing a trilogy documenting the work of The Tavistock Institute of Human Relations.

CHAPTER 19

WATER QUALITY IN THE UPPER COLORADO RIVER BASIN

By Bob Rehm, Rita Schweitz and Elaine Granata

S EARCH CONFERENCES have been used to scope out new domains in Australia, Canada, Scandinavia and elsewhere for many years. In the United States, this is still a relatively new idea. The future search model, that stimulated so much action in this country, was developed largely in the context of single organizations. Bob Rehm, Rita Schweitz, and Elaine Granata are among the first to take that model to another level of work.

Indeed, they push the boundaries in two ways. First, they apply future search concepts to one of the stickiest social/environmental issues in our society—water quality. They offer useful insights in how to work with multiple, shifting sponsors. Eventually, they devise a strategy (still in progress) to move the issue from the courts to the conference table. – MRW

SETTING THE STAGE

This is the story of a search conference that helped contentious stakeholders discover common ground and begin changing the way they relate to one another. The meeting brought together organizations and groups that differ widely on the use of a scarce natural resource—

water from the upper Colorado River basin. The search focus was a highly-conflicted specific issue (water quality) within a regional domain (upper Colorado River). This story describes the planning, management, and outcomes of the conference, and includes our reflections on the process.

BACKGROUND

The history of water conflicts on the upper Colorado River reflects the history of the American West. This river begins as a small stream high in the mountains of Grand County, Colorado. Wherever there has been a limited resource, people have struggled to control it. The struggle for control of the Colorado River began with the arrival of the first white settlers more than a century ago. Traditional foes staking claims for river water include: west slope mountain counties through which the river flows; water providers to east slope cities such as Denver and Colorado Springs; mining and industry; recreational users; dam builders; and environmentalists.

The Colorado State Water Court has been the customary mechanism for settling disagreements over uses and rights to the water. And water law is as complex as the relationships among the stakeholders. The history of litigation and conflict has been expensive and unproductive according to many of the stakeholders.

THE REQUEST FOR PROPOSAL

In 1990, a regional planning agency responsible for the state Water Quality Plan for its region began looking for "a firm to develop and conduct a structured approach to water quality management decision making using consensus and collaboration as tools for updating and implementing its Water Quality Plan."

The Water Quality Plan is required by the state and must be updated periodically. In the past, the regional planning agency met with severe opposition from various stakeholders whenever it applied for state approval. To avoid opposition again, the agency decided to invite stakeholders to assist in updating its plan.

The project, said their Request for Proposal (RFP), would "involve training and facilitating a diverse group of organizations representing varied and sometimes conflicting views and interests from Colorado's water community... in order to organize a forum in which to generate broad involvement and commitment from the organizations which have a stake in the process."

"We recognize that we are in a state of change and we see an opportunity to design a new system."
    — "Proud" statement from Water Quality Conference

"The application of government laws and regulations has made obsolete the old way of resolving water quality issues ... creating a state of chaos and lack of common interest."
    — Search group analyzing Water Quality milestones

As we met with people from the agency, it became clear that they were really hoping for a shift in values and beliefs among stakeholders. We recommended the search conference method as a way of bringing these diverse parties together to discover common values and ideals, as opposed to a more traditional conflict resolution approach. The planning agency saw the method as a good fit and accepted our proposal.

SEARCHING FOR THE CLIENT

One unusual feature of this event was our difficulty identifying a client. Because of past conflict, no group was willing to be singled out. Their concern was that a single sponsor might discourage other stakeholders from participating.

So we chose to consider the whole system as client and to contract with various parts for various purposes. One client group paid the bills, another helped plan the event, another sponsored the event, and others participated in the conference. Despite these shifts, each "client" group retained some responsibility for the outcome. So our contracting was continuous.

This was truly a case of a "problem" becoming an "opportunity." The lack of a central sponsor or client focused the attention of the group on the domain issue itself. The use of a planning group effectively switched the locus of attention from the regional water planning agency to the field of multi-organizational stakeholders who stepped up to the task. So there was little evidence during the conference of fight/flight or dependency behavior.

PLANNING BEGINS

We met with the regional planning agency in June, 1991 to identify broad conference goals. Agency members voiced concern that a conference would not succeed if they were perceived as sponsors, since the agency is sometimes a Water Court litigant. The group also agreed that their primary interest was a "paradigm shift," a new cooperative dialogue among diverse water stakeholders. So we recommended a planning group that would be a microcosm of the whole to assist in setting up and sponsoring the conference.

The agency liked the idea, although it meant changing the conference goal from "updating the Water Quality Plan" to "finding common ground among diverse water stakeholders." The mission became broader and more open ended. The regional planning agency now invited participation from other key stakeholders—two major urban communities, a water conservancy district, a sanitation district, and one county commissioner. The broader planning group proved to be a key factor in the conference's success. They provided the expert knowledge about water issues that the consultants lacked. They helped us frame the appropriate questions and activities. Working with them also gave us an accurate preview of how stakeholders would behave in the conference and react to us as consultants.

While our planners included key stakeholder groups, they were still a partial microcosm of the regional water community. As it turned out, only a couple of people attended from government and agriculture, and no one from the environmental community. Inclusion of these stakeholders in planning may have resulted in better conference attendance.

Several members arrived at the first meeting with their lawyers in tow. So our first task was to gain agreement on ground rules of cooperation and openness, a shift away from the adversarial process. (These ground rules were carried forward into the conference.)

Next, we developed a division of labor between consultants and planners. The planning group would develop objectives, invite participants, and handle logistics. They decided their group would fade away in the conference and they would join in as participants.

We would design and manage the conference. At one point, we considered sharing design and management with the planning group. We decided, however, that these tasks belonged to us. Our job was to provide a safe environment in which people could explore new behaviors together, and that required control of the process.

OBJECTIVES AND INVITATIONS

The planners met three times—to set objectives, handle invitations, and plan conference logistics. They set as their conference goal "to bring together diverse stakeholders to search for common ground regarding the future of water quality on the upper basin of the Colorado River." The focus would be dialogue, discovery, and learning.

The group set modest expectations, realizing that agreement on actions might be unrealistic in such a high-conflict situation. They steadfastly avoided communicating that action items or a specific action agenda had to emerge. Instead, they committed to an open ended process.

Initiator: Regional planning agency responsible for state Water Quality Plan

Conference Task: Common Ground on Future of Water Quality Decision Making

Stakeholders: 48—Agricultural, Industrial, and Recreational Water Users; Local and Municipal Governments; Federal and State Agencies; Water Providers; Water and Sanitation Districts.

Length: Two full days and two nights

Place: Winter Park, CO

Facilitators: Bob Rehm, Rita Schweitz, Elaine Granata

The invitation itself was important because of the history of contention and litigation. The planners spent considerable time perfecting the invitation so as to communicate the inclusive nature of the conference and its goal of searching for common ground. At first they tried to save time by relying on written invitations. In the end, it took personal telephone calls to convince some key stakeholders that their presence was important. Personal contact from the start might have made some environmental and agriculture stakeholders more comfortable with the conference idea, thus increasing their participation.

READINESS AND POTENTIAL FOR ACTION

We assessed the "potential for action" by using the "four-room apartment" from Weisbord's *Productive Workplaces*. This illustrates how people move from contentment through denial and confusion on the path to renewal (See Chapter 9).

From the start we saw that water stakeholders were ready for renewal. The first sign of renewal was the formal request itself, which asked for an innovative approach to conflict resolution. Another sign was the willingness of adversaries to join in a planning group with ground rules and processes very different from past experiences.

During the planning, it became plain that after years of contention, law suits, and lots of money spent on the problem, there was a growing feeling that it was time for a new approach. People were dissatisfied with old ways. We believed the potential for renewal would be high.

THE SEARCH CONFERENCE HAPPENS

The Water Quality Search Conference proved remarkable in three ways:
1. Focusing on a complex issue of broad social concern;
2. Involving a wide range of organizations; and
3 Seeking common ground as a way to address the history of stakeholder contention and litigation.

A SOCIAL ISLAND

The Conference took place off-season at a ski resort condominium in Winter Park, Colorado, over two nights and two full days in early November, 1991. The setting was remote—"a social island" environment, and the 48 participants, virtually the only guests, stayed together the entire time.

We agree with Weisbord that it is not the number of hours and activities that count, but the "soak time." The history of this group made soak time on a "social island" critical. We met in a large open conference room with windows overlooking the mountains. Meals, informal get togethers, and living quarters were provided on site. People ate, drank, worked, and partied together. We stuck to our guns on a two night commitment from stakeholders and discouraged people from coming and going.

We created a temporary community where common ground and values could be explored many ways. The opportunity for people who had met only in court or across a formal table to experience each other in more human ways proved to be an important force for change.

SOCIAL ATMOSPHERE AND INCLUSION

We believe the opening moments of any meeting are critical. It is important to consider people's needs for inclusion. So this conference began with drinks and snacks, an opportunity for socializing, then a formal dinner. We seated people randomly at mixed stakeholder tables.

After dinner, a planning group member introduced the conference, reviewed the historical context of how it came to pass, and turned it over to us. We did an activity that got people walking around interviewing one another to find common ground themes about themselves. From the outset we sought to make sure people felt included, understood their roles and responsibilities, and began to open up to others.

FOCUSING ON COMMON GROUND

With contention and litigation as backdrop, we made a clear goal statement at the start: "We are here to search for common ground regarding the future of water quality decision making in the upper basin of the Colorado River." We made clear that the overall purpose would be dialogue, discovery and learning. It was important that we engage in a search for values and beliefs people could share. We said we thought that in a turbulent, complex environment, our ideals and values are what move people ahead.

So, we would build a common data base, interpret it together, and decide what (if anything) we would do. We were serious about the "if anything." In fact, resurrecting old debates and spending time on resolving conflict was not our purpose. We promised to intervene if necessary to cut off debate and get focused back on common ground. So a firm statement about common ground as a ground rule set the stage.

To provide a safe environment, we were strict at the beginning about structure, instructions, time commitments and a focus on common ground, not old wounds. (As we moved towards implications and action, we became more flexible in our management of the conference. And the group, as it discovered common ground, took more responsibility for its own learning and action. During the last third, the action phase, we became more facilitative than managerial.)

Throughout, we explained in detail the purpose of each activity and how it related to the conference goal. We used a modified version of the "funnel" approach recommended by Merrelyn and Fred Emery plus tasks from Weisbord's "future search" design. We would start with a broad emphasis on global environmental forces, narrowing to water quality implications. It seemed particularly important with a contentious group to discover early on how the demands of a turbulent external environment required them to pull together.

Below we describe each task, the content generated, and our own rationales and learnings.

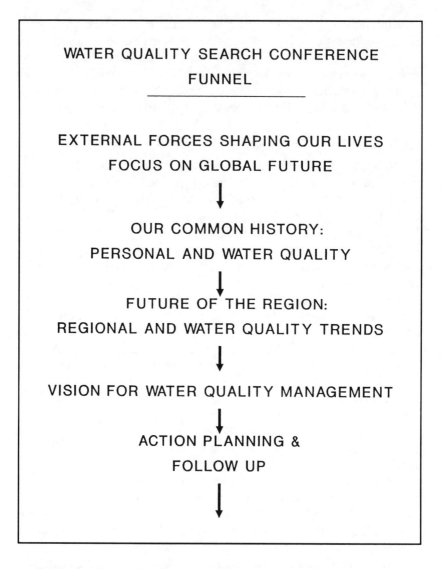

WATER QUALITY SEARCH CONFERENCE
FUNNEL

EXTERNAL FORCES SHAPING OUR LIVES
FOCUS ON GLOBAL FUTURE

OUR COMMON HISTORY:
PERSONAL AND WATER QUALITY

FUTURE OF THE REGION:
REGIONAL AND WATER QUALITY TRENDS

VISION FOR WATER QUALITY MANAGEMENT

ACTION PLANNING &
FOLLOW UP

Step 1. Identification of Trends andFforces

Identification of the trends and forces in the global environment that impact the stakeholders (the "L22"—see page 330, Chapter 28 for more detail), and formulation of probable and desired futures of this environment.

We used a modified nominal group technique to generate trends and forces. Each person privately wrote down some trends and forces they thought were important. Then we asked people to chime in publicly if they desired and we put their contributions on the wall. Almost everyone participated. Then we asked people to take markers and come to the wall to mark the trends and forces they considered "hottest." This activity encouraged a cooperative search for common ground and also created a climate of community in the room from the outset.

The most salient forces identified included federal regulations, population growth, the Clean Water and Endangered Species Acts, human resource needs, tax limitation, and increased demand on limited resources. There was both a sense of pessimism and challenge about these forces. The formulation of desired and probable futures occurred next in small mixed groups. By the end of these activities, a sense of community was developing in the group.

Step 2. Analysis of the common history of the participants

To highlight common ground shared by various stakeholders, we asked people to post personal milestones and milestones in the history of water quality over the last 30 years. One concern expressed by the planners was that people would not tolerate early attention to personal "non water quality" issues and concerns. But this reaction did not materialize. Personal milestone themes included family values, persistence, a sense of humor, public service, career, and a love of Colorado and its natural environment.

For water quality milestones, we also asked that they flag their "prouds" and "sorries." Their "prouds" included the control of water borne-infection, beginning to act on the degradation of the environment, and recognition of a current state of change and an opportunity to design a new system. The "sorries" included the degradation of the environment and the litigious relationships among the water interests.

The personal history activity in fact helped the group uncover individual experiences that made the search for common ground feasible. Regardless of their water stance, nearly every person shared a strong attraction to the Rocky Mountains, the Colorado environment, living and playing in the outdoors, caring about the environment, a high level of education, and enjoyment of life.

There was a strong sense of common values deep within the character of this group. And it was at this point we saw clear signs of the group's readiness to change their way of dealing with water quality. When one participant remarked that it was "time to change our ways," the whole group nodded in agreement. [EDITOR'S NOTE: A related discovery was made in the fishing conference reported by Dick Axelrod in Chapter 23, suggesting that "irrelevant" personal data may sometimes be central.]

Step 3. Stakeholder analyses of regional trends and issues

Following lunch on the second day, we moved people into stakeholder groups, and asked them to tell others in the room their perspective on regional and water quality issues. This analysis was the only task not done in mixed groups.

It was a unique opportunity for every stakeholder perspective to be heard, sometimes for the first time, within a facilitated, controlled process. Arguments and debates were not permitted. It was a time for listening and clarifying only. After this exchange, some stakeholders commented that this was one of the first times they had ever really felt heard.

To their surprise, there were many common issues that surfaced across groups. These included a sense of not having adequate money, feeling the oppression of federal regulations, and frustration with the lack of local control over water issues. This brought us to a turning point. Enough common ground had emerged to suggest moving beyond the modest expectations of the conference planning group. There was a sense of readiness in the group to explore a future vision.

Step 4. Identification of the desirable future for water quality management in the region

Now, mixed groups of stakeholders developed their vision of an ideal future. This turned out to be surprisingly easy to do. An "umbrella" consensus vision/mission statement emerged:

"Regional water stakeholders desire that water quality management be a collaborative process with a structure based on shared data."

The whole group identified the following major needs arising from this statement:

- A structure and process for collaborative decision-making about regional water quality management;
- All stakeholders sharing a common vision;
- An information management process to create a common shared data base;
- More education and information sharing;
- Legislative reform.

Step 5. Action planning and follow-up.

At this point, the outcomes had already surpassed anyone's expectations. It was not a matter of our suggesting action, but of facilitating so as to stay out of the way. On the morning of the third day, as several stakeholders ate breakfast together, one commented, "This must be the paradigm shift people talk about."

FROM IDEALS TO ACTION

Of 48 participants, 30 signed up to work on action groups—one to create a collaborative decision-making process and structure, a second to explore technology and information management systems that support collaborative decision making, a third to study educational needs, a fourth to find funding for recommendations that come out of the other groups' work.

The whole conference agreed to convene again in March, 1992 for two days. They set as goals even broader stakeholder participation, including the environmental community, and to begin to take actions recommended by the action groups. When the group was deciding on a site for the next conference, some people suggested a Denver hotel. Even the Denver people said, "No—let's go back to the mountains."

FACILITATION TEAM

The three of us had worked together on many projects over the past six years so we felt secure in guiding this diverse group through a challenging change process. We share several values, philosophies and beliefs that influence our conference facilitation:

- People make choices and become self-regulating when conditions allow;
- Our job is structuring tasks for people to do, getting out of their way, and using our facilitation skills to help all learn and discover together;
- Energy and commitment to action come primarily from the group not the facilitators; our focus is always the group, not us.
- We are dedicated to continuously assess the needs of the group in the here and now, make adjustments accordingly, and be flexible with time, tasks, and the personal needs of stakeholders.

CONCLUSION

At this point (December 1991), we can report that the task groups that emerged from the search conference are coming together to complete their work. The discovery of a shared vision and the number of volunteers for action task groups exceeded many peoples' expectations. It created an atmosphere of hope and encouragement at the close of the conference. Anecdotal feedback afterwards indicated that there is considerable energy to carry this spirit forward.

We believe five factors proved to be the keys to our success so far—solid planning, stakeholders ready for action, the funnel design, a strict adherence to common ground, and the "social island" environment.

We have evidence that the conference planted the seeds for a multi-organizational, domain based, collaborative water quality decision making process. Only time and the continuous commitment of this remarkable stakeholder group will tell. What we know for sure is that the search conference was an effective method for stimulating cooperative behaviors among a diverse, complex, contentious set of vested interests.

Update (June 1992)

The stakeholders are now calling themselves the Colorado River Headwaters Forum and are meeting regularly. They expanded their ranks to include environmentalists and other groups, agreed on a collaborative model for water quality decision making, and are now implementing their new model. We conducted a follow-up evaluation of the search conference six months later. Participants reported significant improvement in cooperation across stakeholder groups.

NOTE: The authors wish to acknowledge the special help of Merrelyn Emery and Marvin Weisbord, whose advice and encouragement were essential to our success.

ABOUT THE AUTHORS

Bob Rehm consults with communities, businesses, and organizations seeking renewal through participation and democratic values. He worked several years at StorageTek, a Fortune 500 manufacturer of information storage systems, where he led sociotechnical work design efforts throughout the company.

Rehm is continuing the application of the Future Search Conference idea to community issues, such as education, ecology, and human services. He is a certified member of Associated Consultants International (ACI).

Rita Schweitz provides management and communications training and organization development consultation to public and private agencies. She has worked in education, the criminal justice system, and the high technology sector. Schweitz is currently assisting a public school system to change from a traditional centralized system to a site-based management system and implementing work redesign at StorageTek.

Schweitz was the coordinator of the Water Quality Search Conference, providing the interface between the clients and the facilitators. She is a certified member of Associated Consultants International (ACI).

Elaine Granata is president of Patere Ltd., a firm that provides consulting in organization and management development and work redesign, including overseas in a multi-cultural setting. She also consults on sociotechnical work redesign for a hi-tech manufacturing corporation.

Granata has worked as a manager in both public and private sector organizations, is dedicated to community building and does volunteer work in corrections, international relations, and peace organizations. She is a certified member of Associated Consultants International (ACI).

CHAPTER 20

CONTEXTURAL SEARCHING
Cases from Waste Management, Nature Tourism, and Personal Support

Beth Franklin and David Morley

BETH FRANKLIN AND DAVID MORLEY between them have managed numerous search conferences since 1980. They have worked in every mode, with single organizations, advocacy groups, and referent organizations.

They believe that search processes are a major way to facilitate action learning, in particular among diverse parties seeking to act together within complex domains. Their preferred mode is "contextural" searching, a value orientation toward equalizing power and status among participants. Here, they differentiate this mode from traditional and radical approaches to searching.

They also present three "contextural" cases. One relates to waste management in Ontario, a second to nature tourism in the Windward Islands, the third to personal support for individuals who are developmentally handicapped. In two cases they have expert specialists providing needed information in real time, showing how this can be done to minimize dependency and maximize dialogue.

> The waste management case is especially instructive. The facilitators and stakeholder co-designers make the right strategic moves before and during the conference, and involve the appropriate parties. They are dismayed, though, when the initiating agency falls down on follow-up, reverting to old, short-term behaviour. The seeds for this mixing of paradigms exist in every conference. We have little control of such outcomes if those with the greatest stakes are unable to act on their own plans.
>
> Encouraging priority shifts responsive to a fast-changing world is a continuing challenge for those of us committed to discovering and acting on common ground. Franklin and Morley show us one way that "works"—most of the time. This chapter is adapted from a much longer paper. – MRW

INTRODUCTION

The concept of "issues without boundaries" is gaining acceptance in many different sectors in our society as we are challenged by complex problems that reflect global turbulence. Our current organizational paradigm does not have the built-in capacity to deal with such complex, interconnected issues. Here, we illustrate a mode of searching based on action learning, that we believe is useful under these conditions.

Action learning promotes the integration of all interests associated with a "metaproblem"—a tangled web of many related problems—that extends beyond existing organizational boundaries. These interests are, after all, "integrated in the workings of the real world . . . [requiring] . . . a change in attitudes and objectives and in institutional arrangements at every level" (The World Commission on Environment and Development, 1987:62). With an action learning perspective, we continually reframe issues and make new action plans.

Unfortunately, our society places severe economic, political, and cultural constraints on collective action in response to global issues (Morley, 1989). Existing institutional authority structures exert influence to maintain the status quo, reinforcing the old-style learning paradigm. This behavior only strengthens a confrontational attitude between mainstream organizations and countervailing initiatives. Crisis can often generate a climate that supports a greater acceptance for the new paradigm of participative, collective learning, when traditional, reactive responses are no longer seen as effective.

Contextural Searching

A *contextural orientation* aims to create a search conference that encourages learning to occur in the common ground of the problem domain — one that favors no group or position over any other. The name comes from the word "contexture" which means "the process of weaving parts into a whole" (Webster's Collegiate Dictionary, 1983).

Participants representing different interests create a shared perspective of the issues and move towards future action strategies that reflect their mutual understanding. We use the term "contextural" to differentiate this mode from two others that are more commonly used.

One mode is "traditional." It follows a consultancy model incorporating considerable guidance from the lead agency and facilitators. This orientation reinforces mainstream values that determine the power structure of a society (Brundage and Mackeracher, 1980).

A "radical" orientation, by comparison, creates a process that follows more closely a participatory research model. It usually involves support of a group or position countervailing to the establishment. It often leads people to create an advocacy style of process and alters social structures in ways that enhance both individuals and society (Freire, 1973; Mezirow, 1978; Baum, 1978).

A search conference's purposes, and its underlying values, determine which orientation is applied to the learning setting. Purposes and values profoundly affect the nature of the conference itself and the continuing action learning process (Franklin, 1989). Viewed in this way, a contextural search is not dominated by a single lead agency's objectives (i.e., traditional orientation) or those of a countervailing movement or group (i.e., radical orientation); instead, we use it to create interconnectedness among many perspectives. In short, the organizers are committed to creating common ground for action across the *whole* domain. Eric Trist (1985) encourages us to "be alert for opportunities and to *create new spaces*." The contextural search conference is a viable means for creating an alternative learning space. It enables:

1) the exploration of the critical issues associated with a particular metaproblem;
2) the formulation of new ideas, concepts, and values related to the critical issues; and
3) the development of a dynamic methodology that will accommodate this collaborative learning process.

Ideally, all searching *should* be contextural; however, traditional and radical forms of searching are commonly used. It is important in such conferences that we sustain the integrity of the search approach by being explicit about the way the process is oriented in relation to ideology, power, and control—and the limitations that these factors may impose.

Recognizing the inevitable role of ideology and power in the design and application of search conferences, we apply the term contextural to those search events that explicitly subscribe to action learning principles—a process owned by participants and aimed at empowering all the interests involved.

Contextural searching adapts search principles and methodology to the unique needs of a particular domain. In this way, connection with the context (stakeholders, natural environments, history, culture, social structures, and political economy) and a continuing emphasis on contexture (the weaving together of the parts) are inherent throughout.

Here we present three case studies that demonstrate the power, and limits, of contextural searching in three different domains of action.

THE DESIGN OF CONTEXTURAL SEARCH CONFERENCES

Regardless of the focus of the search, contextural conferences always reflect the same basic assumptions and minimum requirements for action learning:

1) the initiating agency(ies) take a broad-based, integrated approach to problem-framing;
2) awareness of the rate of change and uncertainty related to the problem setting;
3) the search conference is viewed as only one part of a wider action learning process (pre-conference and post-conference stages are also of critical concern);
4) initiators involve the full array of stakeholders in exploring the issue — the problem domain;
5) a locally-based group representing the key interests carries out the conference design and participant selection;
6) the conference aims to establish joint directions for continuing collective action;
7) the conference designers agree that the ideological and power structures inherent in the problem will be made explicit in search conference activities;
8) the parties commit to maintaining the domain process — an ongoing dialogue among existing organizations and emerging interests, networks, and groups.

Figure 1:   CONTEXTURAL SEARCH CONFERENCES IN AN ACTION LEARNING PROCESS

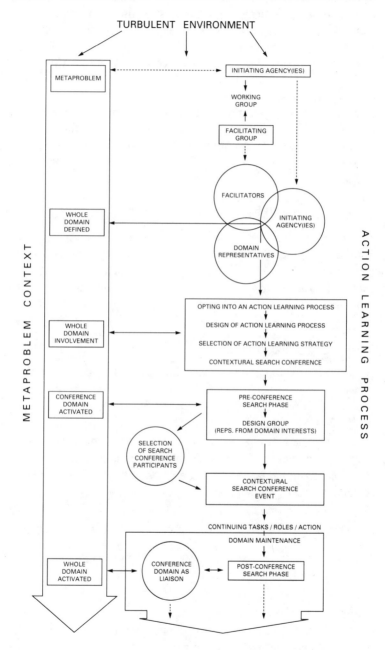

Adapted from : Franklin, Beth.
"Action Learning in a Multi-Organizational Context."
Unpublished Major Paper, Faculty of Environmental Studies,
York University, Toronto, Canada, June 1989, p5.

Figure 1 shows how contextural searching works within an action learning process. Although many of the above characteristics are common to search conferences in general, it is the combination of these elements that establishes an event as a contextural search conference. The application of these contextural search conference characteristics does not imply the existence of a single conference style. Many of these qualities demand the involvement of the participating groups as direct members of the design process.

The role of the outside facilitating team is primarily to guide the process on the basis of the underlying principles of searching. Perhaps the greatest strength of the contextural search conference is its capacity to build directly on the collective experience and needs of the different participating interests.

THREE EXAMPLES OF CONTEXTURAL SEARCHING

The three cases provide distinct examples of contextural search conferencing. These three problem settings are discussed because of their variety and because they reflect outcomes of an explicit attempt on the part of the authors to work with participants in continuing contextural search processes.

NOTE: In each case the external design and facilitating role was performed by a team from the ABL Group (Adapting By Learning), including the authors, based at the Faculty of Environmental Studies at York University in Toronto. We wish to acknowledge the role played by the environmental organization's consultants and the ABL team members in case one, the National Advisory Groups and Project Coordinators in each of the Windward Island countries for case two (a project funded by the Canadian International Development Agency), and our ABL colleagues and the project's Joint Design Group in case three.

CASE 1: FUTURE WASTE MANAGEMENT STRATEGIES IN ONTARIO

Metaproblem

In 1988 Metropolitan Toronto was approaching a serious waste management crisis situation. In response, a major Canadian environmental NGO (nongovernmental organization) decided to bring together representatives of the major waste management interest groups. A contextural search conference was organized to explore the potential role of recycling in Ontario's future waste management strategies.

Domain

To establish a contextural perspective the following interests were involved: municipal works officials, environmental groups, the recycling industry, waste management consultants, citizens advocacy groups, waste management planners, elected municipal officials, private industry, international technical consultants, and policy advisors for the Province of Ontario.

Domain Involvement in Process

This process was part of a long-established grassroots initiative to introduce recycling in Ontario. The lead agency, a well-established NGO, decided to invite international experts (from Germany, Austria, and the United States) to a conference to assist in setting up integrated recycling programs in Ontario.

In discussions with the ABL Group, the NGO recognized that a standard conference style, focusing on presentations by international experts, would not be relevant to local needs. Therefore, it was agreed to involve all of the domain interests in a participatory learning process.

Critical elements in the design of the contextural process included: (1) representing of key interests, (2) changing the role of the visiting experts, (3) linking with senior policy makers, including the Provincial Minister of the Environment, and (4) creating a continuing action learning process for the post-conference phase.

The Design Process

The organizers announced the change in the conference style to the participants *after* they had already registered for a traditional, lecture-style conference:

> "We have changed the format of the forum. . . to make the conference more interactive. These changes result from our experience that long, lecture-style sessions do not address participants' questions and needs. Instead, new small-group sessions have been designed to give you greater access to the technical experts and to allow you to discuss the international examples in the context of your own experiences."

Figure 2 summarizes how contextural search principles were incorporated into the new design. Small networking groups, made up of

**Figure 2:   DESIGN FOR FUTURE WASTE STRATEGIES
MANAGEMENT FORUM**

First Day

MORNING

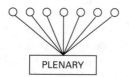

Networking Groups
(small group sessions on
 recycling interests, concerns,
 and priorities)

Plenary:
(international guests respond
 to networking groups)

AFTERNOON

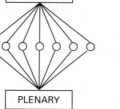

Continuation of morning Plenary

Networking Groups
(pose critical questions for
 recycling in Ontario)

Plenary:
(guests respond to networking
 groups' questions)

Second Day

MORNING

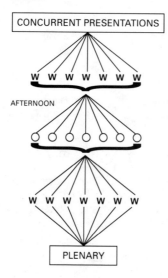

(presentations from guests)

Workshop Sessions 1
(focus on Ontario recycling
 – guests as resources)

Networking Groups
(development of action plans)

Workshop Sessions 2
(future strategies for recycling
 – guests as resources)

Plenary: "Future Directions"
(Comments and questions from
 workshops & responses from
 Minister of the Environment)

people from the different domain interests, met on three occasions during the conference to generate the questions and issues that would guide the process.

To establish the central directing role of the participants, the conference opened with networking group sessions. The issues raised were used to frame the experts' introductory statements in the presentation plenary that followed.

A second networking group session allowed participants to further develop their needs, to propose topics for the upcoming focus workshops that could assist them in addressing these needs, and to suggest the longer term actions needed in Ontario. The groups summarized their concerns and posed questions to an expert panel in a plenary that concluded the first day.

The second day began with the technical experts linking their areas of expertise to the issues identified by the networking groups. These areas of concern formed the basis for the succeeding workshop sessions that initiated the action phase of the search. This phase not only translated the energy and learning of the participants into an action mode at the conference, but also attempted to generate follow-up activities in the post-search conference action learning process. It was intended that the participants would take a new understanding of recycling back to their various municipalities throughout Ontario.

Using Workshops

Workshop sessions examined a broad range of topics that varied from highly technical to more process-oriented. Several workshops dealt with the integration of separate issues and one group chose to examine an international perspective to waste management. Such approaches to waste management demonstrate the contextural orientation of the learning process.

The networking groups met for the last time between the two workshop sessions. Information from the various workshops was shared, unmet needs were identified, and future options were defined (to be incorporated in the second set of workshops). During this final networking group meeting, space also was provided for the writing of statements and the posing of questions to the Minister of the Environment who, with the media, was invited to attend the final plenary.

At the closing session, the Minister expressed his admiration and support for the diverse parties who had come together because of their dedication to recycling as a significant waste management option. He supported the participative approach of the conference:

"It is time that we all break down the institutional barriers and strike out on a new path—one that will close the circle and eliminate the one-way, dead-end waste of our natural resources."

Discussion at the final plenary session was based on the assumption that the action learning process would continue. Participants were asked to generate follow-up activities and were given a form letter to be sent to politicians that communicated the need for all levels of government to take a stronger and broader approach to waste management. Conference proceedings represented a third form of continuing activity that would assist participants in transmitting their conference experience to their constituencies.

Outcomes/Continuing Action

At the conclusion of the conference many of the requirements of a successful contextural search had been achieved. What was required now was the commitment of the lead agency, which had retained full responsibility for extending the conference outcomes to a broader network. The ABL Group designed a post-conference phase that would have continued to involve the broader domain in policy and decision making processes in the various municipalities throughout Ontario.

Unfortunately, due to the demands of other environmental initiatives, the management group of the lead agency discontinued support for the recycling effort. The conference proceedings were not produced, there was no continued funding for follow-up recycling activities, and no staff member was given responsibility for waste management. In the words of a resource management consultant associated with the lead agency:

"[We] blew it. We had created an opportunity to accomplish unprecedented advances in the area of recycling and waste management in Ontario. Never before, anywhere in Canada, has such a diverse wealth of information and expertise in waste management been brought together to examine the various issues and possible courses of action. By not following through, at least with the distribution of conference proceedings to the participants, we have truly lost a great opportunity."

The contextural style of the post-conference phase had been suppressed because the control of the process was left with the lead agency that did not follow through with its responsibilities.

CASE 2: NATURE TOURISM IN THE WINDWARD ISLANDS

Metaproblem

Contextural search conferences were held in four Eastern Caribbean countries during 1991/92 (Dominica, Grenada, St. Lucia, and St. Vincent) as a crucial part of an overall action learning process relating to the national and regional development of nature tourism strategies.

The situation that led to each government participating in this project relates to the serious threat to Windward Islands' banana exports posed by the impending change in trade relations with Britain in 1992. This will lead to an even greater economic dependence on tourism. However, the potential for expansion in traditional tourism (based on sun and sand) is very limited in these countries, resulting in a growing interest in "nature tourism" (also called "ecotourism" and "green tourism").

This alternative form of tourism is based on the attraction of natural, cultural, and historical environments and attempts to balance the economic objectives of tourism with environmental conservation and cultural/historical preservation. Development of this "sustainable" form of tourism poses many problems—particularly to integrate existing local resources drawn from many institutions.

Domain

The domain interests brought together by the project to address this issue include the key governmental agencies (economic development, planning, tourism, agriculture, fisheries, finance, forestry), environmental and heritage groups, community organizations, women's and youth groups, farmers' cooperatives, and private business.

Domain Involvement in Process

The initiation of the action learning process came from key governmental agencies with direct interests in tourism—planning/economic development, tourism, and forestry. Senior officials and politicians played a part in developing and supporting a participatory multi-interest process towards the creation of national and regional strategies for nature tourism.

Although the ABL Group acted as catalysts, the process depended on the involvement of representatives of the domain. In each country, they were brought together through the invitation of the governmental body acting as the lead agency—either tourism or planning. An initial task was to form National Advisory Groups that would direct the process.

Each country appointed a local Project Coordinator to act on Advisory Group proposals, convene meetings, and maintain contacts with the Canada-based ABL team.

The open, participatory style was supported by organizations with statutory rights over tourism policy. They recognized that nature tourism involves many parties and that the project would provide a neutral, middle ground to search for collaborative frameworks for new national directions.

In this sense, the contextural form of the process allowed the political implications to be addressed by the full range of interests involved in exploring key issues_ e.g. environmentalists examining the validity of ecotourism as an economic development strategy; hotel associations incorporating environmental conservation into tourism strategies; and finance officials working with agricultural ministry personnel to support small rural businesses in the provision of local produce for tourist consumption.

Design Process

Search conferences were used by National Advisory Groups to draw together a wide range of interests to establish future directions in the project. The objectives of the search events were to:

1) develop comprehensive national perspectives on nature tourism;
2) connect this alternative approach to existing tourism initiatives;
3) examine the potential of an integrated nature tourism strategy as a basis for future economic development that is environmentally sustainable;
4) discuss the planning, design, and management needs of such an approach; and
5) advise on ways in which the project can assist in creating an integrated and ongoing planning capacity both nationally and regionally.

Figure 3 outlines the basic design that each country adapted to its own needs. Again, the search tradition of alternating plenary and small group sessions was used. Presentations (by local participants with special skills and experience) were used to provide a foundation for conference discussion.

The opening plenary was used to introduce the objectives of the nature tourism project, to assess the characteristics of the domain setting, and to demonstrate support of the process from a key national figure (e.g., a Minister of Tourism). Following the opening session, small

**Figure 3: DESIGN FOR NATIONAL SEARCH CONFERENCES
ON NATURE TOURISM**

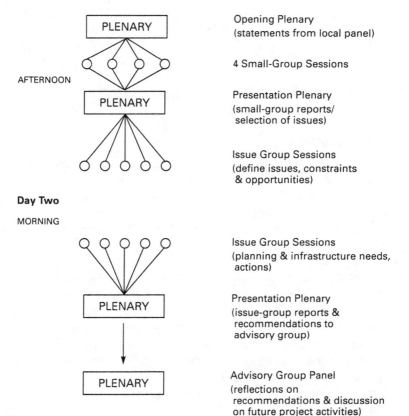

Day One

MORNING

Opening Plenary
(statements from local panel)

4 Small-Group Sessions

AFTERNOON

Presentation Plenary
(small-group reports/
selection of issues)

Issue Group Sessions
(define issues, constraints
& opportunities)

Day Two

MORNING

Issue Group Sessions
(planning & infrastructure needs,
actions)

Presentation Plenary
(issue-group reports &
recommendations to
advisory group)

Advisory Group Panel
(reflections on
recommendations & discussion
on future project activities)

groups scanned the problem context and generated their issues and concerns.

The small groups then reported summaries of their discussions in a plenary and key issues were selected by the participants to focus subsequent small group sessions. The "constraints and opportunities" phase of the search took place during these discussions.

The issue groups met again on the second day to integrate their ideas and concerns into a set of proposals for action in the wider project. These took the form of recommendations to the National Advisory Group to be carried forward into the planning and implementation stages of the process.

Outcomes/Continuing Action

This case provides a clear example of the role of contextural searching. The Windward Island events were closely integrated with an ongoing action learning process. Participants will continue to be drawn into the process together with a wider group that represents more fully the set of interests and organizations that will design and implement a new national strategy. Further search events will take place to sustain the domain activity. Each will be designed from within and will take a form related to particular needs as they are established.

CASE 3: PERSONAL SUPPORT FOR INDIVIDUALS WHO ARE DEVELOPMENTALLY HANDICAPPED

Metaproblem

This contextual search event held in October 1990, brought together 40 people who provide support for individuals who are developmentally handicapped. The objective of this event was to assist in the building of a network organization to link people engaged in personal support activities in a wide range of settings. This domain-based network would also provide a framework for the future stages of this action learning project.

The problem focus of this event was the need to address the boundary between the informal personal support movement and human service agencies that provide formal service for people with developmental handicaps. The action learning project aimed to create a space where the different perspectives on these boundary issues could find common ground. The purpose was to assist in building working networks that would cross social, institutional, and individual boundaries and to initiate tasks that had the capacity to continue after the project is completed.

Domain

The project domain included both formal and informal human service areas—human service workers, community workers, representatives from the Ministry of Community and Social Services of the Province of Ontario, consumers, advocates of personal support, and parents and friends of individuals who are developmentally handicapped.

Domain Involvement in the Process

An action research project had been in operation for over a year prior to this contextual search conference. An actionresearch approach was selected because of its capacity to create settings that encourage collaboration among individuals, groups, networks, communities, and organizations focusing on the vision and practice of individualized personal support—housing, education, work environments, and community involvement.

Therefore, the participants and the ABL research team became co-designers of the research process. The search conference was designed by ABL and a Joint Design Group involving key participants from a variety of backgrounds.

Design Process

Figure 4 shows how the search process was adapted to reflect the needs of the project, in particular, the contextual linking activities. On the first day, after an opening plenary, participants formed small work-

Figure 4: DESIGN FOR WORKSHOP ON PERSONAL SUPPORT FOR INDIVIDUALS WHO ARE DEVELOPMENTALLY HANDICAPPED

Day One

AFTERNOON

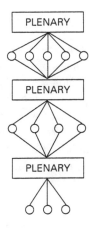

Opening Plenary

Small-Group Session 1
(definitions, issues, role of project)

Presentation Plenary
(group reports, development of common issues)

Issue Group Sessions
(reframe as collective issues,
  possible role of project)

Plenary
(issue group reports, definition & selection
  of action themes)

Action Groups 1

Day Two

MORNING

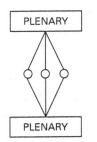

Plenary
(action group reports, re-examination
  workshop objectives & presentation
  by insider)

Action Groups 2
(designing of continuing project activity)

AFTERNOON

Plenary
(action group presentations, discussion
  and reframing of action plans)

ing groups representing the full range of interests. The emphasis was to define key issues of personal support and to establish the continuing role of the project associated with these concerns.

Each group then reported on the questions and issues in a plenary. An extended discussion followed in which the focus for a series of issue groups was developed. The intent was for participants to choose an issue group where they could examine a particular issue and generate follow-up actions that could be initiated by the project.

The schedule of the second day was changed significantly to respond to the expressed needs of the participants. (This is a common occurrence in the adaptive style of contextural searching.) The day began with a plenary in which issue group reports were followed by a discussion of action themes that could be used to extend the workshop's activity beyond the event itself.

Four action groups met until the early afternoon. Their presentations to the final plenary led to proposals for continuing activities to be picked up by the project. The workshop concluded with the participants identifying activities through which they intended to maintain contact with the project.

Outcomes/Continuing Action

The action themes identified in the workshop have all been sustained as major project activities. One theme—the design of an "umbrella organization" for individuals and interests associated with personal support—has become a central focus for the project. In the light of the sensitivities expressed at the search event, this organization seems likely to take a quite innovative form—very close to Trist's "referent organization" (Trist, 1983), the primary objective of which is contextural. This outcome demonstrates a major function of contextural searching—fostering ongoing interaction among domain interests in addressing long-term issues.

CONCLUSION

The three case studies help to demonstrate the capacity of contextural searching in different problem settings. The strength of this process lies in the principles and values that guide action learning and its ability to tap existing resources in a time of rapid change and uncertainty, complex metaproblems, and numerous constraints.

Each time contextural searching is used the methodology and design will adapt to the situation and be unique. What remains constant is the notion of a collective learning approach that can help organize an array of interests and resources to address multi-organizational dilemmas.

THE AUTHORS

Beth Franklin is a Research Associate and Fellow in the Faculty of Environmental Studies at York University and a principal of the ABL Group. Professional and research interests include planning and management in multi-organizational domains, educational design, international development, and social change. She has a particular interest in using the search methodology in ways that reflect action learning principles.

David Morley is Professor in Environmental Studies at York University. He has been involved in many projects that focus on the application of action learning to domain-based organizational change. An original member of York's ABL Group, he has recently coedited (with Susan Wright) a festschrift for Eric Trist—*Learning Works: The Search for Organizational Futures* (1989).

SEARCH CONFERENCES DESIGNED AND FACILITATED BY TEAMS THAT INCLUDED THE AUTHORS

BETH FRANKLIN

Executive Development and Training: An Action Learning Approach (Human Resources Division, Ministry of Health, Government of Ontario) – January 1992.

Metro Toronto and Region Remedial Action Plan Workshop – Towards a RAP Strategy (Environment Ontario and Environment Canada) – May 1991.

Personal Support for Individuals who are Developmentally Handicapped (Ontario Mental Health Foundation) – October 1990.

National Computer Conference – Barbados Microcomputer Network Project (MFC/CIDA) – October 1990.

Shaping the Future: Independent Living for Physically Disabled Persons (The Office for Disabled Persons/Cheshire Homes of London, Inc.) – October 1989.

Health-Environment-Economy: Strategies for a Sustainable Future (Health & Welfare Canada/Environment Canada) – May 1989.

Framework For Support – All Sites Search Event (Canadian Mental Health Association) – March 1989.

Research Futures in Environmental Criminology (Solicitor-General Canada) – October 1988.

Recycling: The Works (Pollution Probe Foundation) – May 1988.

Canadian Executive Service Organization (CESO) Future: A Search Process (Canadian Executive Service Organization) – May 1987.

Anishnawbe Health Conference for Native People (Native Community Branch, Ministry of Citizenship and Culture, Government of Ontario) – January 1987.

DAVID MORLEY

Community Development Strategies (Social Planning Council of Peel, Ontario) – May 1990.

Lake Ontario Organizing Network (Pollution Probe) – September 1988.

International Aid in the Context of Changing Environments (CIDA) January 1987.

Education/Training for Microcomputers and Development in Barbados (CIDA/Govt. of Barbados) – April 1985.

Education and Training for Children & Youth Who Are Mentally Handicapped (Metropolitan Toronto School Boards) – January 1985.

Education/Training for Development in St. Lucia (CIDA/Govt. of St. Lucia) – May 1984.

Planning for the Developmentally Handicapped (Ministry of Community & Social Services, Govt. of Ontario) – December 1982.

Energy Futures for St Lucia (CISA/Govt. of St. Lucia) – June 1982.

Food Futures for Mexico (National Autonomous University of Mexico) – May 1982.

Day Care in Saskatchewan (Dept of Cooperation, Govt. of Saskatchewan) – June 1982.

Demonstration Search Conference (with Eric Trist): Global Futures Conference, Toronto – July 1980.

PART 5

REFERENT-ORGANIZATION CASES

Introduction

> "The model for the peaceful arena is the dialogue. By talking together, out of disagreement we create some synthesis beyond our individual views. Dialogue, or conversation, is democracy." – Sam Keen (1991)

Here are three cases, two from Australia, one from the United States, on conferences in what Eric Trist calls "referent" organizations. This useful term describes entities whose membership cuts across wide networks of people with similar interests. Where the "domain" is a conceptual amalgam of related interests, "referents" have a life of their own. They represent the first wave of a new organizational form—a formal coalition of individuals and organizations—providing a roadmap toward a "politics of interdependence" based on dialogue. Crombie and Davies take us behind the scenes into major issues in Australian society—people with diabetes in one case, a government forum for the aging in another. We see the issues, the conferences, and sample the actual reports written for the sponsoring agencies.

Dick Axelrod's case, though shorter, shows the use in the United States of a future search to establish a new referent organization, the

United Sport Fishermen/Freshwater, an amalgam of private and public interests. He also makes a surprising discovery—how personal histories helped parties in conflict to discover common ground. – MRW

CHAPTER 21

EMPOWERING PEOPLE WITH DIABETES
The Australian Diabetes Foundation

Alastair Crombie

T HIS CASE STUDY shows how search conferences can be used to address social issues involving many diverse parties. Crombie first describes a set of unmet social needs. Then he considers Eric Trist's work on "domains," and of Geoffrey Vickers on "appreciation." He uses these concepts in simple, practical ways to design a conference that has had major impact in Australia on the care and treatment of people with diabetes.

He alternates theory with practice, gives examples of related social problems, and shows the actual output of various parties to a conference sponsored by the Australian Diabetes Foundation, a "referent" organization for this issue.

Those interested in community, industry-wide, international or other forms of inter-organizational development will find this a valuable introduction to how this methodology could advance their purposes. — MRW

INTRODUCTION: CONTEXT FOR THIS CASE STUDY

In rich societies, health is a complex and expensive matter. Once the province of doctors nurses and hospitals, it now includes a galaxy of professions and labyrinth of specialized centres. Many people agree that health systems might be more manageable if their emphasis shifted from curing illness to preventing it, but there is a colossal gap between rhetoric and reality. It is hard to wrestle resources from the vested interests of the curative system and re-allocate them to prevention.

The treatment and care of people with diabetes (*not* "diabetics") represents a small part of health systems. It also presents significant opportunities for prevention and self-management. Lifestyle factors associated with diabetes are now better known, and new technologies help sufferers manage their own condition.

To maximize prevention and self-management, the knowledge and skill once monopolized by doctors, drug companies, researchers, and allied health professionals has to be pooled and communicated to the public and to people with diabetes. This is not the health professionals' traditional role. Some react as though empowering patients would undermine their own status and "professional standards." Each professional group has its own conception of the key issues, and a commitment to defending its own patch. Many patients, on the other hand, have a good deal invested in their dependency, and collude with health professionals to support the "medical model."

It was against this background that the Australian Diabetes Foundation (ADF) asked for a national search conference on "diabetes health care and education in Australia." I propose to use this search conference as a case study in helping a complex national organization fulfill its role to educate and influence its stakeholders. I will do this by interpolating relevant extracts from the conference report with my comments on the underlying theory and practice of searching.

WHY A SEARCH CONFERENCE? – BACKGROUND ON THE PROCESS

The search conference is especially suitable for dealing with future-oriented problems and challenges—what Trist and others call "social ecology." Referent organizations address matters of common concern or "domain development" (Crombie, 1985). Trist identified searching as one of four "processes of domain development," the others being networking, referent organization design, and "flocking."

My impression is that most search conferences are run for individual organizations—private, public, or community—in the service of strategic planning. Searching practice, as a result, is most influenced by searches for a single organization's future.

In this case study I would like to reflect on how searching also can make possible a more complex task: forming a domain to link diverse organizations for common goals.

There are infinite ways to organize people and purposes. Every choice that we make, however, limits our alternatives. If we institutionalize a "nine-to-five, Monday to Friday" work week, for example, we cannot also have good cheap weekend services. Social change and social reform are ways of trying to match human time and energy to our most desired ends. The result is inevitably a set of compromises.

Beyond Networking

Networking, a distinct social phenomenon, goes hand-in-hand with organizational society. We join or create networks for significant concerns that lie beyond the capability of single organizations. Some networks are formally sanctioned; others operate covertly. They are a prime means by which existing organizational boundaries and responsibilities are challenged.

Networks often fall apart. Those that survive eventually institutionalize and re-shape the social fabric. As a rule, networks do not have conventions or Board meetings. They tend to use informal media like "flocking" and newsletters. They may consider a search conference or other strategic planning process when the need is felt to create a referent organization—an ongoing node from which the network can exert itself more purposefully.

Trist argues that advanced western industrial societies "are weak in their inter-organizational capability." We badly need institution-building between organizational domains to cope with complex social issues. He sees such domains as "functional social systems which occupy a position in social space between the society as a whole and the single organization." (Trist, 1983:270).

This "gap" in the social field arises from turbulence—rapid economic, technological and social change. Turbulent social fields are characterized by intractable, complex, long term meta-problems, the solution for which is beyond any single organization.

Examples: the interpenetration of organized crime with legal and financial institutions; reversing land degradation while maintaining rural economies; increasing self-reliance in health care without distorting the system to favor the rich.

Such metaproblems do not yield readily to single efforts, even the might of national governments. They require voluntary negotiations and collaborative agreements among diverse agencies.

Inter-organizational domains can be both cognitive and organizational structures. Restructuring our conventional way of seeing things—a cognitive shift—can be decisive in forming a new domain and organization to embody it.

Closing the Gap—Examples

Following Australia's National Economic Summit in 1983, for example, industrial leaders perceived a serious organizational gap. Thus was born the Business Council of Australia—a Council of the Chief Executives of Australia's largest private companies, to parallel the capability of the trade union movement.

Recently the BCA, along with government and the Australian Vice Chancellor's Committee, helped establish another national body—the Australian Business/Higher Education Round Table—to strengthen ties between business and higher education.

Sometimes new organizations emerge before they are fixed conceptually. Take for example the idea of package holidays in the travel industry. Airlines, transport operators, insurance companies, hotels and motels, tourism authorities and entrepreneurs had to discover their common interests before the packaging of holidays could become an art form and customers pay a single fee.

Similarly, the concept of "open learning" is now taking hold, long after the establishment of the British Open University and the introduction of the elements that make open learning distinctive—self-directed learning, open access, distance education, use of radio and television, computer and video-based technologies, home or work based study with short intensive residencies, local tutors, study leave as a condition of employment, provision of child care.

In this field both cognitive and organizational structures are still evolving, although the contrast with traditional schools is now unambiguous.

What makes inter-organizational domains crystallize is many people recognizing and joining forces to pursue a shared purpose. Their activities become "directively correlated" (Sommerhoff, 1950, 1969) They interact selectively to bring them closer to their shared purpose.

Each organization usually continues to play its original role in other systems. However, they can be re-configured by what Vickers (1965) calls an act of "appreciation" —anticipating the benefits new relationships could bring. This phenomenon has evolved naturally for a long time, often without the benefit of self-conscious domain-building processes.

New Forms Are Essential

Emery and Trist (1965) showed a quarter of a century ago that organizational survival and effectiveness in turbulent social fields requires new forms of collaboration by former competitors, under the rubric of shared values and a negotiated order.

Since then it has become more evident that managing in turbulent times requires vast re-configurations of many social domains. Moreover, the time-scale for working through to new arrangements has been cut down by the closing of critical "ecological traps" (Vickers, 1970). We need many more collaborative domains than we have—in every area of human concern—and we need them fast.

The search conference is an ideal tool for accelerating the identification and development of new domains. Put another way, the search conference is a very effective way of *testing* new domain appreciations, for not all candidates can succeed. A carefully planned search conference can "reality test" the hypothesis that a new inter-organizational domain is needed. If people affirm the need, they can make good progress, right then and there, in developing its operating framework.

I suspect that this has been an implicit objective in many search conferences. I believe now that we need to make it more explicit and to examine the impact of this purpose on search conference design and management.

Getting "Close to the Customer"

This case study of the Australian Diabetes Foundation is an instance of a particular new form of domain development among far-flung organizations with overlapping purposes. The ADF search for new directions and new standards in health care and education for people with diabetes took *the needs of these people themselves* ('PWD's') as its starting point and focus. Its central thrust, one might say, was "getting closer to the customer," one of Peters' and Waterman's criteria for excellence in America's best run companies (Peters and Waterman, 1982).

It has since become the subject of many works under the generic label "service management"—the philosophy, values and techniques for customer focus and high quality services.

My impression is that this movement originated with progressive private firms in competitive industries. Jan Carlzon of Scandinavian Airlines is one of its folk heroes. His recipe for "over-turning the pyramid" is widely-emulated (Carlzon, 1987).

The success of organizations that put customers first is now acknowledged in the human services sector—health, education and welfare—and by public utilities that supply water, electricity, telephones, and postal services. It is widely recognized that to achieve customer focus in human services we need to re-configure existing organizations and create new service domains among them.

The medical, health and education services for diabetes over the past 25 years were created by established institutions in separate States. It is no surprise to find that they are fragmented, uncoordinated, and sometimes in conflict.

They also share with health systems the "illness" paradigm and its institutional expression, the medical model, by which *experts* isolate, diagnose, treat, and cure disease. In short, the needs of the customer can easily drop from sight.

THE AUSTRALIAN DIABETES FOUNDATION

To understand the relevance of this conference, you need to know how the Foundation evolved and its importance to diabetes education in Australia.

The Australian Diabetes Foundation is what Eric Trist (1983) calls a "referent organization," one that provides leadership to a broad spectrum of institutions and interests with reference to a particular social issue. ADF has 13 member organizations—medical, scientific, educational, consumer and community groups involved in preventing, detecting, and treating diabetes. Its board represents them all, and its paid staff works to focus its members' diverse efforts on their common purposes.

Diabetes Mellitus (DM) is a treatable chronic disorder. Persons with diabetes experience complications that often are preventable with adequate care. However many Australians do not have access to helpful information. To remedy this, The Diabetes Federation of Australia (DFA) was formed in 1968 from various State Associations.

In June 1983, the DFA and the Australian Diabetes Society united to become The Australian Diabetes Foundation. The first Diabetes Health Education Committee was set up in 1975 to counteract inadequate resources and the growing realization of the benefits of self-management in diabetes.

In 1981 the Australian Diabetes Educators Association was formed to give professional recognition to personnel and programs in disciplines concerned with diabetes care and education.

Trends in self blood glucose monitoring, early detection and treatment of diabetic complications, and dietary advice, require uniform standards and guidelines. Shifts from hospital to community settings, and a greater emphasis on preventing diabetes are increasingly desired.

Patient care and professional education programs throughout Australia are largely uncoordinated, duplicating resources because program and resource evaluation are lacking. Not all Australians with diabetes are being reached. The incidence of this condition is increasing with unacceptable levels of morbidity and mortality.

The Australian Diabetes Foundation (ADF) has provided new opportunities for cooperation between medical, scientific, educational, consumer and community groups. The ADF's 13 members now include eight State and Territory Associations, the Australian Diabetes Educators Association, the Australian Diabetes Society, the Diabetes Research Foundation of WA, the Juvenile Diabetes Foundation of Australia, and the Kellion Foundation.

To explore national opinion and consensus, Dr. Pat Phillips, Convener of the Health Care and Education Committee of ADF chose the search conference methodology. We invited people with diabetes, parents of children with diabetes, diabetes health care professionals, Diabetes Association administrators, community, government and pharmaceutical industry representatives. This conference was the first national attempt to increase the efficiency and effectiveness of diabetes education and care in Australia.

CONVENER: AUSTRALIAN DIABETES FOUNDATION

Conference Task: Improving Diabetes Care/Education in Australia

Stakeholders: 36 Participants—People with Diabetes, Parents of Children with Diabetes, Nurse Educators, Doctors, Allied Health Professionals, Dietitians, Pharmacy Industry, Administrators

Length: Two-and-a-half days, May 21 to May 23, 1990

Conference Manager: Alastair Crombie

Planning the Conference

The conference was planned in meetings with the Director and other representatives of the Australian Diabetes Foundation (ADF). I asked them to clarify what they wanted to achieve. We sent the following statement to participants three weeks before the conference with an outline of the search process.

Search Conference Aims

1. To make an assessment of the current "state of the art" in diabetes care and education which will illuminate both the strengths and the deficiencies of the present system;
2. To explore:
   - the need for improved coordination at the national level of provisions for diabetic health care;
   - how the need for national guidelines might best be developed; and
   - how such guidelines could best be implemented and monitored.

DIABETES FOUNDATION CONFERENCE PROGRAM

DAY 1

5:00	Introductions, Conference Briefing
5:30	Small Buzz Groups: "Who's Who in the Zoo"
6:30	Dinner
7:40	Introducing Participants and Their Expectations
8:00	Brainstorming our History: "Where Have We Come From?"
9:00	Close

DAY 2

8:30	Plenary: Interpreting Our History
9:10	Plenary: Future Scan Brainstorm
10:00	Small Groups: Major Trends; Current Strengths and Weaknesses (Includes Morning Tea)
11:45	Plenary: Reports
12:40	Lunch
2:00	Five Group Tasks:
	1. Major Trends Synopsis
	2. Needs of People with Diabetes
	3. Strengths and Weaknesses Synopsis
	4. History—Lessons Learnt
	5. Goals for an Idealized Future

4:00	Plenary: Task Groups Report
5:30	Break
5:35	Plenary Statements: "To move toward our agreed goals, we should. . . ."
6:00	Individuals Cluster Statements
7:00	Dinner, Music by Stewart Munro

DAY 3

8:30	Briefing on Clusters, Working Towards 7 Task Groups
9:10	Task Groups:
	1. PWD – Education/Care Standards
	2. Professional Education
	3. Community Education/Awareness
	4. Data/Research/Evaluation
	5. Lay Organizational Issues
	6. Delivery Structures
	7. Goals/Strategies
11:45	Plenary: Task Group Reports and Recommendations
12:30	Lunch
1:15	Reporting Continued
2:30	"What we have learnt, where do we go now?" Interest Groups: Nurse Educators; Lay Organizations; Allied Health Professionals, Doctors, AMES
3:00	Plenary: Reports and Recommendations
3:45	Timetable for Report Delivery
3:50	Acknowledgments
4:00	Close

Conference Briefing – The Opening Session

As Conference Manager, I outlined the aims again at the start for confirmation. There was a request to add a third aim—

3. To examine the needs of people with diabetes.

This was agreed to, and the work done on this issue was to have a significant impact on the whole. Next, I outlined the three main stages of the conference:

A: Exploring and pooling information and views about the various contexts that plans for future directions must take into account:

(1) OUR PAST – Where have we come from? Tasks: Gain an appreciation of the history and development of diabetic health care and

education, and discover what lessons it offers for the future. Recognize the continued value of some components, and that others are now dispensable.

(2) OUR FUTURE – What sort of world are we moving in to? Task: Identify major trends and developments in society anticipated over the next ten years which may affect diabetes health care and education in the future.

(3) OUR PRESENT SITUATION – What are the major strengths and weaknesses of current systems and strategies for diabetic care and education?

B: Identifying critical issues to be addressed in making plans for the future.

C: Making judgments and recommendations about future directions and strategies.

The conference structure was illustrated as follows:

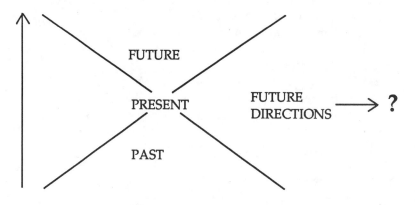

My comments: "This conference is yours. The outcomes are your responsibility, and will belong to you as a group. Judgments will be made and shared by you. As facilitator I accept responsibility for helping to create and sustain conditions for effective and productive work."

Search Conference Implications

In the ADF search one objective was to view diabetes care and education through the eyes of *all* stakeholders. Early in the conference participants were asked to take stock of the present system:

"Identify the main strengths and weaknesses of the present system of diabetic health care and education."

Among the main WEAKNESSES identified were the following:

- poor GP care
- reliance on out-dated medical model
- crisis management rather than prevention
- professional health training geared to illness management
- Federal/State/Local government conflicts in health policies
- no clear standards for professional care of patients
- variable quality in standards of educational materials, programs and professionals
- failure to adequately influence government policies
- lack of management evaluation
- GP's and other health professionals unaware of resources available for diabetes
- no model for integrated health care of diabetes
- no prevention plan
- fragmentation of services—duplication of efforts
- conflicts between health care providers
- fragmentation of funding
- maldistribution of care
- lack of sharing of knowledge
- lack of resources, poor distribution, and inefficient use
- failure to tailor information and care to needs of specific groups
- lack of defined national standards
- lack of definition of GP's role in DM care

Among the main STRENGTHS identified were:

- developing team approach
- evolution of diabetes education systems and professional skills
- unification of groups and associations within ADF and desire for standardization
- this forum
- ADF unification
- diabetes centers training for outreach activity
- endocrinologists recognize and show willingness to modify their role in traditional medical model
- diabetes care teams
- recognition of inadequate education
- better consumer liaison with government, professional and lay organizations
- holistic approach to health care and commitment to community based health care
- multidisciplinary orientation
- formation of relevant national bodies for professionals
- search conference—contributors from wide spectrum

The search conference also addressed itself to an effective health care and education system for PWD's in which meeting *their* needs was the primary criterion. Although implicit in the objectives, this particular search focus actually crystallized at the point that people with diabetes, or parents of children with diabetes, met as a group to summarize and report to us on their needs.

As often happens when we pay attention to others' views of the world, it was not just the words that made an impression, but the power of the voices that spoke to us. The lists that follow include the words. You have to imagine the music.

Summary of the Needs of the Person with Diabetes

[This report was prepared only by people with diabetes and parents of children with diabetes. I have summarized several sheets of newsprint with some of the highlights.]

There were eight major issues. (1) "Training/competence of health professionals" included raising the profile of diabetes training in colleges, and keeping medical officers updated on diabetes management. (2) "Emotional and social support" included the need to consider family psychology in insulin-dependent families, and freedom from guilt for those needing help.

The group asserted as (3) "Rights of all people with diabetes" more medical support for self-managing their condition, the truth about their condition at all times, lower costs for PWD's and families, the rights of aborigines to control their own health care, and research into the needs of the 80 percent of PWD's not represented in the conference.

They called for (4) "Standard procedures following diagnosis" like integrated health care for PWD's, recognizing the special needs of children with diabetes, easy access to experts despite social and geographic isolation, education as essential to treatment in the first 12 months, and continuity in the expert team.

They required (5) "Clear definitions" of the kinds and frequency of periodic checks, and of the differences between diabetic groups–juvenile, adult, teenage–with varying diagnoses. They specified (6) "Standards for food/nutrition" in food labeling, guidelines and measurements, and for (7) "Public awareness/information" to overcome community misunderstanding, and finally a statement that (8) "Cure and prevention is the ultimate goal."

This obviously is a wish list more than a strategic plan. Yet it had the effect of forcing us all to focus on the customer, and to view the world from the perspective of people with diabetes rather than the almost-taken-for-granted perspective of the health system. There is an emotional dimension to appeals for "perspective transformation" that can only be stated authentically by those our systems are supposed to serve. I confess that this session was not pre-planned, but emerged in the conference as a most obvious step to take. As such it highlights that designing a search is only half the job. Staying alert to what actually happens during the meeting is equally important.

If the PWD's report crystallized the focus of the new domain we were searching for, it was the reflections of the occupational interest groups that put substance on how to bring this new domain into being. Here one finds expressed the need to weave together more completely the many strands of activity that are part of diabetes health care and education. One significant proposition to emerge was the desire to overcome the barriers between medicine and the other main players. More, there evolved a shared recognition of the need for deeper collaborative relationships all across the field.

INTEREST GROUP REFLECTION AND RECOMMENDATIONS. WHAT HAVE WE LEARNED? WHERE DO WE GO NOW?

Here I have summarized some of the many learnings and future proposals of each stakeholder group.

NURSE EDUCATORS were cheered by the unification of ADF, the common goals of many different groups, the realization that outside bodies are willing to help, and of the power of the search model for learning. They realized the need for more liasion with lay organizations, a full time National Education Coordinator, and for forming a Health Care and Education Committee.

DOCTORS learned the great value of multi-disciplinary inputs and ongoing mutual collaboration. They supported a National Coordinator for standards of health care and education, a diabetes database, a Health Care and Education Committee of ADF with a core of lay, allied health professionals, educators and medicos. They recognized that lay organizations had a role in health care and education rather than relying only on providers, and offered to discuss the Search Conference report at the Royal Australian College of General Practitioners.

ALLIED HEALTH PROFESSIONALS cited how effective the search conference was for reaching consensus despite initial reservations, acknowledged associated areas/health problems as part of diabetes management, validated a holistic approach to PWD's and their families, rather than just treating the disease, appreciated telling others what they were about, seeing people willing to be accountable, and networking with other health professionals. They saw a future for a watch dog group to ensure follow up, affirmed their personal commitment to act in their own areas, and to continue conferences/networking and to be a resource to ADF.

DIETITIANS supported the proposals of nurse educators and doctors, considered the conference part of a peer review process of their work that demonstrated areas of deficiency and need for improvement including communication with the providers and consumers of diabetes care. They also realized that many diabetes-related initiatives by the Dietitians Association of Australia were not known by people for whom they were designed.

An INDUSTRY GROUP from Ames Pty Ltd. commented on the usefulness of the Search Conference and the need to keep working together, and observed that the pharmaceutical industry does much market research that could be tapped into.

SUMMARY: THEORY IN ACTION

I want to summarize by showing how this search conference functioned to move toward Eric Trist's five "aspects of domain formation," integrating people, ideas, institutions, and social needs in a way that had never been done before in Australia.

Trist's aspects are:

1. Making a shared *appreciation* of the "metaproblem;"
2. Acquiring an acceptable *identity* for the domain;
3. Setting an agreed *direction* for a development pattern into the future;
4. Overall *social shaping* as regards boundaries, size, etc;
5. Evolving an *internal structure* from stakeholder accommodation (Trist, 1983).

The first ADF search conference objective—"to make an assessment of the current 'state of the art' in diabetes care and education"—made the conference's task of *appreciation* quite explicit. As the flip-charts indicate, this was a marked success.

There also are signs of progress on domain identity, future direction, social shaping, and internal structure. Many of the conference recommendations now have been implemented in some form. Clearly the search process is especially suited to the inter-related questions of appreciation, identity and direction, and one should expect that more detailed planning, social shaping, and institution-building will occur—

preferably by processes sanctioned by the conference.

None of this can happen without a broad "appreciation," the discovery of common ground among diverse stakeholders. The search conference is uniquely suited to achieving this goal, probably in a way no other method can.

REVISITING VICKERS

Geoffrey Vicker's seminal study of policy-making has influenced all of us involved in developing search conferences. I find it a useful reminder to look again at Vicker's own account of "appreciation," lest we minimize the importance of this concept in managing under conditions of rapid change.

"An appreciation," wrote Vickers, "involves making judgments of fact about the 'state of the system', both internally and in its external relations. I will call these reality judgments. These include judgments about what the state will be or might be on various hypotheses as well as judgments of what it is and has been. They may thus be actual or hypothetical, past, present or future. It also involves making judgments about the significance of these facts to the appreciator or to the body for whom the appreciation is made. These judgments I will call value judgments. Reality judgments and value judgments are inseparable constituents of appreciation.

"Appreciation manifests itself in the exercise through time of mutually related judgments of reality and value. These appreciative judgments reflect the view currently held by those who make them of their interests and responsibilities, views largely implicit and unconscious which none the less condition what events and relations they will regard as relevant to them, and whether they will regard these as welcome or unwelcome, important or unimportant, demanding or not demanding action or concern by them. Such judgments disclose what can best be described as a set of readinesses to distinguish some aspects of the situation rather than others and to classify and value these in this way rather than in that. I will describe these readinesses as an appreciative system." (Vickers, 1965)

THE CHALLENGE FOR SEARCH CONFERENCE MANAGERS

Appreciation is intrinsic to search conferences. We do it at every step, interpreting external and internal environments, looking at the past, projecting probable and desirable futures, and identifying key issues for future action. Often, however, appreciative processes are dominated by conventional thought-ways and mind maps. Excavating these out of the "implicit and unconscious" so that people know better why they do what they do, is a worthwhile achievement. Sometimes a search conference manager is tempted to settle for this.

When the search aims to explore creating a new inter-organizational domain, however, such curtailing of aspiration is not appropriate. In these cases we need to be more explicit about the critical nature of the appreciative process. Trist asked, "'Can we improve the work of appreciation? Can we learn to speed it up?" I think the answer to both questions is "yes," but we do not yet have reliable processes.

How can we work on this? I suggest that we look more closely at group composition, the design of "scanning" and "scenario" phases, and our responsibilities as search managers in fostering appreciation. The best antidote to conventional wisdom is a broad cross-section of stakeholders, and tasks that make explicit all of their world views, needs and aspirations.

ABOUT THE AUTHOR

Dr. Alastair Crombie trained as a sociologist, with special emphasis on organizational behavior and planning. He is now an adult educator on the staff of the Centre for Continuing Education at the Australian National University, Canberra. He has designed and managed search conferences for more than 20 years, more recently on major environmental and agricultural issues—e.g. rodent plagues, the forest industry, agricultural extension, feral animals, and drylands agriculture. He is married with two teenage sons.

CHAPTER 22

SETTING NATIONAL
AND LOCAL PRIORITIES
Australian Consumer Forum for the Aged
Alan Davies

T his report provides an unusual behind-the-scenes view of
planning processes in a government agency. It details
the adaptation of search processes to national planning
in an agency of the Australian government. The Consumer
Forum for the Aging is a "referent organization" bringing
together diverse organizations and stakeholders. This effort
is especially interesting for its strategy: parallel conferences
in eight regions, involving 120+ people, resulting in regional
priorities AND a national agenda on issues of aging.

More, Davies carries on the action research tradition. He
writes a narrative account of the process and outcomes—a
practice common among Australian search conference
managers. He shows what was done, how it was done, what
the issues and dilemmas were, and the output and possible
uses. Note the overlap in priority issues selected in eight
separate regions, despite some differences in facilitation and
timing.

This account is adapted from the final report. — MRW

"PROCESSES DEVELOPED FOR SEARCHING ARE EXTREMELY POWERFUL FOR OTHER OBJECTIVES..."

"I use the developing theoretical base as a guide, and operate out of 'common sense' judgments about what is possible given the organizational realities. Turbulent environments create the need for participative planning based on open systems thinking. Given this, there are likely to be many planning tools that respond to this need, and the Emery Search Conference is but one, albeit one which has an excellent theoretical underpinning.

"We need to distinguish between Search Conferences and Search Processes. Many of the processes developed for searching are extremely powerful in the pursuit of other objectives such as priority setting, team building, and problem-solving. They are a reality-based means of locating any activity in its broader social context, in making values explicit, in reducing the propensity to fall into the wasteland of fight-flight.

"These national conferences might be called by some 'search conferences,' by others 'priority-setting workshops.' The name does not matter to me. However, the processes used, that I picked up in learning to run search conferences, are very powerful, reliable and reproducible for me as a practitioner, and for the clients, reality-based.

"Australians don't like to play games, they resent being manipulated. I find many people are very wary of the word 'search,' as it has been identified with the 'black plastic and baby oil' activities of the past.

"In that climate, you start with a skeptical group who signal in advance they will be outside the door at the end of the first session if they don't see positive evidence of something constructive emerging. My experience of the last 5-10 years is that people are convinced by the reality of the process and one's preparedness to explain the rationale for the process along the road. You will see some of this in the report."

Alan Davies

SPONSOR: THE OFFICE FOR THE AGED, AUSTRALIA

Conference Task: Setting Local/National Priorities on Aging

Stakeholders: Members, Consumer Forum for the Aged—Returned servicemen and women's organization; care-givers' organizations; councils for the aging; Country Women's Association; Aboriginal Aged groups; Alzheimers Associations; Ethnic organizations; Trade Unions; Pensioners' associations; Superannuees associations.

Length: One-and-a-half Days

Place: Eight sites, regional – Average group: 15 persons

Date: March 4 to April 4, 1990

Conference Managers: Alan Davies (6 sites), Merle Rankin (1), Glen Watkins (1)

SUMMARY

Early in 1990 The Office for the Aged decided to assist the eight State and Territorial Forums in the planning and conduct of their work over the next 12 months. The Office contracted Norsearch to help plan and manage a series of one-and-a-half day workshops and to report on the outcomes and the processes used. The objectives were four fold:

(i) Develop a group identity among Forum members.

(ii) Determine issues of high concern to Forum members.

(iii) Determine priorities for action for each Forum on a 12 month time scale.

(iv) Develop an action plan and strategies for future work on these issues by the Forum.

It is the contractor's view that we met the first three objectives. Each Forum has begun developing action plans, even though in several States the meeting was shorter than planned.

The more important question is whether group cohesion improved and continues as a result of the workshop. That must be judged by Forum members and Department staff who can make before and after comparisons.

This report contains (1) a description of conference processes and how they contributed to the development of group identity while generating information, understanding and decisions; (2) views on the Forums' future development; (3) each Forum's four priority issues; (4) my comments on the content issues raised.

THE PROCESS—GENERAL POINTS

The essential workshop task was planning and priority setting, using the Search Conference as a tool.

This approach has two essentials:

- Planning is set against the future social, political, environmental and technological context.
- It is participatory in at least three ways. All participants are encouraged to contribute their own knowledge and experience; they decide

what, if any, outside expertise they need; and they decide the directions and priorities.

A common reporting format was sought to enable interstate comparisons. However, some differences result from modifications made to process or questions in light of our developing experience and differences in style of the three facilitators.

Each facilitator managed the process through a series of questions, tasks and negotiations that participants worked on in full session (plenary) or in smaller sub-groups.

The subject matter was supplied almost entirely by the participants. On rare occasions they called on departmental officers or other experts where they lacked knowledge or information. The only input from facilitators was to explain the process being used from time to time. The intent is for participants to:

- Set priorities against some realistic view of what the 1990's are seen to hold.
- Understand the values, commitments and view of the future of fellow Forum members. This reduces misunderstandings between Forum members and they are better able to pursue joint purposes over distance and time.
- Become committed to workshop outcomes.
- Remain active and alert during long work sessions.
- Believe their expertise is recognized and used.

The process is not aimed at a consensus view of the future, simply at members knowing each others' views. It is likely that the process produces some convergence, simply because all are forced to look at the perspective of others and consider new information. What follows is a general overview, then comments on specific workshops.

DETAILED EXPLANATION

1. The Overall Workshop Logic

This diagram was given to participants and displayed on the wall as a "road map" to be followed. The facilitator outlined the logic and detailed steps, working back from the selection of priorities.

At the end a "notional" timetable was displayed. The actual schedule depended on the completion of tasks along the way.

Those tasks or questions feeding into the circle aim to achieve three objectives:

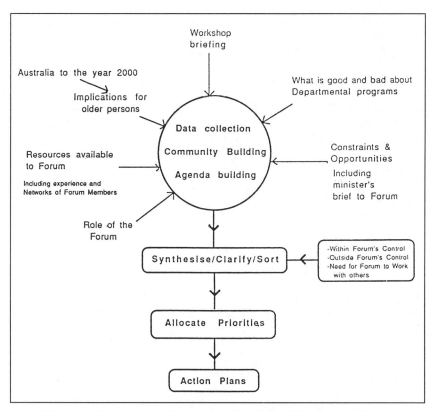

Figure 1: Consumer Forum for the Aged (Workshop Logic)

- A common data base amongst participants, expanding the range of information they can use in their planning.
- Collecting this data so as to build trust and common purpose amongst the participants.
- Using the whole diagram at the start to negotiate an agreed agenda.

Tasks coming out of the circle were used to narrow the focus to an informed selection of priorities.

2. The Role of Specific Processes

A) BRIEFING. The facilitator explained the conference logic and negotiated additions/deletions to the items feeding into the circle. Participants were told that while content could change, the process by which tasks were dealt with was the facilitator's prerogative.

Participants readily understood and negotiated the program using the workshop-logic diagram.

B) INTRODUCTIONS. Forum members introduced themselves, outlined their personal experience with issues related to older Australians, and listed relevant networks to which they belonged. Objectives of this stage were to:

- Make members aware of each others' resources.
- Provide recognition for Forum members' experience and, if necessary, get their burning agendas on the table. Otherwise, they might divert the workshop by pushing these agendas at inappropriate times.

C) FUTURE SCENARIO. The underlying theory for the scenario building was outlined as follows with the aid of Figures 2 & 3.

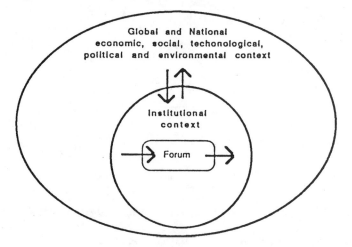

**Figure 2: The Place of Forum Within
the Broader Social Context/System**

It was pointed out that the Forum's issues sit within a broader institutional context that influences what each Forum can achieve. Further, this institutional context sits within a broader global and national economic, political, technological, environmental and social context. This in turn determines in large part what can be done by our institutions.

Our starting point was the outer circle, the broader context, and the prediction of what it holds for Australia. Only after that do we hone in on implications for older Australians and finally for the work of the Forum.

The scenario was built on the assumption that many factors combine to create the context that determines what is organizationally, socially and politically possible. The scenario was then constructed by attempting to predict the factors that will have significance at the time under consideration (see Figure 3).

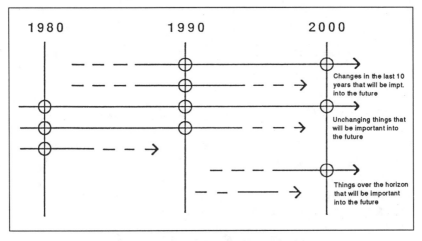

Figure 3: Logic for Brainstorming

It was suggested that one could arrive at these factors by brainstorming answers to three questions and selecting those the group believes will be most important over the next decade.

QUESTION 1. What changes have you seen over the last 10-15 years that you believe will be important into the future? Technological, social , economic, political, religious, environmental, international, national, regional.

QUESTION 2. What unchanging things do you believe will be important into the future?

QUESTION 3. What things over the horizon do you believe will be important into the future?

These activities generated many items. For example:

- Increased medical knowledge, leading to increased human survival, leading to an increased percentage of aged persons in the population;
- Increased periods of time in ill-defined roles, leading to increased alienation amongst older people;
- Increased inflation;
- Increased availability of education, particularly at the post compulsory level;
- Increased use of expensive medical technology;
- Increase in the number of nursing homes and hostels;
- Increase in world travel;

- Increased Asian influence on the world and Australia;
- A breakdown of rural communities;
- Closing of government facilities in country areas;
- Deterioration of the environment;
- Increased cultural change;
- Decrease in older people's income.

Forum members were then divided at random into two or three groups to answer this question:

QUESTION 4. Which six of these do you believe will be of most importance for older Australians over the next decade.

The number six was arbitrary, but deliberately small to give some focus to the scenario and prevent people from avoiding argument and conflict by simply making a long list that means very little. It was pointed out that at this stage smaller sub-groups could more easily discuss important issues than the larger plenary. In earlier workshops groups also were asked to list the implications for the Forum's work. Later this was done in plenary. In Western Australia participants also were asked to provide a quality of life statement.

D) IMPLICATIONS FOR THE FORUM. As groups reported their items, the facilitator combined them into one list. Each item then was screened, since some might have little direct bearing on the Forum's work.

E) CURRENT DEPARTMENTAL PROGRAMS. Next each forum focused on the Departments' programs. Where necessary a departmental officer outlined the programs and answered questions. Then Forum members brainstormed the following:

QUESTION 5. Are there any issues in relation to the Department's Program that the Forum might address?

Items raised in the subsequent discussion were recorded on three sheets of butcher's paper under these headings:

- Those that are going well.
- Those that are not going so well.
- Any gaps that should be filled.

It was pointed out that programs that are running well often do not attract attention and might wither if not recognized and protected.

F) ROLE OF FORUM. A departmental officer outlined the Forum's role and answered questions.

G) IDENTIFYING THE ISSUES. This session's objective was to identify no more than four items for primary attention during 1990. The purpose was to narrow the task to a manageable size and ensure some agreement on the relative priority of tasks.

Using data generated in the workshop, and minutes of previous Forum meetings, the facilitator identified 12 to 20 potential issues for 1990. This list was presented on a white board so that it could be amended during the discussion. People were told that until now we had recorded items not subject to alteration in a non-erasable manner on butchers' paper for ease of reference and to assist in preparation of a report.

The facilitator read out each issue and its sub-issues. During an hour or longer discussion items were added, amalgamated, and/or renamed.

For example, in the A.C.T. "discrimination" and "attitude change" were combined; and in Victoria a new category "Continued personal growth" was coined to include "education," "recreation," "self help groups" etc.

H) ESTABLISHING THE TOP FOUR PRIORITIES. This task was tackled three different ways.

1). Forum members were given 100 votes to allocate on issues according to their priorities. In the first vote, members were asked to distribute the points according to what they saw to be the absolute priorities for older Australians, regardless of the Forum's brief. Votes were tallied and displayed by number of people voting and number of votes cast for each issue, e.g. 5/55 means five members allocated 55 votes to this issue.

This vote allowed members to assess the importance of issues regardless of their relevance for Forum and Department programs. Without this step, subsequent votes could become muddied on this distinction.

2). Next, Departmental Officers weighted each issue on how much influence they thought the Forum had over that item, using a scale from one (virtually no influence) to five (high influence). Ratings were discussed, justified, and if necessary altered.

In the Northern Territory, the department's budget allocated to each of these areas was also rated—as Nil, Low, Medium or High. In the A.C.T. other factors like availability of resources and the extent to which other groups dealt with those issues adequately, also were considered.

Members then allocated 100 votes to items they believed it would be most fruitful for the Forum to put its energies into over the next 12 months. In early workshops this vote was disclosed after the negotiating exercise that followed. The purpose was to heighten awareness of matters over which the Minister, and hence Forum, have some control or influence.

Interestingly, preferences changed markedly between these two votes, usually as potential leverage by the Forum was seen to be increased. For example, in South Australia "accommodation" went up from 90 to 130 (leverage 5) and "economic security" went down from 90 to 32 (leverage 2).

3). Forum members next identified their top four priorities and divided into four groups. Each group also came up with its four top priorities. Then, the four groups were combined into two groups and the process repeated. Next, the negotiation continued in full plenary, often by means of formal debate, until all had arrived at four priority issues.

Any attempt at amalgamation of issues was resisted, in six out of the eight cases successfully. While three or four top priorities often duplicated some of the top six from step two, sometimes an issue that had little support in the first two rounds made the top four as a result of argument and discussion.

Voting by numbers allows one member who feels strongly enough about an issue to catapult it into the top four by allocating all 100 points to it. Thus, the final decision was based on negotiation where a majority was required to carry the day.

I) ORGANIZATION OF THE FORUM AND DEVELOPMENT OF ACTION PLANS. Before setting priorities, the Forum Chairperson, workshop facilitator, and departmental staff agreed to transfer management of the process from facilitator to Chairperson once the four priority issues were identified, and this was done.

In all cases the Chairperson decided to establish separate "Core Groups" around each priority, with the expectation that groups would work on the issues between Forum meetings and report to back to each Forum. Next, each group met separately to clarify the content of their issue. This was then reported and discussed in plenary. The small groups then developed strategies for working on their issue before the next Forum meeting.

At the hand over, the facilitator asked the Forum to consider the characteristics of effective work groups:

- They have an agreed and understood task. (After identifying four priority issues, the task was agreed but needed more definition by the group.)
- The group had the resources to carry out the task. (A Departmental Officer outlined resources available.)
- The group has an agreed way of proceeding. e.g. Appointment of convener; dates of meetings; division of the task; means of communicating; face to face; tele-conference; fax, etc.

In the time left, the Forum worked on action plans under the direction of its chairperson and with help of departmental officers.

In general, members self-selected into groups based on experience and interest. The point usually was made that members could work with more than one group. However it was expected that the core group formed the quorum for each group's operation. Geography also was recognized as a problem.

Workshops varied slightly:

- In total time, and in allocation to tasks. Some groups took no overnight break;
- Later workshops were changed based on experience;
- There were three facilitators;
- There were many different departmental resource staff, at State or Territory and National level;
- The Chairperson was different in each State and Territory.

The main variations were:

- After Perth, facilitators made more explicit reference to an open systems approach. See Diagram 2;
- In Perth more time was devoted to gaining the full Forum's commitment to a detailed definition of the four priority tasks;
- In Perth members were asked to develop an overall "quality of life" statement early, and a "value statement" for the issue they elected to work on over the next 12 months;
- As time went on, more attention was given to the involvement of the State based departmental staff in workshop management and action planning;
- The extent to which, and the way in which, the action plans were developed.

J) COMMENTS ON THE PROCESS. Prior to the workshops, some people expressed concern about the ability of Forum members to concentrate for one to one-and-a-half days. In the event this was not a problem. Many participants already had been meeting or working for several hours before their workshop. It is the facilitators' experience in many workshops that attention is not an issue at any age if the people work on issues of their own making.

The real test of the workshops' value will be the extent to which each Forum achieves its objectives over the next 12 months. Any judgment about how the workshops helped achieve these objectives will be highly subjective. Many management decisions are based on a similar mix of the subjective and objective.

3. Major Issues

Mid-way through each workshop the facilitator identified major issues facing older Australians over the next decade based on the data generated to that point and from the minutes of previous Forum meetings.

This list of 12 to 20 items was presented on a white board and amended over the next hour or so by Forum members in the light of discussion.

A heading for each issue attempted to capture each Forum's major concerns, and subheadings elaborated the main theme.

These categories are not mutually exclusive. They represent one way of slicing the cake of aged persons' issues. However, they do reflect the Forum members' emphasis and perspectives. They appear under "Issues" in each State and Territory report. For example "dementia," "care-givers" and "support" have a common core of concerns but each title gives a different emphasis.

Another example relates to the issues around rural isolation, variously aggregated under the headings "rural isolation," "regional isolation," "distribution of services." One potential confusion is different meanings attributed to "accommodation" and "housing."

To the lay person, some Forum members, some Department Staff these terms are used interchangeably. Yet they have very different policy implications for the department.

While the facilitator tried to capture the Forum's intentions, inevitably categories reflect his/her own conceptualization of issues. This was modified in part by the subsequent discussions. Most sub-headings, however, are a straight transcription of terms used by Forum members.

4. Top Priorities

The Table opposite summarizes priorities in each conference, ranked one to four. This is intended only to give readers of this book a feel for overlaps and differences between conferences—it is not intended to be an accurate summary of content.

5. The Future

The planning workshops are simply one event in each Forum's life. Their success will depend on cooperation between the Forum, each State Secretariat and the National Office for the Aged. This requires understanding the roles, responsibilities and constraints operating on each and how they are interdependent in achieving the overall objectives.

The effective on-going life of each Forum will depend at least on the following:

PRIORITY	TERRITORY							
	NEW S. WALES	SOUTH AUST.	QUEENS-LAND	WEST AUST.	VIC-TORIA	TAS-MANIA	N. TERR.	ACT
ACCOMMODATION	3			2	1	2	1	
HACC'S	4	3	3		1		2	
CARE-GIVERS/RESPITE		2	4	3			1	
HOUSING/ACCOMODATION		4	1					
CONSUMER RIGHTS						4	4	
PHARMACEUTICALS						3	2	
VOLUNTARISM		1						
SUPPORT	1							
ASSESSMENT				1				
RIGHTS	2							
SERVICE DISTRIBUTION			2					
PERSONAL GROWTH					2			
INFORMATION/COMMUN.				3			4	
QUALITY OF LIFE							3	
DEMENTIA								3
NURSING HOMES/DISCHARGE							4	

- The extent to which Forum has agreed priorities, and the resources and strategies to meet them. They have the priorities and sufficient talent, energy and commitment to make it work if the necessary support of the Department is forthcoming and the Minister is seen to give serious consideration to their recommendations.
- The ability to maintain the momentum between quarterly Forum meetings. This depends largely on the work of the State Secretariats and their relationship with the chairperson. They will have to be the organizational glue.
- The ability to maintain a national cohesion and relationship with the minister that does not reduce the State Forums' autonomy and professionalism of State Secretariats.

Based on my observations during the workshops I sense that some attention will have to be given these matters. Firstly, the State Secretariat was not always a full partner in planning and managing the workshop, although this improved as time went on.

If this is true then there is no guarantee that the State Secretariat's understanding of the priorities, or of the way ahead, matches that of the Forum or the National Office.

There are understandable reasons for this. The timing at the start of the year, and the advent of the election; uncertainties about who would service the Forum in each State; no prior meeting between the State Secretariat and facilitator; no role for the Secretariat in the workshop; the imposition of a planning workshop against the wishes of some States; the anxiety of the federal office about the successful outcome.

So there is a danger that the game plan remains in Canberra rather than with, or shared with, the Forum and the State Secretariat.

These issues need to be checked as soon as possible and become agenda items for the next national meetings of the Secretariats and of the Forum.

The broader society keeps changing and so will the issues of older Australians. It is important each year that each Forum undertakes a similar planning process to keep up with these changes, for members to keep in touch with each others' changing views, and to integrate new members or Secretariat staff.

Therefore I recommend that the Office identify or develop staff competent to conduct planning conferences annually. Perhaps some State Forum members might wish to develop such skills. This could be an item for the national meetings.

I also would like to blow away once and for all the myth that older people cannot concentrate for more than one or two hours. All of us have difficulty sitting and listening to talk about matters that are not of riveting interest to us.

However in these workshops, where participants are all actively working on their own issues, the length of working sessions is not an issue. This was demonstrated during March and confirmed what was learned years earlier by the NSW Office of Aged Services when two-day conferences of 12 hours a day were conducted with high levels of participation and activity throughout.

The major problem of these workshops was too little time for action planning, not Forum members staying awake and involved.

6. Comments on the Content

While it is not the facilitator's business to be concerned with workshop content, inevitably she/he takes away a view of how participants viewed the issues and possible directions.

The following, for what it is worth, are what Alan Davies saw emerging from workshops he managed. The issues taken up are not limited to those that fall within the responsibilities of the Minister for Housing and Aged Care. Issues of aging fall across many portfolios and government levels. Perhaps the Minister should be negotiating with his colleagues to develop an expanded role for the Office and Forum and if necessary its relocation.

FIRSTLY, the Forums recognized that the major societal factors determining the course of events for older Australians over the next decade were:

1). The increasing proportion of aged in the total population. The likelihood that the economy would be struggling over the period ahead, not growing at the same rate as the percentage increase in the numbers of aged persons. (This would lead to a reduction in per capita government expenditure on aged services, increased pressure on voluntary services and pressures to do away with the compulsory retirement age and with taxation rules punitive to retirees.)

2). The number of two-income and single parent-single income families would continue to increase (reducing the time those with dependent children could devote to voluntary community activities or supporting aged parents, relations, neighbors and friends).

Coupled with (1), this would pressure voluntary services to expand through increased coordination of existing agencies or by involvement in voluntary service of more able bodied community members who do not have dependents.

3). The cost and ease of volunteering is increasing while discretionary income is falling for those on fixed incomes.

4). There will be continued pressures to reduce hospital beds and occupancy time, making it harder for older people to get elective surgery, that might enable them to live independently for longer. This will accentuate the lack of convalescent facilities that leads older people to return home unable to cope, lose confidence, have accidents, and prematurely lose their independence.

5). The information and communication explosion will continue. This will accentuate the current information overload that older Australians experience, pressures multiplied for those becoming confused.

The answer is not access to more information, but rather access to face-to-face advice on making sense of overwhelming information. The problems are many—medication, finance, accommodation and availability of services.

6). The number of Australians on superannuation will increase and impact on retirement towards the end of this decade. Some pension costs will shift to the private sector. There will also be increased electoral pressures to treat pensioners and non-pensioners "even-handed" in matters of taxation and fringe benefits.

7). Problems of medication for the aged and particularly the confused and lonely aged would continue to increase as medication became increasingly complex and loneliness more prevalent.

SECONDLY, the major concerns that emerged for older Australians and their care-givers over the next decade were:

Support for the care-givers of the frail aged; income security; accommodation; the accessibility of face-to-face advice; remaining independent as long as possible; and a growing sense of hostility towards the aged from younger Australia, contributed to by the media.

Access to facilities and programs that support continued personal growth and a reasonable quality of life.

The right to live a dignified life, as physically and mentally active as body and mind will allow.

THIRDLY, given the above, the things that Forum members considered governments should do were:

1). More formalized arrangements for respite care that allows the large and growing numbers of care-givers some control over their own lives.

2). Coordination of services within and across the levels of government and the non-government sector. Working towards a one stop shop and a single point of contact for services and advice. Strengthening of HACC.

3). Advisory services on all matters effecting the elderly—finance, medication, availability of services, rights.

4). The concept of Neighborhood Care (based on the idea of Neighborhood Watch) that keeps a caring eye on the old, and particularly those living, in the community alone. Meals on wheels and domiciliary nurses were currently seen as providing aspects of such a system, a system which could be built upon.

5). Higher priority for hospital treatment that keeps older people independent.

6). A review of dementia and the implications for accommodation and the situation of care-givers.

7). Some system(s) that reduce over-medication and incorrect medication. The concept of Neighborhood Care could identify and help in problems arising from confusion. The pharmacist could be assisted in providing feedback to the doctor and the patient, for example with computer programs that retain the patient's history, drug interactions and, more importantly, with public and professional sanction to play the role.

8). Greater support and encouragement to programs that encourage older Australians to remain active physically and mentally and involved with others, e.g. activity groups, gentle exercise routines, group housing, university of the third age.

ABOUT THE AUTHOR

Alan Davies lives at Rosebank on the North Coast of New South Wales. He is Associate Professor in the Office of Deputy Vice Chancellor and Chief Executive Officer on planning matters and new projects, University of New England, Northern Rivers. From 1970 to 1990 he was part of the Emery group at the Centre for Continuing Education at the Australian National University. He has managed more than 100 search conferences in the last 20 years, many of which, he notes, "failed to meet their primary organizational objectives. . . but had one consolation in that they have been rich learning experiences for all involved."

CONFERENCES MANAGED BY ALAN DAVIES

Industry Futures
Restructuring of Trade Unions (9 conferences)
Program Evaluation (5)
Organizational and Sub-Organizational Futures
    —public, private, community (60+)
Curriculum Review (2)
Organizational Amalgamations (3)
Community Futures (4)
Priority-Setting Workshops (15)
Multiple Searches—parallel groups (3)

CHAPTER 23

PRESERVING FRESHWATER FISHERIES
United Sport Fishermen
in the United States
Dick Axelrod

T HIS CHAPTER HAS TWO PARTS. The first is an excerpt
from a trade journal news story on a conference that
united seemingly-polarized interest groups—an increasingly familiar story. The result is a new referent organization
representing the interests of freshwater sport fishing.
However, there is more. Reflecting on the experience, Dick
Axelrod is struck by how personal histories buried in the
unconscious of many participants had shaped their interest
in sport fishing. Ultimately it led them to come together on
environmental concerns.

This linkage between our inner and outer worlds represent
for me an important frontier in searching. The environment is
not just "out there." It exists, in some personal form, in every
one of us. This subtle linkage only becomes obvious when we
notice it, as Dick Axelrod has done here. — MRW

FISHING TACKLE INDUSTRY PERSPECTIVE

"According to a Gallup survey, 60 million Americans enjoy some
leisure time fishing. While a once-a-year angler may not be concerned
with protecting water quality or maintaining quality fishing resources,

many in the industry are. Until recently, there was no one organization to answer this need.

"In September 1989 more than 50 spokespersons representing segments of the sport fishing industry—manufacturers, charter boat captains, writers and publishers, and the angling public, launched United Sport Fishermen/Freshwater.

"The meeting was hosted by the American Fishing Tackle Manufacturers Association. It provided a platform for discussion of prominent issues impacting the welfare of freshwater fisheries in various regions and nationwide. Bringing together representatives of so many different groups that had never worked together before, had the potential for disaster. So AFTMA asked Dick Axelrod to design and facilitate the meeting.

"In the past, each fishing organization made decisions regarding industry issues as a single body. There was no unified voice. 'Just getting them to listen to each other was a major undertaking,' said Dick.

"First participants identified those forces that have historically affected fisheries and their use. Then, after examining current problems, the groups began to identify issues of major concern to the future of sport fishing. It is around these issues that a national constituent coalition will be built."

(The above excerpt is from "AFTMA Kicks Off USF/Freshwater," *Tackle Times*, the newsletter of the American Fishing Tackle Manufacturers Association, Volume VII, Number VIII, Oct. 1989.)

SPONSOR: AMERICAN FISHING TACKLE MANUFACTURERS ASSOCIATION

Conference Task: To Establish a New Organization

Stakeholders: Business—Retailers, charter boat captains, manufacturers (15); Sports groups—Salmon Unlimited, Trout Unlimited, Walleye Unlimited (25); Consumer/political groups—National Wildlife Federation, Isaac Walton League (5); Academia and Media (5).

Length: Two Days

Place: Chicago, IL

Conference Manager: Dick Axelrod

DICK AXELROD'S OBSERVATIONS

I want to emphasize the power of having people record their personal histories and tap into their deepest values in addition to exploring the outside environment.

Earlier I had helped to develop a group called United Sport Fishermen/Saltwater (USF/Saltwater), to bring sport fishing interests together and represent their views to Congress. They were primarily concerned about commercial tuna nets that also caught game fish and were destroying the sport fishing population.

The group had fishing tackle manufacturers, charter boat captains, magazine writers, and anglers. The initial meeting was attended by the Under Secretary of Commerce and a subsequent meeting by representatives from the State Department.

I facilitated the organizing meeting for this group prior to reading about search conferences but intuitively used some elements, enabling people with diverse interests to come together around a common cause—protecting the environment and the habitat. Many had predicted it could never happen.

As a result of this success, a decision was made to form USF/Freshwater. This group also had diverse interests who did not believe they could tolerate being together in the same room. Having now read Chapter 14 of *Productive Workplaces*, I decided to explore the past, present, and future with the freshwater groups. IT REALLY WORKED.

People from all over the country who initially did not believe that they had much in common found that they were facing similar issues. Anglers from the Midwest, and from the state of Washington who thought their problems were unique learned that all faced similar issues.

Two things stand out. What brought people together was their concern for the environment and protection of the fishing habitats. Many believed that for fishing to remain a viable sport the environment had to be protected, programs such as catch-and-release had to be instituted, and the fishing habitats had to be maintained.

However, this second conference reached a deeper, personal level in exploring the past. Many of the men talked with great emotion about what fishing meant to them as children—a place and a time alone with their fathers. This experience with their fathers ranked among their most positive early memories, a place where father and son could relate to each other. To them, maintaining good conditions for sport fishing meant preserving a place for others to have this relationship and was part of a legacy that they wished to hand down to their children and their grandchildren.

Both saltwater and freshwater groups achieved common ground in the need to protect game fish. However, the second conference had an added positive dimension. It brought people together at a much deeper level through their personal histories and deepest values, a powerful and memorable experience for all of us.

THE AUTHOR

Dick Axelrod, principal of Axelrod and Associates, Inc., a Chicago management consulting firm, has more than 20 years experience consulting with organizations that seek to address critical issues through empowerment and organizational teamwork. Dick has served as Co-Chair of the Illinois Quality of Life Council and as Regional Chair and Peer Review Committee member of Certified Consultants International. He also has been an adjunct faculty member at Loyola University. His clients include Ford Motor Company, Harley-Davidson, R. R. Donnelley and Sons Co., and Helene Curtis Industries. Dick holds an MBA from the University of Chicago.

RELATED COMMUNITY DEVELOPMENT CASES

Introduction

> "Those of us living in the 21st Century will have to adjust to the reality of interdependence—global, national, personal—whether we like it or not and whether it happens through conscious policies or painful resistance. The paramount issues of human survival require us to move beyond narrow factionalism to a politics of interdependence."
> – Craig Schindler & Gary Lapid (1988, p. 210)

The two chapters in Part 6 share many common features. The first is how they got here. Cliff McIntosh and Pat Tuecke each attended talks I gave in the late 1980's on my adventures with future search conferences. Both identified strongly with the values and processes, recognizing close links to their work in other corners of the world. Each sent me versions of the material that follows.

Both chapters describe highly-successful community building in cultures different from the one I know best. These programs have origins in the 1960's—the same period when Tavistock and NTL Institutes were experimenting with the methods that most influenced me. Each process represents a core technology for a community development organization, Quetico Centre for McIntosh, the Institute of Cultural Affairs for Tuecke.

Each model integrates humanistic values, group processes, and action research methods. Both Quetico and ICA devised planning methods remarkably congruent with the Emery/Trist searches and the Lippitt/Schindler-Rainman collaborative communities. They are alike at the dynamic level with every model I have seen. Both clearly involve everybody in improving whole systems. Given the results, I believe that these models also fulfill Emery/Asch's conditions for dialogue (Chapter 5). Yet neither explicitly uses the global future as its planning context. In that sense they are not search conferences. Yet, the ICA model, 30 years in development, is used effectively to establish common ground in both communities and corporations. And Quetico Centre traces its journey to common ground back to the Danish folk school movement more than 150 years ago.

Despite working in entirely separate venues, and with no awareness of each other's work, these folks have evolved strategies, planning methods, and conference designs remarkably similar to search processes. I believe there are many more models, processes, and cases floating out there, each the tip of a very big iceberg.* If I'm right, we have a great deal to learn from one anothers' experiences. More, we have an opportunity to create together a more unified systems development practice equal to our aspirations and profound technical, economic and social dilemmas.

Despite great success over many decades, these processes are not well understood in the upper echelons of government, education, business, labor, health care. In every sector we rely too much on technical or political models that don't work very well in situations of high conflict or misunderstanding. Here we have further evidence of processes that *can* work if we learn to manage our anxiety about large groups and snowballing issues. – MRW

*NOTE: As I was editing this material, Christina Cross sent me the book by Craig Schindler and Gary Lapid of Project Victory from which the opening quote is drawn. I also am struck by the parallels among these models and the community-building model devised by M. Scott Peck (*The Different Drum*) and applied by the Foundation for Community Encouragement, Inc. of Ridgefield, CT.

CHAPTER 24

NORTHERN ENTREPRENEURS DECIDE THEIR FUTURE
Applying the Quetico Model in Ontario, Canada

Cliff McIntosh and Margaret Wanlin

T HE SIMILARITIES of Quetico Centre's workshop model to ICA's in the next chapter will be immediately apparent—a future vision, the identification of barriers, and action planning. Yet the origins—the Danish Folk High School movement and Canadian Citizens' Forums of the 1930's—illustrate again the many pioneers who have trod similar ground not knowing of each others' work.

Here, McIntosh and Wanlin demonstrate a strategy of interlinking workshops to stimulate major activity by business, government, and labor. They start with nine grassroots conferences. The output from each becomes input to an integrated document that becomes the starting place for a 275 person conference involving all stakeholders in the region. This chapter is based on an article from *The Entrepreneurship Development Review,* Winter 1987/88, No. 4. For this volume, the authors have provided an update and some added reflections. – MRW

BACKGROUND

In the late 1980's Northern Ontario achieved a record of business starts only half that of Ontario as a whole. Big industries, once the major employer in the region, were hiring fewer people, leaving a void that was slow to fill. This chapter describes how we helped people in Northern Ontario develop their own "Made in the North" solutions. In two years 1,000 northerners were involved in a process to replace a culture of dependency with one that supports entrepreneurship, stimulating many new jobs and businesses throughout the region.

They did it through a workshop series and major conference sponsored by The Ministry of Northern Development and Mines and conducted by Quetico Centre. The initiative began in Sault Ste. Marie after Premier Peterson's Conference on Northern Competitiveness in 1986. Though that conference was successful, Peterson realized the need for more dialogue among northerners. In the summer of 1987, a committee led by William Lees, Deputy Minister of Northern Development and Mines, considered the issue. The committee saw three possible options:

1). Train people to start and run small businesses. This idea was discarded because several institutions teach this, yet the problem persists.

2). Create lists of business opportunities, in various areas. This too was scrapped, because lists already exist, and lists do not power change.

3). Focus on developing a culture that supports small enterprises—the strategy that was selected because it could become self-renewing.

Life in Ontario's North had been dominated by big industry, big unions, and big government, resulting in a psychology of dependence. The North was full of entrepreneurial opportunities, and there were skilled people, but northerners had relied on the big institutions. They had not had to take entrepreneurial risks. Local institutions were not sufficiently supportive of business development and entrepreneurship.

Thus, cultural change became the main goal of a series of workshops, culminating in the Premier's Conference on Northern Business and Entrepreneurship.

THE SOLUTION

In 1987 a planning team led by Marc Couse, Senior Policy Analyst, Ministry of Northern Development, designed a workshop series to attack this issue. It was important that we involve local people in identifying, discussing and solving their own issues rather than having outside "experts" come in and tell how things should be done.

It was no easy task to bring together enough people from such a large geographic area to discuss such a complex issue and achieve a coherent response that could be acted upon. The committee built a three phase program:

Phase 1

Each of nine Northern Development Council (NDC) areas, consisting of business and community leaders from all of Northern Ontario, sponsored a workshop. (The NDCs' purpose is to advise the government on policies and initiatives to spur development in the region.)

Each workshop was attended by 60 business people and others concerned with Northern development. The intent was to involve those with roots deep in Northern communities, keeping government people to a minimum. In addition, a young entrepreneurs' conference was held in Sudbury. Two conferences were held for economic development officers, and two for chambers of commerce.

Phase 2

The responses from these workshops were tabulated into nine major issues that could be brought to a Premier's Conference in Thunder Bay.

Phase 3

The Thunder Bay conference was then designed and executed under the direction of Ken Sharratt, a manager at the Ministry of Northern Development and Mines. It was a working conference aimed at creating home-grown solutions rather than listening to speakers. Conference participants met in nine working groups of 30 people. Each group tackled one of the issues. To ensure maximum participation, working groups were divided into study teams of six to eight people. Each team worked on its issue. The aim was to create clear action steps towards a solution.

THE DESIGN: WORKSHOPS

Collectively, northerners knew what was wrong and what needed to be done to improve their economy. What they lacked was a forum to pull their thinking together to understand the problems and identify solutions. The nine regional workshops were led by people local to the various communities and trained by Quetico Centre staff. Groups of six to eight people tackled three questions, putting their ideas on flip-charts:

1. THE VISION: If entrepreneurship and business development are to become important contributors to our region's economic growth, what

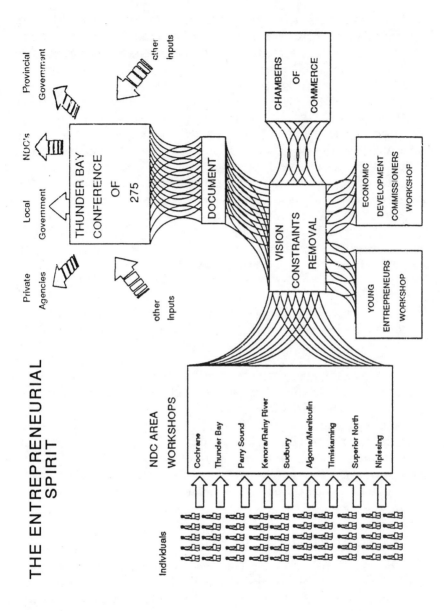

THE ENTREPRENEURIAL SPIRIT

perceptions, attitudes and approaches will be required of these groups: municipal councils, chambers of commerce, labor unions, local media, the general public, local merchants and business people, financial institutions, economic development commissions and officers, educational institutions, big business and physical infrastructure?

2. WHERE ARE WE NOW? Each group examined their area's current state of readiness for entrepreneurship and business development.

3. FILLING THE GAP: Knowing the ideal, and having a clear picture of the current situation, groups would decide on action steps towards achieving their common goals.

THE IDEAS: THE WORKSHOPS

During the planning stages, government people among the planners were worried about this process. It meant investing a great deal of time and expense without knowing what the outcome would be. Despite Premier Peterson's statement that, "[Northern Ontario] needs the leadership of local people," they were worried because they could not predict the "end product."

The workshops, however, successfully developed a clear idea of what Northern Ontario's entrepreneurial culture should be like. They accurately assessed the current situation without "bashing" any particular group. Most importantly, clear aspirations were defined.

1. THE VISION: Groups came up with a host of ideas for a prosperous North. Here are some of them:

- Government would be decentralized, with Northern offices to assist in Northern concerns. Further, access to government would be simpler.
- People foresaw a regional database and improved transportation throughout the North.
- Banks would employ northerners who knew the local economy to loan money to northerners. The Small Business development Corporation's (SBDC) mandate would incorporate Northern needs and conditions.
- Town councils, rather than being reactive, would have clearcut goals that would be communicated to the public. They would use local resources to accomplish these goals.

2. THE CONSTRAINTS: Looking at the North today, however, the groups saw problems. The economy was resource-based with most large companies supplying their needs from outside the region and, in some cases, outside the province. Government seemed very remote and

difficult to access. Schools in the North and elsewhere built on the psychology of dependence and did not support entrepreneurship as a career possibility.

Many Northern communities also lacked adult education facilities to meet the needs of small business education. The enormity of the North created difficulties in transportation and communication. There was a lack of confidence in the abilities of northerners. Companies were buying their products from central Ontario. Many town councils and chambers of commerce were reactive and inward-looking. Limited media coverage, focusing on negative events, created a poor impression.

3. The Action Plans: With these visions in mind, and recognizing current conditions, workshop participants conceived many action steps. Among their ideas were plans for ongoing education of town council members to foster improved long-term planning. Since chambers of commerce are based on entrepreneurship, groups thought they should seek to gain full representation among the business community. Businesses would have to improve training and advertising efforts in the future. Schools would create business competitions and give students assistance in starting summer businesses.

Overview of the Workshop

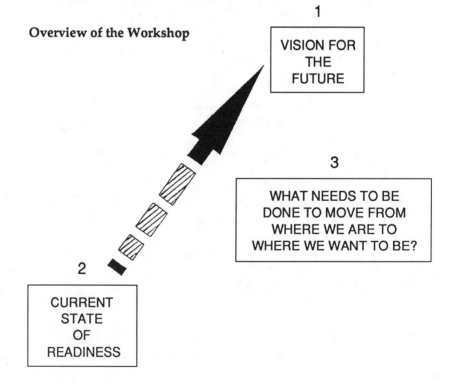

1

VISION FOR
THE
FUTURE

3

WHAT NEEDS TO BE
DONE TO MOVE FROM
WHERE WE ARE TO
WHERE WE WANT TO BE?

2

CURRENT
STATE
OF
READINESS

THE DESIGN: THE PREMIER'S CONFERENCE

The visions and constraints identified in the workshops were brought to the Premier's Conference in Thunder Bay, November 23-25, 1987. They were tabulated into nine areas of discussion:

- strengthening the local economy
- enhancing quick, easy access to government
- education for entrepreneurship
- strengthening regional networks
- enhancing the service sector
- increasing local availability of local capital
- promoting sound labor-management relations
- encouraging community leadership
- improving the Northern Ontario image.

The conference had four goals:

1). Leadership and Vision: Northerners would understand the region's potential and the leading role they must play in developing it.

2). Networking: Northerners would use networking opportunities to establish a regional vision and consensus for business development and entrepreneurship.

3). Strategies: Specific strategies would be created by northerners to remove constraints to business development and entrepreneurship.

4). Actions: There would be a clear understanding of what should be done and by whom.

In similar fashion to the workshops, conference teams dealt with three issues:

1). The Vision: Is the vision for this subject appropriate and complete, considering the whole of Northern Ontario?

2). The Issues and Networking: Using the vision and the constraints identified by the previous workshops, identify the key issues for action and the networks or groups that need to be involved for action to be taken.

3). Developing an Action and Communications Plan: Identify the actions needed to resolve the issues and achieve the visions. Which groups must be involved to ensure that constructive change takes place?

THE VISION: THE CONFERENCE

The delegates' goal was to lay at least part of the foundation for development of a dynamic North, and to that end they generated several ideas:

- The North would be not only self-supporting through local industry, but selling as well to other parts of Ontario and the country. The economy would be diversified.
- The school system would help to create an entrepreneurial culture in the North, fostering self-reliance through programs such as Junior Achievement. Teachers and guidance counselors would have business experience, and schools would offer small business management courses for students and adults.
- Ideally, the service sector in the North would foster economic development. Medical and professional services would exist as well as hydro and other utilities at reasonable rates.
- Labor and management would work closely together, rather than in their traditional adversarial roles.
- The vision included an improved understanding of the North's opportunities and advantages among residents and non- residents alike. Media coverage would support this theme with a strong Northern network.

In the final stage, the means of achieving this vision were tabulated, again in the nine areas mentioned. There were several concrete plans made. Some highlights are:

- Promoting awareness of local assistance programs already available, expanding the availability of capital through government guarantees and SBDC eligibility, and improving the transportation infrastructure;
- Creating a centre for entrepreneurship and information networking among communities;
- Utilizing Northern decision-making, creating one body to replace many agencies, establishing a Northern Ontario Business Centre in Toronto;
- Improving hospitality and highway services to create a positive image;
- Creating co-operative working groups to educate people about promoting and managing technological change.

THE FUTURE

The process worked; the conference achieved its goals. People reacted immediately. Chambers of commerce began creating networks, Northeastern and Northwestern Ontario municipal associations started working together, companies commenced rethinking their strategies, and several new business ideas were conceived in the supportive hot house of the conference.

The Minister of Northern Development & Mines, Rene Fontaine, committed his Ministry of Northern Development to extensive consultations with Northern Development Councils.

This conference was a dramatic change from previous meetings that usually involved outside "experts" explaining what should be done and how northerners should do it. People became committed to the solutions because they were involved in the planning and participated in the decision-making. This process is an example of education for empowerment and action.

In his closing remarks, Rene Fontaine, supporting the process, said, "We brought together not one but a thousand consultants to work on something that is very important—the economic future of Northern Ontario."

EPILOGUE (DECEMBER 1991)

Two categories of significant work were undertaken as a result of the entrepreneurs' project.

1. Government Service Delivery

Some Ontario government departments reorganized their Northern service delivery systems. Government agencies brought together senior bank officials and community business people to discuss decentralizing lending decisions from Toronto to local branches. A major youth out-migration study was funded by the government but done by northern residents. Many of the business assistance programs were reviewed and updated. The entrepreneurship programs in local schools were raised on the priority lists.

2. Increased Local Responsibility

The most significant change was attitudinal. Traditionally, one of the first things northern people asked when launching a new idea was, "Is there a (government) grant?" Now more than ever, people are saying, "If it is going to get done, we have to do it." That stance has been strengthened by the awareness of the huge provincial and federal debt and the annual deficits.

A theme that came out over and over in the workshops was doing more with less. In recent municipal elections, some candidates used that as their campaign slogan.

Another theme rejecting the "one size fits all" government policy for a province as large and diverse as Ontario. The value of that idea is recognized broadly. One of the candidates in the context for the leadership of the provincial Liberal Party is using that as the cornerstone of her platform.

In the last election, the Liberal Party (LP) lost to the New Democratic Party (NDP). The LP has been a middle-of-the-road party with its main strength from small business. The NDP's support comes from unions. The NDP isn't well tuned to broad-based community problems.

All the regional and community organizations supported by previous governments have either been phased out or reduced in stature. The NDP places much greater emphasis on government controlled welfare and other social services rather than community controlled development. As a result, now there are no resources and simple mechanisms available for systematic follow up.

QUETICO'S CONCEPTUAL AND HISTORIC ROOTS
By C.M. McIntosh

The roots of our practice come from two main sources—early 19th Century Denmark and Canada in the 1920's-30's. Both pre-date modern social science and research on participation.

1. The Danish Folk High School Movements

About 150 years ago, Denmark was decimated by wars, its institutions dominated by foreigners. Even the Danes' folk language was seen as inferior. Bishop Grundtvig recognized that for the Danes to be masters in their own house, there had to be an intellectual awakening of the folk, or common people.

Grundtvig believed that the folk had to learn about and take pride in their local, regional and national history. They had to understand how the political and economic systems of their day worked and affected their day-to-day lives. They needed to understand the importance of a healthy mind and a healthy spirit in a healthy body.

Grundtvig and his followers believed that intellectual awakening resulted from addressing national issues within the context of the local experience. To capture the significance of this, one has to keep in mind that the emphasis was on co-operation, not individualism. Life issues were issues of concern to the group, the community, the nation.

Schools of the time were for the elite. They emphasized esoteric, academic learning, what Mao Tse Tung called "book to book learning." That meant learning that went from one book, through the student's eyes and out through a hand-held pencil to another book without catching on any place in between.

Each year for eight months, the time after harvesting and before planting, Grundtvig's folk high school brought together young adult peasants and their teachers in a residential facility. The schools were kept small, 150 to 200 people, to keep the organization on a human scale and focus resources on student learning. The teachers' knowledge, the students' life experiences, the interactions within the school and with the surrounding community were all grist for the learning mill.

Through Grundtvig didn't have the benefit of 20th century science-based child and adult education theory, he applied many principles of experience-based learning that American pioneers systematized and codified in the 1930's and 40's.

The Grundtviggian (he'd shudder at that word) approach was:

- small group discussion;
- connect new learning to the learner's experience;
- help the learner think in terms of systems;
- involve the whole person in the learning;
- build confidence in self and community;
- emphasize cooperation and egalitarianism rather than individualism and competition.

In a Danish Residential Folk High School, there were no examinations, certificate or degrees. Subject mastery was not the issue, intellectual awakening was. To this day, if a Dane tells another Dane that they spent a term at a Folk High School, that is credential enough.

The folk high schools spread through Europe. Today in Denmark there are over 150 with about 7,000 people attending annually. If you and I decided to start a folk high school and could find students, a residential facility and enough money to operate for a year, we could get 80 percent of the cost back from the Danish government. As a result of this simple formula, there are folk high schools organized by people concerned with the arts, athletics, parenting, union, management, and aid to Third World countries.

It is easier to do this in Denmark because of the tradition of co-operation and the legal stance toward mandatory education. The state's role is to ensure that people are educated. As a result, Denmark has compulsory education where Canada and the United States have compulsory school attendance. The Danish approach prevents the administrative and union bureaucracies from getting control of the system.

2. 1920's and 30's Adult Education and the Cooperative Movement

Adult education in Canada was led by the churches and community groups in Canada. Fishing, farming and marketing co-operatives were formed to give a better return for the work. To make the co-ops successful required extensive education programs. The model for many of these programs came from Scandinavia and was pioneered by the Danes.

In the 1930's, activities like Citizen's Forum and Farm Radio Forum were tied to local learning groups where the dominant technique was small-group discussion. As well, an extensive network of traveling libraries and documentary films was used as discussion starters.

Like the Danish Folk High Schools, these were designed to provide people with the information they needed to understand the socio-economic system. To use a current word unknown at the time, people were empowered by their learning.

I began my serious work life as a community recreation director. My job was in a new, rugged mining town. The span of programming included everything from prenatal courses to ice hockey—art and crafts, music, drama, athletics, home and school, anything that enriched the community's leisure life.

There wasn't any money and so it was necessary to find and activate community resources. I tried to apply to all our activities Sun Yat Sen's principle, "A leader is effective if the people say, 'we did it ourselves.'" In the six years I did that, I received 25 years experience in mobilizing community resources to make a better life.

ABOUT THE AUTHORS

Cliff McIntosh came to Atikokan in 1952 as a community recreation director, and co-founded Quetico Centre, of which he is president, in 1958. This residential education centre helps people to cope constructively with change. McIntosh has received the Order of Canada, the Order of Ontario, and Honorary Doctorate from Lakehead University, and other awards recognizing his work in adult education and change.

Margaret Wanlin's experience at Quetico Centre since 1977 includes directing youth leadership and community planning programs, to managing the introduction of computer systems. As manager of Administration and Programs, she has responsibility for youth programs, conference services, support services, and participation in management and leadership training.

CHAPTER 25

RURAL INTERNATIONAL DEVELOPMENT
Using the ICA Model in India and Maylasia
Patricia R. Tuecke

"T HE NEXT DECADE holds major challenges for the planet,"
writes Patricia R. Tuecke, reflecting on her work in Third
World cultures. "It is important to use methods that
bridge cultural gaps and tap the diverse wisdom and experience of cross-cultural teams." In this chapter she describes
global applications of a strategic planning process that
evolved from work in a Chicago ghetto in the 1960's by the
Institute of Cultural Affairs. (ICA's network includes 68
centers worldwide, with 500 full-time community development
staff.)

Both Emery/Trist and Lippitt/Schindler-Rainman started
with small group dynamics in single organizations and found
their way to whole communities. Tuecke made exactly the
reverse trip. She started with planning models developed for
whole communities and discovered how to apply them to
single corporations.

The ICA method has been used with equal success in
remote Asian villages and Fortune 500 multi-national firms.
It reflects this book's central tenet—that finding common
ground is the only practical way to control change, and that
shared aspirations for the future are the best way we know—
so far—about how to orchestrate the search.

Tuecke's central theme—that "western" methods are wholly transportable to other cultures—supports my belief that techniques don't care what we do with them. She also emphasizes the conditions under which organization development methods may be transferred—when we are able to recognize our own cultural biases and can leave them safely at home.

I have edited this chapter from an article that appeared originally in *Vision/Action*, the Bay Area Organization Development Network's journal. — MRW

What do a Westside Chicago ghetto and a village in India have in common with a Chinese banking corporation in Malaysia, a Taiwan subsidiary of a British chemical corporation, and a U.S. fast food corporation? In each of these settings people have used the same "contentless" planning process to shape their own futures, empower and transform themselves.

Here I want to describe a method grounded in transcultural human values that helps people bridge the cultural differences and vastly-different perspectives that so often divide groups. It is a method that allows people, regardless of culture, to develop their own plans, drawing on their unique experiences, dreams, needs, issues, strategies, and goals.

Many people are skeptical that western organization development (OD) technologies are appropriate in other cultures. Working with national and multi-national corporations in Asia, Europe, and the U.S., and with rural development projects in Third World countries, I have found the process I will describe easily transferable. To do it, though, we need to be aware of the many different world views, thinking modes, customs, and business styles of nations and cultures.

To be oblivious to differences in cross-cultural situations can result in everything from embarrassment and frustration to total ineffectiveness and hostility for insults not intended from the people we are trying to help. A consultant's attitude toward the people and their situation is always a major part of any intervention.

I want to emphasize that we don't have to learn totally new technologies to work with different cultures. Some familiar tools are transferable because they empower people at a basic human level. What we *do* need to learn is open-mindedness about their application and how to let people make their own meanings of their experience.

A TRANSCULTURAL PLANNING PROCESS

The transcultural planning process I use was developed in Chicago by the Institute of Cultural Affairs, a research, training, and development institute. The ICA believed that if an effective, self-empowering, general community planning process could be designed, millions of communities would not have to sit in hopeless situations waiting in vain for help to "trickle down." People would have a means for constructively shaping their own destiny instead of being victims of their situation.

Over the last 25 years this approach has been used effectively in communities around the world. In over 30 nations it has helped people deal with basic human issues of self-sustenance, self-reliance, and self-confidence. Though the basic form used was much the same, the process took on the flavor of the particular culture and locale.

The ICA began developing this planning process in the 1960's in a collaborative effort with citizens of an urban ghetto on Chicago's Westside. The neighborhood was full of neglected buildings, vacant lots overflowing with junk, unemployment, babies dying of lead poison, and angry youths running in gangs. The ICA asked groups of citizens, "If you could change all this, what would it be like here? What do you need? What's keeping it from happening? What can you do about these problems so that your future will be different?"

They began to tell us their hopes and dreams—a safe place to live, jobs, good schools. The Institute staff became catalyst, resource, and partner as decisions about need, direction, and action were made by the people who would be most affected by them. Through this group process, solutions emerged and programs were created that met local needs and reflected authentic cultural style.

The ICA learned that a shared vision is key to lasting and effective community change and development. They discovered that when a community sees the interrelationships of problems standing between their current state and their vision and can name the major blockages, it can begin to deal with them. They found that when people in consensus create a plan for themselves, commitment and motivation to actualize the plan comes from within the group.

HUMAN TECHNOLOGIES IN PLANNING

The ICA process represents a very creative, human way to approach change for individuals and groups. It is the way people think in their daily life. "What is it we want and need in our future? What is blocking us from realizing that? What will it take for us to deal with those blocks, and allow that future to come about? What can we do now to start moving in that direction?" This removes the victim stance and replaces it with an empowered stance. "We are in charge of our own destiny." The four basic parts of the process parallel these questions and utilize some familiar OD interventions.

The VISION is made up of the group's hopes and dreams, a picture of what they see going on in their future. The second part discerns the major problems and issues blocking actualization of the vision.

Clusters of related problems are named as the MAJOR BLOCKS or UNDERLYING CONTRADICTIONS that must be dealt with. Then an integrated STRATEGY is designed to deal with these blocks, incorporating proposals that both utilize existing strengths and move in new directions. The final part focuses on TACTICAL PLANS and ACTION STEPS to implement the strategy. The ICA planning process is described in detail in Laura Spencer's *Winning Through Participation: Meeting the Challenge of Corporate Change with the Technology of Participation,* Kendall/Hunt Publishing Company, 1989.

THE ICA STRATEGIC PLANNING MODEL

1. VISION: What are our hopes and dreams for the future?
2. UNDERLYING CONTRADICTIONS: What keeps us from our vision?
3. STRATEGIC DIRECTIONS: How do we get what we want?
4. TACTICAL PLANS and ACTION STEPS: What can we do

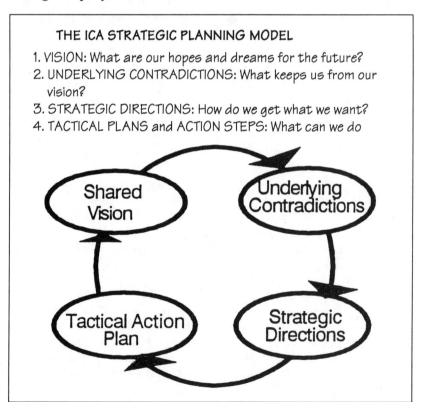

This planning process works well in diverse settings because it is linked with some familiar dynamics essential in enhancing group creativity, commitment, cohesiveness, and motivation. The process, rooted in basic human realities, has seven characteristics that contribute to its effectiveness in highly-diverse groups:

1. Planning is done by the people who will carry it out. This process is not what someone outside the organization or community—a "Euro/American expert," for example, or their own top leadership alone—thinks is needed. However, support of top leadership is crucial if not included in the planning group. This approach assumes that each planning team has the wisdom and experience to decide what they need, and provides a systematic way of making those decisions. Real issues and problems are dealt with, authentic solutions are created, and people become motivated and committed to action.

2. The process is structured, yet highly participative, open and contentless. It assumes each person has a piece of the puzzle, a part of the mosaic the total group is creating. This allows the culture of the group to shape the plan. Various methods used by individuals, small teams and the total group to elicit and share data and make decisions allow all to participate equally in building the consensus of the group. The focus of the discussion is always on the data and the wisdom of the group and does not "spotlight" the persons with the best ideas, most senior position, or most dominating style.

3. Decisions are made by consensus. Many cultures traditionally use consensus to arrive at decisions; Americans have difficulty with it. Yet it is critical for multi-cultural management teams to reach a common ground on which to base their decisions and actions. Many joint ventures have fallen apart because this did not occur.

4. The planning is practical. It is not a case study or theory. It focuses on a major issue that the group faces and must resolve creatively in order to move forward. The future depends on what the group decides to do for itself, not what it hopes someone else will do. Those involved in the planning must invest their time and energy in implementing it.

5. The process deals with the total system and produces an integrated plan. In today's complex world, a system-wide analysis of key issues and multi-dimensional responses to them are necessary to meet the challenges of rapidly changing situations for any organization or business.

6. We employ both rational and intuitive planning methods. They

strike a balance between thinking modes (visionary, analytical, strategic, and tactical), left and right brain activities, commentary, discussion, and workshop. These seem to be effective in many cultures. There is opportunity to reflect on the values, purpose, and meaning of situations, and options as well as to build timelines and action plans. These diverse elements keep the approach from being experienced as totally "Western."

7. The facilitator brings a genuine human concern for the organization and its plans as well as group process expertise. We honor the culture(s) we are working with, but don't "go native," keeping a professional (could we say "global?") objectivity. We're sensitive to the different perspectives and cultural nuances as much as possible, and don't let the tensions get the planning off track or the discussion become discordant. We keep groups focused on common visions and goals, helping them build consensus every step of the way.

"...WE DIDN'T PUT MUCH EMPHASIS ON WHERE THE IDEA CAME FROM..."

"It's difficult for me to give theoretical sources. I became involved full time with ICA in inner-city Chicago in 1968. The task was so overwhelming and the pace so fast, we were very pragmatic. If something worked, we didn't put much emphasis on where the idea came from, so long as it fit our value of honoring the dignity of the people involved. As all of our initial work in this area was so innovative, we didn't think anyone else had discovered this but ourselves!

One of our major theoretical premises we called "Imaginal Education," derived from Kenneth Boulding's book, *The Image, Knowledge in Life and Society.* The basic assumptions are that everyone operates out of images. Our images are our picture of our self and our world. Images control our behavior. Images can change. Images can change through the impact of messages, both inner and outer. A change in image brings about a change in behavior.

So we attempted in our development work to shift peoples images from 'victim' to 'possibility.' We also were much influenced in the 1960's by Susanne Langer's *Problems of Art,* and Viktor E. Frankl's *Man's Search for Meaning.* — PRT

THE VILLAGE AND THE BOARDROOM

Four hundred years ago the village of Maliwada, India, was a thriving agricultural center, producing fruits, vegetables, and wines. In 1975, it had little water, no sanitation, few crops. Over 1,000 villagers barely eked out a subsistence living. Muslims and Hindus of many different castes lived with centuries of mutual distrust. The villagers knew about their prosperous past, but it seemed long gone and hopeless to recreate.

The discussions began based on two questions: "What would it take to have prosperity exist again in this village? What can you do to make that happen?" Gradually, as ideas began to pour fourth, perspectives changed. Hindus and Muslims talked together excitedly about how to clean out the ancient well. Brahmins and Untouchables discovered in a joint meeting that all despaired at the lack of medical care for their sick children. They all wanted to create a health clinic in the village. Hope began to creep into their voices and eyes. What had seemed totally impossible suddenly became doable. People organized and tapped resources they had forgotten they had.

They acquired loans from a bank and received government grants. They built a dam, a brick factory, and the clinic. The shared vision of what they wanted for themselves and their community allowed them to go beyond their personal and cultural differences and continued to motivate them. Each success made them stronger, more confident, more self-assured. Today, Maliwada is a prospering village.

When transformation like this takes place, the news travels. Nearby villages wanted to know how they could do this. The ICA project grew to encompass hundreds of villages in the state of Maharastra in India. Projects were begun in Kenya, the Philippines, Indonesia, and other nations. This effort evolved into one of the most successful micro socio-economic development programs in Third World countries.

Corporations, agencies, and other organizations involved with projects asked the Institute to do this kind of systemic planning. Would it be possible to take this process out from under the tree in a village plaza into the boardrooms and conference centers of the corporate world? Would it be appropriate? Would it break through the barriers that divide people in organizations as it did in communities? With questions like these, three colleagues and myself began working with a modified version of the process. We discovered that some of the basic human dynamics of communities around the world also existed in the culture of the corporate community.

We successfully used the planning process with corporations in Malaysia, with its Indian, Malay, and Chinese workforce, and in Indonesia and in African nations with multi-tribal workforces. It was effective in former colonial nations, where many corporations are owned and managed by Euro/Americans. It worked for agencies with huge multi-levels of bureaucracy and pulled together the thinking of diverse groups, departments, and geographic, regions. It was effective in creating unity between management and labor.

The focus, decided on by senior management with the consultant, deals with any major issue facing the organization. Sears-Roebuck created strategy for the export department in the international division. McDonald's designed a national marketing plan with their regional marketing directors. Indonesia's national Sugar Board created a plan to double sugar production in five years.

IMPORTANT VALUES THIS WORK IS BASED ON

- We are open to and affirming of life.
- Possibilities matter more than limits.
- This organization, with all its strengths and weaknesses, problems and gifts, is received by the universe.
- The future is entirely open to be created.
- Everyone's voice deserves to be heard, based on the worthiness of each individual.
- Concern for the planet. — PRT

IBM designed new training curricula for its planners. Malaysian banks created strategic plans with both corporate and branch management. ICI subsidiaries in Asia used the process to develop strategic thinking and total company responsibility in their national management teams. Time-Life Publishing created a more cohesive team of Asian distributors.

Why Does it Work?

The process is effective when it enables groups to step back from their immediate work and consider long range directions, and to step back from their usual operating modes and consider how they work together. People of any culture experience an approach that honors their ideas and experience, no matter what their role or level within the company. It creates an open space into which new modes of communication and new patterns of information flow.

All levels of management can discuss freely in a neutral place issues they rarely talk about with people they may have never talked with.

They may find themselves teamed with a traditional adversary or rival excitedly planning how to implement a vision they both designed. A common mind develops, a common bond is formed, a new synergy of action infuses the whole management team. A transition time is experienced that bridges the way things were, the no-longer, and what will be, the not-yet. A new perspective on the future emerges.

ABOUT THE AUTHOR...

Patricia R. Tuecke, of San Francisco, facilitates strategic organizational planning which implements breakthroughs in vision, operations and organization. She has worked with corporations, agencies, and institutions in Asia, Europe and the U.S. for 20 years. A current focus is on continuous Quality Improvement from a whole systems perspective and facilitating organizational learning.

PART 7

MAKING SEARCH CONFERENCES EFFECTIVE

Introduction

> "The search is what anyone would undertake if he were not
> sunk in the everydayness of his own life. . . . To become aware
> of the possibility of the search is to be onto something. Not
> to be onto something is to be in despair." – Walker Percy. The
> Moviegoer, Quoted by Sam Keen (1991), p. 125.

The focus of Part 6 is conference management—learning to make search conferences effective. By now it should be obvious that the models presented here "work" under appropriate conditions. Whether a given person wishes to work with them, though, is an entirely different matter. If you have not managed this kind of conference, you may wonder (1) whether this work really suits you, and (2) if it does, how you can gain the required knowledge and skills.

These chapters, written by and for facilitators, offer experience, information, and advice. In Chapters 26 and 27, Tim Hutzel and Tony Richardson tell informally of their backgrounds and values in relation to managing conferences and why they like this way of working.

In Chapter 28 Merrelyn Emery, a key developer of search methodology, tells how she orients people to this work and advocates a theory-practice apprenticeship for learning to manage conferences. By contrast,

Mary Fambrough, in Chapter 28, discusses her thoughtful do-it-yourself first learning project and reflects on Emery's caveats in light of her own experience. Both take up planning/facilitating questions related to how far you can stretch the design boundaries before you are back to the "old paradigm."

If you aspire to facilitate future search conferences, I suggest you read all of this part and the one that follows—Pitfalls—before deciding what to do next. I have one observation, based on my own journey and from 20+ years of consultant training workshops, both as learner and teacher: the hardest part of this work, for those of us steeped in training methods, is learning how to do less of what we think is needed, enabling participants to do more of what they wish. – MRW

CHAPTER 26

FROM ENGINEER TO SEARCHER
The Impact of Values on Personal Practice
Tim Hutzel

Y CALL FOR PERSONAL STATEMENTS elicited several letters from people in various stages of their own search for methods that work. I was particularly taken by Tim Hutzel's experiences, starting as an industrial engineer, to find his way towards humane practices that meet the needs of a high tech business. At this point he had adapted searching to team development in his company. His story strikes me as typical of many people seeking ways to match participative methods with the peculiar demands of relentless change. "I'm very interested in learning what others have done successfully as well as not so successfully with the search conference," Hutzel wrote in response to my request for values statements. "Is there a preferred format? Are the inventors amenable to amendments, enhancements, and other deviations?" This book provides my best answer so far for the questions he raises — MRW

My introduction to the search conference came about like many other things in my career. While engaging in organizational change practices I found some things that didn't work and some that did. One practice that worked significantly well was getting a representative group from an organization together and having them systematically review the past, present and future. It was only after attending a panel discussion on searches and reading Chapter 14 of *Productive Workplaces* that I understood the connection between the methods I was using and the search conference.

The paramount values in our conferences are very basic. I begin each conference by asking participants to share their personal values. The lists they make are remarkably consistent from one conference to another. There are four recurring personal values: first, people's families; second, their relationship to a higher being; third, job security; fourth, health. I believe these personal values are the source of energy for a group's searching for a better future. The teams I work with see that they really do have common ground from which to work together.

There are two primary organizational values that seem to recur: first, pleasing an outside customer; second, assuring a viable place in which to work. Secondary values that emerge (not so consistently) are autonomy, safety, recognition, and egalitarian pay systems. I see the secondary values in most cases as supportive of the two primary ones. It's my observation that the personal values act as both catalyst and foundation for a team to engage in the search process.

COMMON VALUES

Our Family	ЖЖ ЖЖ ЖЖ ЖЖ
Relationship with God	ЖЖ ЖЖ ЖЖ ||
Job Security	ЖЖ ЖЖ ЖЖ ЖЖ ЖЖ
Health	ЖЖ ЖЖ ЖЖ ЖЖ
Satisfied Customers	ЖЖ ЖЖ |||

TYPICAL FLIP-CHART OF VALUES FROM SEARCH CONFERENCE

THEORY BASE

My interest in and devotion to organizational change has been evolutionary. My undergraduate training and experience was in engineering sciences, and most of my industrial experience has been manufacturing management. For 18 years I was an exemplary performer of Frederick Taylor's "scientific management" without even knowing who Mr. Taylor was. As a methods planner I developed work plans for machine operators that limited their skills and contributed to their boredom and stagnation. As a production supervisor I watched over my subordinates and counted their work, and as a production manager I perpetuated the system in which I learned my lessons.

In my engineering roles I designed machinery and equipment without the benefit of involving those who use it. It wasn't until much later that I learned about organization development and sociotechnical systems, and the possibility of improving the quality of work life and organizational effectiveness. For the past five years I've been learning and practicing organizational change, and am now completing a master's thesis at Bowling Green University on what traditional supervisors need to make the transition to leading autonomous work teams.

As a result, my theory now is based in sociotechnical systems. Trist's work began in the coal mines studying the miners' adaptation to technology and environment. Later (I believe) Trist's work evolved to looking at the environment in a broader context, one of society at large and the tools of society within which we must adapt or change.

The act of searching asks participants to become aware of their society (past and present) and, based upon common values, to determine a future they can and want to live in. The act of searching leads to planning towards this future that will, perhaps require changes in society's tools (technology).

My theory is based in action research. After all, we are speaking of assisting a group to *do its own* sensing of where it is in the present (based on data) and how it got there (by looking at the past), thus heightening the group's need to move forward. Further, we now suggest a group develop its own transition plan towards its agreed-upon future and make adjustments as it proceeds. Action research is the method that we use to help a group move forward.

Finally, I believe that my theory is based on team development, and I especially like Douglas McGregor's (1960) theory of effective work teams. In *The Human Side of Enterprise* McGregor listed a set of requirements that I take to apply equally to searching—informal, relaxed atmosphere; lots of discussion with everybody participating; a common task or goal; everyone listening and no idea squashed; conflict put on the table so the group can move on; decisions by consensus, not voting or power; impersonal criticism intended to help the group process; shifting leadership; groups evaluating their own process.

I have been doing conferences with diagonal slices of various organizations, primarily for purposes of team development, often six natural work teams at a time in a single conference. After about a third of an organization's members have gone through that process. We hold these conferences under the title of "Visioning Offsite Session."

ABOUT THE AUTHOR

Tim Hutzel, Program Manager of Joint Ventures at GE Aircraft Engine Group when he wrote this, is now Manager of Organizational Effectiveness.

CHAPTER 27

LEADING SEARCH CONFERENCES
Reflections on Managing the Process
Tony Richardson

I FIND SEARCHING SATISFYING BECAUSE IT IS SUCH A "CLEAN" process. When I manage a conference my role is clear—not to mix up the group's agenda with mine. I like Alastair Crombie's lovely symbol of the facilitator's role. He says we're like umpires of a soccer match who, if we become caught up in the play, quickly run backwards out of action, hands above head, indicating a determination not to influence or manipulate.

Because I am determined not to "run their show," I get more strung out in some critical stages of searches than in anything else I do as a consultant. I must help people do what *they* intend, and not what I wish they would do.

For me, searching succeeds to the extent that the process helps people unbutton their usual "survival" facade and meet each other at the level of their values. When they do that, MOST people will discover a common core of hope that can, for the occasion, cause a transcendence of the quality of the way they relate to each other. This in turn causes what Merrelyn Emery (1982) in her book on searching calls "joy"—the correct word I think.

CASE IN POINT—I managed a search with a union/management group (of 56) who have umbrella responsibilities over 180 local councils. I had previously met with leaders of both labor and management around a board room table where they spent the afternoon haranguing each other. Apparently this was normal "consultation." By the sixth hour of the search conference they were in small mixed groups asking for more time to explore "how society could be by the turn of the century if we got it right."

Most people—when we get it right—also will move out of their well-worn and pre-determined corners.

I think that this is critical because I, and everyone that I know well, has some level of difficulty in giving up being a "corner person." (Someone who operates out of one corner and uses guile to gain power by sucking people into the corner with them—a bit like a spider with a long tongue!)

A search creates a new (temporary) community with values based on vision, not politics. In this community the ground for "life's dealings" shifts from each individual's well-guarded office to something more akin to a village common. To be part of the daily commerce of this community people have to risk leaving their corner to join the rest on the common.

In some searches there are those who can't or won't do this. They end up forming a "smoking group" outside, usually angry and confused because they have, for the moment, lost their usual power base.

STAFFING

I make it a practice to have the client system select two people to join with me in managing the conference. I take an active part in this selection, looking for people who are credible, forward looking and likely to be influential in the future. In the case where there is a serious division of interests, I go for "one of each."

I then spend a few hours with these "assistant managers" coaching them in their role and in the critical ingredients of systems management and work systems. This has seems to have several benefits:

- The leadership offered by people credible within the system often soothes some of the folk;
- Insiders help me ground my own learning from the search management perspective, and they also may become new search managers, making possible the wider use of this process.
- The conference management group then understands and can use the "language" of the system. I, as an outsider, can still question the language if I feel it is important to do so.

INTRODUCING THE CONFERENCE

I feel pretty good about how I introduce this process, both when orienting a possible client and at the start of the event. My main aims are to have people:

- Feel within themselves their potential to explore and share ideals;
- See from their own experience that planning without focus on ideals may lead to frustration around details.

Because I think pictorially, I always describe the conference using Figures 1 and 2 (for which thanks to Alastair Crombie). Let me explain how I use these pictures. I start by drawing up the arrow (Figure 1), from left to right, saying it's about "specificity." Then, beginning with the left side, STRUCTURES, I point out that we can have an infinite number, and

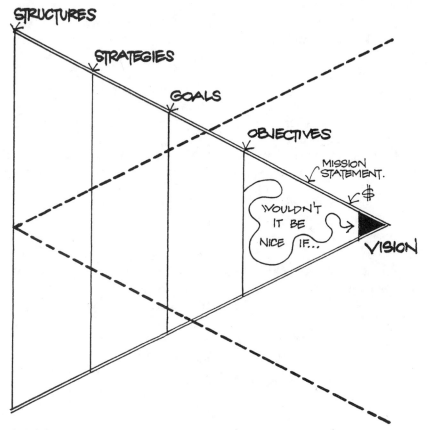

FIGURE 1

that tinkering with them alone doesn't make much difference.

So on to STRATEGIES. We can have lots of these too.

Then to GOALS. I say this means things we can "kick" in the shorter term—like in soccer.

OBJECTIVES on the other hand are longer term and may be the "what" of which the goals and the strategies are the "how." Systems that have searched usually only have three or four objectives.

When we become more specific we enter the RARE AIR of the ideal. "Wouldn't it be nice if?" I usually say, "This is where the more tasky or left brain-oriented folks will find it hardest, because they will want to get back to 'real life' and sort out the details they came here to fix." This is the place we often put most of our time and energy. I take time talking about this so that the key elements that make a search different are appreciated, as much as they can be in theory.

Now, I point out that MISSION STATEMENTS can emerge somewhere up this track. (In general I find most mission statements, although a necessary start, can be described as "too many words written by somebody else.")

Finally, VISION STATEMENTS are really highly-refined mission statements. We cannot have an infinite number of these. But a good one makes all the rest easier to decide. The chart has no redundant words and yet the essence is ALL there.

I first saw a system discover their shared vision near the end of a massive search Alan Davies and I did together. It was for a government support lobby group in Queensland called "Queensland Parents of People with Disabilities." The search was to sort out how to make the best of some new disabilities legislation.

We had 90 people, some in wheelchairs, some parents, some service providers, health bureaucrats and the private staff of the health minister. When they explored for a vision statement it gradually unfolded, lots of words at the start, then fewer as the essence became distilled. When the vision emerged it was greeted with silence, relief, and then a common, "Yes, that's it."

> "Every person in Australia
> has the right to live
> a socially respected life
> in the community
> of their choice."

To me, it seemed like a sort of "birthing." This statement gave a unified focus for objectives, three of which fell out naturally. The goals then fell out of the objectives... etc.

That diverse system, where most participants had a life and death stake to safeguard, had struggled with every issue up to that time, then found an ease of planning borne of a unity of view.

Figure 2 shows the opposite focus of specificity overlaying the original figure. People often see their system in this approach which is very focused on detail, particularly about structures, and a woolly and barely considered idea about "what is the game we are in, why do we exist?" I suggest that in another setting this is the classic recipe for divorce.

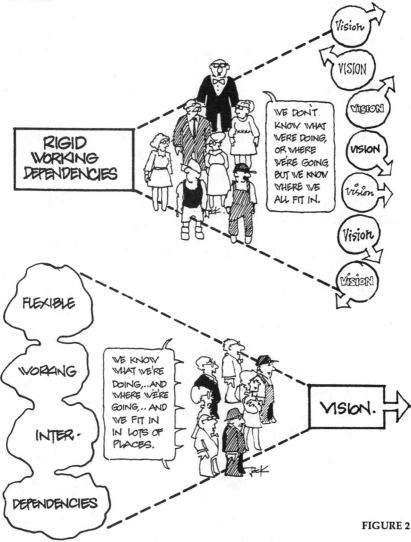

FIGURE 2

I have a couple of other pictures I follow through to depict the difference between "planning out of depression vs. doing so out of the ideal," and "shifting the focus from "what's wrong" to "how would it be if it were good."

All this introducing only takes ten minutes, but appears to set the scene for searching.

CUTTING THE DEPENDENCY ON LEADERS

I find that ESTABLISHING GROUNDRULES helps here and I always do it. I usually get people to do this in small groups to support a movement towards "pairing."

I also make a commitment to MANAGING THE TIMING in such a way that there is the best possible chance of a "resulting product" in written form, with broadest agreement, able to impact on planning and the future.

To be honest, I'm not sure whether I'm just warding off possible "scenes" because I personally dislike tension or I'm being sure the left-brained people know that this "flight of fancy" time will be ended some time.

Anyway if it is a two-day search, starting at 4:00 p.m., ending 48 hours later, I commit myself to ensuring that the group will be focusing on their aim within 24 hours, and that the probability is they will end with an agreed written product. I think that this eases people's anxieties in searching together.

MY PROCESS is rather set right now. I'd like to develop more flexibility and guess that this will come with experience. Like many search managers, I use the picture of a funnel, starting broad, narrowing into the "aim," then broadening out again as participants move into groups planning.

GENERIC SEARCH PROCESS

- LIKELY FUTURE (say in ten years)
- DESIRABLE FUTURE (the ideal)
- POSSIBLE DESIRABLE FUTURE (achievable if we got it right)
- SYSTEM'S HISTORY (sads and happies)
- IMPLICATIONS (of all of this) FOR THEIR SYSTEM
- KEY IMPLICATIONS regarding the AIM
- SELF-SELECTED GROUPS responding to one or more of the implications
- GROUPS REPORT BACK to the plenary which then acts as "consultants" to the groups as they prepare

---

CLOSURE

I have experienced a couple of searches where inadequate thought was given to the stage of planning that must be reached if the client system is to have a "product" that it can build upon and sustain. This has led me to plan towards closure from the beginning. Here are some steps on my personal checklist.

- Discuss desirable outcomes with the client system while planning the search so that the desired level and detail of planning (but not actual plans) to be reached during the event is understood and agreed by all parties.
- When introducing the search, focus upon the second half of the process when "we move from how we would like it to be to how we can arrange ourselves so that we get there."
- Manage the second half of the conference to put some pressure on the participants to refine and re-refine their plans so that they end up with practical ways to the ideal. I have found a few of things can help here:

1. Point out to the group when I see them concentrating on "do better" statements, ie. "We must improve this and that," (this is very much "parent ego state" stuff) and suggest they might get unstuck if they move to "do different" thinking, ie. "What are the two or three (little) things that we can actually start to change tomorrow?"
2. Have planning groups pair up and report back to each other in plenary and become consultants and task setters for each other.
3. End the event with each group reading out their plans (recorded on butcher's paper) so that they all see the fullness of their achievement and get agreement on the breadth of it.

    If it is a complex system with a range of vested interests, it amazes people how much they agree to how to proceed towards their common future and I know this builds confidence in going for it into the system.
4. Have the final plenary appoint a small "caretaker" group to oversee delivery of the conference material into the parent system.

"HAIR SHIRTS"

"Hair shirts" are people who make a profession of being the conscience of the organisation or community. They end up on all the committees that "do good" around the place. They tend to wear their values on their sleeve as they try to confront their various systems to raise themselves to loftier ideals. Please be nice to hair shirts (I tend to be among them).

However, I fear we hair shirts are not being as useful as we would like to think if, by our activities, we become a sort of quasi-professional conscience of our system. We may, unwittingly, set up a situation where:

- The average or very busy person no longer feels a requirement to, or maybe has no time to, examine their own values on issues, inasmuch as we are there DOING IT FOR THEM;
- We advocate so cogently for action that we inevitably hog the action;
- The conscience of the system may be salved but most people are left out.

It is not so much that searching makes a "hair shirt" of everyone. Rather, searching allows everyone to be confident about their quieter hopes. It allows for the democratization rather than the politicization of ideals.

ABOUT THE AUTHOR

Tony Richardson is a self-employed organization and training consultant working in organizations seeking to improve their whole system. Born in Britain, he worked in the paper making industry all over the world before embarking on a varied career as a clergyman, public servant, farmer, visiting fellow at a University, and consultant with a large firm. He has lived in Australia for more than 20 years. His operating philosophy, is that "where executives are committed to improving the whole, are prepared to involve everybody and don't need to know everything, the capacity of people to improve the quality and output of their work is damned near infinite."

CHAPTER 28

TRAINING SEARCH CONFERENCE MANAGERS

Merrelyn Emery

MERRELYN EMERY, has been a major influence on the learning of search methods. She makes a persuasive case for a careful apprenticeship in a theory-based practice. Here she describes how she introduces search conferences to novices, what she believes the critical learning issues are, and how people decide whether this work is for them. Along the way, she provides an overview of the key concepts she considers essential.

She also offers a theoretical rationale for not mixing modes. By that she means mixing task-focused searching with experiential learning exercises, training modules, "ice-breakers," expert lectures, question and answer sessions, or any group activity that takes people away from the central tasks they have come to do. She suggests strongly that "training" and democratic self-management are incompatible as part of the same event, a mixed message that may undercut the search. (Mary Fambrough, in the chapter that follows, speculates on the degree to which this might have happened in her own first conference—and tells us what has happened since.) — MRW

In this chapter I want to show why search conference managers need careful grounding in the concepts and methods of the practice. I'll do this by describing an orientation workshop that makes a good introduction. While few would rush to do brain surgery or psychotherapy without training, many have rushed into running Search Conferences (SCs) lacking awareness of the theory and "know how" required. Yet, SCs have broad social impact, as they encompass cultural and individual mental health. Diagram 1 illustrates the spiraling consequences of bureaucratic structures and also "expert" planning.

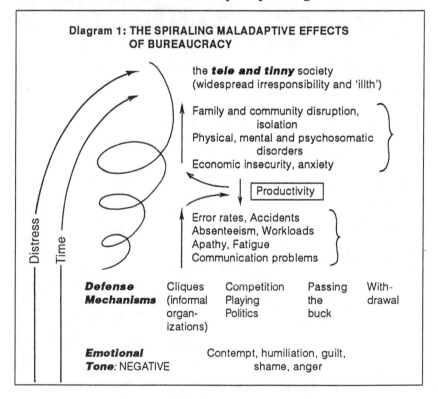

Diagram 1: THE SPIRALING MALADAPTIVE EFFECTS OF BUREAUCRACY

the *tele and tinny* society
(widespread irresponsibility and 'illth')

Family and community disruption,
isolation
Physical, mental and psychosomatic
disorders
Economic insecurity, anxiety

Productivity

Error rates, Accidents
Absenteeism, Workloads
Apathy, Fatigue
Communication problems

Distress
Time

| *Defense Mechanisms* | Cliques (informal organizations) | Competition Playing Politics | Passing the buck | Withdrawal |

Emotional Tone: NEGATIVE   Contempt, humiliation, guilt,
                                    shame, anger

I've been concerned about this issue since the lateseventies, when we began to hear from disgruntled SC participants. It was apparent that enthusiasts had run things called "SCs" which weren't. Some included activities like requiring people to fill in questionnaires at various stages. This cut across the momentum of work, reducing instead of increasing participants' control of the outcome. Others removed what they saw as irrelevant elements (eg. the environmental scanning or L22—global trends) or modified bits so drastically that they became inimical to the progress of the whole. Others ran through the stages as efficiently and mechanically as possible, leaving participants to wonder what had hit them.

By far the commonest mistake was scattering "speakers" throughout the meeting—on the unspoken assumption that ordinary people would not otherwise pool their own experiences to arrive at effective plans or solutions. This tells you something about the parlous state of our culture. Calling in "experts" (while remaining cynical about them) expresses dependency and lack of faith in people's purposefulness, wish to learn and deep need to control their own destinies.

What had gone missing in the rush to use these new, more effective social change methods, was an understanding of the need to ground this work on strong, coherent foundations. So SCs were treated with contempt, just another fad that failed to deliver the promised goods.

Objections to these distortions were met by comments that we were being "antidemocratic" and should "let a hundred flowers bloom," charges that hurt those of us seriously committed to democratic practices and validating individuals' experience. These comments confirmed that the revolutionary mood of those years was strongly laissez-faire. The best we could do was continue practicing the "real thing" in competition with the other flowers. At last we began to pilot introductory training workshops for potential managers and participants, grounded in the works of Fred Emery and Eric Trist and conceptual and practical extensions of their theory and practice since 1959—what I would call "the genuine article."

This history lies behind the introductory workshop I will describe here. In no sense does this design replace an apprenticeship, which I consider essential. It serves only as an introduction and first opportunity to discover whether one really is cut out to be an SC manager. Some people are naturals, others will never make it. Still others will become good managers, but only with enough experience to overcome the many barriers they have internalized from past socialization and education.

THE INTRODUCTORY WORKSHOP

This workshop is designed to provide a basic appreciation of the theoretical and practical dimensions of the SC. It includes, therefore, conceptual presentations and some experience with the process. I have run variations from a half day to two days. During the experiential components the reasons for the manager's comments, questions and moves are debriefed to give a broader understanding of the whole approach and as a lead into deeper questions. In the half-day versions, people experience only the first stages, but we derive as much understanding from this as possible.

It is always difficult to integrate conceptual and experiential sections, and their quite-different dynamics, within a single exercise. This problem results from the unavoidable *mixed mode—the alternation of contrasting design principles*. Too long an opening presentation will induce dependency which later interferes with the growth of the working mode demanded by the experiential component. The longer and more powerful the working phase, the less participants can be bothered with subsequent theoretical discussion. Therefore, one of the skills required for a successful mixed mode workshop is to keep each component short, concise and with many leads and pointers backwards and forwards into other sections, creating both continuities and *"zeigarniks"* (bits of unfinished business). Another skill is that required in Search Conference management itself, namely, to hear the operating dynamic, the "music" or second level message of the group, and manage it towards the most creative learning.

Above all, I need to stress the difference between the workshop and the Search itself. For the workshop cannot model the coherent dynamic of a Search Conference. There is a paradox here that cannot be resolved until those who wish to learn more take the next step of becoming an apprentice.

While some of the components must be conceptual, they must also be presented in ways which encourage interest and learning; with aids like overheads, butcher's paper and invitations for clarifying questions. Extended question and answer sessions must be avoided, however, as these could reinforce an emerging dynamic of dependency on the "expert".

Above all, these "top down" components need to radiate the *excitement* the presenter feels about Search Conferences. This cannot be simulated. If you don't have it, you would be wise not to attempt a workshop like this one or the management of a Search Conference itself. As will be clearer below, the method is predicated on experiencing ourselves as whole systems living within bigger whole systems, within even larger whole systems. Participative methods in general, and the Search Conference in particular, cannot be approached with a view of people as uneasy amalgams of mental, emotional, and physical subsystems. The method is designed on and illustrates the efficacy of *Open Systems* (Emery, F.E), 1981).

It is also necessary to stress here that learning to run a Search requires a working knowledge of the underlying theory of the method *and* serving as an apprentice manager for as many events as it takes to feel confident with the phenomena embodied.

Routine practice without conceptual understanding becomes rigid and dangerous, especially when dealing with groups of people, unpredictable at the best of times, and even more so when they are working creatively with new problems in changing circumstances. This training workshop is only a toe in the water to allow people to get a feel for whether this work is for them.

PLANNING A SEARCH CONFERENCE

Introduction

The actual plan for an introductory workshop depends on the time available, number of participants and their special needs. Sometimes participants come from one organization and need to integrate their abstract learnings about search with their own circumstances and problems. More diverse groups may require the creation of a purpose for the experiential components to make it meaningful for all. This demands quick thinking and flexibility from the workshop manager, just as in an actual SC.

I find I can give a comprehensive overview of concepts and practice in about seven hours. If time is short, I run certain components together, using strict time management to make sure to include high priority concepts.

First Phase

This is always, in sessions of a half day or more, a briefing and "introduction and expectations" session. Small groups compile their expectations of the workshop which avoids these surfacing at inappropriate times and alerts the manager to special issues they may need to address. At the end, it is useful to hold a ten-minute appraisal of whether the many needs have been met and to fulfill, if possible, any that haven't.

Second Phase

This is the first presentation of the theoretical framework and its concepts (40-60 minutes depending on questions).

Content

1. ENVIRONMENTS AND STRATEGIC PLANNING

I use a set of overheads to explain the core concept of "directive correlation" (Sommerhoff, 1969) as both system and environment acting on each other to produce a new outcome and state of affairs. As these change, so must our forms of planning. This leads to the concept of open system, all of whose elements must be addressed in *effective* future oriented methods (see Diagram 2).

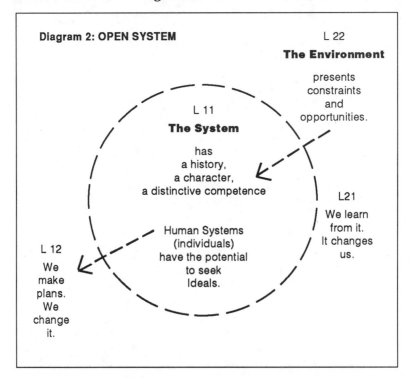

Diagram 2: OPEN SYSTEM   L 22

The Environment
presents constraints and opportunities.

L 11
The System
has a history, a character, a distinctive competence

Human Systems (individuals) have the potential to seek Ideals.

L21
We learn from it. It changes us.

L 12
We make plans. We change it.

There is then a quick run through of at least Types 3 and 4 of environmental causal texturing (Emery and Trist, 1965), the types of planning appropriate to each and ways *not* to do it.

Diagram 3 spells out the relation of each phase to the open systems model, the points at which ideals come into operation, the need for continuity of organizational or community "personality" and the reasons for leaving constraints towards the end, etc. If I have time, I use a real rather than abstracted model, discussing flexibility and the need to custom design for individual circumstances.

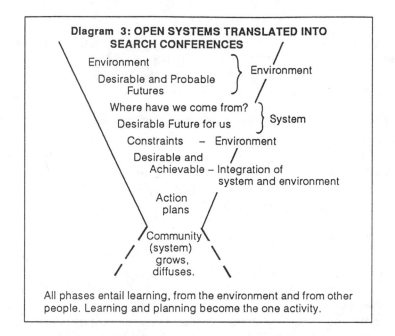

Diagram 3: OPEN SYSTEMS TRANSLATED INTO SEARCH CONFERENCES

Environment
Desirable and Probable Futures
} Environment

Where have we come from?
Desirable Future for us
} System

Constraints – Environment
Desirable and
    Achievable – Integration of
        system and environment

Action plans

Community (system) grows, diffuses.

All phases entail learning, from the environment and from other people. Learning and planning become the one activity.

We then look explicitly at the assumptions and purposes of the Search Conference, alerting people to other concepts to be introduced after some experience (Diagram 4).

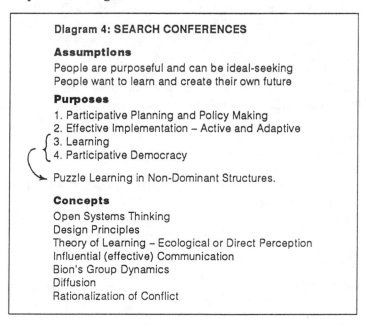

Diagram 4: SEARCH CONFERENCES

Assumptions
People are purposeful and can be ideal-seeking
People want to learn and create their own future

Purposes
1. Participative Planning and Policy Making
2. Effective Implementation – Active and Adaptive
3. Learning
4. Participative Democracy

Puzzle Learning in Non-Dominant Structures.

Concepts
Open Systems Thinking
Design Principles
Theory of Learning – Ecological or Direct Perception
Influential (effective) Communication
Bion's Group Dynamics
Diffusion
Rationalization of Conflict

The Experience with Integrated Concepts

At this point I brief the group on forming a SC community. I stress the importance of careful preparation and planning that must precede the actual event. I emphasize selecting participants so that they cover all aspects of the puzzle to be solved—a crucial success factor.

If participants are a coherent adult education group I might suggest they become, for example, a task force making policy for the future of AE in Australia. If they are diverse, I ask them to become the first national Australian government selected by lot rather than as elected representatives. This allows me to tie more strongly the SC into the concept of participative rather than representative government as a necessary tool for such a venture, where methods for group decision making and the *rationalization of conflict* would need to be used.

So the scene is set and participants then receive a standard briefing for the first Search phase—data collection of changes taking place in the "extended social field" or environment, from which we will prepare desirable and probable future scenarios. The rationale has been explained and the rules for the conduct of this phase are given as "all perceptions are valid, no argument is allowed at this stage. That comes later when you have to make sense of all the data you have perceived."

I add the second ground rule: "You may add to the list at any stage during the Search but only when you inform the community that you are doing so." I also explain the second level of meaning this entails, the democratic leveling achieved by the ground rules and their role in ensuring practice in effective communication. Participants begin to get a feel for the manager's job and the care which must be taken in regard to the subtleties of human communication.

All of this is done in the total group for the good reason that we are building communities; not small "in" or "out" groups but big "many hat wearing" groups who have to collaborate and can diffuse through many networks.

When the environmental data is collected, we stop and examine the following overhead (Diagram 5).

This illustrates the difference between traditional theories of education as *teaching* and the SC which is based on "people *learning* in an environment." We note that the second paradigm is the educational foundation of Design Principle 2 (below) and that the Search Conference integrates the elements necessary for a full-scale learning experience of democracy.

I ask people to reflect on the second paradigm which they have just used to explore the environment. Contrary to beliefs about discrete bits

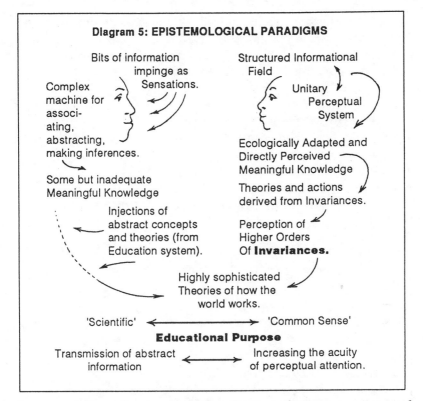

Diagram 5: EPISTEMOLOGICAL PARADIGMS

Bits of information impinge as Sensations.

Complex machine for associating, abstracting, making inferences.

Some but inadequate Meaningful Knowledge

Injections of abstract concepts and theories (from Education system).

Structured Informational Field

Unitary Perceptual System

Ecologically Adapted and Directly Perceived Meaningful Knowledge

Theories and actions derived from Invariances.

Perception of Higher Orders Of **Invariances.**

Highly sophisticated Theories of how the world works.

'Scientific' ←——————→ 'Common Sense'

Educational Purpose

Transmission of abstract information ←——→ Increasing the acuity of perceptual attention.

of sensory information impinging on the central nervous system and requiring integration before meaningful knowledge is available, our perceptual system acts as a unit to absorb meaningful knowledge directly from the environment.

In the first Search session people draw on their perceptions of the extended social field, and they will continue to synthesize these into collective scenarios reflecting their own sophisticated and realistic theories. They are gaining confidence in their ability to self-manage their learning and to value their own perceptions and experience.

Next, we ask people to analyze and synthesize their own environmental data, using their own resources and values. I split them into four mixed groups if numbers permit, with a minimum of four persons in a group. If there are only enough for three groups, it is desirable to have one group work on "desirable futures" and two on "probable futures" as this area is often more conflicted and it is important to surface the groups" commonalities and differences.

The groups then report, discuss and negotiate their scenarios to the point where there is an integrated most desirable and most probable

scenario. This is essential because these scenarios become the bench-
marks for measuring progress during the rest of the conference. Any
item that finally cannot be agreed upon in some form is placed on a "Not
Agreed" list. It cannot then be the basis for further work.

This process can generate a lot of learning. Many people are challenged to explain the values and reasoning behind a particular decision.
Because all participate only as people with something to contribute to the
puzzle solution, nobody can hide behind position, authority or status.
Negotiating skills are also learned here. When any conflict has been
rationalized, I present the following overheads.

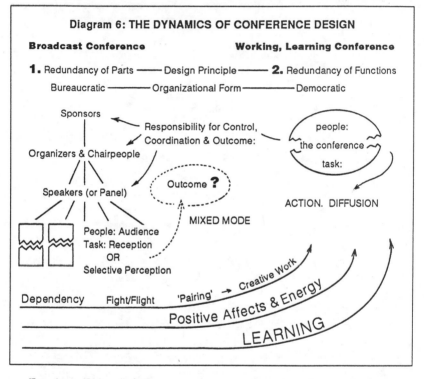

Diagram 6: THE DYNAMICS OF CONFERENCE DESIGN

Design Principles

These two contrasting basic principles, (1) *redundancy of parts* and (2)
redundancy of functions underlie both organizational and conference
(temporary organization) design. Which one we choose determines our
structure (see Diagram 6). And this structure has profound implications
for the outcome of the conference, the amount of learning it generates,
and the potential for follow-through that flows from its emotional tone
and energy level. An SC is the most internally-consistent method de-

signed on the second principle. This highlights the training workshop paradox. To learn *about* SCs puts us in the *mixed mode*, something we as Search Conference managers must avoid in an actual conference.

Conference Dynamics—Group Assumptional and Working Modes

Wilfred Bion discovered that people in groups make assumptions about how they should protect their group as an entity. If conference managers design tasks or act according to the structure portrayed on the left, the group will enter a state of *dependency*. They assume the management is a great and powerful leader who will take responsibility for their behavior, absolving them from responsibility to learn. Very little learning takes place in this mode.

The assumption that a leader or force aims to destroy the group results in *fight/flight*, expressed either as fighting behavior or passive resistance. This is more likely in the mixed mode, but we also see it these days in pure cases of design principle 1. Since Bion's time, we have witnessed a growing awareness of the right to participate. Outright denial of this right—in conferences packed with speakers and little discussion time—for example, can spark dramatic episodes of fight/flight. People learn more in this mode than in dependency, for at least they are active, but their main task becomes removing the threat rather than the original purpose.

In *Pairing*, the third of Bion's assumptional modes, the group may divert itself from the task and shift attention to a subgroup or pair. However, this also can be a prelude to the desired condition, the *Creative Working Mode*.

A group is most likely to achieve this mode when it takes full responsibility for the control and coordination of its work towards the agreed purposes. In fact, once a group establishes this mode it is very difficult to stop them. Managers who feel the need to decelerate or reverse the momentum can find themselves in a great deal of trouble.

The second overhead spells out dependency and fight/flight in greater detail (Diagram 7). This perspective is often useful for people struggling within the confines of bureaucratic structures.

A SC manager must learn to design processes that avoid outbreaks of the group assumptions and to recognize them should they occur. S/he also needs the practical skills to redirect the conference back into the working mode before the assumptions become entrenched. If they arise in the training workshop (as they might), they should be debriefed at the end of that session.

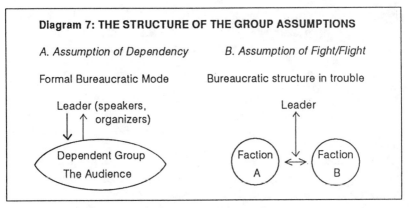

Diagram 7: THE STRUCTURE OF THE GROUP ASSUMPTIONS

A. Assumption of Dependency   B. Assumption of Fight/Flight

Formal Bureaucratic Mode   Bureaucratic structure in trouble

From this point, I continue or curtail the experience depending on time available. When we have time I find it useful to move into the phase that embodies the L11—systemic relationships within the system under study. For creative planning work, we need both internal and external perspectives. This phase offers insight into other features of the method and its underlying theory.

I call this the *History* session, a brief review where participants share perceptions of the past as well as the future. Some people have little or no knowledge of where X has come from and there is often intense disagreement about critical turning points. The history session makes it possible to build into the future continuities deeply valued that mark the character of X. Without preserving what matters most, there is little chance of implementation. These continuities define what people recognize and feel they belong to. Omitting them in standard bureaucratic planing heralds an outburst of active or passive resistance (fight/flight).

In diverse groups, however, this task is better described than attempted. For example, most participants in my seminars will have a working (book) knowledge of Australian history. Rather than recreate it here, it makes more sense to move on and have them decide what to retain of their valued continuities, what to discard and what they feel they should create. This is a critical preparatory step for the task of deciding what a desirable Australia should be.

By this stage the group should be in full creative working mode. Now, it is a good idea, if time permits, to take reports from the small groups on their "keep," "discard" and "create" lists, negotiate these so that the commonalities become conference property, and move straight to the desirable future of X. This confers a partial sense of completion and also allows a demonstration of another interesting aspect of people working together—the dynamics of assigning priorities (more below).

At whatever point we leave the experiential component, we use the time left to outline the remaining process as it would probably happen, deal with the many questions participants are likely to raise and to highlight other concepts employed. I find it best to discuss novel concepts in response to questions asked and to have participants learn them by reflecting on how they actually went about their work.

I always include one major concept concerning the conditions for effective communication, perhaps one of the most misunderstood of all human phenomena (see Diagram 8).

Diagram 8: THE PROPERTIES OF INFLUENTIAL (EFFECTIVE) COMMUNICATION

Theoretical	Design and Management
1. OPENNESS For exploration and checking of opinions and perceptions	Pre-briefing on content and process. Minimize threat to participation. Clarify roles and values. All recording is public (butcher's paper) visual, verbal, vernacular.
2. MUTUALLY SHARED OBJECTIVE FIELD 'We all live in the same world.' It is commonly perceived as background to joint action, taking into consideration, the interdependencies.	Scan the external social field using ground rule – 'all perceptions are valid.' This is analyzed and used throughout as a benchmark.
3. BASIC PSYCHOLOGICAL SIMILARITY 'We are all human with the same human concerns. Each is an action centre, can talk as equals and learn from each other.	Provide opportunities to see common ground – desirable futures based on ideals and use these as basis for cooperative work and the rationalization of conflict.
4. TRUST: THE EMERGENCE OF INDIVIDUALS AS OPEN SYSTEMS Will initiate communication which builds self confidence, therefore vicious circle which generates energy and leads to action and diffusion.	No status difference between participants and managers. No management interference in the content, manages only the environment and process for all the above.

$$4 = 1+2+3$$

$$\text{TRUST} \rightarrow \left(\begin{array}{c} \text{COLLABORATIVE ACTION} \\ + \text{ DIFFUSIVE LEARNING} \end{array} \right)$$

The guidelines for Searching pictured here derive from Solomon Asch's (1952) learnings in this area. They document four necessary conditions for effective communication and how we design them into Search Conferences. Any behavior by managers *or* participants that disturbs these conditions can spell trouble for a Search Conference.

For example, we often are asked why individual note-taking for reports is discouraged and butcher's paper is so important. Basically, this open technology reassures everybody that things are what they appear to be and nobody will manipulate the content. In this practice, as in all others, there must be a high level of consistency.

In discussing these principles and the participant's experience so far, people develop a deeper understanding of what we are about. They are able to integrate bits of the theory and practice verbally and conceptually. For example, gaining meaningful knowledge directly from our own perceptions applies as much to our knowing those around us as it does to our physical environment. Our traditional Western theories may cut us off from learning of our awareness of this knowledge. But the process of the Search Conference itself gives us direct evidence that it is there. The speed with which a group can act out any of Bion's assumptions leaves no doubt that all are aware of what is going on. In any social setting we can go through elaborate, albeit subtle, rituals to learn as much as possible about and communicate adaptively with others.

CONSTRAINTS AND ACTION PLANS

When we have two days for an introductory workshop, it is useful to practice discussing constraints and making final action plans. These steps often induce strong feelings. A group may grow quite depressed as it contemplates what a big job it has in front of it. This is why constraints are left to the end, after a collective direction and positive working mode are established. The trick here is to covert this positive energy into more effective action plans.

For this reason, I never say "List the constraints." Rather, "Bring back the most serious obstacles together with a way of dealing with them! This keeps the emphasis on the positive. In the creative working mode, jokes and asides flow fast from the participants and add to the sense of community. *Serious learning is fun!*

Whenever the experience is terminated *diffusion* must be mentioned. The concept often is misunderstood. Diffusion is more a psychological process of communicating energy and enthusiasms than a mechanical exercise of putting out reports or holding information meetings. Emotions—excitement and joy in particular—drive diffusion every bit as much, and perhaps more than, the actual content of the "message". When people are really "working" towards their purposes they generate high levels of excitement. That is the surest clue they have held a successful Search Conference. This energy is contagious and the driving mechanism for the implementation of action plans. This effect accounts for the diffusion of the concept of the Search Conference itself. (This book is one example—contagious energy among the contributors—Ed.)

OTHER IMPORTANT CONCEPTS TO CONSIDER

Rationalizing Conflict

The complexities of our world render a simple dichotomy between conflict and consensus impossible. The Search Conference aims above all for realistic working relations, and not, therefore, consensus. It aims for the rationalization of conflict as it applies to achieving the purposes of all parties in the venture, in the long term as well as short, for they often will need to continue working and negotiating action plans after the conference ends (Diagram 9).

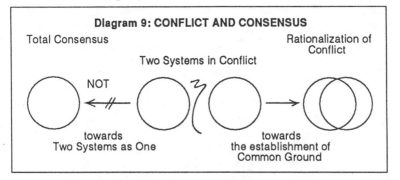

Diagram 9: CONFLICT AND CONSENSUS

Total Consensus

Rationalization of Conflict

Two Systems in Conflict

NOT

towards
Two Systems as One

towards
the establishment of
Common Ground

Some level of common ground is almost always achieved through exploration of areas that lie on the periphery of the conflicted issue, or outside of it. So we always seek our first level of agreement in basic ideals. Once this ground is secured, we seek ways that the parties can work to enlarge its size. This aspiration always will be limited by the degree to which some parties must, by definition, play adversarial roles. Often, however, they will cooperate on significant matters of common interest. The Search works by seeking indirect strategies to negotiated agreements, broadening the sphere of concern surrounding the conflict and enlarging the area of agreement.

In my experience the area of common concerns and agreement is always larger than the parties in conflict or even impartial outsiders had supposed. Indeed it is *much* larger than the stereotypical view we tend to have of conflict. That in itself is one of the most significant learning experiences that can come from a search, and a leveling one too.

SPOKEN LANGUAGE

Similarly, I find it important to discuss spoken language and its role as "social cement" (Ong, 1967). There is a faddish concern now about "verbal aggression," but I prefer to have people yelling at each other than not talking at all. Wars start only after somebody decides to stop talking. Don't be dismayed if people express strong feelings: it means they care. Our worst nightmare should be facing a dissociated and alienated society.

Finally, *deciding on priorities* is interesting. How do *you* get a group to do it? I sometimes do this little experiment in the workshop. I ask them as individuals to use a voting system—e.g. "You have $100 to spend. Allocate it according to the importance you personally place on these issues." The results are recorded. I then put participants into small groups to discuss issues and to choose five out of, say, ten issues for action. Again the results are recorded. Finally I say, "Put a mark against those you are personally prepared to put time and effort into." When the results are recorded this time, we note that they usually are vastly different. What does this mean? I have three hypotheses:

The method the manager chooses has a significant influence
    on the outcome or product;
Group working produces different outcomes to individual
    voting systems;
There is a difference between what people think is important
    and what they're committed to.

I usually would opt for commitment, allowing for group discussion, but each manager and group must be aware of the consequences of their decision-making processes.

I also draw attention to what may happen during the *process of implementation*. How can we maintain the nature and spirit of the Search process? Once the event has finished, many people embrace time-honored formalities, appointing or electing a chair, for example, or setting up rules of debate, only to find a wholesale return to territorial bickering and refusal to address the primary issues. So they waste the gains made during the conference. To avoid this disappointment, we need to understand the dynamics discussed above.

The Strategy of the Indirect Approach

The Search Conference enacts the indirect rather than head-on approach. We progressively secure common ground as we zero in on the issue. The indirect (or "broad front") approach attempts to maximize gains and minimize losses. There is little point in storming barricades or putting all your eggs in one basket. You could lose everything the first time around.

It is better to encircle the enemy. It is critical in the SC that participants span the spectrum of opinion on the issue. As implementation continues, it involves wider and wider nets—"community development" at its best.

At the End

Once the planning phase is complete, we often need to address the question, "How do we organize ourselves to ensure that we meet our long term goals?"

Diagram 10: LOGISTICS—IDEAL

Management. Designs and manages environment, structure and process. Stays out of content.

Venue. Social island for intensive work, preferably residential to aid community building. Comfortable, plenty of wall space. Participants should not have to think about meals, etc. Flexible arrangements.

Timing. Start late afternoon, continue after dinner. Then full day and night, finish lunch or afternoon of next day. One and a half days is possible but really only suitable for very simple situations.

Materials. Simple, butcher's paper, thick felt pens, masking tape. Computerized white boards and rapid WP and photocopying have advantages and disadvantages.

Numbers. Between 15 and 30 or go to multi-search for larger numbers.

We also take up matters of logistics and practicality (see Diagram 10). One important conference practice is carrying tasks over from one day to the next to take advantage of the "Zeigarnik effect"—the spontaneous wish to complete unfinished work. We also discuss the timing of each phase, the best places to meet, reporting findings, and many other matters. While describing ideal conditions, I also point out that we have to make do with the best we can get. [For more detail, see *Searching* (Emery M., 1982), where I also outline the Participative Design Workshop, a method for using these same principles to help people design their own workplaces.]

Numbers often demand special attention. What do you do when the number of necessary participants exceeds the roughly 35 person limit for a SC? The answer is the Multisearch or "Future Directions Model" (Diagram 11).

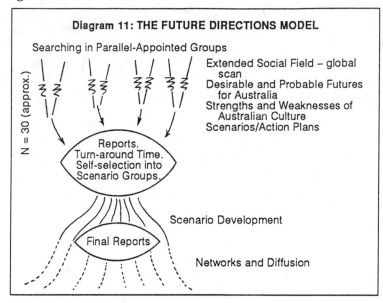

Diagram 11: THE FUTURE DIRECTIONS MODEL

Searching in Parallel-Appointed Groups

N = 30 (approx.)

Extended Social Field – global scan
Desirable and Probable Futures for Australia
Strengths and Weaknesses of Australian Culture
Scenarios/Action Plans

Reports. Turn-around Time. Self-selection into Scenario Groups.

Scenario Development

Final Reports

Networks and Diffusion

The Future Directions Model

This model represents SCs in parallel until the point where all the ground work has been done and self selecting task forces are sufficiently well informed and trusted to do work on behalf of the total search community. The critical element in a multisearch is the coordination and good functioning of the managerial group. (Emery M., 1989).

ABOUT THE AUTHOR

Merrelyn Emery has designed and managed hundreds of Search Conferences, experimenting with the method in small country towns, regional and national industries, local government, businesses and in other cultures. Trained originally as a psychologist, she became more interested in the prevention of individual and social ills through change based on learning.

She is particularly interested in structures that enable people to regain control over their lives. The best known of these is the Participative Design Workshop (in which workers redesign their section of an organization) and the Search Conference. Both are described in her book Searching (1982), now being revised. She has been with the Centre for Continuing Education at the Australian National University since 1970.

CHAPTER 29

DOING BY LEARNING, LEARNING BY DOING
A Practitioner's Experience with Theory and Practice
Mary Fambrough

THIS CHAPTER SHOWS HOW an experienced facilitator and trainer adapted search methods to her own contracting business. Mary Fambrough has worked for large and small corporations, had formal training in group dynamics, and had never managed a search process before.

Drawing on her aspirations for her own firm, she creates a consulting/training hybrid, that includes a planning expert as her co-facilitator. It resembles the "doing by learning" applications many folks have practiced for two decades. She sees no contradiction between personal growth and strategy planning within a global and industry-wide perspective.

In the previous chapter, Merrelyn Emery suggests that "mixing modes" can dilute the search process to the point where people feel manipulated and democratic values are compromised. Yet, many practitioners like Fambrough have mixed modes as they seek to apply these processes. What can we learn from their efforts? What are the risks and benefits?

At what point does the meaning of searching disappear? Can the "Asch conditions for dialogue" (Chapter 5) be established when a facilitator has focused on other objectives? Is the creativity—emphasized by Fambrough and Emery both—qualitatively different in such an event? The case makes clear the dichotomy, the dilemma, and the paradox. Was this event and follow-up process "just another participative management exercise?" Or did Fambrough create a third form, combining participation and searching into something else? Her personal mission, she writes, is "discovering new ways to create a workplace that exemplifies the values of adventure, challenge, creativity, diversity, and love."

Fambrough's case raises critical issues in do-it-yourself strategic conference learning. She points out that a facilitator's working agreement with participants is a key mediator in any event. Under what conditions will a group accept any assigned task as furthering its central purposes? To what extent is "mode mixing" one way we, as facilitators, manage our own (and a group's) anxiety?

This question is especially relevant in a conference based on procedures and concepts that are likely to be unfamiliar to most people. Suppose the facilitator is also a co-owner of the sponsoring organization? Most of us have (unconscious or semi-conscious) agendas that put us at risk to be experienced as manipulative, regardless of what tasks we ask groups to do.

I asked Fambrough to revisit her experience in light of these questions and Emery's caveats. She has provided a thoughtful rationale in the pages that follow, and some ambivalent second thoughts too.

My discussions with Mary Fambrough began with a letter I received while preparing this book. Later she sent me her conference documents, and I've included enough so that readers can appreciate how she changed the future search design, her reflections on the conference itself, and what happened in her company during the year that followed. — MRW

ICOM Mechanical Inc.
571 North 7th St.
San Jose, CA 59112
July 17, 1991

Dear Mr. Weisbord,

I am a principal in a ten-year-old mechanical contracting company, ICOM Mechanical, employing about 70 people. We engineer and install commercial and industrial air conditioning and process piping systems. The company is small, but larger than average for our industry. I'm writing to find out whether you have any interest in the application of Future Search Conferences to small businesses.

The search conference concept fascinated me when I read about it in *Productive Workplaces,* and I was eager to conduct a conference myself. That opportunity presented itself last September. I used a Future Search Conference as an event to launch a strategic planning intervention.

I found it to be a wonderful medium for maximizing involvement, teaching and learning of all participants including myself, gaining insight, building trust, and creating an environment of possibilities and hopefulness. Perhaps the most exciting aspect was the number of participants who thanked me for inviting them and told me that the event had made a significant contribution to their personal growth and self-esteem.

Our conference was attended by employees of all levels, from the president to sheet metal apprentices. It included vendors, customers, and a union representative—about 40 people. Part of what I found intriguing about the ICOM conference was how successful and well-received it was, given the characteristics of the attendees.

Most participants have experience working only for small businesses. Most of our employees have spent their careers in the highly-fragmented construction industry. Many vendors are also small businesses. Our insurance broker attended as well as our certified public accountant, both small business owners. None had ever been to anything remotely like a search.

Few had attended meetings or training situations that were participative, and they certainly never had been asked to discuss personal values or beliefs in a public, work-related environment.

I designed the agenda with this in mind as best I could, but this was still an unusual group, quite different from a group of people working for Procter and Gamble or IBM. The educational backgrounds of group members also was varied, ranging from MBAs and

engineers to plumbers and sheet metal mechanics. In my opinion, all
of these factors might be perceived as reasons not to use the Future
Search Conference approach. I believe they are what made it so
special and powerful.

I have enclosed our conference agenda and the invitations that
were sent to employees and other stakeholders.

Sincerely,
Mary Fambrough

INVITATION LETTER (abridged)

September 4, 1990

Dear Stakeholder,

You are receiving this letter because we think you are someone
who is important to the success of ICOM Mechanical, now and in the
future. Where will ICOM be a year from now?

Where will ICOM be in five years? Even more important, where
would we like ICOM to be?

These are some of the questions the ICOM Board of Directors is
trying to answer as we begin the process of strategic planning. As we
proceed, we will be re-evaluating the basic mission of the company,
the values we represent, the goals and objectives we hope to achieve,
and the strategies we will use to make our vision of the future a
reality.

We welcome and encourage input and assistance in this undertaking from all stakeholders. You are a stakeholder. You have an interest
or share in the future of ICOM. If you are an employee, ICOM's
success means job security, an opportunity to learn and grow with the
company, and contributions to your profit sharing plan. For customers, ICOM's greater efficiency and effectiveness could mean higher
standards of quality and lower prices. To the unions, ICOM's success
represents more jobs for members. We believe that all of you have
something to gain or lose by our success or failure.

We are planning an event. It is called a Future Search Conference
and will be held on Friday, September 14, and Saturday, September
15, 1990. The purpose is to bring together the members of a community who in some way, however direct or remote, play a part in
shaping each others' future and the future of ICOM. Together we will
look at the external and internal environments, trends, and possibilities and opportunities for creating a future for ICOM that we can all
support and benefit from.

Those who attend the conference will be both the actors and

audience. We would be honored by your participation. Details regarding time and place can be found on the attached flyer.

Very truly yours,
Donald G. Isaacson
President

SPONSOR: ICOM MECHANICAL, INC.

Conference Task: Initiate Corporate Strategic Planning.

Stakeholders: Corporate Management Group (5), Engineering Dept. (4), Piping/Plumbing Dept. (3), Sheet Metal Field (4), Sheet Metal Shop (2), Service Dept. (3), Administrative Staff (3), Accounting Dept. (1), Material Handling/Expediting (1), Customers (1), Union Representatives (1), Vendors (9). Total: 37.

Length: Two Days

Place: San Jose, California

Conference Managers: Mary Fambrough and Bill Brickner

A PROGRESS REPORT FROM THE STRATEGIC PLANNING TEAM

October 10, 1991

Dear Friends,

Last month marked the one year anniversary of the ICOM Mechanical Future Search Conference which many of you attended. You may remember that one important purpose of the conference was to generate as much data as possible for use by our strategic planning team who was about to undertake the challenge of creating ICOM'S road map for the future.

The amount of data we actually collected about the company, our customers, the industry, the United States, and the world was amazing. We described ICOM and the environment in which it operates from the many unique perspectives offered by the diverse attendees of the conference. We attempted to project local and global changes we might see in the future and developed an image of how we would like the future to unfold which became a source of inspiration to both the participants, and later, to the strategic planning team.

During this past year we have learned that strategic planning is a valuable activity and must never truly end if it is to be effective. We would like to share some of the things ICOM has accomplished or changed as a result of our focus on strategic planning:

- We created a written statement of corporate values and objectives;
- We conducted an extensive written and verbal customer survey, vastly increasing our knowledge of our customers, how they feel about us, and what we can do to better serve them;
- We initiated and institutionalized a customer satisfaction mail-back "report card." presented to every customer at the end of the project, repair, or maintenance;
- We increased customer response time;
- Profitability increased;
- We recognized that we could not be all things to all people. The process of strategic planning allowed us to develop a clear understanding of the markets we can best serve, our distinctive competencies, and also, the type of work we should decline;
- We learned how to conduct more effective meetings. Understanding increased between departments and a welcome sense of cooperation and teamwork developed;
- We improved our accounts receivable collection processes, which has resulted in a significant reduction in past-due accounts;
- We reduced operating costs and eliminated excess inventory;
- We became convinced of the value and importance of consistent quality service;
- We recognized the necessity of increasing the information, knowledge, and decision-making power of our people who regularly interact with customers in the field if we are to respond more quickly and effectively to the needs and desires of our customers;
- We became more conscious of the need to constantly engage in the process of improvement;
- We identified training of everyone in the organization as the critical factor of our long-term success. We must never lose our desire for knowledge and our ability to learn.

The process of strategic planning has been an opportunity for the members of ICOM to increase and deepen their understanding of the goals, purposes, and values of the organization. We have come to recognize that the conscious choices and decisions we make today will determine the course of the company in the years ahead.

Amidst the incessant cry for immediacy in the contracting business we have been true to our commitment to develop a long-term perspective. Balancing the pressure to react now with the newly-found option of reacting more slowly, with forethought and consistency with our chosen goals is challenging,but the resulting sense of control over our own destiny is a satisfying reward.

Thank you for your contribution to our efforts.

> With Sincere Appreciation,
> ICOM Mechanical
> Strategic Planning Team

Dr. Wm. Brickner, Mary Fambrough, Dan Littleton, Richard Craine, Donald Isaacson, Bonnie Pratt, Nancy Heath, Steve Murphy, Randy Silva, David Luedtke, John Reyna, Tom Radich, Al Glace

(This letter is being sent to our fellow employees,customers, suppliers, and union representatives who have expressed an interest in the outcome of our strategic planning process.)

[EDITOR'S NOTE: Fambrough now takes up the many issues— organizational and personal—that influenced her conference. She also revisits each part of the design.]

REFLECTIONS ON THE ICOM FUTURE SEARCH CONFERENCE
By Mary Fambrough (November 11, 1991)

I agree with Merrelyn Emery regarding the immense importance of the conference manager role. I am also very sensitive to her distinctions between the two modes, searching and training. I am personally fed up with organizations that foster dependency, paternalism, and mindlessly act out their own co-dependence. Still, I conducted a conference that mixed modes and was effective and well-received.

I know that the conference design I created was motivated by a desire to take care of my own needs as well as to support the desired conference outcomes. My personal agenda was to run a successful conference, both in the minds of the attendees (my need for acceptance) and in terms of actual output (my need to relieve anxiety about competence), to provide play, warmth, and fun (my need for fellowship, love, and emotional comfort), and to send participants home with a feeling of personal fulfillment, discovery, enhanced understanding, or whatever might be valuable to a given individual (my need to alleviate my guilt as a company owner asking employees and other stakeholders to give themselves, their time and energy, to benefit ICOM).

Why a Future Search?

I viewed the Future Search Conference (FSC) as a discrete part of a larger process in ICOM: Strategic planning. I wanted maximum participation of all members of the organization. What little was written about participative planning processes typically involved a top management team producing a mission statement, drafting goals and objectives, and then graciously turning these over to the next level below to "sell" them to the managers reporting to them.

This model is often "cascaded" down the levels all the way to the bottom of the organization. Each level is offered the opportunity to develop its own action plans to support the master plan. The rank-and-file are given the "opportunity" to participate in the uninspired work of carrying out a plan derived by the elite group of managers and planners at the top. That is not the kind of participation I had in mind.

My belief is that an organization is a composite of its individual members. The real values of the organization, the values that form a company's character and ethics, and give depth, meaning, and strength to its informal operating systems, are the values of the members.

There is immense power in identifying and writing down these core values. They are an undeniable source of motivation. Ideally the formal structure and systems should be an outgrowth of shared values. Commitment to carry out a corporate vision, mission, and goals based on values common to most organization members will be generated naturally and genuinely with little need for "enrollment," dangling carrots, or negative reinforcement.

I must interject a word on the probability of discovering shared values. I do not naively assume that all people share the same values, even people with similar cultures and vocations. But I did believe it highly probable that we would identify some common values among my fellow-employees at ICOM. I know I am instinctively drawn to others who have values compatible with my own; my hypothesis, based on considerable experience, is that we are most likely to work with, do business with, and socialize with people who share a similar value base.

In addition, the literature (I read a lot of it in graduate school) is full of talk about the necessity of involving stakeholders in the planning process. A lack of involvement of those who would be affected by a plan was cited repeatedly in the research as a cause for unsuccessful planning or for the failure of plans to be implemented. Still I found no documentation of a :planning process that was genuinely participative. Hence, I decided I would create my own.

Obstacles to Participative Planning

I quickly discovered numerous obstacles—everything from the reluctance of top management to relinquish control to the logistics of involving everybody in the process got in the way. I decided:

1). I would probably not get it perfect the first time,

2). Real world constraints, things like limited time and money, must be honored, and,

3). I was really lucky to be in a situation to try something like participative strategic planning at all.

I chose to begin the strategic planning process with a FSC, hoping to realize the following outcomes:

- To generate lots of data about the environment, global and societal trends, the industry, and the company to use in the analysis phase of strategic planning. Traditional methods of uncovering such information would involve many tedious hours of research and would probably produce less meaningful information.

- To begin to infuse the culture with the concepts of collaboration, shared responsibility for future success, and the corporation as a community.

Based on these desired outcomes, I designed a conference (see Box B) that would:

- Create a safe space to engage stakeholders in a dialogue about values, visions, feelings, and other topics not within the comfort zone of most of the participants.

- Create an environment that equalized hierarchical distinctions, existing role perceptions, and emotion-laden labels such as labor and management, journeyman and apprentice, etc.

- Establish common ground among the stakeholders; uncover the places where individual values, visions, hopes and desires intersect, overlap, interconnect, or support.

- Allow participants to experience some of the following:
    A sense of interdependence;
    A sense of possibilities rather than limitations;
    A feeling of personal and collective power to make a difference;
    A sense of personal and shared responsibility for the future;
    Strategic thinking;
    Learning from each other;
    An appreciation of the value of planning;
    Synergy;

An alternative to competition. This might be cooperation,
collaboration, valuing of differing viewpoints, etc.
Stimulation to be creative, to contribute, to share, to support, to
risk, and to be authentic.

Based on my knowledge of the group (at least the ICOM portion of the
group) I also recognized a need to consider the following:

- We have a strong need to produce. In the construction industry this
generally means to create something tangible. Thinking, planning,
and talking are not regarded as work. The value of the search
conference accomplishments must be reinforced.
- *Time is money* is an underlying assumption. Thus, the need for
structure, time management, and agendas is acute.
- A significant level of tension existed about the conference, essentially
fear of the unknown coupled with the inherent tension between
participants. It would be helpful to reduce tension to a manageable
level.

ICOM FUTURE SEARCH DESIGN

Domino Survival Exercise
THE PAST: INDIVIDUALS, COMPANY, INDUSTRY
AND SOCIETY
Best Job/Worst Job
Best/Worst Companies to do Business With
Values Exchange
Personal Vision and Values
STEPPING INTO THE FUTURE:
An Exercise in Imagination and Creativity
THE PRESENT
Strategic Thinking and Strategy Formulation
ICOM'S Strengths and Weaknesses
Opportunities and Threats
Mapping the External Environment
POSSIBILITIES AND OPTIONS
Next Steps

All of this meant to me that I had to impose a structure, complete with
ground rules. The agenda must make active participation a part of the
conference from the onset, interaction between perceived "unequals" or

"enemies" (competing vendors, for example) must happen quickly and naturally, with the goal of moving the group swiftly toward a level of tolerable discomfort.

Fear and Skepticism

An early clue about the level of fear and skepticism was apparent from the moment the first invitation was circulated. Prospective participants phoned and wrote with all sorts of questions: What exactly is this Future Search Conference? What should I do to prepare for it? Why am I invited? Can I just come and watch? Will you be sending out more information in advance? I don't think I was supposed to get this; I'm not a "stockholder" (ICOM is a privately-held corporation).

These clues (or cries for help) prompted me to add a bit more structure to my original conference design and to send an abbreviated agenda to participants prior to the conference.

Use of Training Methods

Starting off the conference, our first activity was a structured learning experience, the Domino Survival Exercise. I decided I wanted to provide this learning structure as an icebreaker. (In fact, its likeness to a game made it readily accepted and understood by this group.) In a way, it was like saying, "Okay, we are going to play a game. According to this game, everyone in the room is an equal. Each of us has one goal and that is to survive. Here are the rules. . . ."

I first experienced this exercise as an illustration of how organization structure develops; a simulation of why specialization and division of labor make sense and tend to develop as an organization strives to operate more efficiently.

I saw countless potential interpretations of the exercise, depending on the context in which it is used. I also have a faith that every group has its own collective theme. I expected this ICOM conference group to discover relevance in the domino activity without being forced or led. I was prepared to lead if necessary, which satisfactorily took care of my own control needs. (I probably did more leading than I remember or than was actually needed.)

Important planned and unplanned learning emerged from the Domino Exercise:

- A game context provided safety for interaction, risk-taking, and successfully equalized the group.
- A sense of team-ness began to take shape as a result of the shared pleasurable experience. The appearance of a group metaphor—the

domino, numerous (unexpected) acts of self-sacrifice, the formation of "strategic partnerships," and an open discussion of why the survival of others was important to the satisfaction and fulfillment of most individuals (win-win thinking) helped this group quickly develop its own identity.

- An observation regarding improved performance and achievement of goals with pre-planning introduced the idea that planning has value in terms of optimizing time and output.
- A frustration with the rules of the game, and the fact that the rules changed throughout the game. The players could not control the rules. This was the only place where I consciously led the group. I drew an analogy of the game rules to our own real-world environment. There are, and always will be, environmental forces that are perpetually subject to change without warning and that are well beyond our control.
- Bill Brickner, my co-facilitator (who had not experienced the exercise before), acted as a participant in this discussion. He drew a delightful analogy. The activity demonstrated the need for each other's dominoes. He saw the dominoes as symbols of each person's unique and individual contribution.

Had I been teaching organization structure and design, I would have been mighty disappointed at this point. Instead of bringing to the surface dysfunctional dynamics, the exercise brought people together! Simply observing behavioral changes in the group during the break following the domino exercise revealed what the activity had accomplished. The room was loud with talking and laughter. There were no visible barriers between individuals, no formality, and no evident discomfort.

The Values Exchange Activity

This was another activity selected to accomplish a very specific goal: Legitimizing a discussion of personal and organizational values in the workplace by creating a safe place to do this. It was less of a "training" technique to my thinking than was the Domino Survival Exercise

The Values Exchange allowed participants to consider and weigh the values they personally hold most important. At times, people were asked to choose between money and values. The atmosphere began as playful and non-threatening. By the end of the activity, individuals were seriously trying to acquire the values they personally coveted.

The purpose was to afford a vehicle to present a broad selection of values to the participants within a safe context. The activity thus provided exposure to an extensive vocabulary of names of values, enabling people to more easily engage in values-talk.

The Values Exchange was a high-minded experience that served to segue participants into the development of a personal vision statement, which was of course, to be values-based. Had the group not already achieved a comfort level with the discussion about values, I think the visioning would have been very difficult.

As I write about the activities used in the conference, I am wondering where to draw the line between the two modes: training and searching—democratic mutual inquiry. Consider the use on Day 2 of collage-making as a way to express and give shape to participants' desired future visions of themselves, ICOM, and the world. Was this a training activity?

Is an activity_encouraging use of a generally foreign medium for non-verbal symbolic expression of ideas—a training technique? I don't think so. I find it to be a vehicle encouraging and enabling creative expression and personal disclosure. Still, I am sure you can find all kinds of guides for trainers that contain descriptions of the use of collage in training.

Maybe the key element in defining what is and isn't training has to do with the desired outcome: Is the product of the activity pre-known by the facilitator/trainer or is the product created or discovered by the participant(s)?

Stimulating Creativity

This brings me to another essential part of this discussion. I wanted the FSC to encourage creativity, to stimulate participants to go beyond the kinds of thinking they were accustomed to, to focus on possibilities rather than limitations. What kinds of processes might be appropriate and effective to facilitate creativity? Certain generally accepted principles regarding the promotion of creative thinking and problem-solving come to mind.

Most would agree on ways to unlock creativity: non-judgment and non-evaluation of ideas; becoming aware of limiting perceptions and enlarging the field; asking "why," again and again, every time a possible conclusion is reached; assuming a different role while looking at a problem and exploring how the definition of the problem and the solution now look different; and looking for multiple acceptable solutions.

Roger von Oech suggests "doing something differently" as one way of promoting creativity. This includes something as simple as the order in which you do routine activities like eating breakfast, combing your hair, and getting dressed. Though this discussion may be simplistic, I think it illustrates one reason why the FSC concept is so powerful as a method of stimulating creative thinking.

Attending a FSC is a break from the daily routine. Participants engage in a different set of tasks than usual, with different people, in a different place. So just by definition, a search conference is clearly fertile soil for creativity. It provides time and space for a group of stakeholders with no collective identity or established norms to conduct some form of inquiry.

In terms of search conference design, are participants most likely to achieve maximum heights of creativity if all activities are rooted in real-life and real-time? Might not a break from the commonplace, routine, real-world biases and constraints—through the mechanisms of fantasy, role-playing, and visioning—help people squirm and wiggle their way into new territory, both internally and externally? Obviously, I tend to find the movement from real-world to make-believe and back again to be freeing, stimulating, and potentially frame-breaking. (ED NOTE—Steven Burgess makes a similar point in Chapter 34).

Interestingly, I think that training approaches may reflect successful use of the strategy of the "indirect approach" advocated by Emery. Nonetheless, the critical issues she identifies must not be lost. I certainly recognize the danger of training technologies promoting dependence, non-acceptance of responsibility, and control and manipulation by the conference manager both of processes and outcomes. But if a facilitator is controlling, that will probably be the case regardless of the design.

Using An "Expert"

A word on our resident expert. Dr. William Brickner was hired by ICOM to assist in developing a strategic plan, something we had not done before. He was selected for a number of reasons. His undergraduate degree was in engineering so he understood the construction industry and mechanical contracting operations. In short, he spoke our language.

Our industry has little use for academics or strategy. Bill was as close as we could come to finding someone with strategic planning experience that fit us. Second, Bill agreed with our desire to achieve a high level of horizontal and vertical participation in the planning process. Third, Bill had years of experience working with high-tech firms in the Silicon Valley. This meant that he had a good understanding of our customers and our environment.

When I decided to use FSC as a kick-off for our strategic planning process, I recognized a need for a second person to help with facilitation and coordination of the event itself. I asked Bill to assist, and together we carved out a role for him as a co-facilitator and presenter of limited information about strategic planning principles.

The goals of his presentations were: 1) to create understanding of what the company was undertaking, 2) to provide a context for the information the FSC was generating, i.e. to communicate a sense of how the data would be used, and 3) to increase the knowledge of everyone about strategic planning, both what it is and why we were doing it. Essentially, we wanted to give the participants a new tool and an additional source of power by helping them understand more about the "big picture."

A secondary goal of involving Bill in the FSC was to demystify the expert. If ICOM was to achieve a truly participative planning process, all members of the organization must acquire the ability to relate as equals, to listen to each other, to learn from each other, and to honor differences.

The whole strategic planning endeavor would be pointless if it were dominated by an expert to whom everyone looked for the answers and a final judgment of right or wrong. Bill operated at times during the conference as a participant, for example in the Values Exchange Activity. Other times he asked questions about the business and the industry, learning from the attendees.

Bill also provided value as an observer trained in group dynamics who had virtually no prior experience with ICOM. His marginality balanced my immersion in the system, which proved to be most effective. I might add that Bill expressed values and attitudes incredibly consistent with those of ICOM's management group. This tended to add credibility to management and further the development of trust.

ICOM Has Changed

I find these questions more compelling now than I would have a year ago. ICOM has changed. Specifically, the expectations of the members have changed. People are less willing to be led or manipulated, and are more willing to accept responsibility for results, trust their own abilities, make decisions, and manage themselves.

Some months ago, for example, I was facilitating an inter-departmental task force that expressed criticism (to put it mildly) of my covert mixing of modes (slipping teaching and lecturing into meetings without clearly presenting the intention to do so and giving them a choice) and of my unconscious use of power (e.g. dominating air time, recording ideas on flip-charts selectively, and enthusing over suggestions mirroring my own thinking).

As a result, I gave up facilitating this group. They have evolved into a self-managing improvement team that seldom consults me. They create their own agendas and facilitate their own meetings. This recent experience at ICOM suggests some positive long-term changes for which the FSC may have been a catalyst.

But the crucial point—from the standpoint of my own learning is that if I were planning an ICOM search today, I would be dealing with a different set of cultural norms. And these certainly would influence my conference design. It would be harder for me to facilitate, because I could rely less on modes I have used in the past and would be forced into new territory.

I wonder to what extent I would consider using training activities? With or without training, I still believe that when somebody who is called something like conference manager, facilitator, or coordinator provides the operating structure, the risk of creating dependency exists just as surely as if that person were a content expert.

ABOUT THE AUTHOR...

Mary Fambrough is a founding partner of ICOM Mechanical, a San Jose, California, contracting firm started in 1981. It provides engineering, design, fabrication, and installation of mechanical systems to high technology corporations. She has been involved in most phases of the business including labor relations, training, engineering and sales, and corporate effectiveness and quality improvement.

Fambrough has taught courses in management and supervision, and serves on two plumbing industry joint apprenticeship training committees and the South Bay Piping Industry Labor Management Committee. She is a former president of the Santa Clara Chapter of the American Institute of Plant Engineers, and was honored as "Plant Engineer of the Year" in 1988.

She holds a Master of Science degree in Organization Development from Pepperdine University, and has recently entered the doctoral program in Organizational Behavior at Case Western Reserve University in Cleveland, Ohio where she will study and consult for the next several years.

PART 8

PITFALLS IN ORGANIZING SEARCH CONFERENCES

Introduction

> "Learning to do it right the first time probably means doing it wrong at least once." – Weisbord's first paradox of quality

While there is quite a bit of "give" to search methodologies, every conference situation has its limits. In this part four practitioners describe pitfalls that anybody organizing conferences might encounter. They review a variety of unwelcome problems, some avoidable, some not. Their admirable willingness to make their dilemmas public provides us a rare gift of learning.

In Chapter 30, Maurice Dubras and Ivar Brokhaug team up to propose an ambitious community conference on the future of the Isle of Jersey in the Channel Islands. Their efforts stir political anxieties among key people who accept and then reject the plan—an object lesson for conference enthusiasts.

James Cumming in Chapter 31 unfolds a lesson of another sort. He discovers the importance of having diverse stakeholders, especially the "power people," if the conference is to make progress on tough issues—and what might happen if you don't.

Finally, in Chapter 32 Chris Kloth an experienced consultant then new to searching, reflects on a design sequence change that had unanticipated consequences. – MRW

CHAPTER 30

THE ISLE OF JERSEY FUTURE SEARCH
Pitfall – Whose Idea Is This Anyway?
Maurice Dubras and Ivar K. Brokhaug

"Lé changement est nécessaithe, mais i' faut nos asseûthé que tout changement est pouor le mus." In the words of the Island's ancient language, Jersey French, *"Change is necessary, but we must ensure that all change is for the better."*

I N THIS POST MORTEM (that may yet prove premature), two experienced consultants describe how they invested considerable effort in planning a conference that could not be brought off. While the community desperately needed a way to plan together, no local leaders were calling for a search, or indeed seeking outside help. The driving force came originally from one of the authors, not from the community. Dubras, in his zeal to bring this good process back home, became the prime mover. In the event, he had little leverage. This reality was hedged, initially, by bringing in "an expert from out of town," Brokhaug, whose impressive European experience reduced local anxiety. However, the anxiety soon went higher than ever when it became clear that both "experts" intended to have the key decisions and leadership in community hands rather than their own. That was not the way the game began, nor did it match local expectations. – MRW

THE CONCEPT

In the spring of 1988 Dubras floated the idea of conducting a future search process with key government and business leaders on the Isle of Jersey, one of the Channel Islands between Britain and France. It was offered as an innovative alternative in a climate of press criticism of political inaction and inertia at a time of rapid global change. There had been lots of debate in official circles but few results. The conference was offered as initiating a whole new way of doing things in systemic terms.

Dubras, a native of Jersey living in Canada, had recently visited the Island while in Europe on business. Through informal and social discussions he learned of the frustration of key business people and officials. This was confirmed by a series of local news articles entitled, "Whither Jersey?"

Dubras' initial proposal to the people he had met was enthusiastically received. He then involved Brokhaug (see Chapter 8), who had run many similar conferences in Norway, to help plan and manage the event.

Brokhaug's experience in community search conferences carried considerable influence in gaining acceptance of the concept by the steering group. After much discussion, it agreed to the proposed search conference going ahead. Three years later, as we write this, it has still not happened.

Whether it is on the back burner or dead and buried is still unclear. The point of interest is the series of delays, all linked to forces outside the planners' control.

We want to examine this so as to highlight some of the pitfalls of introducing a process into a small community that is part of a much larger system, and that has no existing structure for doing joint planning and strategy. We believe our experience can help those who believe in the benefits of this form of community action to be more aware of the pitfalls. Questions for ourselves:

1). Was the system ready for this or any other approach—that is, readiness in terms of Claes Janssen's four-room apartment model (see Chapter 9). Was the island in either a state of "contentment" or "denial," such that the time (state of mind) was inappropriate? In short, was our timing off in offering this event?

2). Were the people initially approached to sponsor the process the "right" ones? Did we miss some key political clues?

3). Were the political leaders involved to the extent that they had ownership and commitment?

4). Were the motivations of the people most involved appropriate (including the lead consultant's, who in mid-1989 decided to set up business in the island)?

5). Was it simply a matter of an interpersonal conflict between the steering group leader and the consultant?

Our analysis is bound to be subjective. Yet, to learn from the process and its outcomes we need to do this evaluation of the situation and our roles in it. To begin at the end, our conclusion is that this process only got to the initial stage of preliminary planning and "arm's length sanctioning" for several, interlinked reasons, of timing, leadership, commitment, AND conflict.

In this article we want to lay out the facts, as we see them, then postulate some things we would do differently to improve the prospects for implementation in a future or different situation.

THE FACTS
(Emergent From the First Nine Months of Discussion)

Dubras first approached four key influencers in the Island—the editor of the local newspaper; a key advisor to the States of Jersey (the legislature); the managing director of a major bank; and Dubras' brother, a local businessman and honorary officer of the Town of St. Helier.

Based on a written proposal, the key four embraced the idea as a different and interesting concept, and of potential benefit. Private sector funds were promised but not committed. Public sector funds were neither sought nor offered. The four sponsored the creation of a steering group of 12 people, representing major sectors of the community, that began to meet regularly. The newspaper publisher was nominated as leader. He formed a small executive team of four, including three of the original key influencers. The minutes of the first meeting noted that "the majority present were very enthusiastic" in response to the question, "Does Jersey need a Search Conference?" Timing was considered key, and the group considered two windows, early January and mid-March.

So, our answer to Question One is that we believe the timing was right, even though the window of opportunity closed sooner than we had anticipated. At the time of our first discussions, we now know, a major UK consultant was doing a study on revising the "machinery of government." This study led to the committee, the creation of which would influence our efforts a year later. Change was seen to be needed by many local leaders.

At the same time, a lot of people were very content with the way things had been. Their major issue was the slowness of government decision-making. So the "denial" we experienced in Jersey is similar to that heard in many institutions and cultures. It took the form of, "You know, of course, that Jersey is unique and the ways we do things here are not like North America. We are very skeptical of the process you are proposing. . . ."

So, having Brokhaug, with his long experience working in small European communities, was important. A second form of denial was the belief that if decisions are not being made now, nothing is likely to change that. The fact that the search concept was accepted so well by our initial contacts leads us to believe that unfolding events and the way we handled the verbal presentation had more impact on the outcome than the timing.

Responsibility for raising funds was transferred from the lead consultant to the steering group and its leader. He proceeded to tap the local business community with mixed results. As more people became involved, the consultant indicated the total cost was likely to go up, given the increased amount of time allocated to planning. This upset some people. In the event, early sponsorship covered most of the expenses but we took no fees despite several trips to the island—a risk we were prepared to take because of the highly-interesting project.

Meantime, the political structure changed. A new, influential government committee became responsible for Jersey's overall policy direction. This led to a delay and, at the same time, an official entity whose sanction for a search process would be vital to its success. However, it became clear subsequently that the government would neither formally endorse nor provide public funds for the conference.

Meanwhile the steering group continued to meet. We believe we had the right people involved, with the possible exception of a key union executive. He decided to stay on the sidelines, predicting that the conference would not succeed. In the fall of 1988 they addressed the conference objective. It would be "that participants would be from all walks of life who share the common denominator of all caring where Jersey was going and wanting it to be a better place for future generations" (minutes of September 12).

The newspaper owner made it known to the steering group executive team that he had political ambitions, and was expecting to run for election to the Legislature. (He was in fact elected in November 1990.) Meanwhile, the initial time frame—the spring of 1989—was moved to the autumn. Through a series of steering meetings, quite a number of local leaders developed a stake in having a good conference. There was considerable ownership in addition to the consultants. However, though the idea found favor, the process remained controversial and misunderstood by some.

THE UNFOLDING STORY

In December 1988 we made a face-to-face presentation of our detailed design for the search conference. The executive team rejected it. They were not used to informal proposals intended to be developed more fully together with the "client" group. As a result of our commitment to collaboration, the whole project was at risk of being stopped! In a particularly tense meeting in January of 1989, several people expressed "a loss of confidence" in the whole process. One said the consultants' initial paper "spelt complete anarchy, and there was very little in it that could be used." Another called for a document that would be at once "simplistic" and also "well-researched," that "could be presented to the politicians" (minutes of January 5).

The subsequent "formal" written proposal (an excerpt of which follows this analysis) was accepted in February 1989 and submitted to the politicians. By April the steering committee minutes noted "that everyone felt comfortable with the proposals and content. It was easy to understand, more down to earth than previous papers and seemed a very workable design which hopefully would produce an ongoing system after the conference had taken place." Agreement was reached in May 1989 to proceed and the sponsors set the conference date for November.

FURTHER DELAYS

In early summer of 1989 the process was again aborted when the executive team learned that the Institute of Directors, a group of local business chief executives and operating officers, had planned a conventional conference on the future of the Island in the same time slot. This was in reaction "to criticism of their otherwise very successful conference last year, that nothing actually happened as a result" (minutes of May 31). The steering committee proposed an integration of the two events, the Search to follow the IOD conference by two or three months. No agreement could be reached to integrate the two events in a collaborative way.

We were not involved in these later discussions, and the process was put on hold again. Suddenly, it was 1990, an election year in the Island. After that, nothing further happened.

WHY DID THE SEARCH CONFERENCE NOT TAKE PLACE?

As we talked with our executive committee, the original lead figures, this is the behind-the-scenes portrait that emerged. The primary balker turned out to be the owner of the newspaper, who, invited at first only to provide support funds, became leader of the steering group, and then decided, after the decision to proceed, that the risks outweighed the benefits.

While at first he saw in this process a worthwhile opportunity to sponsor and be associated with a potential success, as time went on, in part, he lost confidence in the consultants. He was one of several people who felt success was so important it almost had to be guaranteed. It appears we did not convince the leadership that the process would work.

This only became manifest towards the end of the first year. However, it was key to events surrounding the informal approval process. Eventually, the leader withdrew his personal and corporate sponsorship. This change of heart developed after the rejection by the executive team of the consultants' first detailed design presentation.

He had in fact expressed a desire then to withdraw as leader of the group, but agreed to continue after a discussion with the committee. He continued only because the other committee members insisted he was the most appropriate leader. Subsequently, the pattern of indecision that the search process hoped to challenge and change actually enveloped and stalled the conference planning process. For various reasons, the lead figures withdrew their support and the conference did not proceed.

THE LEARNINGS

The principal learnings for us are:

1). To initiate a search conference process in a situation where there is no established structure is fraught with difficulty and is very time-consuming.

2). The political impact of an innovation such as this process, both formally and informally, has to be anticipated and coalitions built early among all the key players. A key influencer was involved at the outset. Yet, the changing situation among top politicians and the individual ambitions of sponsors were tough to anticipate and work with, especially when the steering group itself had somewhat unclear and parallel goals. The group never took the time to work through these to arrive at well-articulated, common goals.

3). Our process depends on collaboration and a non-traditional design, based on consultants as process managers, not experts on local culture and affairs. That is a notion not easily adopted by business people and politicians used to "expert" consultant presentations and methodology.

4). The basic principles of this method—a democratic strategy-forming process—are that all "parties" or constituencies contribute and cooperate in searching for a preferred future, and then share responsibility for creating it. This concept was unfamiliar to the power structure of Jersey. It represents a cultural gap in understanding that the consultants so far have not succeeded in bridging. In retrospect it appears that people found they could not relate to the concept—how it would work. Apparently we did not do a good enough job of translating the "theory" into "reality."

5). Another learning is that the Steering Group wanted to maintain secrecy until they were ready to have a press conference to announce the event and the process. Once they started to get cold feet, there was no groundswell of public opinion. Nobody called out "we want it" when the leaders withdrew. Would we have had such support if the conference had been announced despite the initial skepticism and discomfort? We will never know.

EPILOGUE

There is evidence that there continues to be an interest in holding the Future Search. Once again it is believed to be a question of timing; the recent identification of a changing economic situation may indeed cause the "climate" to be more appropriate for resurrecting the concept.

November 30, 1990
"A WAY TO THE FUTURE" is the title of the document that "sold" the planners. It is a 3,000-word summary of how the search conference could meet Jersey's needs. It included a short history of the effort, the consultants' credentials, a history of searching, examples of conferences around the world—Australia, Kenya, St. Lucia, Norway, the U.S., Canada—an account of the process, and a detailed design. The paper emphasized the conference as one step in a continuing planning process. The material that follows shows how a generic conference design was adapted for the Isle of Jersey. —Adapted from "A WAY TO THE FUTURE: An Initiative for Action Involving the Total Community in a Search for the Future," Jersey, Channel Islands, February 1989.

OUTLINE OF THE SEARCH PROCESS & CONFERENCE

The overall search process and the conference are built on two key principles—first, that learning is a continuous process and second, that the present is shaped by past happenings and decisions are influenced by expectations of the future. The design of the preparatory phase, the conference itself and the follow-on activities therefore take these into account. The plan is as follows:

- an extensive preparation stage will be required to ensure that the sponsors are fully informed and committed. During this time the delegate selection process and community communication activities will be planned and implemented.
- the four-day conference will be conducted to start the actual search process:

    DAY 1 – (afternoon and evening) Official opening and orientation, followed by a look at the Island's history and significant past events;

    DAY 2 – Emphasis is on the present situation in the world around Jersey and the major factors affecting life within the island;

    DAY 3 – Focus is entirely on the future, moving from examining trends and exploring scenarios, to deciding what the key issues are that will determine the future direction of Jersey. Areas for action are identified and planning starts.

    DAY 4 – (morning only) "Action Plans" are presented by delegate groups who have taken responsibility to investigate and execute a specific activity. The whole conference provides feedback and the group continues its work by scheduling their next meeting (after the conference), etc.

- a follow-on stage of action-oriented activity of about 12 months, which translates the ideas developed at the conference into meaningful decisions and tangible results.

Thus, in about 24 hours of concentrated discussion and debate, the representatives of "the whole island in one room" review their history, the present situation and what sort of future they would like to see for their and future generations. Having determined all that with a high degree of consensus, the people present decide which activities or projects have the greatest interest for them and most benefit for the Island. They then set about developing action plans to begin the process of "checking out" their findings and preliminary plans with people not present which leads to the implementation phase.

A proposed design for the conference is presented on the next page. It must be stressed that the design is based on a well-proven generic model combined with the experience of the consultants. It is their intention to continue to work closely with the sponsoring group throughout to ensure that this process will work effectively and successfully in the unique milieu that is Jersey. The overall process is initially scheduled to last about one year, during which there would be three quarterly review meetings lasting about half-a-day each to measure progress and assess results along the way. Depending on the level of success attained and the willingness of those involved to continue such a social experiment, the process could continue in an appropriate way beyond one year.

THE JERSEY FUTURE SEARCH CONFERENCE
Proposed Design

DAY 1 – Evening

5:00 Official welcome and introductions. Orientation from the staff on the conference concept and way of working
6:00 Group work – identifying main events during the last 50 years that changed the history of the Island.
7:00 Dinner
8:30 "The History of Jersey." A special, prepared presentation by a local historian.
9:30 End of Day 1.

DAY 2 – Morning

9:00 Group work – preparing for presentation of selected main events followed by plenary session with a short presentation from all ten groups.
10:45 Coffee break.
11:15 Group work – analysis of the various forces or pressures on the Island and on each sector within it. Definition of the "present" as seen by each group.
1:00 Lunch
– Afternoon
2:00 Plenary session – short presentation from each group. general discussion.
3:30 Tea break.
4:00 Group work – developing a deeper understanding of the present followed by further general discussion.
6:00 "From the past through the present to the future" – a prepared presentation.
6:30 End of Day 2.

DAY 3 – Morning

9:00 "A search into different possible futures:" – a presentation suggesting some alternative scenarios.

9:30 Group work – identifying both the most desired future and what will happen if "things go on as now." Working out important "areas for action" from the difference between "the preferred future" and the "passive future." (Coffee during this period).

11:30 Plenary session – presentation of the main "areas for action" and why these are selected.
– Afternoon

1:00 Lunch. During lunch the staff and the steering group integrate the various inputs to this point of time into a more cohesive and limited number of potential areas for action.

2:30 Presentation to plenary of the potential areas for action to achieve consensus. Discussion. New self-selected cross-sector groups are formed.

3:00 Group work – ideas for projects and activities within the different areas for action (break for tea included).

4:30 Plenary session. Short presentations of the different ideas with some discussion.
– Evening

5:30 "Happy hour" followed by dinner at 6:00 pm. During this period the staff with assistance from participants will select what appear to be the most important and common ideas to start the work towards the desired future.

7:30 Presentation of the selected topics. Discussion. Orientation about the final action planning part of the conference. Formation of "high interest" task groups.

8:00 Group work – new groups start planning how to convert their idea(s) into reality.

??? End of evening.

DAY 4 – Morning

9:30 Deadline for groups to be ready to make brief statements and present their initial plans.
Plenary presentations begin – action plans setting out first steps to further exploration and implementation.

11:00 Discussion and evaluation.

12:30 Celebratory closing followed by lunch.

ABOUT THE AUTHORS

Maurice Dubras is a consultant living again in Jersey, Channel Islands, where he was born in 1939. He has consulted widely in North America and as part of a network of associates in Europe and South Africa. During the "Workplace Australia" conference in 1991 he managed one of the 20 Search groups. Dubras received a mechanical engineering degree in the UK, and worked for 25 years in Canada as an engineer on nuclear power projects and as a human resource and organization development practitioner for Atomic Energy of Canada, Ltd., a crown corporation.

Ivar Brokhaug is a Norwegian consultant who heads up a leadership and management development program at the Norwegian Institute of Technology in Trondheim. He has managed dozens of search conferences and also is the author of Chapter 8.

CHAPTER 31

THE CENTER FOR INTERNATIONAL EDUCATION
Pitfall – Missing the "Power People"
James A. Cumming

A FIRST PRINCIPLE for encouraging new actions is creating a new temporary system. In future search conferences, this means having people come together as peers who would not ordinarily meet. They must agree to stay together the whole time, and do all the tasks together. The broader the invitation list, the more probable will be new future scenarios and implementation plans.

When James Cumming, a graduate student at the Center for International Education, proposed a conference be organized, he was aware of this need. At the same time, he wished to increase student involvement in decisions about the future of the center. A student committee was authorized to plan the conference with the help of one faculty member. Cumming actively participated in the planning. The lone staff member rarely attended. This proved to have unintended consequences. The students, none of whom had experienced the search before, with great enthusiasm found a site, got financing, and recruited an experienced facilitator (who also had not run this kind of conference).

On the next page are shown the purposes of the conference and the invitation sent to potential participants.

Eventually, 50 people accepted invitations. There were five

alumni, but no university administrators from outside the Center. All four of the faculty members, one of whom held a high administrative post in the School of Education, did attend. However, during the conference the faculty members missed important sessions. So the meeting was largely organized, planned, run by and for students. They had almost no interaction with others in their system who controlled resources, and whose commitment was essential to the future. The facilitator led the "right" tasks, generating little energy or commitment.

James Cumming provides this honest, and bewildered, post mortem. He raises good questions about political and ideological agendas. Many of them are addressed in earlier chapters of this book. Those of us raised on issues of power and conflict, cannot see how powerful the structuring of meetings and conference tasks in a new way can be for creating change in "real time." For that reason, the planning phase—especially the selection and invitation of stake-holders—is a crucial task.

"Were we too naive to expect the conference to succeed without the full support of the faculty?" asks Cumming. The answer, supported by many cases here, is probably "yes."

— MRW

SEARCH CONFERENCE 89

**Center for International Education
Hills House South
University of Massachusetts
Amherst, MA 01003, USA**

INVITATION

We are delighted to invite you to participate in Search Conference 89, to be held from September 15-16, 1989.

THE CIE

The Center for International Education is one of the several programs at the University of Massachusetts' School of Education. Drawing on its own faculty and graduate students, as well as on outside resources, the

Center offers graduate level professional training, service and research opportunities in the areas of Third World Development Education and Nonformal Education.

CONFERENCE AIMS

- To bring together as many members as possible of the CIE's community and together focus on the future.
- To map the networks of people and external pressures that influence the CIE.
- To draw out the CIE's history, the constraints on change, and the values to be carried forward.
- To work together to develop preferred visions of our educational roles in development work.
- To do action planning to implement the values and visions chosen paying attention to questions of technical and social feasibility.

SEARCHING FOR OUR FACULTIES: SOME PERSONAL NOTES ON THE CIE'S SEARCH CONFERENCE 1989
– James A. Cumming

"The danger with calling the university a democratic, independent institution is that students and the faculty might take the assertion seriously and demand the right to ideological diversity, self-governance, and an end to complicity with the Pentagon and with corporations that invest in South Africa" (Parenti, 1986).

I was the main instigator and one of the principal organizers of the Search Conference. During the actual event I was tired and found it hard to participate as well as I would have liked. I was reminded of the way weekend retreats are organized by people doing the Japanese martial art "Shintaido." The people who organize the intensive workshop or retreat are not expected to participate much in the event and it is up to other people to implement the workshop.

Perhaps this has something to do with the organizers' wish for the event to succeed as they have envisaged it. It may be hard to give that up and respond to the here and now of the actual conference. I don't know what the reasons might be, but I think it is something which could usefully be explored in connection with search conferences.

During the conference it was very difficult to produce a map of the external environment. Again I am not sure why that it is. It may be because it is very complex. As a small group of people trying to learn about and promote non-formal education in international development projects, our environment consists of such things as a large formal educational institution which is subject to all sorts of political and social pressures, and our international development work is heavily influenced by US foreign policy.

In addition, we are an international group of people located in the USA environment. Trying to get that out and discuss what it all means for us as an organization may be asking people to do too much during the conference. Perhaps some sort of basic environmental framework could have been prepared and discussed before the conference to give this part of the discussion more clarity and focus.

Another reason why the external environment mapping may have failed is because of the role faculty played in this event. The decision to hold the search conference was made at a meeting which represents the interests of the CIE as a whole (both faculty and students). An organizing committee was formed which included a member of staff but it was difficult to get his participation in meetings. Essentially the conference was organized by the students without much commitment from the faculty.

The major part of the first day of the conference was spent "Looking at the Past." The last session of the day was when all the sub groups came back together and we tried to discuss what all this data means for the CIE. It was then we noticed that none of the four faculty members were present. We discussed what their absence meant and during that discussion the energy of the group dropped significantly.

For various reasons I have come to experience the CIE as a "mom and pop" organization which tends to reinforce the adolescent behavior of some of its students. Those internal organizational dynamics were recreated to a certain extent during the search conference in the way some people responded to the facilitator. I felt my anxiety rising and became worried that the conference would fall apart.

Then, at one point, I noticed that all the people presenting out from the small groups to the larger conference had black faces. It was as though the international students took on some leadership roles and enabled people to act in more mature ways.

This event points to yet another level of complexity we were trying to deal with.

Given all this complexity, it was incredible that the conference worked at all. Most participants spoke of it as a positive experience even though we did not generate sufficient energy to start the implementation of real changes.

Clearly, the conference model is very powerful. I would like to have greater clarity as to under what conditions it is most likely to be successful. What are its weaknesses and strengths as a tool for change? It seems that our conference was pushing the model to its limits in some ways. What additional peripheral activities would have supported the implementation of the conference itself? Were we too naive to expect the conference to succeed without the full support of the faculty?

Yet, once you have started planning the conference it is hard to stop that process without the organizers' losing face. Is it easier in the business world to map the external environment because businesses have to be sensitive to external forces if they want to succeed? Isn't trying to change the culture of the culture makers (the universities, etc.) the hardest sort of change to accomplish? In that case, don't we need to bring a more political perspective into the discussion?

Is it easier to mask political forces in business rather than in education? Do all search conferences have to deal with issues of having many different interest groups present, a concealed ideological and political agenda, authoritarian interpersonal relationships and so on?

Just a final thought: If we can address these issues, then wouldn't we have a model to help organizations in communist countries change?

THE DEVIL: What is the use of knowing?
DON JUAN: Why to be able to choose the line of greatest
          advantage instead of yielding in the
          direction of least resistance.
          – George Bernard Shaw, *Man and Superman*

ABOUT THE AUTHOR

James A. Cumming is a Language and Training Specialist at the Continuing Education Center, Asian Institute of Technology, Bangkok, Thailand. His work is organizing ways to improve intercultural communication through the medium of the English language in the context of non-formal technical education in international development work. He holds degrees as Master of International Administration and Master of Design Engineering and is a Ed.D. Candidate at the Center for International Education, University of Massachusetts.

CHAPTER 32

OHIO CHILDHOOD DEVELOPMENT CONFERENCE
Pitfall – Starting in Ohio, Not Globally
Chris Kloth

CHANGEWORKS

3440 Oletangy River Road
Columbus, OH 43202

January 17, 1992

RE: Search Conferences

Dear Marv,

During our Cape Cod seminar last summer we discussed whether there is a "right way" to do a Search Conference. Your position, as I recall, was that this is an emerging technology, and that there are minimum critical specifications that you feel more committed to than "one right way." You also invited us to share our experiences with you.

I am writing to highlight a recent conference and to ask for your feedback. We plan to work on other conferences this year and would like another perspective on a dilemma we faced.

This conference was sponsored by the Governor of the State of Ohio and the Ohio Head Start Association. It was intended to support a strategic planning process facilitated by another consultant. The plan will address the Governor's goal that, by the year 2000, *all* children in Ohio will start school ready to learn. The Search was to address the more specific question, "How will we be sure that all of the groups addressing early childhood development in Ohio are collaborating effectively in meeting the needs of young children?"

There were a number of barriers we had to overcome that diluted the "purity" of our work. The conference was an afterthought in response to a letter I sent to the Governor regarding the state's request for Strategic Planning Consultation Services. It was decided that a Search would help address the concerns I raised. However, since the planning calendar was set, we had only a short time to plan/design the event.

Fortunately, the two key people from the Head Start Association and the Governor's office know their constituent groups very well. They understood quickly what would be needed to make our project work and had the energy to make it work. Thus, while we did not have the time to put together our ideal planning committee, we got most of what was needed in two Head Start Association meetings and several with the two key people.

Four critical variables were present from the start:

- sincere commitment from the Governor and the Association to act on both the goal and the input from the Search;
- a shared sense of importance and urgency about the issue by all involved;
- a commitment from the Governor to continue to involve those at the Search in reviewing the plan to assure that it met their concerns;
- and a willingness to stretch far beyond the usual boundaries of inclusion (they invited Head Start parents, business, state and local government agencies and departments, diverse advocacy groups with contrary interests—64 people in all!).

With these critical variables in place, we felt confident that we could have a productive session. However, as we planned the conference, I and the two colleagues who would assist me found ourselves in a hot debate about whether to start with the "three decades/ history" activity that you use, or the "trends/priorities" activity. [EDITOR'S NOTE – This refers to a task where the whole group is asked to brainstorm present trends affecting the focal issue, and then to select stakeholder group priorities.]

My position was that I had used the decades exercise in several other settings, felt comfortable with it and that it made sense to me based on our experience and discussion in Cape Cod. I also felt it created an opportunity for people to actively participate in discovering the common ground in the group. It was also my position that either approach would get us where we needed to be and that I wanted to listen to my colleagues.

Terry Swango agreed that it built common ground and added that it helped address the inclusion and orientation needs of people in new groups. He also felt the trends were "too cognitive" and that, without the decades, lacked an adequate context. He was afraid it would create a deep, dark pit that would become an obstacle later.

Julie Harmon preferred to lead with the trends activity because it was "safer" in an early stage of group growth. She had heard me describe the level of disclosure that occurred when I used the decades activity elsewhere. She also felt that it was more "here and now" and would help create a context for "why we are here" and why our work is important. Since all of us felt that we would get where we needed to be in either case, we chose to go with trends.

HOW TO START?

The results of our experiment were instructive. First, the final results of the Search were powerful—values based statements of minimum critical specifications for the strategic plan that the entire diverse group endorsed. We believe this occurred because the right people with the right energy worked hard and well to assure that the needs of young children are met. *Starting with trends did not help!*

All three of us believe that starting with decades would have been a better choice in this situation. The group identified over 100 trends, about ten themes and four priorities that appeared to outweigh—in the polling—the other issues. However, the fact that all the trends had to do with the lives and safety of young children resulted in a strong resistance to "letting go" of those trends that got few or no votes. Some participants resented how the selection process seemed to force them to exclude important issues. (This is consistent with my experience working with similar child welfare populations in other settings.)

We worked our way through this situation, but it came back to haunt us in subtle ways later. It did create an imposing symbol for "the big mess" that was always on the wall. It was also symbolic of the conflict between the rational, structural approach of "the system" and the powerful, visceral experience of the people who see kids at risk each day. While we found ways to use the symbol constructively, we had to remain alert to its impact throughout the search.

The decades activity became part of our recovery. It created energy, excitement and a deep discussion of the values and value conflicts that act on people as individuals, as people with specific

roles in the system and as citizens responsible for the system. People
became involved in the process on a deeper level.

The energy that went into the future scenarios was helpful too.
Several scenarios were exceptional. However, there was a lack of
attention to the priority trends. This did not turn out to be a problem,
but we believe that reversing the sequence would have been more
effective.

We do not have enough experience to generalize yet. We suspect
that there might be groups or search tasks that might benefit from
starting with the trends. Our strong inclination is to start with the
history in most situations.

We would like to know what you and others you are in touch with
have learned about how to start. Have criteria been developed for
determining when to vary the sequence? Is this a dialogue worth
having?

We are especially excited by the public policy implications of
Search Conferences. We will continue to document our experiences
and want to share them with you and others if there is an interest and
a vehicle for sharing.

Searchingly,
Chris Kloth

Marvin Weisbord
119 Sibley Avenue
Ardmore, PA 19003
January 26, 1992

Dear Chris,

Thanks for contributing to our discussion on what makes these
conferences successful. I find it helpful and timely for two reasons.
First, I think it validates a basic minimum critical conference specifications—building a community before focusing on problems. Second, it
makes plain a pitfall that may not be obvious. Third, it suggests to me
that the task sequence DOES matter.

You frame the issue as whether to start with a "three decades
exercise" OR "trends/priorities." The answer, I think, is *either* SO LONG
AS you enable people to explore the larger context—the common
ground. The "three decades" task you learned in Cape Cod asks
people to list and interpret *three* kinds of data—global, personal, and
focal issue. They are to find common themes, meanings, future
implications, etc. In substituting the *particular* "trends/priorities" task
that you used, you jumped immediately to the problem domain.

That is, you started by building data about outside influences on the *problem being searched*. That is step 2 of the "future search," usually done as a group "mind map" of the open system. In so doing, you jumped right into the problem, and invited people to establish their turf. The search task in the Emery design, for example, is not simply a "trends/priorities" activity. It is quite specifically the GLOBAL trends, the broadest possible context for ANY organization or issue. Then people specify ideal and probable futures for key trends.

I think it's important to note that you recovered some of the common ground when you moved in the second phase to a review of the past in both global and personal terms (the "three decades/history"). At least that's my hypothesis on what happened.

Your story confirms for me an important principle that Emery and Trist set out in the Barford search in 1960 (Chapter 3). To have a successful search we must put in place minimum conditions for dialogue, namely that the whole conference experiences that we are all living on the same planet, with similar stakes and concerns as human beings. An environmental scan in relation *to the issue being searched* doesn't meet that minimum specifications. It does not create the wider "objectively-ordered field" as backdrop for the issue at hand.

COMMON GROUND IS THE ISSUE

My personal preference is not to have a group brainstorm of global trends as an opening activity, finding it more cognitive and passive an exercise than I like (so I invented an alternative I could run with more enthusiasm). However, that's not the issue. Whatever technique is used, the opening activity needs to help people establish a common base for further exploration (or discover they have none). I believe any successful search model must accomplish that task.

The Emery/Trist model is an elegantly simple set of tasks matched exactly to the criteria Fred Emery derived from the work of Solomon Asch many years ago [EDITOR'S NOTE—See Chapter 5]. The first four tasks explicitly establish the "objectively ordered field." The next three are designed to help people experience that they are "equally human," the next three (with slight overlap) that people share the same psychological field, that we all have the same basic needs and wants. Emery and others in our book show that when these basic conditions are established, people, regardless of previous conflicts, are capable of genuine dialogue. They can then form a temporary planning community able to take creative action.

Not incidentally, it's important that the opening activities be done in mixed groups. That way we arrive at interpretations that reflect a cross-section of the conference, rather than harden up particular positions.

That leaves a puzzle I have been musing on for some time. Some search practitioners believe that personal data (and individual work prior to small group discussion) tends to separate, fragment and individualize what should be a collective experience. Yet many appliers of the "future search" model have found it to be a powerful community builder, regardless of organization or issue. That, I take it, has also been your experience, and the reason you wanted to use it.

Why does making three lists alone and analyzing them in small groups—the past from personal, global, and an organization/issue perspective—also contribute so dramatically to the establishment of common ground? The explanation I like is quite unrelated to the actual technique. This exercise ALSO meets the minimum critical specs derived from Asch. It enables people to experience their common stakes in the future of the planet, to create order from a chaotic, apparently random set of data points, and to acknowledge their common humanity.

Thanks for your timely contribution. Clearly, we need to improve our discussion of minimum specifications in future orientation workshops. I am enormously encouraged by your willingness to make public your experience. It will help others avoid the same pitfall, the best possible way for us to help each other.

Best regards,
Marv Weisbord

ABOUT THE AUTHOR

Chris Kloth, a senior partner of Harmon, Kloth and Associates, is a futurist and an organization design and development consultant. He has consulted throughout the United States, especially in public policy development. He and his partners work with communities, businesses and organizations seeking renewal through participation and Democratic values. They also have helped to start a consulting venture in St. Petersburg, Russia. He is active in the World Future Society, Organization Development Network and Ohio Policy Issues Network. Julie Harmon and Terry Swango who co-facilitated the Ohio conference, also are senior partners in Harmon, Kloth and Associates.

PART 9

FUTURE DIRECTIONS

Introduction

> "What were you looking for?" Kennedy asked. "Besides tracks."
>
> "Nothing in particular," Leaphorn said. "You're not really looking for anything in particular. If you do that, you don't see things you're not looking for."
>
> — Tony Hillerman
> *Talking God*, Harper Paperbacks, 1991, p. 23

We come at last to a new beginning. These methods have been used consciously for about 30 years. That's a long time for you or me, but only an eye-blink in the long scheme of things. We have learned quite a bit about suspending judgment long enough to discover, along the path, vital things we were not looking for. But these words, despite the great number of them, are in my opinion far from the last ones on the discovery of common ground.

The closing chapters suggest quite diverse ingredients of future scenarios for search conferences. Together they challenge us to take these processes of open-ended inquiry from outer space to the innermost nooks of the unconscious, from headlines to breakthroughs, from conference room to livingroom, and to whatever other places we can imagine.

I find it fitting that Fred Emery, that erstwhile innovator, has gone out on a limb again in Chapter 33. Here he speculates on how democracy and telecommunications (the social and the technical) might become more compatible traveling companions through the medium of search conferences. In the chapter that follows, Stephen Burgess takes the search model to the arts community, describing efforts, still experimental, to unlock unconscious processes and creativity through these meeting methods.

Finally, in Chapter 35, I wind up my own speculations on this subject—for the moment—by imagining applications triggered by my reading, as I have almost daily for the last 50 years, diverse periodicals.

– MRW

CHAPTER 33

EFFECTIVE DIALOGUE AND THE NEW TECHNOLOGY
Can Closed-Circuit TV Enhance Democracy?

Fred E. Emery

WHETHER WE WORK WITH 30 PEOPLE OR 80, face-to-face
conferences impose limits of time, cost, and distance on
issues and organizations. Yet our systems are increasingly
globalized as people become more interdependent. In this
chapter Fred Emery, who pioneered searching 30 years ago,
speculates on whether the requirements for face-to-face
dialogue could be preserved as we transcend time and space
through teleconferences.

The issue has practical consequences. Enormous resources are being invested in teleconference facilities. To
adapt this technology to searching would be a major advance
in our aspirations for getting everybody involved in discovering
common ground and improving whole systems. This chapter is
adapted from his book *Toward Real Democracy* (1989).

— MRW

THE "TYRANNY OF DISTANCE" HAS BEEN CONSTANTLY INVOKED
as the reason why only representative democracy is practical.
Now we are told that new communication and computer technologies are shrinking distances until we are all living in a "global
village." There is enough truth in this to consider what it might mean for
achieving a stronger democracy.

If there are any doubts about technology's role in shrinking distances, one has only to reflect on how the world stock exchanges went down like dominoes after the Wall Street break in October 1987. Even the lag imposed by different opening hours of exchanges in various time zones did nothing to delay international movements of capital. While it was happening, the rest of the world could follow the widely distant events hour by hour. Investors around the world were tightly linked in an almost instantaneous, interactive network.

Given this capability, one has to ask whether nations could greatly strengthen their democratic procedures if effective dialogues could be held via telecommunications to reduce the costs and time losses of face-to-face meetings. Travel and housing costs impose severe constraints on the level of democratic dialogue in voluntary organizations, professional and trade associations, corporations, and administrative services.

There are main areas where new telecommunications capabilities might strengthen democracy:

a) interactive distance learning;
b) video conferencing;
c) community networking.

To succeed, as a minimum, participants must be able to (a) control the medium being used and not be the playthings of the media, as in TV conferences, and (b) determine the ends to which the medium is being used.

This is a start, and may be sufficient for distance learning and community networking. They are, after all, concerned primarily with information exchange. They do not seek to resolve differences to viewpoint and arrive at common agreements about things to be done.

THE POTENTIAL OF VIDEO CONFERENCING

Video conferencing, I believe, offers the most potential for stronger democracy. At the moment, 1001 arbitrary decisions are defended because, "We simply cannot afford the expense to have a conference on this matter." Or, "The people who should confer will not give up the time for this." Or, "The decision simply cannot be delayed longer."

Video conferencing, *if it created the conditions for effective, democratic dialogue*, would cut through these defenses and, in the long run, establish a new mode of social decision-making. Instead of Australia, for example, having 300-plus search conferences as in the five years 1972-77, it might be having 3,000 per year. The big *if* is whether video conferencing can create the conditions for effective dialogue.

For some 15 years people have striven to "make a success of video conferencing." That has always meant creating a viable market for corporate and administrative video conferences. The demands for such conferencing are less than what is required for effective dialogue. No one to our knowledge is even claiming to have found a successful formula. The rest of this chapter is devoted to solving this problem.

First, let us examine theoretically what this task involves.

Video conferencing in particular imposes critical demands. Conferencing usually aims to achieve a higher quality of decision-making by allowing individual viewpoints to be *enlightened* by an understanding of the views held by others. For the purposes of distance learning and community networking it is often enough just to *instruct* or *inform*.

If the purpose is only to instruct or only to inform, then it can be served by a communication system that is "serial" in nature, i.e., an ordered linear sequence of communication events. In human communication systems the dominant features of seriality are i) *asymmetry* of social control of the communication process; ii) *ego-centrism*, in that the process is guided to serve the ends of the controlling party, not mutually agreed ends; and iii) a "*them-us*" polarization of the communicators. Bureaucratic systems favor seriality. They have been well served by modern communications technologies, since seriality can be so readily modeled mathematically.

But the explicit purpose of conferencing is to allow different parties to arrive at *mutual* understanding of each other's views and purposes. For mutual understanding to emerge, the exchanges between parties A and B about task X must both inform and instruct. That is, A and B must arrive at a shared understanding of X, and they must appreciate what the alternative courses of action, with respect to X, mean for each other.

Here are the conditions for an effective dialogue between A and B in regard to X:

a) ABX presents an objectively ordered field open to the inspection of all of the participants.

b) The mutual confrontation of A and B attests to their basic psychological similarity.

c) Continued communication leads to the emergence of a mutually shared field.

d) The participants become more open and responsive to the objective requirements of the situation, more sensitive to what ought to be done, and less dominated by what they would individually like to do.

These conditions form an ordered sequence; each presupposes that the preceding conditions have been established. Failure at any stage, e.g., that continued communication is not seen to be converging on "a mutually shared field," would inevitably lead to questioning of whether the preceding conditions had in fact been achieved.

These matters are not just of theoretical interest. Technical systems for teleconferencing have been on the market since the late 70's. Yet, as of early 1990, only five percent of the Fortune 500 companies had "bought" the product. Given the wealth and far-flung operations of these companies, we have to assume a great deal of market resistance.

The reason is simply that the focus has been on the technology, not on how it should be used. The technologists have been guided by simplistic notions about what is required for fruitful interactive communication. When teleconferencing did not achieve what they expected, they could only guess at what they should do next.

A TECHNICAL SYSTEM MUST MEET ALL FOUR CONDITIONS

The four conditions for effective dialogue can be taken as the *minimal critical specifications* for video-conferencing technology. Thus, for a technical system to provide what human beings can achieve in face-to-face contact, it must meet all four conditions. The cost/benefit ratio of a new technical system could be measured that way.

With these specifications in mind we can take a closer look at how remote conferencing via electronic media differs significantly from face-to-face conferencing. Perhaps we can pinpoint the electronic technologies and/or developments that offer the most cost-effective solutions.

Condition (a) of the conditions for effective dialogue—an "objectively-ordered field"—is usually expressed as a striving for realism. It is important to note, however, that the aim is not that a remote group should appear as if they were really present, across the room. That degree of "realism" would actually be the height of illusion, giving the impression that one could walk over and touch people hundreds of miles away.

The remoteness of the other group (or, to put in another way, the presence of the other group at that other remote location) is a *part of the reality* of conferencing. It cannot be disguised.

> "The height of reality in remote conferencing would be the conviction of individual participants that the conversation could not have proceeded more satisfactorily if they had all been in the same room." — FEE

That is, that the cues they might have missed because of the remoteness would not in any case have materially helped the constructiveness of the conversation.

In the past, this degree of reality has not usually been achieved. The most striking deficiency has been in the use of voice-actuated switches that keep the auditory channel clear for one-way transmission. This allows for clear and controlled transmission, unless of course people talk at the same time, in which case babbling confusion reigns. Even operating normally this system is like the game children play of communicating down a long pipe. There is no communication if both parties have their mouths to the pipe openings or both have their ears there. It is only by volunteering to take turns that communication can be achieved.

PSYCHOLOGICAL SIMILARITY

Even with a telephone that is not limited like a pipe, people feel constrained to take turns. This constraint can lead to the negation of condition (b), "basic psychological similarity." The person who initiates the call or seizes the initiative on the phone line, can readily establish a me-you position of dominance.

Reports on video conferencing based on this sort of one-way audio transmission consistently refer to egocentric posturing or role-playing, channel-grabbing, and lecturing down in a me-you, them-us fashion. These features are appropriate to serial but not interactive communication.

Hence if remote conferencing is to approximate the reality of interactive communication then, *there must be open, bi-directional audio transmission at all times.*

"Open bi-directional transmission" could lead to confusion and a breakdown in meaningful communication. The safeguard against that is to be found in the human regulator(s) understanding what is going on in the groups, not in a technician, or in automatic switching mechanisms.

To be realistic there should also be a match between the acoustic image of spatial location of voices and the subvocal "buzz" with the location of others in the video image of the remote group. Thus, if someone is seen to be speaking from the right side of the screen, then that voice should appear to come from the right. This calls for stereo sound.

Finally, there is the mismatch that can occur between loudspeaker-reproduced voices and buzz and that which is picked up in face-to-face groups. This is quite noticeable with loudspeaker reproduction of telephone quality speech. Existing digitalized high-fidelity sound systems probably can achieve a quality similar to what participants would experience if they actually were face-to-face.

THE IMPACT OF VISUAL CUES

So far we have considered only the sound—what people with their eyes shut would need to achieve an "objectively ordered field open to inspection." Suppose they opened their eyes? Then what would we need to sustain or enhance this sense of reality? First, participants would want "to put a face on the voice" and, sometimes, a nametag on the face. To maintain the correlation of face and voice they should have the same spatial location. They also should have the same temporal location, i.e. if X is angrily denouncing some proposition his (or her) lips should be moving, the face should be seen as angry, sneering, or stony, and the others in the remote group should be seen to be behaving as if listening to somebody angrily denouncing something.

Here is the crunch for remote conferencing.

We are supersensitive to the merest flicker of emotion in the human face, or even just the eyes. (Franklin Roosevelt, for example, once recalled how he broke the ice at the Teheran conference. He "whispered to Stalin, 'Winston is cranky this morning, he got up on the wrong side of the bed.' A vague smile passed over Stalin's eyes, and I decided I was on the right track.") So sensitive are we to these cues that Tompkins (1962), arguably the outstanding authority on human emotional expression, recommended the ultra high speed Schlieren camera, used for ballistic studies, to detect the fainter cues that humans respond to.

There is also a large body of research establishing the important role of visual, non-verbal cues in communication. The findings together appear to establish an almost impenetrable cost barrier to achieving interactive remote conferencing. Video as compared to audio transmission is so very expensive that practical applications to date seem half-baked. The realistic transmission of every flickering facial expression that the eye can detect is too expensive to contemplate.

Yet, there is a technical growth curve. Special landline connections could give a TV quality image of, say, three people sitting at a table. However, broadcast connections could provide only a couple of consecutive stills per second. Computer programs for coding into and decoding out of digital signals have emerged (codecs). These enable us to transmit, on even low capacity channels, a realistic representation of the grosser facial and gestural movements. Yet, the details are lost.

REFLECTED VS. RADIANT LIGHT

To this particular limitation on visual information must be added a limitation inherent in cathode ray display technology. The visuals in

CRDs are radiant light, but the human eye has evolved to extract information from light *reflected* from surfaces. If the human eye is directed toward a radiant light source, it will *stare* and the stare quickly becomes a glazed stare. If the radiant source is unpredictably flickering and colorful, as with a wood fire, the glazed effect may be delayed, but even a wood fire will not evoke looking behavior. By contrast, visual information in face-to-face situations is seen in radiant, reflected light.

The natural response to varying reflected light is to *look*, and to look more actively, with rapidly changing focus, if the picture is changing.

The implication of this is that even if visual recording and transmission were improved significantly, the gain in received picture by a human viewer would still leave us with a very marked mismatch between the visual transmission of the remote group's non-verbal communication and what would be available to someone who was physically present.

The limitations we have just discussed are well founded. It would seem therefore that aspirations for remote video conferencing are as ill-fated as those we have had for video telephony.

Let us go back over the evidence that has brought us to this point. There is no doubt about the powerful impact of non-verbal communications and of human sensitivity to the merest flicker of emotion. However, it has been assumed, traditionally and without question, that non-verbal communication serves to amplify and enrich the inadequacies of speech. On this assumption talking on the telephone could of course be only an impoverished form compared with talking face-to-face. By this same assumption, the videophone should be one of the most-welcomed technical innovations of our age. The facts are otherwise and the assumption false.

Non-verbal communication in fact is used to constrain conversation by constantly reminding the other of person and place: who is being spoken to and in what social setting. Even the language of illiterates is too rich and too free-wheeling to be given totally free rein. Non-verbal communication warns the speaker to practice restraint in speaking and to be careful about the construction placed on what is said.

SPEECH AND THOUGHT

The point is that speech becomes more powerful as it is freed from the context of non-verbal communication: powerful, that is, as an expression of what people are *thinking*. It does not become more socially powerful unless the social context is defined as allowing mutual interaction. Thus the Roman Catholic confessional has been traditionally designed to minimize the role of non-verbal communication and to maximize free expression, but the dominant role of the confessor remains inviolate. Where mutual interaction is socially acceptable, people have more influence over the attitudes and opinions of others when they are restricted to telephone conversation than they have face-to-face (Short, 1976).

These findings are of fundamental importance for remote interactive conferencing. The clear implication is that *maximum video communication is not after all a desirable design goal.* What is now unclear is how *much* video communication, if any, is desirable.

Some of the minimal desiderata for visuals have been mentioned above, e.g., to put a face on a voice and to see spatio-temporal events that match the spatio-temporal characteristics of the audible field.

A more general requirement is to remind participants, by visual means, of the longer-term constraints on the apparent openness of the interactive process. Participants are always going to ask for more visual, non-verbal information than is good for mutual interaction because of their concern about getting off-side with their superiors or treading on colleagues' toes. However, this is a regulatory function that should not be solved mechanically. It should be a tool in the hands of the human regulator(s). Without such regulation it is likely, as has been experienced with computer conferencing and electronic mail systems, that people will become unduly reticent in subsequent conferences.

REMOTE, INTERACTIVE CONFERENCING – A MENTAL EXPERIMENT

One could go from the theoretical principles to an idealized design of a remote interactive conference. However, we are not concerned here with long-term technical development. Our concern is whether existing technologies permit a commercially viable form of remote interactive conferencing. Let us then take a recent interactive conference and see how and whether it could have been conducted with widely-separated groups linked by telecommunications.

An important point is that the conference being subjected to this mental experiment is a "search conference," i.e., it was deliberately designed to maximize interaction. The designers of traditional conferences will always claim that they are aiming at maximum interaction but in practice they design to give one paradigm superiority over contenders to allow one set of statused persons to assert their superiority.

In other words, they implicitly deny the first two basic conditions for effective dialogue. Veteran conference-goers reduce the negative impact of this by maximizing their informal face-to-face contacts. The formal conference becomes the excuse for being at the same location. Remote conferencing can easily do what traditional conferencing does because it only involves serial communication. However, the absence of conditions for informal face-to-face get-togethers reveals such conferences for the charade they really are.

By contrast, a search conference strives to meet the first two basic conditions for communication by minimizing the tendencies to protect one's territory or to stand on one's dignity. Insofar as they are successful, search conferences minimize the need to use informal, face-to-face channels, and hence the necessity for all participants to be in the same place.

THE SEARCH CONFERENCE
– COMPARING METHODS

Let us rerun mentally an actual search conference on management education for small business. For each phase, we will describe the way it was done face-to-face, followed by how it might have been done with participants at several remote places. In imagining a video conference, we will impose two constraints. First, randomly-selected groups and task forces will be organized without reference to their location. (Most organizations would be trying to arrive at conference outcomes that were not just the product of horse-trading and power-dealing between special interests held by different locations.)

Second, a remote conference, where technical media are open to filibustering and confusing overload, puts special demands on conference managers. A conference manager would need to be present at each location and the management team would need its own teleconferencing facility.

These constraints automatically raise the cost of remote interactive conferencing. So, at each phase we will try to identify the most cost-effective ways of carrying out the conference tasks. Here is the basic pattern:

Phase 1 – Introduction

FACE-TO-FACE – The purposes are spelled out by someone who is in a position to sanction the exercise socially. Participants are introduced to each other so as to identify their interests and allow their subsequent contributions to be identified. The managers spell out the planned program and the resources available to the conference.

REMOTE – Best done by video. The requirements are: (a) "talking head" for the sanctioning speech, (b) roving camera for the interactions so that people can put face to name, (c) video of white-board as manager outlines program and organizational details.

All participants should get hard copy of at least the last two matters.

Phase 2 – Perspectives Session

FACE-TO-FACE – Whilst still in plenary, participants are asked for their views about what is currently happening that could have a meaningful impact on the human future. Each view is recorded, in telegraphic form, on flip charts by the managing staff. As charts are filled they are taped to walls where they are open to the inspection of all.

REMOTE – This would best be done by electronic bulletin board and would probably be more effective than in face-to-face conferences. There is no reason, for example, why it could not be spread over 24 hours before moving to Phase 3, allowing much more time for reflection.

Phase 3 – Major Trends in the Perspectives

FACE-TO-FACE – Three randomly selected groups examine the flip charts they have generated and try to identify the five or six major trends that are shown by the data. Each group prepares a flip chart for presentation of their views.

REMOTE – There seems to be no need for these groups to meet face-to-face. They could probably do this task by means of phone-conferencing and fax to consolidate their presentation.

Phase 4 – Comparison of Trend Evaluations

FACE-TO-FACE – In plenary the groups present and compare their analyses. The purpose is to let the participants find out whether they are all in the same "open, objectively ordered world." If it appears they are not, then they can try to identify what it is that divides them and agree upon whether it is in fact worthwhile to continue further.

REMOTE – Video of white-board and talking head of manager could well manage this phase provided there was a phone-conferencing facility operating at the same time. If the faces of discussants could be put up as stills it might help participants keep track of who is pushing for what.

Phase 5 – Probable and Desirable Futures

FACE-TO-FACE – Within the context that they have created for themselves, the participants are asked to consider what would happen to their common concern—management education for small business—if things were just left to go along as they are, i.e., Probable Future, and, if all went well in the current situation, what might possibly be achieved, i.e.,

Desirable Future. One randomly selected group works on the first task and another works on the second.

REMOTE – The groups working on probable and desirable futures could probably do this quite effectively using phone-conferencing with fax facilities.

Phase 6 – Identifying the Planning Challenge.

FACE-TO-FACE – In plenary the two scenarios are presented and compared. If there is no significant difference, that is, if the desirable future is the most probable future, then there is no need for planning. In this unusual case the conference could repeat the previous phase, with differently constituted groups.

If they confirm the findings, the conference would be disbanded. Someone would then need to ask about what misunderstandings led to the unnecessary conference. Clearly, the discrepancy between the probable and the desirable scenario is what normally defines the agenda for the rest of the conference.

REMOTE – Video is desirable for this plenary but it might be enough to provide talking head with white-board. (Slow scan is assumed throughout to be adequate for the talking head where that is simply the manager presenting the views of others, not arguing his own.) Phone-conference and fax are assumed.

Phase 7 – Inherited Constraints

FACE-TO-FACE – At this point it is usual for a search conference to suspend its future orientation and take stock of where the organization has come from and where it currently is. The strengths and weaknesses they have inherited are the starting point for future change. This is done in plenary with one or two individuals making the major input.

REMOTE – Video of talking head and maybe white-board. Phone link for questions and other inputs.

Phase 8 – Idealized Designs for the Future

FACE-TO-FACE – Working in parallel, several randomly selected groups try to come up with an organizational design that would realize the desirable future scenario. These are called "idealized designs" because participants are asked to design in the required capabilities without consideration of where those capabilities are going to come from. Following Phase 7, it is not usual for totally unreal expectations to enter these designs.

REMOTE – Groups meet via phone-conferencing and fax facilities.

Phase 9 – Reconciliation of the Idealized Designs

FACE-TO-FACE – This is done in plenary with the expectation that the process will continue till one design emerges. Whilst still in plenary, the participants divide up the task of preparing *operational* plans, and select the groups that will work on each task. It is expected that by this stage the conference has sufficient unity and identity that the groups will accept the duty of acting as task forces of the conference, whatever their other organizational loyalties.

REMOTE – Plenary with facilities as for Phase 6.

Phase 10 – Working in Task Forces

FACE-TO-FACE – Task forces set their own plans for working, within the time and space constraints of the conference, and are expected to present their proposals on flip charts to a plenary.

REMOTE – Task forces use phone-conferencing and fax.

Phase 11 – Plenary on Task Force Proposals.

FACE-TO-FACE – The plenary allows for presentation, critique, and coordination of the task force proposals. The plenary should finally agree on plans and allocate responsibilities for the final report/presentation.

REMOTE – Plenary with facilities as in Phase 6.

SOME OBSERVATIONS

Several observations may be made about this conception of remote interactive conferencing:

a) To cope with the remote extension of conferencing we need to allow more time. It may in fact be easier to fit with organizational timetables and thus achieve some improvements in quality of product.

b) In this method, the electronic bulletin board could be used for a final review process. Perhaps, as a stringent test of the conference process, the geographical groups should do their own reviews and debate unresolved issues, as groups, through the electronic bulletin board.

NOBODY HAS DONE IT – YET

This is a mental experiment. We have experienced video conferencing and phone conferencing. There is a body of knowledge building up on electronic bulletin boarding. We do not have experience of the combination suggested here. In particular we do not have a feel for the time demands nor a proper sense of the demands that would be placed on the prime regulatory mechanism—the conference manager sub-group.

This in *not* an attempt to find an alternative path toward stronger democracy than representative forms. Rather, it is an attempt to find a powerful multiplier effect, one that would cancel the all-pervasive privatizing effects of television and the equally iniquitous deprivatization effects of mainframe computers and their centralized data-bases—the early stages of the telecommunications revolution.

ABOUT THE AUTHOR

Fred Emery's work is discussed in Chapters 3 and 5. He is an independent action researcher living in Cook, Australia.

CHAPTER 34

THE CREATIVE SEARCH GATHERING
A Story of Creative Action-Learning from the Arts

M. Stephen Burgess

F OR MORE THAN A CENTURY our world has grown more linear, wedded to "hard" data and statistics, and faithful to processes that provide structure and control over our own affairs. In strategy conferences, this process has reached a dead end. Despite our best efforts to stay on top of things, we increasingly experience our world as unpredictable and out of control. To alter this experience, and our satisfaction with life, we need to learn of things that we know but don't know that we know. Search conferences give us a means to test out new forms. For they involve people and agendas that CANNOT, by the rules of the traditional meeting game, come together this way.

Now, Steve Burgess pushes the boundaries of the search conference itself. Here he takes us on a journey into the realm of the expressive, non-linear, and unconscious, a realm that is just as assuredly "there" as it is impossible to measure. Burgess began his experiments by drawing on ideas from the Craigmillar Festival Society in Scotland, in the 1960's. This is a community arts organization that has opened a floodgate of local creativity and social action.

Working with Eric Trist, a pioneer of search conferences (Chapter 3), Burgess began by having groups make their

reports of what would normally be linear information in
creative and expressive ways. Eventually, he teamed with
actors and artists to extend creative feedback to include
dreams, drama, and art forms that elicit archetypes, the
common experience of our species through many millennia.
These come from deep wells of human experience, what Carl
Jung called the "collective unconscious."

In this chapter Burgess reports his experiments. He
speculates on the future implications of the "creative search
gathering" as ritual and celebration, two community processes now in short supply. His work complements that of
Wheatley (Chapter 10) and Bohm (Chapter 11). Others are
dipping into this stream as well—as shown by examples in
Part 3.   — MRW

In Canada and Scotland in the 1980's some of us began to elaborate the
search mode to incorporate a wider range of creative expression. I
consider the effort still experimental. The impetus came from long
experience in Scotland where we found that "engagement in community
arts is a main pathway to community development" (Burgess, 1980). In
this article I want to tell you of our early experiences, and how we drew
on them for search conferences. At the end, I add a brief essay on the
research and theory that supports this work, and the philosophical
implications.

ORIGINS IN SCOTLAND

The original setting was the Craigmillar Festival Society in Edinburgh,
a distinctive grass roots community organization. It started with a local
festival in 1964 in which people expressed and celebrated their talents,
traditions and community life. They translated their creative expression
into social and political initiatives—involving most aspects of local life
from social care to transport, from education to town planning, from
employment to environment, from housing to health. Throughout its
history the founder, Mrs Helen Crummy, and her associates have
maintained that the touchstone of their activity is "the creativity that is
in everyone". The Festival Society's constitution calls this integration of
creativity and social action, "cultural action."

The Festival people have spread their networks extensively into other
institutions, including the European Economic Community. They arrived at concepts of "creative shared government" and "communiversity"
to describe activities designed to bring about a locally-desired future.

The Festival Society's work has substantially increased the number of locally-run projects and programs.

The Society's work attracted widespread attention:

Said The New Statesman, (August 18, 1972), "By its pioneering example the Craigmillar Festival Society may do more for Edinburgh's social balance sheet than all the tourist millions the International Festival has earned in the last 20 years."

Wrote Albert Cherns (1982), "I am quite sure that this organisation represents a most useful model for the containment, if not the solution, of many of the social problems that crowd upon us."

THE PATHWAY THROUGH THE ARTS AND SEARCHING

Our first opportunity to elaborate "the pathway through the arts" was a 1983 search conference in Toronto on the future of the York Action-Learning Group, developed by Eric Trist and his colleagues. The conference took place high on the bluffs overlooking Lake Ontario, a site adorned with objets d'art and artifacts from old Toronto buildings. It seemed a veritable "dreamscape," highly conducive to creativity.

One group, a mix of men and women, accepted the suggestion that they might vary their feedback to the plenary session by dramatizing their understanding of "action-learning." Several members knew of the community arts developments in Scotland and had discussed "the pathway through the arts." The group also had two women facilitators especially good at drawing out members' contributions and helping them resolve conflicts.

THEORY NOTES: BION AND JUNG

At the unconscious level the creative feedback group worked under Wilfred Bion's "basic assumption" of "pairing" in a positive way ("BaP") (Bion, 1961; Emery and Emery, 1978, pp. 299-300; Emery, 1981, p. 467). In Jung's terms both male and female group members projected positive "anima" and "animus" (Jung, 1966, p. 197). Both unconscious "pairing" and "anima"/"animus" projections could have negative valences. I believe we did not see this side because of the ambient search conference setting, skillful facilitation, and balance among men and women. There is always a risk, as Eric Trist has observed, of hierarchical male dominance inducing female negative animus. This is less likely the more collaborative and egalitarian the work setting. — SB

The small group launched into its improvisation with spontaneity and enthusiasm. The 12 members moved freely, playfully exploring, criss-crossing, meeting each other and the audience, removing eyeglasses, handbags and other items from audience members. Eric Trist was given several overlapping pairs of glasses to wear upside down. Gradually most of the audience were drawn from their seats into the process in a live demonstration of collaborative of collaborative networking. The merriment, laughter and joyousness persisted for some minutes. I believe it enhanced the atmosphere for the rest of the conference.

Soon other small groups began to tell stories or use graphic expression in their feedback. The final application groups were unusually prolific in their action recommendations, and the conference set up a steering group to process the recommendations and facilitate the network.

The same small group that initiated this burst of creativity introduced another creative element. A story was told of the Senoi people of Malaysia (Stewart, 1935) whose cultural practice includes family members sharing their dreams each morning, giving gifts to any with whom the dreamer had been in conflict, and the telling of "big dreams" to the whole village. People were invited to share any big dreams they might have.

The next day one woman graphically drew a dream where a dark cyclone caught up Eric Trist and blew everything about. The dreamer saw herself as expressing anxiety about the future of the Action-Learning Group, especially in relation to Trist, its principal founder, who was due to undergo surgery. The conference acknowledged the dreamer's warning for the future, a manifestation, perhaps, of Jung's collective unconscious in action. Reflecting on this conference later, I saw how we in this group had evolved a process that might be called a "creative search gathering." It included the cognitive and procedural elements of a traditional search, plus a means of expression that tapped into deep unconscious processes.

"CREATIVE FEEDBACK"—SCOTLAND, 1983

Back in Edinburgh I told this story to an actress friend in the Traverse Theater. She suggested I study a work by British actor Keith Johnstone (1981) who uses various techniques to elicit creative improvisations from people who think they have no imagination. I experimented further with creative feedback in a conventional (non-search) conference on education for health and safety. By now I was using the term "creative feedback" to mean a group conference report expressed imaginatively by drawing upon one or more of the arts.

In this event, Janet Fenton and Angie Rew, both experienced in professional theater, introduced to a group of 20 a series of exercises, each increasing the degree of free expression. The experiment was to see whether people could capture other conference session content creatively, from scuba diving to hang gliding to yoga. In a surrealistic stroke of genius, Ms. Fenton instructed the hotel staff to provide a fully-set dining table near the entrance to the large room, including table linen, candles, flowers, lacking only dinner plates.

On the table were two identical notices reading: "YOU ARE INVITED TO TAKE PART IN A FEAST OF CREATIVITY. THE INGREDIENTS ARE ON THE OTHER TABLE." Nearby was a table laden with art materials—colored pens, crayons, paints, modeling clay and a stack of paper plates. The facilitators suggested at the start that participants feel free to wander over to the tables.

All took part in the table art work, producing beautiful mandalas drawn on the paper plates, for example, or placing exquisite clay models of symbolic figures upon them. Each then placed his or her work on the dining table in one of the set places, providing an effect that illuminated the entire conference for all.

I now believed for sure that we could integrate creative feedback into "creative search gatherings" that would provide immense enhancement of the visionary planning and action processes of a search, a kind of analog of the more variegated community arts processes exemplified in the Craigmillar Festival Society. The next section describes our earliest attempts.

A CREATIVE SEARCH GATHERING ON THE FUTURE OF THE EASTERHOUSE FESTIVAL SOCIETY, GLASGOW

Our first "creative search gathering" took place March 15-16, 1985, with the Easterhouse Festival Society in Glasgow, an organization inspired by Craigmillar. Easterhouse leapt at the opportunity to engage in creative searching as a natural concomitant to their own search for greater financial self-reliance. Two experienced search facilitators were joined by two arts professionals from Craigmillar.

The gathering became a happening, eliciting creative feedback in many phases through improvisations, games, dramatizations, pictures, graphics (including tree symbolism), sharing of dreams about the gathering, poetry and song culminating in one group depicting a joining of

Easterhouse and Craigmillar Festival Societies with youth, the elderly, the excluded people and a crumbling establishment to share the creative endeavor of making a better life for all. The participants concluded with a dramatic circular dance and a unison chant: "The future is unity."

I have many more examples. Following the first search phase— emergent trends in the wider environment—one woman reported a dream in which "everybody, all of us, were in one great big bed all together. . . It was everybody really enjoying and coming together and helping each other. . . a great, great feeling. But somebody in the dream threw a glass of water over everybody in the bed. And they just jumped and dispersed. They split up and I awoke with a terrible fear.

"The funny thing was that I had a glass of water on the shelf by the bed and I must have pushed it and spilt it on the bed! So it was actually the water that woke me up. . . I felt quite negative about everything we'd said last night. But in talking about it in the group, Tom said to me that perhaps I shouldn't be negative. That, perhaps the water was positive, was a positive step. I'm not quite sure what he meant."

Added Tom, "I think there's a danger though. As Mary was saying, she's not going up blindly and accepting all this positive stuff. She's also realizing that there can be drawbacks. That things can happen to disperse that [optimism].

"But if you've got that bit of awareness about you, and you kind of know [bad] things can happen, you're a wee bit more prepared if and when they do. So I was trying to put that to you, Mary, in answer to a negative thing."

Another notable burst of creativity came during the final plenary on "constraints", "opportunities" and "action" regarding the desirable future for Easterhouse Festival Society. One group proposed a set of "positive fists" to break the various "blocks" identified during action planning. People were given "fists" like "sharing of skills," "education, training and experience," "Do It!" or "tapping our resources."

Blocks included "fear of failure," "no time for the young," "lack of skills," "pressure." With advice from the group, those holding fists used them to cover blocks posted on the wall. The exercise stimulated a much deeper understanding of the issues. For example, here's an exchange sparked by the phrase "DO IT!"

REG: "Can I just give a bit of background to that 'Do It!' one? Our group actually experienced it this morning. We were thinking that to move forward within Easterhouse we have to actually get into action. But what holds us back often is fear of failure or, fear of being visible. And we thought that what's really needed is to do something that's risk-taking for ourselves. We decided that we were too frightened to do that playlet this morning, for example. Then we realized it's that precise fear stops all of us from moving forward. Unless we start now, we're lost...So we thought, right, we're going to do a play although we're frightened and nervous. That was us actually 'doing it'!"

JEAN: "I was scared to suggest that we do the play again and all take part. And because of that ('fist') I 'did it.' I think that it's important to keep training yourself to take risks. And I try to do something regularly when I'm scared, just to keep myself in practice."

This process continued until all the "fists" had been applied. Another group drew an elaborate tree as an organic metaphor for the future growth and development of Easterhouse Festival Society, branches representing its different aspects. The group attempted to develop the symbolism to mythological proportions reminiscent of traditional myths. Near the end of the gathering one woman said, "A dead tree produces a beautiful piece of wood. No matter what's done with it, it doesn't change further. It's the living tree that changes."

Another group's creative feedback was in the form of an interrogation of an imaginary Mrs. Positive by a Mr. Roadblock. The transcript shows an entire group connecting and integrating a disparate set of "issues" into a dynamic whole with exciting action possibilities.

REPORTER/M/5: "Oh yes! My apologies! My name is Mr Road-block. And this is –"

REPORTER/F/1: "I'm Mrs Positive. I've got all the answers. [LAUGH-TER] Well, give or take a few."

ROADBLOCK: "My first block was communication." (1)

POSITIVE: "Communication. Move to better facilities to enable some freedom in communication, freedom in participation, freedom in creativity... Within our group it came up that there were isolated groups, single parents, for example, but we were reluctant to slot them into separate categories. So, for a suggestion: things like nurseries, further social facilities, without anybody setting any preconditions for these facilities, that would lead to better communication."

ROADBLOCK: "But to set up things like nurseries you have to go through 'red tape'." (2)

ROADBLOCK: "You have to face red tape."

POSITIVE: "Well, how do we face red tape? First of all, we caaa..nn get a community college where we can learn about structures, or perhaps create our own structure."

ROADBLOCK: "What about 'apathy' or the fact that we have no

voice?" (3)

POSITIVE: "Provide platforms for self development. We felt very strongly that the word 'apathy' is used rather widely when it's not actually apathy but lack of knowledge about how to go forward. We don't like the word apathy. We decided to cross that off the list altogether and educate."

ROADBLOCK: "How do you overcome institutionalized education?" (14)

POSITIVE: "Identify alternative skill instructors, everybody teaching and everybody learning regardless of age."

ROADBLOCK: "Lack of available jobs." (15)

POSITIVE: "Actually we got a bit mathematical here. We did a new sum! There are needs in our community. There are holes in the roads. We need our windows repaired. We need our landings painted. We need our gardens tended. There's lots of practical needs. Take these needs and take the skills that we also have in our area. And we take the empty facilities that we also have. And we take the available finance, of which there is a lot about. . . we do a wee sum and add them all up and we come to a wonderful conclusion. We have everything that we need to develop jobs in our area. So after identifying all the needs, all the skills, all the finances, all the facilities, we can create jobs in our own area."

The 49 Steps

In the end, five small groups produced 49 action steps. They emphasized face-to-face community contact, "getting out in the streets," taking risks, seeking employment initiatives, building the local economy, self-development workshops, child care facilities, and being aware of the need to turn local frustration and anger into positive energy for constructive actions.

A sub-group was formed to bring the action steps to the attention of a Special General Meeting of the Easterhouse Festival Society. A second agreement was for people to make themselves highly visible in the community, examples from the conference being several public displays—"the mosaic, the banner, the shops, the jigsaw, and the market."

Finally, all agreed to actively spread the word about the gathering and its planned actions. In subsequent months the Festival Society encountered severe difficulties both externally and internally. Yet, the spirit of the creative search permeated the community, as evidenced by the following excerpts from a Christmas letter.

EASTER HOUSE FESTIVAL SOCIETY
To All Our Friends and Associates

Greetings for 1987. May it be a productive and peaceful year for us all. As many of you will know, 1986 was a very difficult year for the EFS with the loss of our building, staff and major funds. It was a year full of political problems and conflict. However, the year ended very differently to the way it began and the purpose of this letter is to bring you up-to-date with what is happening and to seek your support. . .

From being devastated by the problems the Society, like the proverbial Phoenix, has risen again. Funds have been raised to ensure the continuation of the work until next October. . . The first event of the re-vitalized EFS was a Christmas pantomime and art exhibition. Over 2,500 children in 11 schools saw the show. . . The cast involved several new members and starred Teresa Cochrane, who is well-known to some of you. Alongside the show Teresa organized art exhibitions in every school—800 children participated. This was the show that not many people thought would happen! . . . Now plans are being made for events at Easter and Mayday, summer activities, a rock concert, street celebrations and a major production, written by Freddie Anderson from Easterhouse, which will also be performed at Glasgow's Mayfest and Edinburgh's Fringe Festivals.

The political problems are not over and the Society is being denied access to public facilities in Easterhouse, including the park! The context of poverty within which the Society operates is, if anything, getting worse with severe problems affecting all residents of Easterhouse. Poverty is becoming more individualized with anger, bitterness and resentment on the increase.

Yet the EFS continues to attract people with vision, commitment and determination to see things change for the better. Our work is needed and is even more important than eight years ago. Without vision, people perish. . .

Grass-roots community action is a major cutting edge of change in the world today. It is essential that we continue to communicate with each other and co-operate wherever possible. It is necessary, therefore it is possible.

OTHER EXAMPLES

I want to cite two other examples of creative processes at work in search conferences. Then I will conclude with a summary of theoretical and philosophical underpinnings for this development.

In September 1985, staff from various parts of Scotland took part in a brief creative search gathering at St. Andrews College of Education, Glasgow on the future of guidance in the educational system—"Guidance 2000"—for people over 16 years of age.

Sub-groups were given art materials, and two tables were arranged in the plenary room, one heaped with earth and surrounded with plants, on the other were materials for making "flowers" and other "plants" for "the garden" that expressed the growing and nurturing explorations of the search gathering. The whole was enhanced by dramatic lighting arranged by Ms. Fenton.

I was struck by how fast small groups came to brief, profound and powerful expressions of their findings in the various search phases when they used improvised drama, creative and symbolic art work, enacted dialogues, games and mimes. For example, one group dramatically portrayed guidance in an ideal future as a quality diffused in everyone so that the need for specialized guidance staff disappeared. Another imagined the diffusion transcending normal boundaries via newly-acquired capacities for extra-sensory perception and telepathic communication between people. Still another group dramatized in dialogue the tension between hope and despair in the wider environment.

My second example comes from Orillia, Ontario, at an international seminar: "Explorations In Human Futures," in October 1985. One small group developed through members telling stories of working in various settings, especially, where they had become stuck or had overcome difficulty. The stories, openly told and deeply shared, accentuated the intense interest by members in the fate of their own human processes.

The group decided to have its report to the plenary made by a mime depicting the personal story-telling and its impact. I believe this decision was more easily taken because this group included members of the York Action-Learning Group search conference, who had experience with creative modes, and also included several women, meaning that a positive "BaP" or "anima"/"animus" projection was possible.

The mime had considerable impact. Some were quite moved by a non-verbal "report" of a verbal process, while others appeared threatened by this non-traditional mode. A deep discussion followed on the significance of creative arts for visionary planning. When people reached the severe constraints on making the visions happen, one group created a vivid graphic showing a breaking out from a center of creative visions by modes of "contagion," "infection," "temporary systems," "blood-letting," chance, and "breaking the rules" through a dark cloud of constraints, especially economic ones (Figure 1).

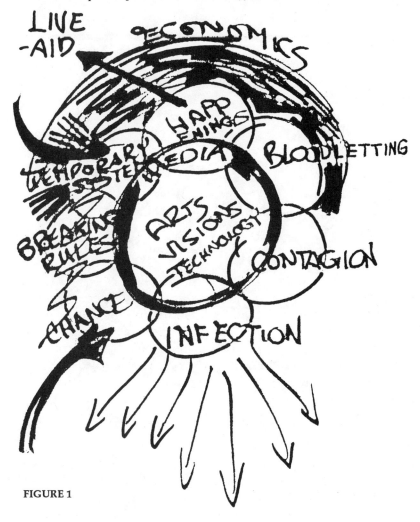

FIGURE 1

The same "process group" used both dramatic and graphic modes to report its conclusions about how young people and women, often alienated from traditional ways of working, engaged in very creative processes of their own. The group's women members began exploring the constraints to self-expression they experienced in male-dominated organizations. They also spoke of the liberating effects their own expressiveness could have. The group produced Figure 2 to symbolize their conclusions, and their plenary report took the form of a continued dialogue between two women about the drawing.

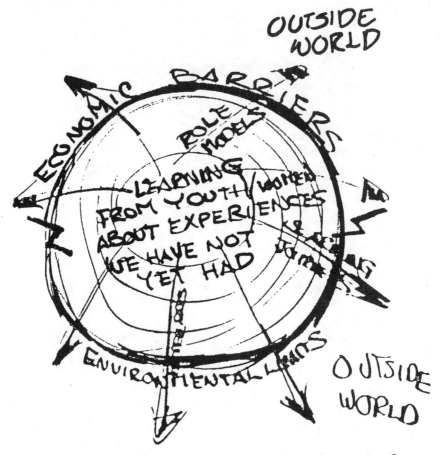

FIGURE 2

A: "I always have a dilemma working with males who stereotypically act like lions and roosters in large groups. Should I become a lion or a rooster to compete effectively? A law professor colleague of mine was instructed to dress for success, in blue and white, and make grand gestures and talk loud and stand up. Should I do that to be effective? I think of the female or expressive side as being like a butterfly. If you put a butterfly with lions and roosters, can the butterfly be itself and be taken seriously?"

B: "Yeah, I know. (To A) Your [earlier] stories about teaching remind me of my role as parent. I'm thinking here about 'the youth' and 'women' and the fact that sometimes as a parent I'm able to put things together because of my connection with youth through my son. It's a different relationship than I have with others in the male world. . . like your stories of how you feel relating to kids in your classes."

C: "I agree. I think the parenting role is a very interesting one because people see it as static. In fact, if you negotiate through from a baby to a teen-ager to a young adult, being appropriate to the situation as it comes up, that's an incredible balancing act. . . that's very similar to other change processes."

In the plenary discussion, one person observed that this same issue—women and youth—had come up in a recent search on the future of the nation of Peru, suggesting that similar findings in different cultures must have wider significance.

THE BENEFITS

What then are the benefits discovered thus far of creative search gatherings? I note three major ones:

1) There seems to be a deeper, richer and more powerful communication taking place that consequently has a more lasting effect.
2) The impact of such gatherings upon non-participants is greater because of the feelings aroused in, and enthusiasm of, participants in communicating with them (and not just the words, or action plans). I note a contagion as outsiders "tune in" or "resonate" to the participants' excitement—a kind of celebration that catches people up and carries them along.
3) The participants are so vibrant that they develop powerful visions, myths, images of the future and proceed to elaborate these into highly energetic strategies and detailed creative initiatives.

For me, these developments are still very much at the experimental stage. I see no practical limits to the ways in which the forms of communication that emerge from creative search gatherings can be enhanced. So long as people have something important to say to each other that emerges from their getting together, the "media" they use to express themselves can take many new forms that remain to be discovered.

SEARCH FESTIVALS?

When I let my mind wander to such wider creative expression in the context of "multiple searches in parallel" (e.g., four or six or 20 simultaneous conferences) or other configurations, then it's not a far leap to imagine the "search festival" and even a "global search festival" as a way of embodying human aspiration.

THEORETICAL INTERPRETATION

I referred briefly to Wilfred Bion and C.G. Jung who have provided me some theory for explaining the phenomena of creative search gatherings. I have found numerous other languages and models that support this way of working. It seems clear that creative feedback deepens participants' experiences in searching. People open up faster, and the group is able to explore and act on its environment in richer ways.

The importance of story telling as evoking archetypal, or even "alchemical," processes has been developed by Gregory Bateson (1979), William Irwin Thompson (1978), Donald Schon (1980), and Thomas Berry (1978), in addition to Jung (1944, 1955, 1956). Dreams, of course, are a direct route to the unconscious or "primary process" (Freud, 1900, P. 588), and people who report their dreams in creative conferences may well be articulating what Jung called the "collective unconscious." This can be a powerful process for solidifying experience, establishing "reality," and stimulating constructive joint action.

In creative search gatherings we deliberately return to "the ground," to cultural democracy, so that new "figurations" may emerge. The holographic theories of Carl Pribram (1971) and David Bohm (1980) suggest that reality, the brain, and the universe may be basically holographic in process and pattern. In this vein, then, one could say that creative searching provides a threshold to a higher system level where the "interference patterns" of the intersecting wave vibrations are richer, resulting in greater wholeness.

In addition, there is a growing literature on the engagement of "right brain" processes, for example the work of Sperry (1975) and colleagues, and the complementary nature of linear, structured work and more expressive free-flowing processes. At the group or systems level, there is evidence that "negative feedback" damps down discovery and learning to keep things the same, while "positive" or "deviance amplifying" feedback establishes new patterns or "figuration" aiding in transformation (Maruyama, 1962).

BEYOND CREATIVITY

The significance of what takes place in the broader creative communication of creative search gatherings may run far beyond our imaginations. We encourage the expression of inner, unconscious, deeply-rooted creative processes. We allow these processes to emerge, creating meaningful figures, symbols, patterns, stories, and myths. In that way we create a cultural democracy that enables people to produce and, in so doing, reveal their own "worlds," their own "societies," their own reality. Above all, we reveal ourselves to each other and as individuals and in groups, become makers of reality—our own trans-universes.

I believe this is why we can see the greater significance of a community in festival mode. For in its festival mode a community or a society actually re-creates itself and reveals to itself the open, vibrating, sharing process by which it does this creating and reality-making. By encouraging unconscious rooted expression, as in the community arts, we are not just giving "play" to a wider range of frequencies of vibration or balancing conscious and unconscious expression, left brain and right brain, etc., we are opening the door, the way to a transformative reorientation of our lives, our "worlds:" a newly re-emergent context, pattern or paradigm of seeing and being.

In physicist David Bohm's terms we re-establish the primacy of the "implicate" holographic order. This is a highly complex order, an order which the esoteric spiritual paths, orientations, philosophies, religions, crafts, and practices reveal is highly discernable. It is this "world"—"the kingdom of god within"—which is abundant with "riches" available to everyone—the transforming of the everyday world—thereby overcoming the distortion of the elite, centre-periphery model, the "sin" of the ego only at the center, rather than the ego in the context of the transcendental Self or All or Ultimate.

I believe the "esoteric" arts are pathways into and through the transcendental, implicate order. My hypothesis is that we find in these processes the evolving human and universal development towards wholeness or the Holy. If we can sense, intuit, feel, and grasp the correspondences between these systems, myths, stories, images and metaphors, our individual and mutual collective lives will be greatly enhanced.

To find such levels of creativity in ourselves with others is not just "art." The expression of creative, unconscious processes through various evolving arts is the most direct human activity, the primary manifestation of our lives, our individual, mutual and collective, transcendental Selves.

To encourage broader creative searching, therefore, would seem to have as yet unfathomable and inestimable significance for the human prospect. For it shifts the *raison d'être* of self and society to manifestation and celebration. In so doing we may glimpse a vision of society and universe as festival.

ABOUT THE AUTHOR...

Steve Burgess is an American who has lived in Scotland for 25 years. He is a consultant and researcher interested in creative organizational ecology. He was formerly a Senior Research Fellow at the University of Edinburgh and consultant and research coordinator to the Craigmillar Festival Society-European Economic Community Programme of Pilot Schemes and Studies to Combat Poverty. He has been consultant to community groups, voluntary agencies, local government, government organizations and businesses. He spends part of each year in North America.

CHAPTER 35

Applied Imagination + Current Events
= UNLIMITED POSSIBILITIES

Marvin R. Weisbord

PICK UP ANY NEWSPAPER OR MAGAZINE AND YOU WILL SEE plainly the scope of potential for search conferences. To read the daily press is to dip into a bottomless well of need. As I write, people are proposing future search conferences as a way of improving race relations in large cities, assisting urban tenant action groups, rescuing a YWCA from bankruptcy, building links between museums and inner-city neighborhoods, and bridging cultural barriers in large corporations. I learn of new applications weekly. What follows are examples of *potential* conferences I have culled from a few days of routine reading. So far as I know, nobody is using the future search in any of these situations. However, in every case we have issues that—

1. Frustrate many people.
2. Will consume enormous resources of time
   and money in meetings anyway.
3. Call for broad stakeholder interaction.
4. Have few or no precedents for successful resolution.
5. Put many parties into conflict.
6. Need bold leadership and new initiatives.

Here are ideas for you to drink in. Maybe you have more influence than you think.

1. HOMELESSNESS

A *Times* editorial applauded the Bush Administration for organizing a Task Force on Homelessness and Severe Mental Illness. "With the recent appointment of an advisory panel of experts, the group has begun work in earnest." The writer points out that New York and other states now have considerable experience with the problem, one that involves an estimated 200,000 mental patients who might cost $3 billion a year to care for. Of the task force, says the *Times*, "Whether its work will lead the White House to act constructively remains to be seen."

CONFERENCE IDEA: Convene into a cross section of federal, state and local officials, legislators, mental health and homelessness advocates, the panel's experts, and some mentally ill homeless people, establish the global perspective, and pool the ideals, experience and ideas of this diverse group.

POSSIBLE MODEL: Rodger Schwass's Pakistan conservation strategy, Chapter 16.

[Source: "Republicans and the Homeless," *The New York Times*, , August 16, 1991, p A22]

2. SECONDARY EDUCATION

One promising movement in secondary education is the concept of "community building." That's defined as collaborative learning, team teaching and learning, joint learning projects among diverse students, the classroom as learning laboratory for both individual accountability and shared responsibility. Reading about this development, it struck me how congruent would be the use of search processes as a strategy planning tool for improving community building—at the level of one school, a whole district, or a region.

CONFERENCE IDEA: Stakeholders—parents, teachers, administrators, students, community members—design their ideal "Classroom of the Future," or "School of the Future" in a global context. This would make a useful annual start-up conference, a direction-setter for a whole district (each school team is free to implement what, how, and when it wishes), and a dramatic public policy influencer if done nationally with prominent stakeholders from government, business, labor, education, etc.

[Source: Kitzmiller, Beverly. "Reflections on Community in Education," *Community Notes*, (Publication of the Foundation for Community Encouragement, Inc.), Vol. 3, Spring 1991, pp. 1-4]

As I was editing this, I received a packet of materials from a colleague, Jan Williams, reporting on a successful conference with the Chatham,

MA Public Schools and the local community. She also described plans for four more education conferences in New England. More information: Janice A. Williams, 52 East St., Hopkinton, MA – Telephone 508 435-5196.

3. INTEGRATING COMPUTER SYSTEMS

If ever an issue cries out for a room full of stakeholders, it's the thorny, knotty, tangled, frustrating, ambiguous, anxious-making, confounding, moving target called "systems integration," or how to get all your hardware wired up so people can talk to each other, and merge words, pictures, numbers, charts, graphs, and ideas in an ongoing, seamless fabric of instantaneous and continuous enlightenment. Oh well, you get the idea.

The question is not which techniques work—they all do, or they don't. Rather it is, in the words of this special report, "What integration strategy should we adopt?" Here the focus is on different models adopted by James River (bottoms up) in operating 20 different paper mills, General Dynamics' Convair Division (top down) in speeding up the development of aerospace products ("five to ten years is just not acceptable any longer"), BP Research Laboratories (case by case) to make computer resources accessible to research scientists.

"It's a very painful process," says Toby Choate of Arthur D. Little. "People must get together across functions, and discuss matters of their business in an open and forthright way...negotiate a common understanding of the enterprise's optimal operating environment, and then take on the responsibility for implementing the changes required."* Search idea: It's so obvious is needs no elaborating. The search process makes an ideal way for any company, regardless of overall strategy, to find a way based on broad knowledge and shared commitment.

POSSIBLE EXAMPLE: Software Process Program of the Software Engineering Institute, Carnegie-Mellon University, that brought together defense contractors, Pentagon, academics, programmers, systems designers and users, to develop scenarios for the improvement of software development processes by the year 2000. Said one participant, "This is the first time some of us have ever been in a room together without fighting!" For more information, Stan Rifkin, Master Systems, Inc., Box 8208, McLean, VA 22106. Telephone (703) 883 2121.

[Source: Lindgren, R. "No one best way: Strategies for integrating systems run the gamut," *Enterprise,* Digital Equipment Co. magazine, Spring 1991, p. 20-28]

4. MERGERS

They're going on everywhere. Toyota and General Motors. Banks. Insurance Companies. Software. One of the more newsworthy (and difficult) strategic alliances is that between IBM and Apple. Two distinct cultures, markets, product lines differing in look, feel, operation, basic assumptions. Together, they represent formidable resources.

"But can they outlive the demise of the machine put on the business map by their 1980's rivalry?" asks the author. . "At the moment the alliance resembles nothing so much as two former rivals huddling together for comfort as their world breaks up around them."

He points out that the merger symbolizes the end of the PC and "the birth of something new, a greater revolution in which visions dreamed a decade ago could finally become reality." He believes it will be the "small upstarts," not the "old giants," who are most likely to shape the future of computers.

"The best companies see innovation as a function that needs managing—and then they manage it by basing new products on customers' needs, encouraging employees to use the expertise of the whole company, giving workers incentives for successful innovation, and refusing to punish those gamble don't pay off. One key lesson: Good ideas don't go very far unless they are nurtured and developed."

[Source: Saffo, Paul. "Farewell, PC—What's Next?" *The New York Times*, October 13, 1991, p. 9.]

CONFERENCE IDEA: This is what is called in corporatespeak a "no brainer." I can think of no better way for merging cultures to create joint future plans than through strategic conferences. These situations call for not one but dozens of such strategy meetings, say one a week, for several months. The strategy would be bringing together all the players in multiple combinations over time, to educate each other, commit to common purposes, and make joint plans. They *will* spend the time and money anyway in meetings anyway. Whether they will realize the full potential of their alliance remains to be seen.

MULTI-CONFERENCE EXAMPLE: Alan Davies, Consumer Forum for the Aged, Chapter 22.

5. CORPORATE COMMUNICATIONS

The business press has discovered teamwork, employee involvement, participation and democracy in the 1980's, largely because that's what chief executives talk about these days (in addition to global business, lean structures, total quality, and customer focus). In one article on the new norm of more open exchanges between management and labor, the following examples are cited:

1. A toy company CEO puts out quarterly results in a rap number delivered to an employee assembly. He is backed by the "Rappettes," a secretary's group.

2. An insurance company CEO invites personal electronic mail from 5500 people, reads it each night, and often responds with personal phone calls.

3. A railroad CEO holds town meetings via satellite with employees in 24 locations across the United States, answering their questions and rapping with them on any subject they wish to bring up.

"The lesson," says reporter Faye Rice, is that "talk back and forth within the organization, up and down the hierarchy—may well be more important to a company's success than external communications, what PR types loftily used to style 'dialogue with major constituencies.'"

[Source: Rice, Faye. "Champions of Communication," *Fortune*, June 3, 1991, pp. 111-120.]

I think the dichotomy between internal and external communications is unnecessary. Both forms of communication are important. More, it's possible—through strategic futures conferences, to do both at once. CEO's love the forum, and so do other stakeholders.

CONFERENCE IMPLICATION: Strategic futures conferences have the potential to accomplish ALL the objectives noted—dialogue within the company, between levels, and across customer, community, and supplier lines. Such conferences could be organized in parallel and linked by satellite (see Chapter 33 for Fred Emery's speculation on this).

POSSIBLE MODEL: Gary Frank and Bob Rehm's StorageTek case, Chapter 14.

MAKING A DIFFERENCE

Who is likely to hold conferences that would lead to breakthroughs in all these situations? I have no idea. We can all benefit from good diets and exercise, but not all of us will eat right and jog. Maybe one of these issues is close to your heart, pocketbook, or idealism. Maybe you have still other ideas. By now, I hope so.

I've based this book on my belief that "making a difference" is partly concept, partly method, partly window of opportunity, hardly ever a technique, and entirely a matter of human will. If the book proves anything, it is that whatever people can imagine, people can do. Could YOU make a difference using future search conferences? If your answer is "yes," remember the minimum specs. You will still need the right sponsors and courageous leadership. You will need broad collaboration and an important task. Above all, you will need leaders and co-workers who believe that the best action plans come from people in dialogue finding common ground in the future of our planet. What you will discover remains to be seen. Let me hear from you!

References

Ackoff, R. L. (1981) *Creating The Corporate Future*. New York: John
  Wiley & Sons.

Argyris, C. and Schon, D. (1978) *Organizational Learning: A Theory of
  Action* Perspective, London

Asch, Solomon E. (1952) "Group Forces in the Modification and
  Distortion of Judgments," pp. 483-4, Chapter 16, *Social
  Psychology*. Prentice-Hall, Englewood Cliffs, NJ.

_____ (1987) *Social Psychology*, (Prentice-Hall, New York, 1952.)
  Oxford University Press.

_____ (1956) "Studies of Independence and Conformity." *Psychological Monographs*, No. 416.

Ashby, W. R. (1956) *An Introduction to Cybernetics*, London

Bartsch, W. and Paulson, W. (1989) *Practical Visionaries: Innovators in
  Learning and Change*, 2nd Ed., Quetico Conference and Training Centre, P.O. Box 1000, Atikokan, Ontario POT 1CO.

Bateson, G. (1979) *Mind and Nature*. New York: E.P. Dutton,

Baum, G. (1978) "Adult Education as a Political Enterprise." Address
  to the alumni of the Department of Adult Education, Ontario
  Institute for Studies in Education, Toronto.

Berry, Thomas (1978) "Comments on the Origin, Identification and
  Transmission of Ideas". In *Anima*. Winter, 1978.

Bertalanffy, L. von (1968) *General Systems Theory*, New York

_____ (1952) *Problems of Life*, New York: Wiley, p. 176.

Bion, Wilfred (1959) *Experiences in Groups*. London: Tavistock.

Bohm, David. An Interview by John Briggs, *New Age Journal*, September/October 1989, pp. 44-49, 110-115.

_____ (1980) *Wholeness and the Implicate Order*. London: Routledge & Kegan Paul.

Boorman S.A. (1971) *The Protracted Game*. OUP.

Boulding, K. E. (1962) *Conflict and Defense; A General Theory*. New York, Harper and Row.

Bridges, W. (1980) *Transitions: Making Sense of Life's Changes*. Reading, MA: Addison-Wesley.

Brundage, D. & Mackeracher, D. (1980) *Adult Learning Principles and Their Application to Program Planning*. Toronto: Ministry of Education.

Buckley, W. (1967) *Sociology and Modern Systems Theory*, New Jersey

Burgess, M.S. (1980) "A Giant Step. An Appraisal of the Craigmiller Festival Society's Approach to Community Development Relative to the Craigmillar-European Economic Community Programme of Pilot Schemes and Studies to Combat Poverty". Brussels: EEC Commission, Directorate General for Social Affairs.

Burns, T. and Stalker, G.M. (1961) *The Management of Innovation*, London

Carlzon, J. (1987) *Moments of Truth*, Harper, Sydney.

Cherns, Albert (1982) (Professor of Social Science at Loughborough University) Letter to the Rt. Hon. Lord Young of Dartington, 2nd August.

Chopra, Deepak (1989) *Quantum Healing*, New York: Bantam Books.

Craigmillar Festival Society (1978) *The Gentle Giant Who Shares and Cares; Craigmillar's Comprehensive Plan for Action*. Craigmillar, Edinburgh: Craigmillar Festival Society.

Crombie, Alastair D. (1985) "The Nature and Types of Search Conferences." *International Journal of Lifelong Education*, 4, 1, pp. 3-33.

Dunn, E.S. Jr. (1971), *Economic and Social Development: A Process of Social Learning*, London.

Emery F.E. (1989) 'Educational Paradigms'. In Emery M.

_____ (1977) *Futures We Are In*. Martinus Nijhoff

_____ (1991) *Per Una Democrazia Della Partecipazione*, Rosenberg & Sellier, Turin.

_____ (1981), "Searching for Common Ground". In Fred Emery (Ed.), *Systems Thinking, Vol 2*. Harmondsworth, Middlesex: Penguin Books, Ltd.

_____ (1989) *Toward Real Democracy*, Ontario Quality of Working Life Centre, Toronto.

Emery, F.E. and Trist E.L. (1965) "The Causal Texture of Organizational Environments," *Human Relations*, 18, 1, pp. 21-32.

Emery M. (Ed) (1989) *Participative Design for Participative Democracy*. Centre for Continuing Education. Australian National University. Canberra.

_____ (1982) *Searching: For New Directions, in New Ways for New Times*. Canberra: Centre for Continuing Education, Australian National University.

Emery, M. and Emery F.E. (1978) "Searching," in J.W. Sutherland (ed.) *Management Handbook for Public Administrators*, New York, Van Nostrand Reinhold.

Etzioni, Amitai (1968) *The Active Society: A Theory of Societal and Political Processes*. New York, Free Press.

_____ (1975) *A Comparative Analysis of Complex Organizations: On Power, Involvement and Their Correlates*. New York, Free Press, 2nd Edition: Glencoe, Ill., Free Press.

Evans, W. M. Ed. (1971) *Interorganizational Relations*, Philadelphia, University of Pennsylvania Press.

Franklin, Beth (1989) "Action Learning in a Multi- Organizational Context". Unpublished Major Paper, Faculty of Environmental Studies, York University, Toronto, Canada.

Freire, Paulo (1973) *Education for Critical Consciousness*. New York: Seabury Press.

Fox, Ronald F., Ronald Lippitt, and Eva Schindler-Rainman (1973) *The Humanized Future: Some New Images*. La Jolla, CA: University Associates.

Goleman, Daniel (1991) "New Way to Battle Bias: Fight Acts, Not Feelings, *The New York Times*, July 16, p. C1, C8.

Gruber, Howard E. (1990) "The Cooperative Synthesis of Disparate Points of View," pp. 143-158, Chapter 9, *The Legacy of Solomon Asch: Essays in Cognition and Social Psychology*. Hillsdale, NJ: Lawrence Erlbaum Associates, Publishers.

Hage, J. and Aiken, M. (1970) *Social Change in Complex Organizations*. New York: Random House.

Harrison, Roger (1983) "Strategies for a New Age," *Human Resource Management*, Vol. 22, No. 3, pp. 209-235.

Haugen, R. (1984) "A Local Community in Search for Futures", Work Research Institutes, Oslo

Herbst, P.G. (1980) "Community Conference Design", *Human Futures*, New Delhi

Janssen, C. (1982) *Personlig Dialektik,* 2nd Ed. Stockholm: Liber.

Johnson, R.C. (1990) *Open learning,* National Board of Employment, Education and Training, Australian Government Publishing, Canberra.

Johnstone, K. (1979) *Impro.* London: Faber & Faber.

Jung, C.G. *Collected Works,* Volumes 12 (1944), 13 (1955), 14 (1956). Princeton, New Jersey: Bollingen Foundation.

_____ (1966) *Two Essays on Analytical Psychology,* Second Edition, Princeton, New Jersey: Bollingen Foundation.

Katz, A.H. and Bender, E.I. (1976) *The Strength in Us: Self- Help Groups in the Modern World.* New York, New Viewpoints.

Keen, Sam (1991) *Fire in the Belly.* New York: Bantam Books. p. 115

Kotler, M. (1969) *Neighborhood Government.* Indianapolis, Bobbs-Merrill.

Maruyama, Magoroh (1963) "The Second Cybernetics: Deviation-Amplyfying Mutual Causal Processes". *The American Scientist,* Winter.

McEwen, Malcolm (1972) "The Other Edinburgh". In the *New Statesman,* August 18.

Mezirow, J. (1978) *Education for Perspective Transformation: Women's Re-entry Programs in Community Settings.* New York: Columbia University Teachers College, Center for Adult Education.

Mintzberg, H. (1985) "Of Strategies, Deliberate and Emergent," *Strategic Management Journal,* pp. 257-272.

Morley, David (1989) "Frameworks for Organizational Change". In: Wright, S. & Morley, D. (eds) *Learning Works: Searching for Organizational Futures.* Toronto: ABL Publications, Faculty of Environmental Studies, York University. pp 163-190.

National Conservation Strategy (1984). IUCN, Gland, Switzerland.

Oech, R. von. (1990) *A Whack on the Side of the Head: How You Can Be More Creative.* Revised Edition. New York: Warner Books.

Parenti, Michael (1986) *Inventing Reality,* St. Martin's Press, p. 245.

Parsons, Talcott (1960) *Structure and Processes in Modern Society.* New York: The Glencoe Free Press.

Perls, F., R. Hefferline, and P. Goodman (1951) *Gestalt Therapy.* New York: Julian Press.

Peters, T.J. and Waterman, R.H. (1982) *In search of excellence,* Harper and Row.

Pribram, Karl (1974) *Languages of the Brain.* Englewood Cliffs, New Jersey: Prentice Hall.

Qutub, Ayub, ed. (1986) *Conservation Strategy in Pakistan, Proceedings of the Search Conference on a Conservation Strategy for Pakistan,* Islamabad.

Schindler, Craig and Gary Lapid (1988). *The Great Turning*. Santa Fe: Bear & Company.

Schindler-Rainman, Eva (1981) *The Creative Volunteer Community, A Collection of Writings*, Vancouver Volunteer Centre, Canada.

_____(1981) *Transitions: Strategies for the Volunteer World*, edited by Val Adolph, Vancouver Volunteer Centre, Canada.

Schindler-Rainman, Eva and Ronald Lippitt (1972) *Team Training for Community Change: Concepts, Goals, Strategies and Skills*, University of California at Riverside.

_____(1977) *The Volunteer Community: Creative Use of Human Resources*, Second Edition, University Associates, San Diego.

_____(1980) *Building the Collaborative Community: Mobilizing for Citizen Action*, Third Printing.

_____(1988)*Taking Your Meetings Out of the Doldrums*, Revised Edition, in Collabortion with Jack Cole, University Associates, San Diego, California.

Schon, Donald (1980) "Framing and Reframing the Problems of Cities". In David Morley, Stuart Proudfoot and Thomas Burns, *Makng Cities Work*. London: Croom Helm, Ltd.

Schwass, Rodger (1986) *Conservation Strategy in Pakistan: The Basic Issues.*

_____(1984) *Report of the Task Force on Northern Conservation*, Government of Canada, September.

Schwass, Rodger (1988) *Circumpolar Conservation Strategy, Proceedings of the Vancouver Search Conference*, Banff Centre, Banff, Alberta, Canada, February.

Selznick, P. (1957) *Leadership in Administration; a Sociological Interpretation*. Rowe, Peterson & Co., New York.

Sheldrake, Rupert (1988) *The Presence of the Past: Morphic Resonance and the Habits of Nature*, New York: Vintage Books.

Short, J., et als. (1976) *The Social Psychology of Communications*, Wiley, London.

Smith, Lethem, and Thoolen (1980) "The Design of Organizations for Rural Development—A Progress Report," World Bank Staff Working Paper No. 375, March.

Sommerhoff, G. (1950) *Analytical Biology*, Oxford University Press, London.

_____"The Abstract Characteristics of Living Systems." In F.E.Emery (Ed), *Systems Thinking*. Penguin, London.

Sperry, R.W. (1975) "Left Brain, Right Brain". In *Saturday Review*, August 9.

Stewart, Kilton (1969) "Dream Theory in Malaya". In Tart, C.T. (Editor) *Altered States of Consciousness*. New York: Wiley.

Tannenbaum, R. and R. W. Hanna (1985) "Holding On, Letting Go, and Moving On." In R. Tannenbaum, N. Margulies, F. Massarik and Associates, *Human Systems Development: New Perspectives on People and Organizations.* San Francisco: Jossey Bass.

Thom, Rene (1975) *Structural Stability and Morphogenesis,* Trans. D.H. Fowler. Reading, Mass.: The Benjamin/Cummings Publishing Company.

Thompson, William Irwin (1978) *Darkness and Scattered Light.* Garden City, New York: Doubleday Press.

Trist, E.L.(1985) After-dinner remarks. Conference on Explorations in Human Futures. Orillia, Ontario, 17 October.

_____(1983) "Referent Organizations and the Development of Interorganizational Domains", *Human Relations,* Vol. 36, No. 13, pp 269-84.

Trist, E.L. and F.E. Emery (1960) *Report on the Barford Course for Bristol/ Siddeley,* July 10-16, 1960. Tavistock Document No. 598, London, September.

_____(1975) *Towards a Social Ecology.* Plenum Press.

Trist, E.L., Higgin, G.W., Murray, H., and Pollock, A.B. (1963) *Organizational Choice.* London: Tavistock.

Vickers, G. (1965) *The Art of Judgment,* Methuen, London.

_____(1970) *Freedom in a Rocking Boat,* Penguin, London.

Weisbord, Marvin R. (1987) *Productive Workplaces: Organizing and Managing for Dignity, Meaning, and Community.* San Francisco: Jossey-Bass, Inc.

Wheatley, Margaret (1992) *Leadership and the New Science—Learning About Organization from an Orderly Universe,* San Francisco: Berrett-Koehler.

Williams, T.A. (1982) *Learning to Manage our Futures,* New York.

The World Conservation Strategy, (1980) and *The World Conservation Strategy* 2nd Ed., (1989) IUCN, Gland, Switzerland.

World Commission on Environment and Development (1987) *Our Common Future: The World Commission on Environment and Development.* United Kingdom: Oxford University Press.

Authors

David Angus
1931 Eisenhower St.
Louisville, CO 80027
Phone (303) 666-5202

Dick Axelrod
Axelrod & Associates, Inc.
723 Laurel Avenue
Wilmette, IL 60091
Phone (708) 251-7361
FAX (708) 251-7370

Oguz N. Baburoglu
Bilkent University, Management Dept.
Bilkent, Ankara, Turkey 06533
Phone (90) 4 266 4164
FAX (90) 4 266 43 06

David Bohm
20 Gibbs-Green
Edgeware, Middlesex
London HA8 9RH, UK

John Briggs
Barnard Road
Granville, MA 01034
Phone (413) 357-8830
FAX (413) 357-8830 (10 pm-7 am EST)

Ivar Brokhaug
Center for Management Education
The Norwegian Institute
    of Technology
Alfred Getz Vei 1
N-7034 Trondheim, Norway
Phone (47) 7 59 34 05
FAX (47) 7 59 36 03

Stephen Burgess
2 Rothesay Place
Edinburgh EH3 7SL, Scotland, UK
Phone (44) 31 226 4961

Alastair Crombie
The Australian National University
Centre for Continuing Education
G.P.O. Box 4
Canberra ACT 2601 Australia
Phone (06) 2494038
FAX (06) 2574498

James A. Cumming
P.O. Box 1535
Brattleboro, VT 05302
Phone (802) 257 5218

Alan Davies
Office of the Principal,
University of New England,
    Northern Rivers
P.O. Box 157
Lismore, New South Wales 2480
Australia
Phone (61) 66 23 0788
FAX (61) 66 22 1789

Maurice Dubras
Dubras & Associates
5 Great Union Road
St. Helier, Jersey Channel Islands
JE2 3YA UK
Phone (44) 534 36403
FAX (44) 534 68442

Fred E. Emery
42 Skinner Street
Cook, 2624 Australia
Phone (61) 06 251 2373
FAX (61) 06 257 3421

Merrelyn Emery
The Centre for Continuing Education
Australian National University
GPO Box 4
Canberra 2601 Australia
Phone (61) 06 249 2384 [office]
(61) 06 251 2373 [home]
FAX (61) 06 257 3421

Mary Fambrough
ICOM Mechanical Inc.
571 North 7th St.
San Jose, CA 59112
Phone (408) 298-8108
FAX (408) 292-4968

Gary Frank
796 West Birch Court
Louisville, CO 80027
Phone (303) 665-8797

Beth Franklin
The ABL Group
Faculty of Environmental Studies
York University
8 Admiral Road
Toronto, ON M5R 2L5, Canada
Phone/Fax (416) 920-0797

M. Andy Garr, III
2672 Browns Mill Rd.
Atlanta, GA 30354
Phone (404) 622-9625

Elaine Granata
Patere Ltd.
2071 Grape
Denver, CO 80207
Phone (303) 321-2735

Rolf Haugen
NSB Hovedhontoret
Personal/organisajon
P.O. Box 1162 Sentrum
0107 Oslo, Norway
Phone (02) 36 80 00
FAX (02) 36 62 18

Tim Hutzel
Manager of Organizational
    Effectiveness
General Electric Aircraft Engines
1 Neumann Way, Mail Drop 0231
Cincinnati, Ohio 45215
Phone (513) 243-8257
FAX (513) 786-2176

Chris Kloth
Harmon, Kloth and Associates
3440 Olentangy River Road - Suite 103
Columbus, OH 43202-1556
Phone (614) 263-7093
FAX (614) 421-2019

Kathie Libby
1320 Maryland Avenue
Washington, DC 20002
Phone (202) 398-4374

Cliff McIntosh
Quetico Centre
P.O. Box 1000
Atikokan, Ontario POT ICO, Canada
Phone (807) 929-3511
FAX (807) 929-1106

David Morley
Faculty of Environmental Studies
York University
4700 Keele Street
North York, ON M3J 1P3, Canada
Phone (416) 736-5252
FAX (416) 736-5679

Bob Rehm
1460 Judson Drive
Boulder, Colorado 80303
Phone (303) 499-1607

Tony Richardson
5 O'Hara Street
Marrickville, NSW 2204, Australia
Phone (02) 559-4230
FAX (02) 558-8917

Dr. Eva Schindler-Rainman
4267 San Rafael Avenue
Los Angeles, CA 90042
Phone and FAX (213) 257-8962

Rodger Schwass
71 The Kingsway
Toronto, Ontario, Canada M8X 2T3
Phone (416) 233 8386
FAX (416) 233 8246

Rita Schweitz
720 Vine Street
Denver, Colorado, 80206
Phone (303) 399-0130

William E. Smith
Organizing for Development
2134 Leroy Place NW
Washington, DC 20008
Phone (202) 483-6344
FAX (202) 234-1392

Eric Trist
P.O. Box 1654
Carmel-By-The-Sea, CA 93921
Phone (408) 626-3881

Patricia R. Tuecke
651 Scott #7
San Francisco, CA 94117
Phone (415) 921-3655
FAX (415) 626-3325

Margaret Wanlin
Quetico Centre
P.O. Box 1000
Atikokan, Ontario,
POT ICO, Canada
Phone (807) 929-3511
FAX (807) 929-1106

Marvin R. Weisbord
Block Petrella Weisbord
119 Sibley Avenue
Ardmore, PA 19003
Phone (215) 649-7272
FAX (215) 642-5768

Margaret Wheatley
The Berkana Institute
226 North 1900 East
Mapleton, Utah 84664
Phone (801) 376-8540
FAX (801) 489-8404

John Wooten
1320 Maryland Avenue
Washington, DC 20002
Phone (202) 398-4374

Index